REVOLUTIONARY ETHIOPIA

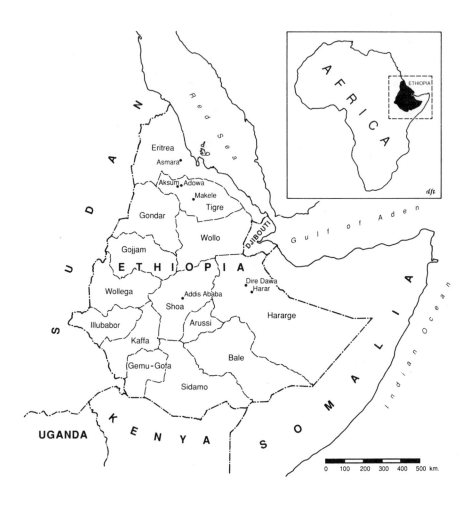

REVOLUTIONARY ETHIOPIA,

From Empire to People's Republic

EDMOND J. KELLER

INDIANA UNIVERSITY PRESS
Bloomington and Indianapolis

Manufactured in the United States of America

Library of Congress Cataloging-in-Publication Data

Keller, Edmond J. (Edmond Joseph), 1942–
Revolutionary Ethiopia.

Bibliography: p.
Includes index.
1. Ethiopia—History—Revolution, 1974.   2. Ethiopia
—History—1974–   I. Title.
DT387.95.K45   1988   963'.07   87-46090
ISBN 0-253-35014-X

1 2 3 4 5   92 91 90 89 88

For Genny, Vern, Erika, and Mom

CONTENTS

LIST OF TABLES   viii

ACKNOWLEDGMENTS   ix

INTRODUCTION: REVOLUTIONARY ETHIOPIA   1

Part One: Toward a Theory of the Revolutionary Transformation of the Ethiopian Empire

Chapter   I   Ethiopia as a Bureaucratic Empire   15

Chapter   II   The Structure of Politics   45

Chapter   III   Policy and the Politics of Survival in the Absolutist State   65

Chapter   IV   The Political Economy of a Modernizing Bureaucratic Empire   94

Part Two: The Genesis of Revolution

Chapter   V   Development and Social Contradictions The Seeds of Revolution   131

Chapter   VI   Politics, Economics, and Class Conflict The Precipitating Causes of Revolution   164

Part Three: Revolution in the Revolution: The Dilemmas of the New Order

Chapter VII   The Quest for a New Social Myth   191

Chapter VIII   Socialism from Above? Power Consolidation in a "Soft State"   213

Chapter   IX   Toward Economic Socialization   245

Chapter   X   Feudalism Is Dead! Long Live Dependence!   264

NOTES   273

INDEX   303

TABLES

4.1 Public Expenditures as Percentages of GNP for Selected Years
in Millions of Ethiopian Birr 102

4.2 Distribution of Private Foreign Investment in Ethiopia, 1966 108

4.3 State Revenues from Land Tax, Tithe, and Cattle Tax,
1956/57–1965/66, in Millions of Ethiopian Birr 116

4.4 Total Value of Imports, Exports, and Re-Exports and Visible
Balance of Trade in Millions of Ethiopian Dollars 120

4.5 Ethiopia's Six Most Important Import Trading Partners by
Commodity, 1967 121

4.6 Balance of Trade with Selected Countries, 1967 and 1972, in
Millions of Ethiopian Dollars 122

5.1 Students Enrolled in Primary and Academic Secondary
Schools by Province and as a Percentage of Total
Population, 1972–73 139

5.2 Distribution of Health Services by Province, 1973–74 141

5.3 Distribution of Total Cultivated Area between Owners and
Tenants in Private Tenure and Communal Areas (1963–67)
by Percentage 145

5.4 Organization of *Gada* among the Oromo according to
Number of Years in the System and Age of Individuals 159

7.1 Estimated Red Star Campaign Expenditures, January 1982–
September 1983, in Thousands of Ethiopian Birr 209

8.1 Students Enrolled in Primary and Secondary Schools by
Region and Percentage of Total Population, 1972–73 221

8.2 Students Enrolled in Primary and Secondary Schools by
Region and Percentage of Total Population, 1979–80 222

8.3 Doctor/Population Ratio in Selected Regions, 1974 and 1980 224

9.1 Peasant Associations, Service and Producer Cooperatives by
Region, 1984 260

ACKNOWLEDGMENTS

Ethiopia has historically captured the imagination of outside observers who have been fascinated by its enigmatic aura. While most of the colonies of Black Africa were rushing to independence, Ethiopia remained Africa's "Hidden Empire," perceived to be more akin to the medieval empires of Europe than to the colonial states of the Third World. Emperor Haile Selassie cultivated abroad the image of a strong, able, and benevolent monarch dedicated to the twin goals of maintaining the independence of the only state in Black Africa to have successfully resisted European colonialism and easing his empire-state toward modernization. Until he was deposed, when most Westerners heard the name "Haile Selassie" they tended to reflect on the emperor's impassioned plea before the League of Nations in 1935 for the assistance of other member states in ousting the Italian Fascists from Ethiopian soil. Or, they imagined his triumphant return to the throne in 1941. Few Western observers—laymen and scholars alike—saw beneath the mystique that surrounded Haile Selassie and the Ethiopian Empire. As a consequence they did not fully understand the factors that contributed to the collapse of the empire-state and to the ensuing protracted struggle to reconstitute society on the foundation of a new social myth. The present work was inspired by this realization.

I came to the study of Ethiopia and the Ethiopian Revolution quite by accident. In 1976–1977 I was based in Addis Ababa as a visiting research associate with the United Nations Economic Commission for Africa. The project I was concerned with was a baseline study of nonformal education policies and programs in East and Southern Africa. One of the countries in the study was Ethiopia. In graduate school I had read a few books and articles on Ethiopia, and I had been acquainted with some Ethiopian student colleagues. Yet I did not really understand Ethiopia. Living through what was perhaps the most traumatic and formative phase of the Ethiopian Revolution, however, forced me to try to understand the process that I was witnessing. One could not live in Addis Ababa at the time without being emotionally drawn into what was happening. I was forced to ask "Why?" and "To what end?"

On my return to the United States I dedicated myself to the scholarly examination of the causes and consequences of the Ethiopian Revolution. The first phase of this project was facilitated by a semester of released time from the Department of Political Science at Indiana University and by two summer research grants from the university in 1978 and 1980 that enabled me to return to Ethiopia for the purpose of gathering data. The major funding for the project, however, was provided by a postdoctoral fellowship from the Ford Foundation and the National Research Council, 1981–1983. Four further research trips were sponsored by the University of California, Santa Barbara, after I joined its faculty in 1983. Without the generous support of each of these sources, the book I have produced would not have been possible.

As the project unfolded I realized that it would be insufficient merely to understand what caused Ethiopia's anachronistic empire-state to collapse. I had to understand the process of revolution itself and to understand the structural factors that influenced both of these interconnected processes. Through careful research on the history of Ethiopia and on the phenomenon of revolution, I hope that I have been able to produce a volume that is useful not only to Africanist scholars but to students of revolution as well.

In my effort to understand Ethiopia I relied on the wealth of knowledge and experience of a large number of nationals from the region. The list of those to whom I owe a debt of gratitude is much too long for me to relate here. However, special thanks are due to Hailu Habtu, Sisay Ibssa, Ruth Iyob, Ismail Ali Ismail, Kassay Legesse, Neway Amare, Dessalegn Rahmato, and Addisu Tolesa, who all in one way or another patiently steered me away from pitfalls in my analysis and contributed to my fuller understanding of what is by any standard a complex story.

John Cohen was introduced to me through his work on Ethiopia, and when I turned to him for help in unravelling the Ethiopian puzzle, John generously shared with me not only his insights but also his impressive library. For this I am especially appreciative. Other colleagues who deserve warm thanks for generously critiquing my work on Ethiopia over the past decade include Gwendolen Carter, Ruth and David Collier, Sylvia Curtis, Richard Greenfield, John Harbeson, Bonnie Holcome, Laura Kullenberg, David Laitin, Patrick O'Meara, Marina Ottaway, Louis Picard, Angela Raven Roberts, Pearl T. Robinson, Elliot Skinner, Deborah Toler, and Crawford Young.

A good deal of the manuscript represented here was initially drafted while I was a visiting research associate at the Institute of International Studies at the University of California, Berkeley, in 1981–1982 and 1983. Carl Rosberg, professional colleagues at the Institute, and all the staff deserve special thanks for their counsel, encouragement, and support.

As is often the case, graduate and undergraduate students were the victims on whom I first tried some of the ideas presented here. In many cases, they were instrumental in helping me to do the research that was involved. Among those who deserve special recognition are Ed Brown, Kelly Brown, Erika Keller, Vern A. Keller, Cy Reed, Karen Schulman, and Jackie Vieceli.

On the production side, heartfelt thanks are due to Muriel Zimmerman, who graciously read the manuscript and offered suggestions for fine tuning it for publication; to Eloise Martzen, who patiently and expertly put the whole thing into the word processor for the final draft; and to the numerous clerical assistants who helped me in so many ways over the years of this project.

Many helping hands contributed to the making of this "cake," and they all deserve to share in whatever praise is given for the insights the book is able to provide. However, any flaws that may appear in these pages may be attributed only to this author. I alone am responsible for whatever faulty analysis, misinterpretation, poor judgment, or omissions the astute reader might detect. In spite of whatever shortcomings there might be, I hope the reader at least gains a better understanding of Ethiopia and the Ethiopian Revolution.

Edmond J. Keller

INTRODUCTION

REVOLUTIONARY ETHIOPIA

On September 12, 1974, Emperor Haile Selassie I of Ethiopia, the Conquering Lion of the Tribe of Judah, King of the Kings, Elect of God, was deposed by a revolutionary coup d'etat staged by young commissioned and noncommissioned military officers and policemen, culminating what has been termed the "Creeping Revolution." With the demise of Haile Selassie came the end of his dream of molding Ethiopia into a modernizing constitutional monarchy, an empire built on refined principles of royal absolutism. What Haile Selassie had failed to realize was that such political arrangements are exceedingly difficult to establish in the twentieth century given worldwide trends toward more participatory forms of government, toward more egalitarian social and economic relationships, and even toward revolution.

Haile Selassie always felt that he had time to ease Ethiopia into full integration in the world community of nation-states. He primarily emphasized diplomatic and military policies but was more cautious in his domestic—economic, social, and political—policies. As a result, Haile Selassie's domestic policies were generally a failure, but his international policies did much to establish the legitimacy and viability of the Ethiopian Empire.

Ethiopia came to be regarded as the only Black African state, along with Liberia, to have escaped the ravages of European colonialism. During the most critical phase of the struggle for African independence under Haile Selassie's tutelage, Ethiopia sought to establish itself as the ultimate champion in the cause of African independence and self-determination. Indeed, an effort was made to portray Ethiopia as the epitome of African independence, a stable and integrated community amid a continent of new states characterized by chronic political instability.

These were, however, myths that could not stand the test of time. They had been introduced mainly for the symbolic support they might elicit for the legitimacy of the Ethiopian Empire in the world community and for the promotion of the desirability of unified, multi-ethnic African nation-states. Haile Selassie seems to have believed that if these objectives gained widespread acceptance, the transformation of Ethiopia's historical bureaucratic empire into a modern constitutional monarchy would be greatly enhanced.[1]

By late 1974 most if not all of the myths about the stability, unity, and uncolonized nature of the Ethiopian Empire that Haile Selassie had at-

1

tempted to foster were being vigorously challenged. Ethiopia was on the brink of balkanization as it reeled under pressures from within and from outside the polity. The most severe challenges came from Eritrean nationalists in the north; certain segments of the Oromo in the south-central part of the country; and from Ogaden Somali irredentists in the southeast. The Ogaden Somali and large segments of the Oromo people had been incorporated into the empire mainly during the age of European colonialism in Africa from roughly 1884 to 1957. This period coincided with Ethiopia's own twentieth-century colonial expansion. Eritrea was annexed only in 1962. As was the case with its European counterparts, Ethiopia maintained control over its colonial possessions largely through coercion, and as a result, such groups as the Eritreans, Somalis, and some of the Oromo were never fully integrated into Ethiopian society. Ethiopia has had to contend with demands for independence among the Eritreans ever since the region was federated with Ethiopia as a result of a United Nations resolution in 1950;[2] with Oromo dissidence since the south was incorporated into the empire between the mid-nineteenth and the early twentieth centuries;[3] with Ogaden Somali irredentism since the 1890s when the forces of the empire first attempted to establish effective control over the area;[4] and with various forms of protest by other politically subordinate minorities periodically since the inauguration of the empire.

Despite the fact that regional and ethnic resistance was historically endemic to the Ethiopian Empire, not until the final days of the regime of Haile Selassie did any of these potential threats to national political integration intensify to the degree that dismemberment seemed a serious possibility. Throughout his long reign, Haile Selassie had skillfully manipulated his domestic and foreign policies to ensure the survival and perpetuation of imperial authority. To this end, he cultivated both national and international strategic alliances and constantly attempted to strengthen those elements of authority that improved his position in relation to other centers of power in the country and the world.

An important aspect of the emperor's style of leadership was image management. He wanted to be seen as a consummate statesman, a benevolent and progressive autocrat, a modernizer. In the end, the social, economic, and political contradictions that emerged inevitably from Haile Selassie's attempts to modernize royal absolutism proved to be his undoing. In order to survive conditions of severe political pressures on imperial authority or periods when there exists a high demand for rapid and radical social, economic, and political change, any monarch must possess the ability to neutralize emerging contradictions. When this proves impossible, the king or emperor is doomed.

Haile Selassie was unable to resolve the cumulative contradictions that confronted his regime between 1973 and 1974. Opposition movements challenged the very integrity of Ethiopia's national boundaries. Drought, famine, and inflation tore at the social and economic fabric of society.

Conflicts between monarchists and republicans in the political arena added to an already charged political climate. The coup that actually deposed the emperor was merely a partial manifestation of the revolutionary sentiment that had blossomed in the wider society.

The revolutionaries pledged to liberalize policies toward freedom of political expression and democratic political participation. But whatever gains were made in this direction were minimal and short-lived. Social reforms were much more sweeping and permanent, not the least of which were the urban and rural land reform programs introduced in 1975.

In spite of efforts to initiate the new order and to have it accepted, two years after the dethroning of the emperor, the new military regime itself was being widely regarded among intellectuals and some culturally subordinate ethnic groups as illegitimate. Opposition forces, however, were not monolithic; they lacked coherence. For example, although there was some cooperation in resistance movements among the Somalis and some Oromo groups, these movements were largely autonomous and never linked up with similar movements elsewhere in the empire. This contributed to a situation of widespread, continued civil strife in both urban and rural areas. Coordination of such activities was extremely localized, and as a result, opposition to the new regime remained fragmented over the three years of its greatest intensity.

Publicly, the new regime committed itself to "One Ethiopia," "Ethiopia First!" but was unable to convince large segments of the population that this commitment was real or that such a condition was desirable. Failing to overcome its difficulties through political negotiation, the new regime responded with massive military force and coercion, finally choosing (at least in the short-run) a policy of political control rather than democracy and political integration. In short, despite the success of revolutionary toppling of the old order, the revolution did not immediately result in the establishment of a viable, legitimate, new order. The struggle continued over the character of the new Ethiopia. What values, what programs, what ideology would be most appropriate for building the new society?

Such a condition is not peculiar to the Ethiopian Revolution. In his analysis of the English Revolution of 1640, the American, French, and Russian revolutions, Crane Brinton identified the convulsive crisis periods that often seem to follow the initial act of revolution as "reigns of terror and virtue." During such periods moderation is abandoned in favor of a zealous and uncompromising attempt to impose the new order by force.[5] Commenting on the reasons for such a period of unrest, Peter Amman suggests that "if an insurrection has been successful in toppling an established government, yet is unable to assume the traditional monopoly of power peculiar to the state, the very dynamic of the state *qua* state will prolong the contest."[6]

The first decade of the revolution was characterized by the new regime's consistent attempt to assert the authority of the state and to establish society on new foundations. When the tenth anniversary of the revolution was celebrated and a "vanguard party of working people" introduced, leaders could reflect on a period of transition in which many of the people most historically oppressed had witnessed a qualitative change for the better in their lives. They were more literate, more independent, and had better access for formal education, modern health care, and other social services. Yet the regime lacked widespread legitimacy. It was constantly challenged on ideological grounds or by nationalist groups demanding their right to self-determination. Rather than being disposed to share power with civilian elements or to consider the possibility of a federated Ethiopia, the "men in uniform" clung desperately to power and in fact attempted to institutionalize their rule under the guise of a people's democratic republic. They pursued a statist development strategy, and under the auspices of a reconstituted state dominated by a segment of the military, the party and bureaucracy attempted to lead and shape economic development and to closely manipulate sociopolitical development.

The Revolution in Perspective

To come to grips with the causes and consequences of the Ethiopian Revolution it is necessary to understand both the processes that led to the formation and perpetuation of the bureaucratic empire as well as the forces that contributed to the protracted period of civil unrest after the initial act of revolution. To this end, several basic, interrelated questions must be addressed. What factors, for instance, enabled Haile Selassie's anachronistic bureaucratic empire to survive as long as it did, given long-standing worldwide trends away from such forms of governance? What factors explain the timing and pattern of the transformation of the Ethiopian Empire? Why was the revolutionary alternative chosen instead of the reformist alternative? How can Ethiopia's protracted civil unrest in the wake of the demise of the ancien régime be explained? When will the social revolution be consummated?

Answers to these questions and others are many and varied. What is clear is that Ethiopia and the Ethiopian Revolution do not lend themselves to simple explanations. Traditional Ethiopian society was extremely complex, and the efforts of Haile Selassie to selectively alter tradition while introducing elements of modernity only added to an already complex picture. Feudalism or quasi-feudal socioeconomic arrangements and gross socioeconomic inequality were always considered potential sources of conflict.[7] Yet both inside and outside observers generally agreed that as long as the Church, the aristocracy, the bureaucracy, the military, and existing foreign military and diplomatic alliances remained intact, the empire would survive.[8] Some observers link the collapse of the Haile Selassie regime to the immediate socioeconomic effects of widespread drought, famine, and inflation.[9] There is no doubt that these were precipitating events, but focusing only on such catastrophes ignores the deeper underlying causes of the revolution. Ethiopia had always been characterized by periodic drought, famine, and pestilence and by widespread poverty. While there had been rebellions that tended to grow out of such circumstances, there had never been such a decisive act as revolution.

Others identify elite disaffection and conflict as the primary causal agents.[10] Still others, taking an explicitly Marxian perspective, point to the corporate grievances of various elements in Ethiopia's peasant and incipient working and middle classes.[11] They argue that the most important determinant was the nature and timing of the introduction of Ethiopia into the world capitalist economy after World War II and the contradictions resulting therefrom.

These are but a few of the most commonly offered explanations for the demise of the Ethiopian Empire. While each provides an adequate partial explanation for the revolution, few have attempted to place this process of transformation into a broad theoretical framework.[12] The present work is a preliminary attempt to fill this void in the literature by analyzing the Ethiopian Revolution in terms of those factors that led to the formation, perpetuation, and transformation of Ethiopia's modernizing empire, and those forces that best explain the nature and timing of the revolutionary process in Ethiopia. The intent is not to advance a general theory of how change occurs in modernizing bureaucratic empires or a general theory of the relationship between revolution and the presence of bureaucratic imperial systems. The goal here is a more modest, middle-range theory that allows us to place the Ethiopian Revolution into critical perspective. From this it might be possible to draw implications that are relevant to understanding the potential for revolutionary change in other similar state systems.

My basic argument is that there was a dialectical relationship between the multiple contradictions that grew out of the attempts of Haile Selassie to centralize and modernize his empire, while initiating only limited changes in existing institutional forms and relationships, and the timing and nature of Ethiopia's revolutionary transformation.[13] I argue further that the protracted period of widespread civil unrest even after the demise of the ancien régime can be explained, as it has been elsewhere, as a natural outgrowth of the revolutionary process. Revolutions do not end with the deposition of the old order but continue until a new regime is accepted as legitimate and a new social myth is accepted as a guide to social, economic, and political relationships in the new society.

Some Relevant Concepts

Three concepts will be of particular importance in this study: bureaucratic empire, revolutionary transformation, and social myth.

Bureaucratic Empire. S. N. Eisenstadt notes that, historically and analytically, empires are states that belong somewhere between what we might classify, for lack of better terms, as "premodern" and "modern" political systems.[14] Historically, most empires were governed by monarchs whose claims to authority and legitimacy were established by sacred traditions. However, there was also a conscious attempt by emperors of bureaucratic empires to secularize certain aspects of their authority.

Historically, bureaucratic empires such as the Egyptian, Ottoman, Roman, Persian, and Ethiopian empires developed from city states, patrimonial or dual conquest-sedentary empires, or from feudal societies. They usually emerged at the initiative of rulers who wanted to centralize, unify, and solidify their conquests or to restore order to a clearly circumscribed territory, with a monopoly over political decision making in the area. To accomplish these ends, emperors were forced to erect bureaucratic, financial, political, and military institutions that facilitated their efforts to centralize rulership in themselves. There was a constant need for the monarch to marshal resources in support of the state system and its territorial integrity. He also had to attempt to balance his desire to use these institutions for his own (mostly exploitative) purposes and his need to respond to sociopolitical demands emanating from the political environment. It is important to remember that such bureaucratic institutions were created not only to facilitate exploitation but also as a counterbalance to traditional elements that remained extremely powerful. The ultimate objective was to foster royal absolutism. Political conflict was somewhat moderated through the establishment of formal or semiformal arenas of political struggle such as court cliques, royal councils, or quasi-representative assemblies.

The emperor could not completely ignore or subjugate traditional elements even if he desired to do so. One important reason for this was his heavy reliance on such elements for his legitimization. Traditions, their symbols and their agents, were what made such societies cohere. The legitimization of the rulers of historical bureaucratic empires was mainly religio-traditional; and the criteria for evaluating such rulers usually combined political and religious value orientations. The designated rulers of these societies were either members of hereditary ruling groups or charismatic personalities thought to embody the society's "sacred" values and symbols. Over time, however, secondary patterns of legitimization evolved in bureaucratic empires based on legal-rational criteria. Examples of these include bureaucratic institutions acting on behalf of a ruler.[15]

When bureaucratic empires changed it was in response to cues emanating from the domestic as well as the international political environment. But the particular form chosen during the process of change from the historical bureaucratic empire to a more modern form of political system was generally determined by the economic and social conditions existing in the given society undergoing transformation and by the political issues, organizations, and activities that characterized that society.[16] Instead of being a spontaneous process, this change grew out of a cumulation of contradictions in society and the prescriptive structural adjustments attempted by rulers to cope with such challenges.

Those bureaucratic empires that survived into the middle of the twentieth century faced similar challenges of modernization; they each attempted to cope in similar ways—centralizing and modernizing the bureaucracy and the military, developing stable and reliable military alliances, reducing the power of traditional elements, and strengthening the hand of secular authorities.[17] In order to survive, monarchs had to engage in policies of economic development and political control. They also had to be sensitive to demands for alterations in power distribution and flexible enough to respond in the most advantageous manner. How well a monarch managed to face up to challenges to his authority and to accomplish his own policy objectives determined his ability to survive. When he failed to survive, idiosyncratic features determined whether he was replaced by a new emperor or by a totally new order. The convergence of the very predictable functional characteristics of bureaucratic empires and the not-so-predictable idiosyncratic or contextual elements best help us understand the Ethiopian Revolution, its timing and its nature.

Revolutionary Transformation. Revolution is more than an event; it is a process. Although factors that trigger this process vary from situation to situation, the objective of all revolutions is generally the same: to radically transform society so that it better conforms to the changing needs and aspirations of its people. Revolutions differ from other types of social transformation in that the change wrought results in the sudden, radical reordering of fundamental values, relationships, and the social myths on which society is based. This is the essence of revolutionary transformation.

The causes of revolution can be grouped into two main categories: underlying causes and precipitating causes. The former might include historically based inequality and exploitation, cultural cleavages, disputes over land tenure, and elite conflict. These are typical fundamental factors that could give rise to a sense of relative deprivation or indignation among segments of a population that feel sufficiently large or powerful enough to challenge existing authorities in revolutionary activities. However, before this happens, precipitating events must occur and facilitating factors must be present.

Precipitating factors might include military defeat, economic crisis, severe political turmoil, and the contagion effect that spreads from other revolutions. Like our list of underlying causes, this list is not all-inclusive. Precipitating causes are highly situational or idiosyncratic variables and depend in large measure on conditions in the immediate political environment.

Facilitating factors are those that separate revolutions from other types of violent rebellion. Chief among these are the emergence of inspired revolutionary leaders, the formation of revolutionary organizations, the acquisition of a revolutionary ideology, and support for the revolutionary ideal by a critical mass of aggrieved members of the populace. These facilitating factors may occur in any combination, and the strength of revolutionary potential of each varies from situation to situation. The success of any revolution is highly contingent on environmental circumstances. But even if environmental circumstances are favorable, there may clearly be a revolutionary potential without there being revolution.

Numerous theorists have identified the transfer of the allegiance of intellectuals as the master symptom of revolution, since intellectuals are the primary upholders of the myths of society, and their support is crucial to any regime.[18] Transfer occurs as a result of two major factors. First, conflicts emerge between ruling elites and intellectuals over contradictions or failures in the policies of the regime. Revolutions represent at least the political failure of a government and its policies. Increasingly sharp and widespread opposition to the existing political system—particularly among intellectuals—culminates in overt political attack on the government.[19] Second, in response to its loss of support among intellectuals, the government turns to force and violence. When this happens, the attitude of the state military is critical. As long as the military is loyal and monopolizes coercive power, the regime is able at least to maintain itself. However, when the military is inefficient, disloyal, or otherwise incapacitated, not only is the potential for revolution much greater, but also the chances for successful revolution are much greater. Revolutions that take place without counterrevolutionary activity on the part of the state military or that involve the military as a revolutionary actor are the most likely to succeed. Charles Tilly correctly notes that "the most crucial coalitions over the whole range of revolutions surely link challengers directly with military forces."[20] The Egyptian and Turkish revolutions are classic examples of revolution involving the military. In both instances, soldiers came to dominate coalitions comprised of intellectual dissidents and civilian resistance movements.

Social Myth. Once the revolutionary act of overthrowing the ancien régime has been accomplished, revolutionaries must be able to establish themselves as a legitimate, new government in the eyes of the majority of the population through a new, viable, and legitimate social myth. Unless this happens, multiple, competing power blocs emerge, and the "period of no government" is protracted. George Pettee has suggested:

> the constructive phase of revolution requires the power of common will guided by common ideas. Every revolution develops such common ideas, or a myth, before it accomplishes positive political action.
>
> A community cannot shed its old form and reintegrate itself by new purposes, without an accepted expression of these purposes in a myth. This means no more than that a new social order is real only when men behave regularly and coherently in the new pattern, which thereby are made the new institutions. . . . Innovations cannot be habits, and so must be ideas.[21]

The political (as opposed to the social) dimension of revolution prevails until the state's monopoly of power is reestablished. During this "period of no government," intellectual struggle is over which new myth will predominate.[22]

The Plan of the Book

The intention of this book is to analyze the transformation of the Ethiopian Empire in terms of its historical and cultural antecedents and to attempt to place the continuing revolution into its proper context. Ethiopia's bureaucratic empire was established in the mid-1800s. The centralization process, however, did not really begin to take hold until the early twentieth century. The height of the development of the bureaucratic empire coincided with the reign of Emperor Haile Selassie I (1930–1974). Attempts by his regime to transform Ethiopia into a modern nation-state fell short mainly because of flaws in the policies he pursued. This led to the revolutionary transformation of Ethiopian society. The political act of revolution did not, however, lead directly to permanent social, economic, or political changes. The struggle continued for more than a decade over the design of the new society.

The book is divided into three major sections. Part One provides a conceptual framework for understanding what factors contributed to the revolutionary transformation of Ethiopia's bureaucratic empire. Chapters 1 and 2 deal with the process of statebuilding, the historical and cultural aspects of society. Special attention is devoted to identifying the structures of power, authority, and conflict in traditional Ethiopian society. These relationships in some cases differed in the core and the periphery of the empire. This had significant implications for the pattern of change during the periods of modernization and revolution.

Chapter 3 focuses on the leadership style of Haile Selassie and on his politically motivated policies. In order for the empire to survive under international and domestic pressures for change, it was necessary for the emperor to be open to adaptation and innovation. Critical choices had to be made about what was to be changed in traditional society; what was to remain the same; what new values and technology to introduce; and which new values and innovations would have to be rejected. In the process of optimizing policy choices, the emperor was constantly confronted with contradictions, some of which could challenge the very survival of his regime. Therefore, he had to become adept at the management of such pressures. To the extent that he was successful, he survived and even prospered. But to the extent that he was unsuccessful, he could be destroyed. This chapter critically analyzes Haile Selassie's policy performance and attempts to identify where and why he failed in managing the contradictions he faced.

Chapter 4 concentrates on Haile Selassie's attempt to transform Ethiopia's feudal economy into a hybrid capitalist economy. This process was fraught with contradictions that contributed greatly to the demise of the ancien régime.

Part Two deals with the actual genesis of the Revolution, its underlying and precipitant causes respectively. Chapter 5 identifies critical areas of political, economic, and social contradictions that characterized Ethiopian society at the time of the revolution and that were rooted in history: the tendency toward royal absolutism, feudalism, and ethnic and class tensions.

Chapter 6 deals with the immediate causes and the process of the revolution itself. Drought, famine, and economic crisis were the main precipitants of revolution, coupled with the underlying factors already mentioned. The facilitating factors of greatest import were the defection of a significant segment of the military from support of the imperial state and the immobilization of traditional elements such as the aristocracy and the church.

The process of revolutionary consolidation is covered in Part Three. Chapter 7 concentrates on the efforts of the new regime to achieve ideological definition and to use ideology as an agent for unity and social cohesion. Even though the regime proved to be quite flexible and adaptive in ideological terms over its first decade of rule, it was unable to secure widespread acceptance. Opposition based on ideology and on claims of self-determination continued, yet the regime forged ahead in its efforts to recast Ethiopian society.

Chapter 8 analyzes the impact of the new state's social policies and institutional innovation and reform on establishing its authority to rule. Social policies introduced over the first ten years of the revolution changed the lot of many of those who had been most deprived and oppressed during the imperial era. However, because of the profound poverty and underdevelopment that characterized Ethiopia and the limited resource capacity of the state, the symbolic and material impact of social policy was limited. The state was more successful at enhancing its bureaucratic capacity. The state bureaucracy reformed and expanded, and a vanguard party that owed its allegiance to the state contributed greatly to the consolidation of a statist development strategy that went far beyond what Haile Selassie was able to achieve.

After a brief flirtation with populist socialism, the new regime declared its commitment to scientific socialism based on the principles of Marxism-Leninism. Chapter 9 critically assesses the efforts of the new regime to socialize the economy under conditions of scarcity and limited state capacity.

Chapter 10 attempts to place the Ethiopian Revolution in the context of other revolutions and of Ethiopian history. While the Ethiopian Revolution had characteristics similar to the "great revolutions" that occurred in France, Russia, and China, it was perhaps more like the modern social revolutions that have occurred in Africa and other parts of the Third

World. Such revolutions did little to change the weak, dependent character of those states. At the same time, it is unreasonable to attempt to place the revolution in the framework of some general theory of revolution. A middle-range theory informed by the peculiarities of Ethiopian history and culture as they relate to more global phenomena appears to be more appropriate and useful.

Part One

Toward a Theory of the Revolutionary Transformation of the Ethiopian Empire

I

ETHIOPIA AS A BUREAUCRATIC EMPIRE

The state of Ethiopia can trace its origins back more than two thousand years. But what we classify as the Ethiopian Bureaucratic Empire was largely a product of the past one hundred years. Between the mid- to late nineteenth century and the mid- to late twentieth century, the state increasingly took on the characteristics of a highly centralized and bureaucratized empire. The state structure that emerged over this period was not modern, and yet it was not wholly traditional. Traditional institutions, symbols, and sanctions continued to be extremely important, but authority became more secularly based than it had ever been throughout the history of the Ethiopian people.

Perhaps the most important distinguishing features of the classical bureaucratic empire are the centralization of the authority in the office of the emperor and the establishment of a salaried bureaucracy that becomes the permanent representative of the crown in subjugated areas.[1] In the process, political and administrative roles become increasingly differentiated. Authority, for instance, becomes more decentralized and compartmentalized. Institutions tend to take on the separate functions of administration and tax collection, maintenance of order, economic organization and trade regulation, and adjudication. Although in some cases these functions might still be fused in one office, as bureaucratic empires entrench themselves, the tendency is toward a higher degree of functional differentiation. However, the degree of bureaucratization falls short of being equivalent to that found in a modern state. In Ethiopia, as in other historical bureaucratic empires, emperors, in their efforts to centralize authority in themselves, were concerned with increasing the absolute nature of their authority. Bureaucratization and the maintenance of a strong state military of course facilitated centralization, but there was always the need to engage in additional political and economic policies that bolstered such efforts. For instance, Ethiopian emperors from Tewodros to Haile Selassie attempted to achieve continuous control and regulation of economic resources; and they attempted to maintain political control over different groups in society through such economic policies as the direct conscription of labor, the

15

promotion of state enterprises, taxation, and various financial and monetary policies.[2] In other words, the Ethiopian emperors who contributed to
the establishment of the bureaucratic empire were all aware of the critical
need to exapnd their reservoir of flexible resources in order to increase
their autonomy and to strengthen their authority in relation to other
groups in society. Flexible resources were simply diplomatic, manpower,
monetary, and secularly based institutional resources that could be exclusively manipulated by an emperor.

This chapter traces the historical development of the Ethiopian Bureaucratic Empire and attempts to show how successive emperors, beginning with Tewodros, continually bureaucratized and secularized the state
and increased the autonomous authority of the crown. Throughout this
process, considerable political acumen was needed to prevent the state
from regressing into the fragmented patrimonial, semifeudal entity from
which it had emerged. If Ethiopia was to survive, it would have to be
nudged toward modernity, even if this meant defensive modernization.

Historical and Cultural Antecedents

Present-day Ethiopia owes its heritage to the ancient kingdom of Aksum,
which grew out of a northern Ethiopian city-state of the same name. The
core of the kingdom encompassed the Tigre highlands, but its sphere of
effective control stretched through Eritrea down to the coast of the Red
Sea. The kingdom emerged around the sixth century B.C., flourished
between the first and eighth centuries A.D., and was finally decimated in
970 A.D. by hostile neighboring groups.[3]

At this time we could not speak of a centralized bureaucratic empire but
of a patrimonial conquest empire held together by force, particularistic
loyalties, and trade. Then what we now know as Ethiopia was peopled by
more than fifty distinct and distinctive ethnic groupings. Wars of conquest
and expansion were common, but few of the groups in the area entertained
notions of establishing permanent political and cultural hegemony over
groups far removed from their own. In this sense, the Aksumites, a semi-
ticized North African people, were different. Donald Levine suggests that
the Aksumites relished the thought of spreading their culture to the peoples they conquered and also the prospects of collecting tribute from
them.[4]

Vigorous Aksumite expansion began around the first century A.D., and
by the sixth century nearly all of the principalities of northern Ethiopia
were under the rule of Aksum. More tentative control was established in
peripheral areas to the south and west. The rulers of Aksum came to
regard themselves as King of Kings, a symbolic reference to the expanded
scope of their authority through conquest.[5]

During two separate phases of Aksumite expansion of the kingdom the

Crown was able to establish control over what is present-day Yemen on the Arabian peninsula. This enabled Aksum, or Abyssinia as it was known by then, at least for a time to control shipping lanes on the Red Sea. At no time, however, were Aksumite kings able to erect a highly centralized, bureaucratized administrative state.

Abyssinia maintained relatively close trading links with the Roman Empire, and this may have contributed to the adoption of Christianity as the official religion during the middle of the fourth century.[6] From this point on the Christian religion and the Greek language—the language of the Church—became the vehicles through which the Aksumite culture spread to conquered peoples.

Soon after the Aksumite conversion to Christianity a controversy emerged over the true nature of Christ.[7] The Greek and Roman branches of the Church held that the deity and the human spirit had been brought together in the person of Christ but not fused. Some representatives of the Syrian and Egyptian wing of the Church, on the other hand, argued for the single, divine nature of Christ. The latter group came to be known as the Monophysite or Coptic Christians. As a result of this conflict, known as "the Great Schism," the Church split into two. The Ethiopian Church identified with the Egyptian Monophysites and the patriarch of Alexandria. The Church continued to be closely allied with the monarchy, crowning kings and lending to the symbolic legitimacy of the office.

Toward the end of the sixth century, the Abyssinians were driven from Yemen and from their possessions along the western shore of the Red Sea by the Persians.[8] This did not, however, totally destroy the kingdom. In fact, it merely forced the Abyssinians to concentrate the focus of their influence south, east, and west. For a time, they were able to establish new trade routes to the sea, even gaining control of a new seaport that allowed them to begin trading with Yemen again. The Abyssinians also temporarily succeeded in converting adherents of traditional religions in peripheral areas to Coptic Christianity.

The revitalization period came to an end with the sacking of Aksum in the 970s. Churches were razed, and most of the royalty were killed. From this period until 1135, the Christian kingdom fell on hard times. Muslim Arabs threatened it from the north, Muslim Somalis threatened it from the southeast, and it was otherwise surrounded by hostile neighbors who entered the territory either bent on ritualistic conquest or in search of land.[9]

By 1135 what remained of the Aksumite kingdom had been pushed to the south. It was able to reconstitute itself, although in a weakened condition, as the Zagwe Dynasty. The capital of this kingdom was established not in Aksum, but in the province of Lasta. The rulers of the Zagwe Dynasty, who ruled for some 135 years, were recognized by their subjects as legitimate, but they were not of the same royal line, the Solomonic line, that had ruled the Aksumite kingdom until its fall.[10] However, in 1270 Yekunno Amlak, an Amhara king who claimed to be a direct descendent of

King David and King Solomon, led a military expedition that resulted in the toppling of the Zagwe Dynasty and the "restoration" of the Solomonic line. Ethiopian tradition suggests that the sole royal survivor of the sacking of Aksum had fled to the south and had taken up residence in Menz.[11] There he is said to have fathered the lineage that was destined to restore the Solomonic line of kingly authority. Yekunno Amlak claimed to be from that line. During his reign Yekunno Amlak inaugurated a cultural revival and made limited improvements in administration.

Despite his claim to legitimacy, Yekunno Amlak, who took the name Tesfa Iyesus (Hope of Jesus) when he ascended the throne, was unable to secure absolute control over the kingdom or to expand it to its previous size and greatness.[12] Resistance flared up immediately throughout the kingdom. Other competing Christian kingdoms in the north gained in strength and provided severe challenges to the restored Solomonic dynasty. Several powerful Islamic kingdoms in the southeast also came to present a threat. Still, the influence of the Amharas expanded under Yekunno Amlak and the Amhara kings who succeeded him. The greatest expansion occurred between 1314 and 1344 under Yekunno Amlak's grandson, Amde Siyon.[13] He was able to subdue independent Amhara and Tigre kingdoms in the north and south as well as in the west. He was also able to bring some Muslim and Falasha (Oriental Semitic) peoples under his control. This expansion and consolidation continued throughout the fourteenth century and into the fifteenth century. Significantly, although force played a central role during this period of expansion, there was also a conscious effort to infuse conquered peoples with an appreciation for Abyssinian culture. Amharic became the primary medium of communication in the provinces of Shoa, Gojjam, Begemdir, and most of Wollo—the Amhara core—and it became the official language in all captured areas. Along with Amharic, acceptance of the Orthodox religion became the primary informal requirement for full incorporation into Abyssinian society. Whether or not conquered peoples became completely Amharized,[14] they were often forced to abandon their animist beliefs and to adopt Christianity. Religious conversion was supported by the state, but the major responsibility for this activity was left with Abyssinian clerics. In addition to the political dimension of the Abyssinian expansion during this period, religious propagation had a tremendous impact in etching out the beginnings of the modern Ethiopian state, a state that ultimately came to incorporate peoples other than the original Abyssinians—the Amharas and Tigreans.

By the beginning of the sixteenth century the Abyssinians were again severely challenged by hostile peoples also in the process of expanding their own domains—the Ottoman Turks, the Somali, and the Oromo. The Ottomans were truly a world power at this time, and their African possessions stretched from the Red Sea and the Gulf of Aden into the East African interior as far west as Sudan and the banks of the Nile. For the most part, in the early half of the sixteenth century the Turks confined their activities in the Horn of Africa to control of the seas, but they did for the first time provide some Muslim neighbors of the Abyssinians, the Afar and the Somali, with arms that enabled them to wage their own separate campaigns of expansion. Led by the charismatic Somali leader Ahmad Gran (Imam Ahmed Ibn Ibrahim El-Ghazi), a coalition of Muslim invaders consisting mainly of Somali and Afar pastoral warriors waged a *jihad* (holy war) in 1527 against the Christian Abyssinians that wreaked havoc on their heartland for the next fourteen years.[15] Pressed by the Muslim leader and his warriors, the reigning king was forced to remain on the move, fleeing one mountain retreat after the other. Gran's fury was particularly directed at shrines and churches, but he was also bent on crushing the Abyssinian state as a political force in the area. The complete destruction of the Abyssinian state, however, was prevented when Ahmad Gran was killed in a battle in 1543 against Portuguese and Abyssinian forces.

The Portuguese were interested in forestalling the advance of the Ottomans in the Horn and had dispatched a small force of soldiers with firearms to assist the Abyssinians in repulsing the Muslim invaders.[16] This demoralized Gran's forces and lifted the morale of the Abyssinian warriors who proceeded to drive out the invaders. The Abyssinians had survived this epic challenge to their political and religious integrity; but, like the enemies who had besieged them, they emerged from the struggle impoverished and debilitated. Yet by the end of the century the Abyssinians were able to lay waste the sultinate of Harar which had been Gran's staging ground.

By the mid-sixteenth century, the Turks had decided to establish a permanent presence on the western banks of the Red Sea. In 1557 they captured the Eritrean seaport of Massawa.[17] The Ottomans were even successful in penetrating the fringes of the Tigre highlands, destroying Christian communities as they went. For the most part, they confined themselves to coastal regions.

The Turkish invasion coincided roughly with a series of invasions by the Eastern Cushitic Oromo people. The Oromos, rather than adhering to Islam or Christianity, were mainly animist in religious orientation. Their expansion, which was mainly into north-central Ethiopia and Kenya, began in the early sixteenth century and has been described as one of the greatest such movements in African history.[18] Even as the Christian Abyssinians and the Muslim Somalis spent themselves in suicidal struggle, the Oromos were making inroads into the territories of both contestants. Some Oromo warriors had penetrated into the Abyssinian core as far north as Shoa by the 1550s, and by the 1560s others devastated the Muslim stronghold of Harar. By the end of the century, the Oromos had penetrated as far north as Begemdir and Gojjam. They did at times encounter strong resistance, particularly in the Abyssinian highlands, but they usually skirted around areas known to have strong rulers, choosing to victimize weaker ones. This was facilitated by the strength of patrimonial and regional bases of power in the Abyssinian core at this time. The Oromos did not possess superior military technology, but in the face of a nonmonolithic enemy they could rely on the might of numbers to win battles.

There is some disagreement among scholars about why the Oromo migration occurred at the time it did, but there is little doubt that Oromo penetration into the Abyssinian core significantly influenced the future course of Ethiopian history.[19] At the height of their expansion, the Oromo occupied as much as one-third of the Abyssinian heartland. Levine notes that prior to this time it was customary for the Oromo to engage in hit-and-run attacks against their enemies. But factors such as population pressures in their traditional areas, the increasing length of their campaigns, and the distance of raids away from their home areas influenced Oromo warrior bands to settle in the territories they conquered.[20]

The Oromo established their own enclaves mostly in the central part of Abyssinia, and although they preserved much of their traditional culture, they selectively borrowed and adapted a great deal of the Abyssinian culture to suit their needs and tastes.[21] As long as they remained in their own enclaves, the Oromo were able to preserve some elements of their traditional culture and thus to maintain their distinctiveness. But in certain instances where they penetrated Abyssinian strongholds such as Gojjam and Begemdir—usually as prisoners of war or as royal retainers—they were more fully integrated into Amhara society, often intermarrying with the Amhara and accepting the Christian religion. The door was then open to direct Oromo influence in Amhara life and politics. Significantly, in the late seventeenth and early eighteenth centuries the already substantial political influence of Oromos in the Amhara heartland increased dramatically as a result of the ascent of Emperor Asman Giorgis to the throne in 1721. Asman Giorgis had taken refuge among a segment of the Oromo during an intense period of internecine warfare within the royal family, and when he became emperor he welcomed Oromos to his court. Asman Giorgis was bent on breaking the power of the Amhara nobility. He recruited Oromos into his army and even employed some of them as close confidants.[22] From this point on, the influence of the Oromo in the royal court grew. There was a good deal of intermarrying between Amhara royalty and people of Oromo origins, and this eventually resulted in the emergence of nobility and even emperors who were not of purely Abyssinian stock.

The growth of Oromo influence in the court had an enormous unsettling influence on the viability of the Abyssinian state. Toward the end of the reign of Iyasu II (1753), the son of Asman Giorgis who had married an Oromo, the state was on the verge of complete collapse. The Amhara royalty struggled to maintain its superior position in the royal court but continued to lose ground. With the ascendency of Ioas, the son of Iyasu II, the Amhara nobility was rendered completely powerless at the expense of the Oromo nobility in the court.[23] This led to bloody civil wars and the steady loss of power by the central authorities.

Between 1769 and 1855 the Abyssinian Empire became moribund and eventually ceased to exist in all but name. This was "The Era of the Princes" *(Zemene Mesafint).*[24] Political power became decentralized as the state regressed into feudal, regional compartments. Local warlords and the traditional nobility competed among themselves for supremacy. The main political divisions at this time were Tigre, Wag-Lasta, Simen, Begemdir, Gojjam, a number of small provinces in the central part of the empire, and Shoa. Of these, only Shoa, which was separated from the other Amhara-Tigre provinces by an Oromo enclave, remained relatively stable and unified.[25]

Abyssinia was then only figuratively a unified state, being nominally ruled by fifteen different puppet emperors during the period. The emperorship changed hands twenty-seven times in seventy-one years, several individuals holding the throne on multiple occasions. Only one emperor (Eqwala Seyon, 1801–1818) during this era ruled for more than five consecutive years. Several served for no more than a single year, and one (Baeda Mariam III, 1826) for only four days.[26]

This period coincided with the dominant influence of the Yejju Galla (Oromo) dynasty. The Yejju dynasty was headed by the reigning governor of Begemdir. The first of this line was Ras (Duke) Ali Gwangwil, Ali the Great. Six other members of the dynasty reigned before the line was deposed by Ras Kasa (Tewodros II) in 1855. While it held sway, the head of the Yejju dynasty became a king-maker, controlling all higher appointments, especially that of King of Kings or emperor.[27] The rulers of this dynasty did not pretend to be of the Solomonic line. They merely referred to themselves as *ri'ise mekwanint* (head of the great men).[28]

Tewodros II

Tewodros II is credited with crushing the Muslim-influenced Yejju Galla dynasty. He is variously described in literary accounts of his life and times as "a revolutionary," "a unifier," "an innovator," "a tyrant," "a thief," and "a villain." At the same time, there is general agreement that he was, more than anyone else, the founder of the modern Ethiopian state. This assertion becomes more credible when one considers the context in which Tewodros II emerged and prospered.

Tewodros was born in about 1820 in the northwestern frontier province of Qwara. He was given the name of Kasa. Kasa was the son of a local chief whose connections (if there were any) with the Solomonic line were obscure. His father died when he was young, leaving his mother destitute. These humble beginnings were to prove a source of great sensitivity for

Kasa, who seemed throughout his life always to be struggling to establish his identity. In his childhood, Kasa was educated at an Orthodox Christian monastery but left at a young age to become a warrior. By the time he reached adolescence, Kasa had proven himself as an able soldier in the service of the provincial administration.

Qwara was situated between Lake Tana and the Sudan border. During the *Zemene Mesafint* the region was constantly challenged by Islamic forces from Egypt who sought to bring its people under the control of Egypt's expanding secondary empire. In contrast to the Ethiopians they confronted, the Egyptians were armed with advanced military weaponry, and their battalions were extremely disciplined. As a result, when Egyptian and Ethiopian forces engaged one another, the former were usually the victors. Kasa, needless to say, lost his share of battles, but he learned the value of modern weaponry and military discipline. These lessons were to have a tremendous influence on his own emergence as a successful warlord.[29]

Kasa's rise to power began in the early 1840s, a period in which he was considered no more than a common *shifta* (bandit). In fact, however, there is evidence that he was more than a mere shifta. Kasa's behavior seemed more akin to a "Robin Hood," a *social* bandit, who was opposed to the established order, but who would go out of his way to see to the needs of the poor.[30] Through such deeds an individual could traditionally assume legitimacy in the eyes of common folk.

Tewodros hijacked caravans, sacked enemy villages, and acquired a wide variety of booty—money, horses, mules, sheep, goats, cattle, grain, and slaves.[31] He is said to have shared his booty generously with the common folk he came into contact with in Qwara and encouraged them to devote their efforts to improving their farming techniques. Kasa, along with his soldiers, went so far as to teach by example, clearing forests and cultivating the land.[32] Through his military prowess, and as a result of the popularity of his social outlook and behavior, Kasa had attracted a sizable number of loyal followers by 1845.

At this time, Qwara was under the jurisdiction of the governor of Ye-Maru Qimis, Menen, the mother of Ras Ali. Menen came to view Kasa's activities as embarrassing and attempted to bring him under her authority as a vassal. Initially Kasa refused, but Ras Ali intervened with an offer that was more acceptable to him. Ali, interested in securing the loyalty of such a powerful warlord in the strategic border region, offered Kasa his daughter Tewabech and acknowledged Qwara as Kasa's own fiefdom, under the governorship of Menen. In spite of this very significant turn of events, relations between Kasa and Menen did not improve. Through her words and actions the governor made it clear that she had no respect for Kasa. Within a year Kasa was engaged in rebellion against Menen. The *Zemene Mesafint* was in full force, and Ras Ali was involved in a struggle of life or death. In more normal times Ali would have sent military aid to his mother in order to quash Kasa's rebellion, but he was engaged on multiple fronts in more important battles of his own.[33] Menen instead sent troops to aid those of Ali against the powerful Tigre king, Wibe, thus weakening her own defensive capacity. In January 1847 Kasa seized this opportunity and invaded Menen's capital, Gondar, demanding that the subjects there pay taxes and tribute due to Menen and Ali to him instead. Once this was done, Kasa set up his own administration not only in the city but also in adjacent districts to the east and south of Lake Tana.

By June the forces of Menen and Ali had succeeded in defeating Wibe's army, and she was then able to turn her attention to the rebel, Kasa. In the battle that ensued, Menen as well as her husband Ase-Yohannis were captured. Ras Ali initially sought to negotiate the release of his mother. Kasa countered with a demand for Menen's governorship. This was an unreasonable request in Ali's eyes, and he then attempted to free Menen through force. But his mother cautioned Ali to liberate her by the safest possible means, and the king agreed to Kasa's terms. Kasa became governor of Ye-Maru Qimis and in the process attracted a large number of new followers. He then turned his attentions west, to the Sudan frontier, and made war on the Egyptians once again. But again he tasted defeat at their hands.

Although Kasa and Ras Ali cooperated in battle from time to time, their relationship was always very tentative, each man being suspicious of the other. By 1852, Ali had decided to make his decisive move against Kasa. He sent his most trusted ally, Goshu, to face Kasa in late November at Gur Amba.[34] In spite of being heavily outnumbered, however, Kasa was able to repulse Goshu's attack. Following this, he attempted to negotiate a peace with Ali, but Ali refused. Each leader then began to organize his forces in preparation for the final showdown. When the series of battles in this sequence began in April 1853, Kasa was able to subdue the initial wave of the combined forces of Ali and Wibe. In May he took the initiative and moved on Ali's capital, Debre Tabor, sacking and burning the city and sending Ali's forces into flight. By late June, Ras Ali himself was finally defeated, taking refuge in Yejju. Kasa was soon able to gain control of Ras Ali's entire domain, and he proclaimed himself king. This marked the end of the reign of the Yejju dynasty. Kasa now controlled Begemdir, Gojjam, Lasta, and Amhara.

Buoyed by his success against Ras Ali and strengthened by the arms he had captured and the warriors he had attracted to his ranks, Kasa dedicated himself to crushing the kings of Tigre and Shoa, Wibe and Haile Melekot, respectively. Wibe had already proclaimed himself emperor and was in the process of preparing for his official coronation. The final confrontation between Wibe of Tigre and Kasa came in early 1855. Wibe was resoundingly defeated, stripped of his fiefdom, and imprisoned.[35] Although he had not yet subdued Shoa, Kasa was prepared to have himself crowned emperor. The ceremony took place on February 7, 1855, under the auspices of Abuna Solama, an Egyptian and the highest ranking official of the Orthodox Church in Ethiopia. He took the name Emperor Tewodros II, and thus his claim to the throne was sanctioned and legitimized. At the time, however, this appeared to be a revolutionary act in that Kasa's pedigree was not clearly linked to the House of David.[36] According to Ethiopian legend, the only individuals who held true claim to the emperorship were those who could claim a direct relationship between themselves and the Solomonic line. Even though Tewodros claimed to be of the royal line well before he was crowned, doubters remained.[37]

The choice of the name Tewodros, however, was of great significance and tended somewhat to stem criticism of Kasa's questionable lineage. According to one of the religious documents that form the basis of Ethiopian myth and custom, the Fikkere Iyesus (The Interpretation of Jesus), Jesus is said to have a prophesied that after a prolonged era of evil deeds among the chosen Ethiopians, a period of divine punishment would ensue.[38] Many people looked on the Zemene Mesafint as the wrath of God that was heaped upon Ethiopia for its corruption. Legend had it that there would emerge a righteous, just, and popular king, Tewodros, who would reign for forty years and restore Ethiopia to its former unity and greatness. Toward the end of the Zemene Mesafint, many claimed to be Tewodros, but none possessed the credentials of Ras Kasa. He wasted no time before attempting to prove that he was indeed worthy not only to be emperor but also to be called Tewodros.

After his coronation Tewodros turned his attention to subduing Shoa, which under the leadership of Saleh Sellassie (1813–1847) had remained fairly stable and unified throughout the most bitter phase of the Zemene Mesafint. To do this, Tewodros had to defeat Haile Melekot, Saleh Sellassie's son, and the Wollo Oromo. (Significantly, the Shoa dynasty wanted to create at least a fictional link to the Solomonic line and to legitimize the notion that the grandson of Saleh Sellassie, Saleh Maryam, would become a unifying emperor.[39] At birth Saleh Sellassie gave his grandson the formal name Menelik, after the mythical founder of the Solomonic line.) Tewodros's advance into Wollo and Shoa met with some opposition, but this was not always coordinated resistance. He subdued the Shoans in late 1855. Haile Melekot was ill and died of dysentery before the battle with the forces of Tewodros. Besides the might of Tewodros's army, Melekot's death perhaps explains why Shoa fell so easily. Ten days after Melekot's death his forces surrendered.

After restoring order in Shoa, Tewodros returned north, taking with him Haile Melekot's young son, Menelik (Saleh Maryam), as hostage. With the capture of Shoa and the subduing of the Wollo Oromo, Tewodros established the ultimate territorial limits of his empire. It is important to note, however, that control over this domain was far from permanent. But the idea of a unified Ethiopia had begun to take hold, and Tewodros attempted as much as he could to bring this about through the policies he pursued.

From his earliest days on the throne, Tewodros envisioned his mission as nothing short of the total unification of the historical Abyssinian Empire under his absolute monarchical and bureaucratic control. W. Plowden, who was the British consul assigned to Ethiopia during part of the reign of Emperor Tewodros, noted at the time that the emperor desired "to discipline his army, and has in part already succeeded; to abolish the feudal system; to have paid governors and judges; and to disarm the people."[40]

Keys to his centralization efforts were the strengthening and professionalization of his military and the establishment of a bureaucracy loyal to him alone. These were his most critical flexible resources. Such assets had to be complemented by a reduction in the power of the traditional nobility and the Church and by an active foreign policy that strengthened his hand against his enemies.

Tewodros attempted to establish a regular paid and professional army. He forbade his soldiers from victimizing peasants in the areas he captured, but this practice was not always followed. There is evidence that Tewodros was constantly involved in disciplining and training his army.[41] He often employed Europeans—and even Muslim Turks—with military expertise to train his men. In addition, he either bought, made, or captured modern weapons to strengthen his arsenal.[42]

Tewodros was an innovator who realized that the very survival of any military man depended upon his ability to adapt to changes in the politico-military landscape. A successful military leader needed not only a loyal army but also the most modern weapons. Tewodros did all he could to encourage European craftsmen, engineers, and skilled technicians to take up residence in his court and to provide him with needed equipment and expertise. His primary concern was military weaponry.[43]

The military became Tewodros's most important bureaucratic instrument and was used not only to suppress rebellions and to control the traditional aristocracy, but also to create a centralized bureaucratic presence in all reaches of the empire. His most trusted followers became provincial governors. Military governors collected tithes and taxes on behalf of the Crown and were instrumental in Tewodros's attempt to break the power of patrimonial feudal lords. He succeeded in jailing most of his potential enemies. This facilitated the maintenance of law and order in the countryside and buttressed the centralizing effort. Even so, military governors were not officially charged with adjudication. Justice remained largely in the hands of local traditional authorities. Tewodros did, however, set up a limited, centralized judicial system, with judges paid from the imperial treasury. It was possible for any case to be deemed worthy of being heard by the emperor himself.[44]

Despite the fact that Tewodros inaugurated a veritable "industrial revolution" in Ethiopia, it is important to remember that his predominant concerns were always *control* and the establishment of Abyssinia's *territorial integrity*. He never succeeded in consolidating his possessions. He innovated out of necessity for survival. Tewodros introduced new technology and

built roads, but these were mainly to support his military capacity. The local
landed aristocracy was a source of constant pressures. He had to put down
one rebellion after another. In spite of such problems, Tewodros was bent
on establishing a unified state in the highlands of Ethiopia.

To a degree, the emperor attempted to use the Orthodox Christian
religion as an instrument of national political integration, but his domain
was never secure enough for this to happen. Indeed, Tewodros considered
political supremacy *the* prerequisite to christianizing the subjugated populations in the periphery of his empire and recasting his domain in a
renewed sense of moral and spiritual commitment. Chief among his enemies in this process were the adherents of Islam who threatened him from
within and without.

A key element in the establishment of Tewodros's political supremacy was
the improvement of the state's taxing capacity and the consequent expansion of the imperial treasury. With more liquid assets, he could afford to
pay the salaries of bureaucrats and soldiers, to expand the bureaucracy, and
to improve the technological basis of his army. Tewodros spurned the idea
of taxing the provinces more heavily for fear that this might encourage the
escalation of rebellious activities. Instead, he attempted to extract what
finances he needed from the clergy. The Church possessed vast tracts of
land but paid no taxes. Moreover, Tewodros viewed many of the clergy as
pretentious and corrupt and thus fair game for his reform efforts.[45]
Tewodros declared that each church should possess access to only enough
land to feed two priests and three deacons.[46] What land was left was to be
redistributed among local peasants. His intent was not only to expand his
treasury but also to weaken the clergy. Needless to say, this reform met with
much resistance, and it was a full four years before it was finally enacted.
He was successful in marginally increasing the finances at his disposal, but
he had alienated the clergy, a flexible resource that was often critical in
buttressing the authority of the crown.

Throughout his reign, foreign policy preoccupied Tewodros. He wanted
to have his regime recognized on an equal footing with the great powers of
Europe. He appealed specifically to Britain, France, and Russia, as Christian nations, to aid him in whatever ways possible in his fight against the
Muslim Turks and Egyptians. However, the emperor never developed
satisfactory relations with any European power. In fact, he was particularly
incensed at the apparent lack of respect accorded him by Napoleon III and
Queen Victoria.

In an effort to force Britain to recognize Abyssinia as an equal and to
secure the manpower and technology needed to hold his empire together,
in 1865 Tewodros in a fit of desperation incarcerated several British subjects, including the British consul. At first, an effort was made to negotiate
the release of the prisoners. But after more than two years of negotiations,
the British decided to free the prisoners by force.

In March 1868 a military contingent of thirty-two thousand men from

Britain's Indian Army moved from Massawa through Tigre to Tewodros's capital of Magdala. This force met with little resistance and even secured some logistical support from *Dejazmatch* (General or Count) Kasa of Tigre. Significantly, the Church chose not to rally the people in defense of Tewodros. The British forces outnumbered his defenders, and they were superiorly armed. In addition, Tewodros's army was already spread thinly in order to maintain a semblance of domestic political stability. The demise of his rule came relatively easily on April 10, 1868. During the course of the battle, Menelik managed to escape, finding his way back to Shoa. Rather than suffer the humiliation of defeat, the Emperor twice attempted suicide, succeeding the second time. The British, ironically, were not interested in establishing a permanent presence in Ethiopia, and after a few days the invading forces withdrew. This event, along with the defeat and death of Tewodros, could have led to the balkanization of the empire once again, but it did not.[47]

At the time of Tewodros's death three rivals emerged to stake claim to the throne: Menelik, the King of Shoa and the son of Haile Melekot; Ras Gobeze, ruler of Amhara and Wag-Lasta; and Dejazmatch Kasa of Tigre. Each of these individuals felt they had a claim to the emperorship. Gobeze went so far as to have himself crowned King of Kings at Gondar within a month of Tewodros's death. He chose the name Tekele Giorgis.[48] Menelik and Kasa also claimed the throne. Although neither had actually proclaimed himself King of Kings, each could trace his lineage to the mythical House of David, a requirement for Ethiopian kings. To firmly establish himself as emperor, Tekele Giorgis had to secure the vassalage of his most powerful rivals. Unfortunately for him, he proved unequal to the task and was defeated by Kasa at Adowa on July 11, 1871. Kasa's victory was made possible in large measure by the better weapons he had acquired from the British for his support of their campaign against Tewodros.[49]

Yohannes IV

When the British decided to rescue the British subjects held hostage by Tewodros, they required security along the planned route to Magdala, and they also needed reliable communications and supply routes. Kasa agreed to aid them on the conditions that they would withdraw from Ethiopia as soon as the captives had been freed, that they would not assist the Egyptians in gaining the upper hand in Ethiopia, and that no British consul would be appointed in Ethiopia.[50] Kasa provided security for the British forces, ensured the operability of telegraph lines, and delivered an average of more than thirty thousand kilograms of grain per week to each of the two camps the British set up as staging grounds for the Magdala campaign.[51]

After Tewodros had been defeated, Kasa actually sought to have the departing British recognize him as the emperor of all Ethiopia, but the leader of the expedition, General Napier, chose not to do so out of fear that this might be considered an indication of a formal alliance with Britain. But in appreciation for the help he had provided, Napier presented Kasa with a battery of mountain guns and mortars and a large quantity of smooth-bore muskets.[52] This greatly strengthened Kasa's military capacity, and even though he was substantially outnumbered by Tekele Giorgis's invading army, he did possess enough relatively modern armaments to enable him to repulse the attack.

On January 21, 1872, at Aksum, the ancient capital of Abyssinia, Kasa was crowned Emperor Yohannes IV. He chose not to meet immediately in combat his lone remaining rival of any significance, the Shoan *Negus* (King) Menelik II, but attempted to gain his submission as a vassal through diplomacy. This set the tone for Yohannes's rule.

In personality and as a ruler, Yohannes differed from Tewodros as night from day. He was more patient and less impulsive than his predecessor. An extremely devout Christian and an even greater patriot, Yohannes, like Tewodros, envisioned a united, Christian Ethiopia. But they were very different in their approaches.

Tewodros had sought to develop an extremely centralized and nationally oriented professional bureaucracy. He was especially concerned that those he appointed governor not remain in one post too long for fear they would develop independent bases of power that could eventually pose serious threats to his rule. In contrast, while Yohannes valued an efficient bureaucracy, he valued political stability even more. Periodically reassigning governors, Yohannes realized created insecurity among the peasantry and thus should be avoided at all cost.[53] The supreme value for the peasant is security, the kind of security provided by stable and reliable patron-client relationships between lord and peasant.[54] Yohannes wanted to maintain as widespread a base of support for his rule as possible. He chose to rule provinces, districts, parishes, and villages through existing traditional authority structures. Rather than jailing his subdued enemies as Tewodros had done, he secured their fidelity through submission and allowed them to continue to govern their people. Yohannes felt that this would aid him in repulsing foreign invasion. He would not have to rely upon unpopular, appointed petty rulers to mobilize the masses in time of crisis and could depend on men who had already gained the trust of the people in their regions.[55] This policy even applied to Yohannes's most serious rivals, Menelik and Tekle Haymanot, the powerful rulers of Shoa and Gojjam respectively. Yohannes gave each of these men important responsibilities, allowing them to expand their own dominions while they protected the territorial integrity of the empire in the periphery.[56]

Yohannes's most outstanding accomplishments were in the field of foreign policy. Whereas Tewodros brazenly demanded respect and the recognition of Ethiopia by European powers, Yohannes followed a course of patient diplomacy. This was a time of heightened European interest in

African bases for colonial expansion; yet the image of a united and relatively strong Ethiopia deterred reckless European adventures into Abyssinia. A more serious challenge was presented by the Egyptians.

At the time of Yohannes's accession to the throne, Egypt had already begun to penetrate into historic Abyssinia along the Sudan border and down the Red Sea coast. By late 1875, the Egyptians, who had become extremely active in the Horn region after separating from the Ottoman sultanates, decided to launch a full-scale invasion of the Ethiopian core. The first wave of invaders, an expeditionary force of a few hundred men, was decimated by the Ethiopians in mid-November at Gundet. In March 1876 the Egyptians again attempted to assault the Ethiopian core, this time with a larger and better armed force of 5,200. Of this number, as many as 3,270 were killed in the decisive battle that took place between March 7 and March 10 at Gura. Even though their losses were much higher, the Ethiopians outnumbered the invaders and emerged victorious.[57]

Yohannes regarded his war against the Muslim Egyptians as a holy crusade to preserve the Christian dignity of a free and united Ethiopia. The victories at Gundet and Gura in this respect did much to consolidate his position. It showed potential challengers such as Menelik that he was a power to be reckoned with; and indeed in 1878 Menelik, who had for ten years claimed the title of emperor, withdrew his claim and recognized Yohannes as emperor. These victories also had the effect of creating a widespread sense of national unity and heightened self-esteem: A powerful invader that had threatened to subjugate all of Ethiopia had been repulsed by a force of Ethiopians from all regions. From these struggles, Yohannes emerged a hero.

Yohannes succeeded in getting Britain to mediate a peace between Egypt and Ethiopia. A treaty was signed on June 3, 1884, at Adowa and for the moment represented a significant diplomatic coup for Ethiopia. The treaty included agreement that Britain would act as a mediator in any future disputes between Egypt and Ethiopia; that Yohannes would allow whatever Egyptian forces remained on Ethiopian soil safe passage back to Egypt; that goods (including arms) bound for Ethiopia and passing through British occupied Massawa would not be subject to tariff or otherwise controlled; and provisions for the extradition of criminals between Egypt and Ethiopia and Egyptian cooperation in providing Ethiopia with Orthodox Christian bishops.[58] Ethiopia was also given control of the province of Bogos on Sudan's northeastern border.

Other than the symbolic impact of Yohannes's diplomatic and military successes, the emperor was also able to achieve a measure of national integration through his policies toward religion and culture. Yohannes sought to establish religious uniformity within the Ethiopian Orthodox Church and in society as a whole.[59] This became necessary because religious controversies carrying political undertones had emerged among religious leaders largely as a result of ideas introduced by Catholic missionaries. These new ideas found supporters among the Ethiopian clergy but generally conflicted with existing Orthodox doctrine. Yohannes saw this growing disunity within the Church as a potential impediment to a concerted military effort against Muslim invaders. He convened the Synod of Borumeda in Wollo not long after his second victory over the Egyptians and attempted to have resolved whatever doctrinal disputes existed. He also committed himself to completely Christianizing the core of the empire, including the largely Oromo province of Wollo, where Islam was strong and growing, and the areas of the southern periphery, where the people generally adhered to traditional religions. Yohannes made the leaders of various areas of the periphery contingent on their renunciation of Islam or other non-Christian religions and on their conversion to Christianity. Realizing that they could be replaced by others who would do the emperor's bidding, many of these leaders consented to conversion.[60]

Despite his desire to Christianize his entire domain, Yohannes took a calculated approach to religious conversion. For him politics was primary. This could be seen in the fact that he assigned some Muslims to his court. He considered Islam a threat, but in his mind an even greater threat to the political survival of Ethiopia was European expansionism. At one point, Yohannes even attempted to form an alliance with the Muslim Sudanese Mahdists against the potential European threat. His worst fears were confirmed when within one year after the signing of the Treaty of Adowa, Britain allowed Italy to take control of Massawa and otherwise to expand its presence in the area. In effect, the treaty was thereby abrogated, and Italy fully intended eventually to claim Abyssinia as its colony.[61] The Italians had already begun to plot Yohannes's demise by concluding a treaty of friendship and commerce with Menelik. Although threatened by the Italian presence along the Red Sea, Yohannes hesitated to attack. He was faced with the more immediate challenge of the Mahdists who had penetrated as far as Gojjam, wreaking havoc and sacking Gondar. Yohannes turned his attention to fending off the Mahdists and led his forces to the fateful Battle of Metemma in March 1889. At first the campaign went well for the Ethiopians, but on March 10, Yohannes was mortally wounded and died the next day, demoralizing the Ethiopian troops and inspiring the Mahdists. An apparent Ethiopian victory turned into a Mahdist rout.[62]

Menelik II

With the death of Yohannes, the way was finally open for Menelik to stake his claim to the emperorship he felt destined to hold. Although at no time during the reign of Yohannes did he feel completely strong enough to seize the throne by force, he had taken care to structure his relations with the emperor as well as with other pretenders to the throne to ensure the legitimacy of his claim. He did so by publically pledging his loyalty to

Yohannes; paying tribute to him; agreeing to the marriage of his daughter to the son of Yohannes; and finally, in 1882, after demonstrating that he was the most powerful of the potential claimants to the throne, securing Yohannes's blessing that he should be the next emperor. Yet Menelik was always a reluctant vassal who struggled not only to survive but also to maintain his own kingly identity. He did this at the risk of arousing Yohannes's suspicions of his intentions. For instance, he concluded independent treaties between Shoa and Italy in 1883 and 1887 that were essentially "friendship and commerce" agreements. Italy initiated these agreements, and Menelik viewed them as convenient mechanisms to allow him to secure arms and ammunition. He had nothing to lose. In an 1887 treaty, however, Menelik did agree to remain neutral in a dispute that was raging between Italy and Yohannes over Italian encroachment into the Ethiopian hinterland.[63]

Toward the end of Yohannes's reign, Menelik came to fear that Yohannes would attack him and attempt to remove him as a potential threat to the emperor's authority. Consequently, he responded favorably to the overtures of the Italian government to supply a large quantity of arms that would enable Menelik to fend off any possible attack from Yohannes and perhaps even to dethrone the emperor. This agreement was different from the previous ones in that it clearly cast Yohannes and Menelik as enemies. The Italians were also now in a position to secure territorial concessions from Menelik should he emerge victorious in his impending war with Yohannes. This was the climate in which the infamous Treaty of Wichale (1889) emerged.

Negotiations surrounding the treaty began in late 1888, but it was not concluded until May 2, 1889, only seven weeks after the death of Yohannes. The treaty was officially described as the "Wichale Treaty of Perpetual Peace and Friendship." With Yohannes out of the way Menelik apparently had nothing to gain from such an agreement, but he thought differently. Menelik again felt he had nothing to lose and might even gain some insurances against foreign as well as domestic enemies.

According to the terms of the treaty, the state of war that had existed between Yohannes and Italy was officially ended, and Italy recognized Menelik as King of Kings. This was important to Menelik, since he wished to neutralize the claim of Yohannes's son, Ras Mengesha, to the imperial throne. Having recognized the supremacy of Menelik it would be inappropriate for the Italians to enter into any types of agreements with his vassals.

A second article in the agreement allowed Ethiopia duty-free privileges for any goods passing through the Italian-occupied port of Massawa. In effect, Italian rule of Massawa was recognized as long as Ethiopia itself could use the port freely for trade. Italy also agreed to give Ethiopia a substantial loan and to continue to supply Menelik with arms.

In terms of Ethiopian concessions, the treaty called for the ceding of part of the Tigre highlands as a buffer safeguarding Italy's interests at Massawa, and for certain commercial, industrial, and judicial privileges for the Italians. The sphere of the Italian occupation and influence, however, was to be confined to a small, well-circumscribed area down to the coast that was already occupied by them at the time the treaty was signed. Significantly, the handing over of this territory was agreed despite the land in question being part of the dominions claimed by Ras Alula, who had been Yohannes's most trusted and reliable general.[64]

Seemingly this treaty had something good in it for both signatories, and hardly anything bad for either. Both Italy and Ethiopia were guaranteed a measure of security and trading privileges. This would have been true if the drafting and execution of the terms of the treaty were carried out in good faith. This was not, however, the case. Before a year had passed, Italy had penetrated deeper into Ethiopian territory than Menelik had agreed to.[65] The two governments had agreed to amend the treaty in an Additional Convention concluded on October 11, 1889, but not ratified by Menelik until February 25, 1890. This addendum allegedly gave Italy the rights to territories they actually occupied at the time the Additional Convention was finally ratified by both parties. In other words, it was a supplement to the language of the original treaty. Between the signing of the Additional Convention in Rome and Menelik's ratification in Addis Ababa, Italian forces moved from Massawa occupying territory as far inland as the districts of Hamasen, Akala Guzay, and Serae, enlarging the extent of their new colony, Eritrea, substantially.[66] Although Menelik's representative in the last rounds of negotiations, Dejazmatch Mekonnen, had willingly approved the addendum, he was then unaware of the potential duplicity in the term "actual possession." During this same period, an additional area of conflict arose over the treaty, which had been drafted in both Italian and Amharic. Both drafts were virtually identical except for one important detail, Article XVII. The Italian translation of this article read:

> His Majesty the King of Kings of Ethiopia consents to avail himself of the Government of His Majesty the King of Italy for all negotiations of affairs which he might have with other powers or governments.[67]

Although the term "protectorate" was not used, the idea of Ethiopia agreeing to become the protectorate of Italy was implicit in the wording of the Italian version of this article. The Amharic version, however, merely implied that Ethiopia *might* seek the aid of Italy in its dealings with "other powers and governments" if it felt this would be advantageous. In other words, there was no obligation to go through Italy in diplomatic matters as the Italian version stipulated. Yet the message Italy conveyed to the world community was, "Ethiopia is now a protectorate of Italy." This contention had immediate repercussions for Ethiopia, as Menelik found. Each time he attempted to interact with European powers as a sovereign head of state, he was referred to the treaty and Article XVII. This proclamation, however, was by no means unquestionably accepted by other world powers, and both Ethiopia and Italy had to work hard to have their respective positions on the matter understood.[68]

Menelik made it clear that he had absolutely no intention of surrendering any portion of Ethiopia's sovereignty. Initially he attempted to iron out the disagreement over the intent of Article XVII by diplomacy. Negotiations continued for more than three years, and in early 1893 Menelik notified the Italian government that the treaty would cease to be effective as of May 1894. A one-year notice by either party had previously been agreed upon as an acceptable manner in which to cancel the treaty. Menelik had made his decisive move. The next move was up to Italy.[69]

Realizing, as soon as difficulties arose over the treaty, that a war with Italy might be inevitable, Menelik began to prepare for the impending conflict. He was being severely criticized at home for having "sold-out" a portion of the Ethiopian state, and he could not let it be said that he had even gone so far as to "sell the entire state"! Rhetorically Menelik attempted to present the image of a true patriot, and as Italy's appetite for large amounts of Ethiopian land became more apparent, leaders from all corners of the empire began to rally around the symbol of Ethiopian independence, the emperor. Even Ras Mengesha, who since the death of his father had been functioning virtually as a independent king in Tigre in defiance of Menelik, decided in 1890 to submit to the emperor's authority.[70] Once again, the threat of a formidable foreign invader united the disparate peoples that made up the empire.

Even as these difficulties with Italy unfolded and expanded, Menelik strengthened his defensive capabilities by purchasing modern arms and military equipment. Some of these came from private concerns, but European governments such as Russia and France and even Britain and Italy were particularly important suppliers for Menelik. He already possessed a substantial battery of armaments that had enabled him as King of Shoa to expand his territorial possessions as far north as Wollo, and as far south as Kaffa even before the demise of Yohannes. In the process he sowed the seeds of much future upheaval. By 1895 Menelik's combined army possessed as many as two hundred thousand rifles, including about sixty-five thousand automatics or machine guns and forty-two cannons.[71]

Italy refused to acknowledge that Menelik had terminated the Treaty of Wichale as of 1894, and by the following year it was clear that Italy did not feel obliged or willing to limit its inland possessions to the Eritrean plateau. Between March and April 1895 Italy annexed a portion of Tigre, sending Ras Mengesha into flight. Menelik then began to prepare in earnest to defend Ethiopia's territorial integrity. He informed his subjects and their immediate leaders of the gravity of the situation and of the prowess of the enemy. He also attempted to gain public sympathy for the difficulties he had confronted as a leader—avaricious foreign powers clawing at Ethiopia's gates; rebellious vassals; and even severe calamities of nature such as famine, drought, and plague. In September he issued the call to arms.

The first skirmish leading up to the Battle of Adowa occurred on December 7, 1895. The Ethiopian forces of Ras Makonnen, who had come all the way from the recently conquered city of Harar, resoundingly defeated an Italian war party at Amba Alaji, leaving some two thousand dead.[72] From this point on, Menelik's ranks began to swell as many regional leaders gained confidence that it was possible to defeat the Italians.

In January Menelik moved north toward Adowa, choosing not to attack the Italian forces in their fortified position at Addigrat but to lure them into a less protected struggle. The plan worked, and the Italian forces numbering twenty thousand well-armed soldiers moved toward Adowa to confront Menelik's army. Menelik's forces numbered about one hundred thousand but they were not as well armed as the Italian forces. After a "war of nerves," the decisive battle erupted on February 29 and lasted for six days. Once again the Ethiopians were the victors. The Italian casualties included: almost seven thousand dead, and fifteen hundred wounded, and three thousand prisoners of war. In addition, they lost a large quantity of modern weaponry including fifty-two pieces of heavy artillery. The Ethiopians lost between four thousand and six thousand soldiers, and about eight thousand were badly wounded. On both sides, then, the casualties were enormous, but in relative terms the Ethiopians fared much better than the Italians.[73]

The vanquished Italians sued for peace, and a treaty was signed at Addis Ababa on October 26, 1896. The impact of the Ethiopian victory at Adowa was profound, sending shock waves throughout Europe and causing the reigning Italian government to fall. Menelik was agreeable to the Italians maintaining their Eritrean colony, but he opposed giving up another inch of Ethiopian territory. The first of his conditions was the abrogation of the Treaty of Wichale.

As a result of this agreement, Italian penetration south could not go beyond the Mareb River, and Ethiopia was recognized as a free and independent country.[74] For the first time, European powers realized that Ethiopia was an African power to be reckoned with. Moreover, the victory at Adowa proved that in spite of endemic internecine warfare among Ethiopian elites, the character of the state as a centralized entity had emerged to a point where unified resistance in the face of external aggression was indeed possible. With the acquisition of further and more sophisticated weaponry—an opportunity that largely escaped other peoples in Black Africa during this period—it was possible for Ethiopia to defeat the most formidable of aggressors.

Having defeated the Italians, Menelik directed his attention toward establishing the legitimacy of the boundaries of his possessions among those powers who held colonial interests in the areas adjacent to Ethiopia. Moreover, he harbored designs on half of Sudan, all of Somalia, and parts of

Kenya. Menelik found that his neighbors were now ready to normalize relations with Ethiopia after Adowa. This was significant in that both of his major predecessors had been continually rebuffed by the European powers. Now Britain, France, Russia, and Italy flocked to Menelik's court to arrange the exchange of ambassadors and to conclude diplomatic agreements establishing their spheres of influence on the Horn of Africa in relation to Ethiopia. Even the Sudanese Mahdists sought to stabilize relations with Ethiopia at this time.[75]

A loose pact of commerce and cooperation was concluded between the Mahdists and Ethiopia in 1896. This relationship, however, soon proved extremely tenuous, as Britain and France began to exert pressure on Ethiopia concerning its relations with Sudan and their competing interests in the western regions of the upper Nile basin.

On January 29–30, 1897, France and Ethiopia signed two treaties. One treaty specified that Ethiopia had the right to use the French port of Djibouti as an official outlet for its trade. The second stipulated that any arms shipments passing through Djibouti that were bound for Ethiopia would be allowed passage on a duty-free basis.[76]

On March 20, two additional Franco-Ethiopian concords were ratified, one public and one secret. The public agreement established that France would relinquish a large tract of land to the east of Menelik's domain known as the French Somaliland Protectorate (Djibouti excluded) to Ethiopia. In effect, this established the border between Ethiopia and France's colonial possessions on the Red Sea coast. The treaty assured Menelik access to land that he had coveted but did not actually hold claim to.[77] The secret compact was a treaty of alliance, and it committed Menelik to support unconditionally France's efforts to bring the region of the upper Nile under its sphere of influence. In fact, Menelik did virtually nothing to assist the French cause in that area. His duplicity seems to have been calculated not only in his dealings with France but also with the Mahdists and Great Britain. For instance, when Menelik concluded a treaty with Britain in 1897 concerning their respective policies toward Sudan, the prior agreement with the Mahdists was more or less obviated.[78]

The British mission to Menelik's court at this time, like the French mission, was concerned with establishing firm geographical boundaries between British and Ethiopian spheres of influence on the Horn. Over a period of several months the two countries agreed that Menelik would not enter the conflict in Sudan on the side of the Mahdists or aid them in any way, that commercial relations with most-favored-nation status would be established between Britain and Ethiopia, and that the borders between Ethiopia and Sudan and the Somaliland frontier would be formalized. Menelik did not contest any of the British or Egyptian claims in Sudan and readily agreed that the border should be set according to whatever effective occupation existed at the time.[79] The Somaliland border, however, was another matter. After a protracted period of intense negotiations, Britain ceded to Ethiopia 13,500 square miles of land in historic Somaliland. This was a mere one-third of what Ethiopia actually claimed. But even this fraction of territory was not (and never had been) firmly under Ethiopian control. This was to prove the source of bitter disputes between the Somalis and the colonizing Abyssinians for years to come.[80] We shall return to this point later.

By the end of 1897, the current boundaries of Ethiopia—except for Eritrea and part of the western border—had virtually been set. It was clear that Menelik had exercised considerable diplomatic acumen, playing off one power against the other as pawns in an effort to ensure the sovereignty of his country. In achieving diplomatic recognition by the European powers, he had succeeded in accomplishing not only what his Ethiopian predecessors had failed to do but also what most of the leaders of Black Africa during this era had to achieve. This contributed greatly to the almost mythical image of Ethiopia as the epitome of African independence, an African country that never suffered under the yoke of European colonialism. What is generally ignored, however, is that in large measure Ethiopia, particularly under Menelik, was itself a participant in the colonial "scramble for Africa," enlarging what we know as Ethiopia substantially between 1882 and 1906 and more or less permanently incorporating these newly acquired territories. Until this time, boundaries on the Horn between one state and the next were fluid and had never been rigidly defined.

In order for Ethiopia to survive, Menelik realized that he had to be concerned with more than international diplomacy. He also had to engage in domestic policies that brought about political control and stability and economic progress and prosperity. To do this he had continually to strengthen certain flexible resources such as his army and his territorial bureaucracy. And he had to create new, flexible resources such as financial institutions, a modern educated class, and an effective and efficient communications system. Thus, under Menelik, the first signs of an emergent modernizing bureaucratic empire began to appear.

The armies of individual Ethiopian leaders were extremely important, offering them the means to acquire and hold power and territory. The more territory a leader had under his control, the more men he could raise for military campaigns and the more money or economic resources he had in his coffers. Menelik, from the moment he returned to Shoa from exile, desired to be emperor, and he realized that to accomplish this he had to acquire a large dominion and to construct a sizable and disciplined army.

On becoming King of Shoa, Menelik immediately set out to expand the territory under his control.[81] Between 1868 and 1876, he succeeded in bringing Wollo under his control. Then he turned his attention to the south and west. By 1882, he had conquered the provinces of Gudru, Horo, parts of Leqa, Botor, Badifolla, and the kingdoms of Luma-Enarya, Guma, Gera, Goma, and Jimma-Kaka. By the end of 1887, Menelik had added Gurage, Arussi, and Harar to his possessions. These latter conquests allowed Menelik to control the most significant southeastern trade route and provided outlets to the sea that were independent of Yohannes's sphere of influence. With this route under his control and able to tap the vast wealth of gold, ivory, and agricultural produce obtainable in his southern and western conquests, Menelik was in an ideal position to begin to assert his autonomy as a leader based upon his territorial possessions as well as the wealth at his disposal.

After he became emperor, Menelik continued to bring more and more territory in the south and east under his control. Through conquest and diplomacy, between 1890 and 1906 he added the Ogaden, Bale, Sidamo, Wollamo, Kaffa, and Illubabor to his domain, thus extending the state of Ethiopia almost to its present configuration.

A key element in territorial expansion, as has been suggested, was the ability to raise a large army. After the mid-nineteenth century, how well armed a force was became a critical variable. Yohannes and Menelik needed large armies to be successful in conquest, but as access to European arms became easier for Christian rulers in Africa, it became clear that the successful leader would be one who also concentrated on arming his troops well enough to repress all challengers, including foreign ones. The records of Yohannes and Menelik in resisting the Egyptians and Italians respectively provide ample evidence of this.

By the turn of the twentieth century, Menelik's army consisted of approximately six hundred thousand riflemen and innumerable traditionally armed warriors.[82] Some attention was given to professionalizing the army and to centralizing the chain of command, but neither of these efforts had substantial impact. Command of various units was still left largely to regional notables as it had traditionally been. Every Ethiopian peasant, as was customary in feudal societies, was a potential soldier. If called upon, social mores made it mandatory that he respond positively to a call to arms from his lord; the lord to a call from the governor; and the governor to the call of the emperor.[83] Very few men were professional soldiers in traditional Ethiopia, but by the time of Menelik's reign the number of professionals, or those who could be classified as members of a standing army, numbered an estimated two hundred thousand.[84] Of this number, between ten thousand and twelve thousand were at the direct disposal of the emperor.[85]

In addition to using foreign military aid to enhance the technological aspects of his military, Menelik also used such aid much more effectively than Tewodros or Yohannes for training his soldiers.[86] Even before he became emperor, Menelik invited Europeans to his court to assist in training his men. These trainers were mainly French and Russians, and their activities were largely confined to instructing Ethiopian soldiers in the use of certain types of weapons. Some of these individuals even accompanied Ethiopian military units as advisers during campaigns of conquest in the south. Although there was some effort to train Menelik's soldiers in the organization, strategy, and tactics of European militaries, there is no evidence that such efforts had a profound impact. Traditional patterns dominated throughout Menelik's reign. The first European-style military academy was not established until after the accession of Haile Selassie I.[87]

Besides introducing the notion of a standing army in Ethiopia, Menelik also contributed to the centralization and professionalization of the army by beginning the practice of paying soldiers a salary.[88] Traditionally, soldiers were rarely paid. Military service was seen as an obligation. Anyone refusing to serve when called upon could be excommunicated or even put to death.[89] Soldiers were expected to live off the land they passed through and whatever loot they might acquire as the spoils of war. The need among the traditional soldiery to loot in order to survive exacted a heavy price upon friendly as well as hostile peasantry. Tewodros and Yohannes had both attempted to restrain predatory soldiers, but not with much success. Menelik was only marginally more successful.[90]

The army played an integral part in the initiation and establishment of a centralized bureaucratic authority during Menelik's reign. Given the ever-present threat of European colonialism and the vastly expanded domain of the empire, Menelik realized that a permanent administrative presence had to be established, especially in the periphery of the empire. The most trusted generals of the emperor's forces were appointed governors-general of the provinces, which constituted the largest administrative divisions in the empire. Below the governor of a province were district governors, also appointed by the emperor. District governors were responsible for appointing the heads of the lowest administrative divisions who were called chiefs or *shums*. The *shum*'s jurisdiction consisted of either one large village or a cluster of small villages in the same general area. A *shum* had first to be nominated by the citizens in the area. In certain cases where a village was considered to be of strategic or economic importance, its leader could be appointed by the emperor himself. The appointment of the *shum* was only for one year, during which time he was paid a token salary and exempted from tax and tribute obligations.[91]

Anyone appointed by the emperor was responsible to him as well as to his immediate superiors, but only the emperor could remove his own appointees. This appointive and removal power, often referred to as *shum-shir*, was another significant flexible resource wielded by the emperor that enabled him somewhat to control potential threats to his authority. Governors were frequently moved to prevent their becoming too politically entrenched in an area.[92] This was normally done as a matter of procedure but could also be used as an instrument of reward or punishment. Menelik was better able to do this in the newly conquered areas of the south than in the north where certain aristocratic families were well established. But, at the height of his power, he could effectively demonstrate the absoluteness of his authority even in the north. For instance, when Tekle Haymanot, the King of Gojjam, died in 1901, Menelik broke up his kingdom, leaving only a small portion to his son.[93] The administrative jurisdiction of anyone who served at any level in the imperial bureaucracy was not secure, nor was it hereditary. An individual could be appointed or dismissed according to the whim of the emperor.

Imperial authority was further exercised and demonstrated through *ketemas,* or garrison towns, that were erected throughout the country but became particularly important in administration of the south.[94] These towns housed soldiers dispatched to certain areas to act as "watchmen" for the Crown and to suppress opposition as necessary. *Ketemas* became administrative centers in the periphery during the time of Menelik and housed the delegates of the Crown, their families, and other settlers. In the south, the contrast between the indigenous population and the agents of the state (most of whom were foreign to them and who resided in or around *ketemas*) was exceedingly sharp. This in large measure inhibited the development of a sense of national identification with the Ethiopian state among the peoples in the newly conquered areas.[95] In an environment in which might was right, conquered peoples tended to acquiesce in Ethiopian authority rather than to accept it because they considered it legitimate.

The agents of the state in the newly emerging centralized state bureaucracy, from the highest to the lowest, were primarily responsible for tax collecting and military control on behalf of the Crown. This did not necessarily mean that the system was so rigidly centralized that no autonomous decision making could take place at the provincial, district, or local level. On the contrary, during most of Menelik's reign appointees of the emperor could in turn appoint their own lower level functionaries, administer justice as they saw fit, and even use their own discretion in the collection of tribute and taxes.

The governor's main responsibility was to defend his province or district and its people against external and/or internal threats. In addition, when disputes arose within his own realm, the governor was the highest court of appeal below the emperor himself. Toward the end of his career Menelik reformed the judicial system in order to make it more efficient and independent.[96]

Monarchs in Ethiopia, as elsewhere, traditionally relied on the tribute paid to them by their subjects, but Menelik was perhaps the first to introduce the idea of paying taxes or tithes to the state.[97] Peasants were also expected to contribute a certain amount of labor each year to the state. Taxes and tribute were collected at each level of administration. The *shum* collected such resources—mostly in kind—at the local level; he kept a certain designated portion of his receipts for himself and passed the rest on to the district level. The provincial governor forwarded two-fifths of his collection to Addis Ababa. Tribute and taxes went to the emperor not from individuals but from the different administrative entities. Branches of the imperial treasury were eventually established at the provincial level. This system was crude, but it manifested a conscious attempt to regularize and bureaucratize the collection of economic resources needed to sustain the expanded state.

The military people stationed in the south received their portion of state revenues largely from specified peasant families in the areas where they served. The peasants provided them with produce and with labor. The important point is, however, that soldiers were forbidden from making arbitrary and excessive demands upon the people as they had done so often in the past.[98]

In addition to strengthening the administrative and judicial capacity of the state in the periphery, Menelik saw a need for differentiating the office of emperor to a degree at the center. In 1907 he announced to foreign powers that he was contemplating the formation of a cabinet. Eventually nine ministers were appointed: the ministers of justice, war, interior, commerce and foreign affairs, finance, agriculture, public works, and the ministers of the court and of the pen.[99] The minister of the pen was the emperor's personal assistant and chronicler. Significantly, Menelik did not feel obliged to appoint powerful aristocrats to these posts. Instead, he appointed to his first cabinet men who were not widely known but who were doggedly loyal to him. This was another way in which Menelik hoped to strengthen his own absolute authority and that of the emperorship.

Menelik relied on his ministers only to a token degree, but the creation of these posts set in motion forces that led rapidly to the emergence of a nascent secularized central bureaucracy. The ministers hired staff to aid them in carrying out their responsibilities. All employees of the various ministries (including the minister himself) were paid a salary out of the imperial treasury.

Following the pattern set by emperors of other great empires, Menelik attempted to enhance his international prestige as well as his domestic control through his monetary policies. Perhaps the most important of these had to do with money and banking. Beginning in 1894, Ethiopia began to mint her own currency, to replace the use of other internationally recognized currency such as the Austrian Maria Theresa dollar.[100] This proved to be a challenging task, and by the time of Menelik's death the Ethiopian dollar still had not gained widespread acceptance at home or abroad as a viable national currency. The first coins were minted in Paris and were limited in number. After 1903 Menelik achieved the capacity to produce most of the currency he desired locally, but the new money still could not compete with the Maria Theresa or even traditional currency for that matter.

Another aspect of Menelik's monetary policy was to establish a national bank. In 1905 the National Bank of Egypt was given a fifty-year concession to establish and operate a banking company, the Bank of Abyssinia. The Bank of Abyssinia was initiated with foreign capital and was an affiliate of the Egyptian bank. The bank was given exclusive privileges to provide banking services in Ethiopia, produce and issue coins and notes, set up bonded warehouses, assume custody of all money belonging to the state, and receive preferential rights to all state loans.[101]

Like the new currency, the Bank of Abyssinia got off to a rocky start, and it was not until 1914 that it realized its first profits. The important point is, however, that Menelik had the foresight to realize the advantages of setting up such financial institutions as a national currency and a national bank that could facilitate his efforts to centralize his empire and solidify his control over most of what went on in the empire.[102]

Menelik is best known for his positive attitude toward innovation. He is credited with building schools, hospitals, postal and telephone systems, bridges, roads, and even a railroad. His concern, however, was not so much the equitable spread of the fruits of change to the most distant hamlet, but the maintenance of the strength, security, and viability of the Ethiopian state, and to the maximization of his extractive capabilities. Roads were needed to ensure the easy movement of troops and administrators into the newly acquired and unstable areas of the empire, aiding in the establishment of the authority of the Crown in recalcitrant areas of the historic core of the empire and securing national boundaries. Roads were also needed to transport the gold, silver, coffee, wheat, ivory, and slaves that produced the wealth needed to swell the imperial coffers. Other innovations in communications also enabled the state to solidify its control throughout the empire.

In order to consolidate and perpetuate his absolutist rule, Menelik saw the need to encourage the development of a new educated class steeped in selected western values and progressive in outlook. Such a class was critical to the functioning of the state bureaucracy, the diplomatic corps, and the economy. "We need educated people," Menelik is said to have claimed, "in order to ensure our peace, to reconstruct our country, and to enable us to exist as a great nation in the face of the European powers."[103] As early as the 1890s, young Ethiopians were sent abroad to Europe, Russia, and Sudan to study.[104] Menelik also encouraged the establishment of crude primary schools in Addis Ababa after the turn of the century, even though he was initially opposed in this effort by the Church. For the most part there were virtually no school facilities and no instructional materials. Children were usually educated in the open, under the tutelage of Ethiopian Orthodox or Catholic clergy. The first modern school was actually a school for the children of the nobility and had an enrollment of about one hundred. Among the initial class were two would-be emperors, Lij Yasu and Tafari Makonnen (who later became Haile Selassie I). Schools were also opened at about this time in such regional capitals as Harar and Dire Dawa.[105] Students learned Amharic, various European languages, reading, writing, mathematics, science, and other subjects. Most young people who were fortunate enough to receive a formal, western-style education either entered government service or became interpreters. Other opportunities for them to use their education had yet to be created. The impact of the educated on politics and government at this time was also limited.

Even as Menelik engaged in consolidating his empire and introducing various innovations into Ethiopian society, he was a sick man. He suffered several strokes and eventually paralysis. After 1908 his condition steadily declined until he died in December 1913.

Menelik had designated Lij Yasu, his grandson, as his heir, but this move was vigorously opposed by his wife, the Empress Taitu, who preferred her daughter Zauditu. Even before Menelik's death bitter internecine struggles raged among the members of the royal family, one faction wishing to reorient the focus of the empire to the north and the other choosing to maintain the southern and central focus Menelik had fostered. A group of Shoan noblemen who supported Lij Yasu won out. They installed a regency government that ruled in an advisory capacity to Lij Yasu, who became *de facto* emperor in 1910 at the age of sixteen. During his brief reign Lij Yasu conclusively demonstrated that he was not cut from the same cloth as previous great Ethiopian leaders.[106] He made many enemies among the clergy and the nobility. He made many mistakes, but his overtures to the Muslims in his domain appear to have been his undoing. Lij Yasu wanted to integrate the Somali and other Muslims of the now vastly expanded empire more fully into Ethiopian society. He appointed some of them to high administrative posts, gave them prestigious titles, and even went so far as to contract marriages with their daughters and to claim an ancestral relationship to the prophet, Muhammad! These and other activities that Lij Yasu's aristocratic enemies considered reprehensible and heretical led them to brand him an apostate, and after securing a release from their oaths of loyalty by the Abuna Mateos, the head of the Ethiopian Orthodox Church, they proceeded to plot his dethronement. Lij Yasu was excommunicated for being an apostate, and in late September 1916 a thirteen-point proclamation was issued listing his wrongs and justifying his demise.[107] The conspiracy was headed by Tafari Makonnen, whom Lij Yasu had stripped of his governorship over Harar some months earlier.

A meeting of aristocratic conspirators chose Princess Zauditu, Menelik's daughter, as the most acceptable replacement for Lij Yasu. There were other claimants to the throne, including Tafari Makonnen himself, but in the interest of a unified front against Lij Yasu, the princess was selected as a compromise. Forces loyal to the conspirators began to move immediately on Harar, where Lij Yasu had been attempting to establish friendly relations with the Muslims. By late October, hundreds of Somalis had been massacred—some by advancing troops and others by Christian civilians—and Lij Yasu had been driven into flight. He remained a fugitive for five years, being captured and imprisoned until he died in 1935 on the eve of the Italian invasion.

Zauditu was crowned empress in February 1917. Tafari Makonnen was made regent to the empress and heir to her throne. He was also given the title of Ras. A traditionalist nobleman, Fitwarare Habte Giorgis, was made minister of war. This triumvirate created an informal system of checks and balances that gave the government enough stability and cohesion to wage ten years of struggle against powerful provincial noblemen who perceived a power vacuum at the center as an opportunity once again to strengthen their autonomy or semiautonomy in relation to the crown.

The Rise of Ras Tafari

As regent, Ras Tafari envisioned carrying out the modernizing efforts initiated by Menelik. A key to his success would be his personal army. Ras Tafari expanded his army and provided it with the most modern weaponry his money could buy. He also attempted to expand his reservoir of other potential flexible resources. For example, he accumulated a substantial personal fortune and deposited the money in foreign banks.[108] He recruited members of his own family to serve as his closest confidants and a cadre of young, educated individuals to aid him in the more technical aspects of administration. Tafari also continued Menelik's efforts to have Ethiopia considered on equal terms with the European powers. His most notable diplomatic accomplishment as regent was to secure Ethiopia's admission to the League of Nations in 1923.[109]

Tafari demonstrated that he was as much (if not more) a progressive as Menelik, but for the first ten years of his tenure as regent he was somewhat bridled by the other members of the triumvirate, particularly Habte Giorgis. But on the death of both the minister of war and *Abuna* (Archbishop) Mateos in 1926, the time had finally come for Tafari to make his move to gain more power. In a bold preemptive gesture, Tafari dismantled Habte Giorgis's personal estate and redistributed it to some of his most loyal followers; further, he absorbed his personal army into that of the regent.[110] This action in effect reduced the possibility of another powerful lord utilizing Habte Giorgis's power base to threaten the regent or the Crown.

Abuna Mateos, the powerful religious leader, had been a conservative thorn in the side of both Menelik and Tafari. His successor, however, posed no immediate threat to the regent, who began at once to attempt to break down the power of the Church in relation to the Crown. We shall return to this point later.

Princess Zauditu realized that Tafari had begun his drive to power, and she plotted to have the regent deposed. Tafari put down this conspiracy and forced the empress to crown him Negus (King) in October 1928. The government was now under Tafari's complete control.[111] In a desperate bid to halt Ras Tafari's imperial machinations, the husband of the empress, Ras Gugsa Wolie, tried to defeat the regent's army on the battlefield in 1930. He was unsuccessful, losing his life in the process. Zauditu died mysteriously two days later; Ras Tafari was crowned Emperor Haile Selassie I (Power of the Trinity) in November 1930. His reign, beginning when he was only thirty-seven years old, would last some forty-four years, and he was to be the last Ethiopian emperor of the Solomonic line. Haile Selassie had a design for the creation of a stronger, more modern bureaucratic empire, and he immediately began to etch out his strategy. His plans were briefly interrupted by the occupation of Ethiopia by the Italian Fascist forces of Benito Mussolini between 1935 and 1941, but surfaced again with renewed vigor in the wake of World War II.

The most formative period of Haile Selassie's efforts to modernize Ethiopia's autocracy came between the zenith and nadir of European colonialism in Africa. The "winds of change" set in motion in other parts of the Third World, coupled with Haile Selassie's seemingly dogged determination to perpetuate royal absolutism in Ethiopia forever, were in large measure the catalysts that led to the emperor's demise. Yet in spite of incredible odds against him, Haile Selassie skillfully engaged in policies aimed at preserving the absolute authority of the imperial crown for more than forty years, well into the late twentieth century—a time when the bureaucratic empire as a common state form had all but disappeared. To understand his achievement, it is necessary to understand the political-sociological context in which Haile Selassie operated; the structures of power and privilege in traditional Ethiopia need to be brought into sharper focus. This is the purpose of the following chapter.

II

THE STRUCTURE OF POLITICS

The historical bureaucratic empire inherited by Haile Selassie was characterized by two extremely important features that served to influence his
style of rulership and the structure and content of politics throughout his
reign. First, traditional Ethiopia was a feudal society in which religious and
aristocratic power and position could be used either to support or to
challenge imperial authority. The bureaucratic state had been constructed
from multiple regional fiefdoms, and initially it was held together solely by
the fact that regionally powerful lords "submitted" to the King of Kings or
emperor. At any point a lord might choose to renege on his pledge, or even
to challenge the emperor for his crown. By the same token, the blessing of
the Ethiopian Church was a prerequisite for relatively secure imperial
survival. Given this situation, the emperor's primary task of rulership was to
find ways of either harnessing or destroying these traditionally powerful
institutions. In other words, he found it necessary to work gradually toward making his personal authority absolute. This tendency was not unique
to Haile Selassie, nor was it unique to Ethiopia's bureaucratic empire; but
because of certain historical developments, Haile Selassie was able to consolidate his absolutist position much more than his predecessors had.

Second, the Ethiopian state as we know it was constructed as a result of a
unique case of African imperialism. As I have already shown, between the
late 1800s and early 1900s substantial amounts of new territory were added
to the emperor's domain. In large measure the people who inhabited these
areas differed from the Amharas in religion and cultural affinities. Moreover, in the process of colonization, rather than consciously attempting to
integrate subject peoples into the dominant culture, the emphasis was
mainly on exploitation and control. This policy created a class structure
with distinctive ethnic undertones. The subjugated ethnic groups became
landless peasants and the tenants of politically, economically, and culturally
dominant Amhara-Tigre overlords. A direct consequence of the process of
colonization, then, were contradictions based not only on social class but
also on ethnicity.

Before turning to consider the style of Haile Selassie's rule and the factors that enabled his anachronistic regime to survive well into the twentieth century, it is necessary to consider briefly the nature and significance of those factors that most structured his political environment: 1) the Crown's relations with the Church and the national religion; 2) the significance of land in Ethiopian society along with the Crown's relationship with the landed aristocracy; 3) feudalism; and 4) colonialism, class, and the national question. Power and authority in traditional Ethiopia was in part based on myth and custom, and in part on land and access to land. As Ethiopian colonialism penetrated into peripheral areas, an effort was made to graft the values and customs of traditional Ethiopia onto subject peoples, while at the same time denying them the rights, privileges, and opportunities open to members of the dominant group.

The Crown and the Church

Christianity was introduced into Ethiopia by Frumentius, a monk of the See of the Christian or Coptic Church of Alexandria (Egypt) in the fourth century, during the reign of the Aksumite monarch, King Ezana. Among the first converts were the king himself and the royal family.[1] Gradually, common people in the Kingdom of Aksum were also converted. Significantly, from this early date a linkage was specifically drawn between kingship and divine ordination, as Ezana proclaimed to the world that he was given his authority, "By the power of the Lord of heaven and of the earth."[2]

Frumentius was appointed the first archbishop or *Abuna* of the Ethiopian diocese by the Patriarch of Alexandria and given the authority to ordain lesser bishops and priests from among the local population. From this point on a firm bond was perpetuated between the Ethiopian Church and the Coptic Church in Egypt. In order to secure the appointment of an Abuna, historically the monarch had to pay the government of Egypt a significant fee.[3] But in the early days this was of small consequence, as the Ethiopian monarch valued the Church and the Abuna for the legitimacy they conferred on him and for the unity they seemed to foster within his domain.

Although the parent church was responsible until 1950 for appointing and removing the Abuna, its chief representative in Ethiopia, traditionally it allowed the local church to administer itself and even to make decisions with regard to certain aspects of doctrine. What resulted was a church that was only nominally unified and only nominally adhered to the tenets of Egyptian Christianity. Rather than being disciplined and hierarchically organized, for more than fourteen centuries the Ethiopian Church was characterized by regionalism and a low level of discipline among its clergy. In practice, Ethiopian Christianity became a syncretic religion, blending elements of local custom and belief with elements common to orthodox Christianity.

The thread that most clearly links the Ethiopian Church with the Church in Alexandria is its adherence to the Monophysite doctrine. This doctrine holds that Christ had but one true nature, a divine one, as opposed to the Roman Catholic creed which maintains that Christ had two separate natures, one human and one divine. The former position suggests that Christ's human body was different from other human bodies, in contrast to the latter which argues that Christ's human body was just like everyone else's body but that his spiritual nature made him unique.

The Monophysite creed caused quite a bit of controversy in the Roman Church in the fifth century, and it was eventually condemned as heresy at the Council of Chalcedon in 451. With this the Coptic and Ethiopian churches separated from the Roman Catholic Church and continued to adhere to the Monophysite doctrine.

This tendency was reinforced in Ethiopia in the aftermath of the Chalcedon conference by a group of Syrian monks adhering to the Monophysite position who fled to Aksum and began to write and teach according to the proscribed doctrine. Among these were nine clerics who came to be known as the Nine Saints of Ethiopian Christianity. Their reputation was mainly based on their contribution institutionalizing Ethiopian Christianity. They translated the Bible into the Semitic-based ecclesiastical language of the Ethiopian Church, *Geez,* and introduced Alexandrian liturgy and music into existing church ritual.[4] In addition, they founded monasteries and built churches, all of which helped to entrench the Church as an agent of national unity.

From the fifth century to the thirteenth century, the Christian Church survived in Ethiopia in spite of repeated challenges from adherents to traditional religions in the region who were bent on destroying it. When Aksum declined, the center of the Christian kingdom shifted to Tigre and Angot and came to be dominated by the Agaw-speaking ethnic group instead of the Semitic-speaking peoples. In 1270, however, after a series of bitter struggles, the Agaw Zagwe Dynasty was overthrown and replaced by a Semitic monarch, Yekunno Amlak. On ascending the throne Yekunno Amlak claimed to have restored the Solomonic Dynasty.[5] His right to the throne was confirmed by the Church, and from this point on it began to play an increasingly significant role in the political affairs of Ethiopian society. Moreover, the reign of Yekunno Amlak marked the beginning of a cultural revival that would last for five centuries.

Over the next century the Church became the chief legitimator of the Crown. The Church's role was enhanced, in part, by the writings of monks who introduced the Ethiopian national epic, the *Kebra Nagast* (The Glory of Kings), which documented for the first time the mythical origins of the line of monarchs begun by Yekunno Amlak's restoration. The *Kebra Nagast* was written by six Tigrean clerics and completed in the early fourteenth century.[6] There is some disagreement as to the origins of the legend, but the chief author of the Ethiopic version of the document claims to have translated it from Arabic. The text, however, consists of 117 chapters containing quotations and illustrations from the Old and New Testaments, the Koran, and elsewhere.

The basic argument of the *Kebra Nagast* is that the Ethiopian people, not the Jews, are the "chosen people" and that Ethiopian monarchs who can trace their pedigree to the House of David through King Solomon have the right to rule not only the Ethiopian people but all the world.[7] The major body of the text is devoted to telling the story of the Queen of Sheba, Makeda, and the wise Hebrew king, Solomon. According to this legend, the Queen had heard of this good, wise, and just king and had journeyed to Jerusalem to share in his wisdom and to learn of his style of rulership firsthand. Makeda was extremely impressed by Solomon, and she agreed to adopt his religion and to bring it to her people. But before leaving on the return trip to her own kingdom, she accepted the king's invitation to dine with him. During the course of this encounter, Solomon succeeded in seducing the Queen and left her pregnant with his seed. Makeda returned home and gave birth to a son, Ebna Hakimor, Menelik I.

When he was of age, Menelik himself journeyed to Jerusalem to visit his father. On this visit he was crowned King of Ethiopia by Solomon and given the name David II. Menelik eventually returned to Ethiopia in the company of the firstborn sons of the Hebrew nobility and secretly stole the sacred Ark of the Covenant. Divine power allowed Menelik and his entourage to escape Hebrew forces, who followed in hot pursuit.

The *Kebra Nagast* goes on to discredit Solomon, his descendants, and the Jews in general as being corrupt and unworthy of being the chosen people. When the Jews rejected Christ, it holds, the light of God left Israel and began to shine (as it will forever) over Ethiopia. A point made throughout the document is that the greatness of Ethiopian kings is contingent on two factors: possession of the "Tabernacle of Zion" (the Ark of the Covenant) and a genealogical link with Christ through Solomon and the House of David. The *Kebra Nagast* established the principle that no one except the male progeny of a direct descendant of the House of David could claim the title King of Kings. Significantly, however, the legend did not establish a formula for deciding who among the many who claimed such a pedigree was most deserving of the crown at any given point in time. Needless to say, this absence gave rise to competing claims and bitter succession struggles.

An effort was made, about the same time that the *Kebra Nagast* was published, to codify the law of Ethiopian society and to spell out clearly not only the duties and obligations of the masses to the state but also those of the king to his people. The most notable example of this effort was the *Fetha Nagast* (The Law of Kings). The importance of this document was that its codes were believed to flow directly from God to the people through kings.[8] In actuality, the *Fetha Nagast* was not of Ethiopian origin but derived from the codified rules of the Coptic Church.[9] Since the Ethiopians accepted the Coptic Church as the only true Church, they also accepted the code of law. Among other things the *Fetha Nagast* established the fact that anyone who claimed to be king and was so designated by the Church had to adhere to Orthodox Christianity; to do otherwise would be tantamount to heresy, thus warranting excommunication and the stripping of the crown. This document also confirmed the king as the *de facto* head of the Church.

In practice the Church had two heads—the king and the *Abuna*. For all practical purposes, however, the king was the most powerful of the two. For example, the *Abuna* was traditionally a foreigner who did not know the local language and did not understand much of the local custom. He was merely responsible for lending legitimacy to the Ethiopian Church and to the reigning monarch. Emperors were known to have jailed, exiled, and even executed *Abunas*.[10]

Local priests and monks came to wield more real power than the *Abuna*, but even their authority was subservient to that of the Crown. Chief among these was the *Echege,* the chief monk in the Ethiopian Church and the ecclesiastical assistant to the imperial throne.[11] Traditionally the *Echege* and other important indigenous clergy resided at the court and were expected not only to be the upholders of sacred traditions but also to be the chief supporters of the king. For their support, high church officials, including the *Abuna,* could rely on the king to enhance their wealth through land grants and other benefices. But their well-being was totally at his disposal. The Church had no central treasury and no bureaucracy capable of commanding a base of financial support that would allow it to become collectively independent of the monarch.

This is not to say that the Church and its representatives had *no* power. The higher echelons of the clergy were extremely dependent on imperial largesse and the bulk of the clergy comprised poor, uneducated, and politically powerless individuals. Still, the clergy to this day is accorded a great deal of respect throughout highland Ethiopian society. It might even be suggested that historically the Church did (albeit in a limited way) wield a measure of power in relations with the monarch. For instance, the *Abuna* was responsible for crowning the emperor, blessing him with special prayers, and sanctioning controversial decrees; and he also had the authority to declare whether or not a given emperor was deserving of the continued support of the masses or the nobility. The ultimate weapon of the *Abuna* was of course excommunication. Moreover, by assuming the role of defining, articulating, and interpreting the cultural myth of society and the heritage of its rulers, the Church became a real political power. One has only to refer to Ethiopia's recent political history to find support for this proposition. The fate of both Tewodros and Lij Yasu was in part directly related to their loss of Church support.[12] The failure of the coup of 1960 was likewise largely due to the failure of the conspirators to secure the support of the Church.

Realizing that the Church was at least potentially powerful because it served an important legitimizing function, Ethiopian emperors as a rule tended to emphasize the interdependence of Crown and Church. Consequently, like emperors elsewhere, they tended to support religio-cultural institutions that buttressed their own authority. There is a good deal of evidence for this. For instance, it was quite common for an emperor to use a churchman as a mediator between himself and a recalcitrant lord or between two feuding noblemen. Also, the Church was systematically used as an agent of education and for the transmission of Amhara-Tigre culture and values to peripheral areas of the empire. Wherever the emperor's soldiers set up their garrisons, churches and priests followed shortly thereafter. In this sense the Church participated fully in the spoils of conquest. The most obvious manifestation of this was the huge holdings of *samon* (Church) lands given to the Church by the Crown.

As suggested earlier, the support of the Church was guaranteed by the granting of certain rights and privileges to important or influential clergymen in return for their services to the Crown. The Church received rights to land and other property, and from time to time it had its holdings enlarged through imperial grants and grants from members of the landed aristocracy. By 1974 between 20 and 30 percent of all arable land in the empire was held by the Church.[13] The Church was also allowed to collect tithings on a local basis from anyone who resided in a given parish. More detail on *samon* land rights will be given in the next section.

The important point here is that although the Church's power was generally passive, it was real. No emperor who valued his political survival could ignore this.

The Crown, Land and the
Landed Aristocracy

In Amhara mythology the king, the Church, and the nobility were thought to have critical roles to play in ensuring the good life of the people. Therefore, each was accorded preeminent status. The good and just king was responsible for preserving civil order; the nobility (*makuānnet*) was responsible for the fertility of the land; and the Church (*kāhenāt*) was responsible for the spiritual well-being of society. At the same time, however, there was the fiction that the king rightfully predominated over the nobility as well as the clergy. The *Fetha Nagast* invested him with ultimate rights over all land within his domain, and this in large measure justified his absolute authority. In practice this was not often the case, as the monarch had always to be capable of demonstrating his power and authority in order to be effective. Weak kings often found their positions undermined by both groups. In periods of intense provincialism, such as the "Era of the Princes," or at times when the state was thrown into disarray by foreign invasion or bitter succession struggles, the Crown found much of its authority diminished at the expense of powerful regional lords or the Church. The successful monarch was the one who could find mechanisms for diluting or curtailing the power of these two groups and enhancing the absolute authority of the state.

Prior to Menelik's reign, Ethiopian society was extremely unstable, as the nobility could never be completely controlled or manipulated. Even though a man might claim the title of King of Kings, he had to be aware of the constant need to cater to the potential military power of lesser kings and regional lords and also of the sanctioning power of the Church. Should a recalcitrant noble-vassal of the Crown feel that he was powerful enough to challenge the authority of a given monarch, it was accepted that he had license to do so. The Church, on the other hand, could weaken a ruler's position simply by questioning his fitness to rule.

As has been demonstrated above, emperors traditionally maintained their authority, ultimately, through their military prowess and through the effectiveness of their bureaucracies. At the base of the effectiveness of both these instruments of control, however, was the emperor's fictional control over all land. Through his ability to dole out land and tribute from land (extremely valued forms of political patronage) the emperor could reign in potential enemies while at the same time enhance his own absolutist position. No Ethiopian emperors were more successful at using this strategy than Menelik II and Haile Selassie I. Both men achieved great success in placating the *makuānnet* and the *kāhenāt* even as they used these institutions to strengthen their own positions. To appreciate how this occurred and what implications this process had, it is necessary to understand both the place of land in traditional Ethiopian society and the role assumed by land as Ethiopia moved from its premodern feudalist phase to a modern, largely capitalist phase. The land tenure systems of Ethiopia's highland core formed the basis for the tenure patterns that characterized the whole of Ethiopia at the time of the 1974 coup. The essential elements of this system can be traced to antiquity, but over the centuries significant alterations occurred as the centralizing tendencies of the state took hold.

Historically there were five basic types of land tenure found in the Ethiopian core, each conveying certain individual rights to land. These were kinship land, village land, private land, church or *samon* land, and government or crown land. By far the most common was kinship land, land belonging to a lineage, not to individuals, by virtue of it having been claimed by a founding ancestor by right of first cultivation. Individuals could not own land, they could only use it, and they could theoretically claim use rights over land wherever they could prove their birthright to be common with others on the land. Such rights were called *rist*, and were based on the principles of ambilineal descent. That is, *rist* could be claimed through one's mother or father.[14] One result of this practice was that individuals often claimed rights to widely dispersed land parcels. Since *rist* rights could not be owned in the conventional sense, theoretically such land could not be sold. John Cohen and Dov Weintraub note, however, that peasants in *rist* areas reported that wealthy and politically powerful individuals did in fact often buy *rist* land through a variety of fictions.[15] Frequently the fragmented nature of one's *rist* holdings forced individual peasants to lease at least some of their land.

From the time of antiquity, *rist* rights characterized the land tenure system of the Abyssinian core. Such rights were most common in Amhara areas, but variations of this system could be found in other parts of the core as well. *Risti*, for example, was very similar to *rist* and was common in Tigrean regions—Eritrea, Tigre, Begemdir, Gojjam, and some parts of the Shoa and Wollo.[16] Although *rist* rights were considered hereditary, there were conditions under which an individual could lose these rights. In ancient times, when the state was held together only tenuously, the *Fetha Nagast* established the principle that though every individual possessed *rist* rights, the king possessed the right to collect tribute from all land in his domain. Over time the emperor came to claim ultimate dominion over all land, a claim made possible by the ever increasing centralized power of the state.

Confiscation of *rist* land was seldom done in an arbitrary manner. In fact it was customary for the emperor to provide a pretext, a justification, for such actions. A lord might, for example, be accused of treason or heresy and legitimately stripped of his *rist* land. Such imperial sanctions were not restricted to the nobility, however. Peasants could also lose their *rist* rights if they failed to honor tribute obligations, vacated *rist* land over a long period of time, or were involved in capital crimes or rebellions. *Rist* lands could also revert to the Crown if a *rist* peasant died and left no heirs.[17]

The right of the king to demand tribute from all land under his dominion was a very significant factor in determining the pattern of land tenure that evolved over the centuries in Ethiopia. Originally it was not solely the King of Kings who could demand *gult* from *gabbars* (tribute payers) who tilled the land. Any king or lord who both demonstrated that he was a power to be reckoned with in a given area and entered into a patron-client relationship with a group of peasant cultivators could legitimately claim *gult* from their land. As the polity became more and more centralized and hierarchically ordered, the emperor became the supreme *gulteñya* (one who has the right to claim tribute), with successive layers of *gulteñyas* beneath him. For his part, the lord provided the peasant family with protection, emergency relief, a system of justice, and sage advice when needed. The peasant in turn was responsible for paying the lord tribute in kind: a certain number of days of labor on the lord's estate each year and service in the lord's army in time of war. Significantly, the peasant in the earlier phases of this system was an autonomous cultivator who had exclusive rights to the land he tilled and the authority to make all decisions relating to cultivation. His tribute obligations, however, were determined for him by the lord. This vassal-lord relationship is thought by many to have given Ethiopia its particular feudal character.[18] This point will be dealt with in more detail in the following section.

Gult, then, was essentially an overright to dues from land. Since the Crown had ultimate *gult* rights over land, once the monarch conquered territory or succeeded in gaining the submission of other nobility, he then had land which could be dispensed as *gult.* In other words, the monarch surrendered his *gult* rights to others and thereby allowed the *gulteña* to collect tribute from certain specified amounts of land inhabited by a certain number of cultivators. The most desired *gult* land was the most fertile, inhabited by large numbers of peasants, and under intense cultivation. The benefiting *gulteña* could further surrender a portion of these rights to individuals he might hold in his service.

Gult rights according to this system were not held in perpetuity, although in the case of certain powerful regional families such rights became quasi-hereditary in practice.[19] Usually, however, *gult* was a temporary grant contingent on loyal and satisfactory service to the dispenser of the *gult.* This being the case, successive emperors developed this system into an effective instrument of reward and punishment in the process of centralizing the bureaucratic empire. The tendency was for the emperor to grant revenue from the land he controlled by waiving his own *gult* rights to members of the royal family, other nobles, individual clergy, the Church, distinguished soldiers, and local rulers. The revenue they received was not rent in currency, but tribute. By the early twentieth century, as Ethiopia moved from what could best be described as a feudal mode of production toward a nascent form of agrarian capitalism, *gult* became payable in currency and, as we shall see, was eventually transformed into taxation.[20]

Menelik was responsible for introducing another variation in this system which provided the basis for the eventual privatization of large amounts of *gult* land under Haile Selassie: *rist gult.* With the expansion of the state to include large areas outside of the highland core, Menelik came to possess land that was not rigidly subject to Abyssinian custom. Most of this land was dispensed as *gult* land in the process of consolidating the expanded bureaucratic empire, but certain amounts of it were given as hereditary *gult, rist gult.* The holder of such rights could theoretically extract dues in perpetuity from the peasants who worked the land, but the *rist* or tenancy rights of the cultivator were protected as long as he continued to pay the required tribute. If the peasant defaulted from his obligation, the *gulteña* was justified in seizing his land.

In contrast to the *rist* system of kinship tenure, under the village tenure system the village was regarded as the corporate holder of use rights over land. The family or descent group played no official role in deciding how land would be allocated. Rights to land were determined by residence in a community, and each individual was entitled to an equal share of village land. Land was held under village tenure, and periodic adjustments were made in the distribution of village land to ensure the equity of the system. For the most part, village tenure was practiced only in parts of Eritrea and Tigre.[21]

During the period that the state was confined to the Abyssinian core, private tenure was rare.[22] However, in certain cases, even a peasant could gain ownership of land. For example, a peasant who farmed government land and paid a tax in kind for a number of years could theoretically ask for the right to own the land he farmed. Local level chiefs and soldiers who kept a portion of the tax paid on government land, however, tended to discourage this practice, as they preferred to have their own revenues uninterrupted.[23]

The private ownership of land did not become common until the period of Menelik's colonial expansion, when the boundaries of the state were broadened. Menelik doled out land in conquered areas as private tenure and *gult* tenure holdings. He gave land and access to tribute to soldiers who helped him conquer the land; to settlers and local notables, *balabats*, who helped him administer it; and to members of the nobility and royal family as gifts. Private holdings were mainly administered under *rist gult* and *gabbar* tenures, both of which amounted to a form of freehold tenure. Both were eventually abolished by Haile Selassie and transformed into freehold land.

Maderia land was land given to lower-ranking soldiers and government employees in place of a salary or pension. Normally this grant was temporary, valid only over the period the individual held office, but it could also be for life.[24] The individual simply had to pay tax on the land, and he could collect rent from persons settled on it. This practice became widespread after World War II when Haile Selassie attempted to consolidate his hold over the south while at the same time rewarding Ethiopian patriots who had fought so gallantly in defense of the motherland during the Fascist occupation.

Balabats in the south held similar rights to tribute from land as did the holders of *rist gult*. They were given a certain portion of land for their own use (*balabat meurt*) and the right to collect tribute (and ultimately taxes) from a certain number of *gabbars*. This type of *gult* was called *siso gult*. With the abolition of the *gult* system in 1966, much of the land held as *rist gult* land, *siso gult* land, *maderia* land, and crown land became private land, and those who occupied it were given freehold title. Until this time, however, private ownership had been relatively limited.

In addition to the nobility and the imperial bureaucracy, the Church held special rights to land and to the fruits of the labor of those who worked the land. *Samon* land was traditionally land that was under the obligations of tribute to the Church.[25] In practice there existed two basic types of *samon* land: land held directly by the Church in rights of permanent possession and land held indirectly by the Church through persons responsible for paying tribute to the Church rather than to a lord. The right to such land was known as *samon gult*. Whereas similar secular *gult* could be withdrawn at the emperor's pleasure, *samon gult* was permanently in the hands of the Church. Significantly, however, this land was not held by the Church in a monolithic fashion, but instead by individual parishes or monasteries. It could even be held by certain high-ranking individual clerics, such as *Abunas* and *Echeges*.[26]

Ethiopian legend holds that the Church is due at least one-third of all land in the empire, but this rule has never been followed consistently.[27] In fact, it is not certain just how much land the Church actually possessed by the time of the 1974 coup. John Cohen estimates that by that time the Church held no more than 5 percent of the total land mass in Ethiopia and no more than 20 percent of all arable land.[28] The largest Church holdings could be found in the south. As with the nobility and the soldiery, Menelik and Haile Selassie saw the clergy as having a crucial role in the consolidation of the bureaucratic empire through proselytizing Ethiopian Christianity among conquered peoples. As a result, provincial governors were encouraged by the Crown to give out large tracts of land to the Church as inducement to aid the colonizing mission.

In addition to doling out land for private use and as *gult* tenures, the Crown also held land of its own, known as crown land. This land was farmed by tenants who in return were given land for their own use, usually under terms of temporary tenure.[29] Cohen and Weintraub estimate that by 1974 about 47 percent of the total land of Ethiopia could be classified as crown land and about 12 percent of all arable land.[30]

On the Existence of a Feudal Society

Prior to the period of expansion and consolidation of the bureaucratic empire, Ethiopian land tenure patterns were characterized by a peculiar form of feudalism. It differed from classical European feudalism in several respects, but there were several similarities as well. The similarities appear significant enough for me to characterize Ethiopia as it existed from roughly the time of the Zagwe Dynasty until the early twentieth century as predominantly feudal. The degree of feudalism varied, of course, from time to time and from region to region. But I think it can be demonstrated that what existed was a feudal society. This position goes counter to that of scholars such as economist Gene Ellis who contend that the feudal paradigm is a "hindrance" to understanding Ethiopia.[31] Certainly it is, if we consider as a feudal society only one that resembles Medieval European feudal society in every respect. To do this, however, would suggest that it makes no sense to attempt comparative historical or political analysis, since every society is unique. Instead, I would contend, as do Marc Bloch and others, that feudalism is not an event that occurred only once in world history.[32] The fact is, the basic human relationship we call feudalsim—that method of governing and organizing economic activities—occurred in several parts of the world and at different times. It was not a widespread phenomenon; yet it was not unique to one place either. That feudalism existed in Ethiopia and was an outgrowth of the peculiar type of political economy found in the region for about eight or nine hundred years can be demonstrated if we contrast the basic features of classical feudalism with the most salient elements of the Ethiopian system. This will allow us to comprehend better the politico-economic implications of the social relationships that emerged around land use, surplus extraction, and political dominance.

Classical feudalism developed in Medieval Europe. It is generally acknowledged as the outgrowth of a "profound weakening of the State, particularly in its protective capacity."[33] This coincided with the fact that traditional kinship ties were unable to address the security needs of the affected populations. Centralized bureaucratic states had yet to consolidate, in large part because a viable money economy had not developed that would have allowed for the establishment of a salaried central bureaucracy.[34]

The most basic features of classical feudalism were: 1) land held as a fief; 2) a dyadic personalistic bond of political dependence between a lord and vassal; 3) the delegation of monarchical authority through intermediaries widely dispersed throughout the state; 4) a secular elite that was first and foremost a military class; and 5) a weakened state struggling for survival.[35] In Medieval Europe land was of supreme value because it enabled the warrior-lord to subsist; but most important, it provided him with a ready supply of men who could be his warriors in time of war. The lord provided his vassals with protection and generally maintained public order within his domain.

Rushton Coulborn has defined feudalism as primarily a method of government rather than an economic or social system.[36] He bases this contention on the fact that the essential relationship is between lord and vassal. To the extent that this is true, I would contend that this explains only the lord's role in the dyad.[37] Feudalism cannot be understood without acknowledging the importance to the overall functioning of the system of the extraction of economic surplus from the vassal. Rather than considering feudalism merely as a method of government, then, we must also consider it as a method of resource extraction that characterized certain precapitalist societies at a given moment in their historical development.

In order to apply the feudal paradigm to Ethiopia, certain anomalies that contrast the classical model must be addressed. The first anomaly relates to the role of land and land ownership in Ethiopia as compared to Medieval Europe. Ethiopia was never characterized by a strict manorial system where serfs farmed land on a lord's estate. As outlined in the foregoing section, in the preexpansion phase of the state, land rights were vested in Abyssinian or highland Ethiopian peasants themselves, although they did owe tribute and service to their lords. At the same time, however, when a lord held *gult* rights these could be considered a form of fief. Although the existence of a fief usually implied the existence of a piece of land in the lord's possession, it did not always have to, even in Medieval Europe. What was more important was vassalage. A pool of vassals was essential to raising a military force sufficient to defend a given community, and it was needed to provide the professional warrior-lord with his subsistence needs. The personal estate was not essential to those relationships.[38]

During the phase of expansion and consolidation under Menelik and Haile Selassie, the traditional Amhara systems of *rist* and *gult* were transferred and adapted to serve the needs of colonizing peripheral conquest areas. Noblemen and bureaucrats were given *rist* rights to land on which peasant families were already engaged in cultivation. These settlers, then, were made instant lords with their own estates that they owned in perpetuity. In addition, those who acquired *rist gult* privileges could benefit from the labors of vassals permanently assigned to them. *Gult* provided a temporary but nevertheless important form of vassalage. A similar situation obtained with respect to *balabats* who possessed *balabat meurt* and *siso gult*. In the periphery the possibility of the fief being land held by the lord in right of permanent possession was not only much greater than in the core areas but also an essential component of the pattern of rulership the state was attempting to impose as it consolidated itself.

Related to this is a second critical anomaly. Feudalism in highland Ethiopia appears to have developed much slower than in Medieval Europe, to have lasted longer, and to have matured less. F. C. Gamst traces the origins of Ethiopian feudalism to the collapse of the city-state of Aksum in the tenth century.[39] Between that time and the early twelfth century, the state was besieged by one enemy after the other and was barely able to survive. The weakened Abyssinian state reconstituted itself around 1135 A.D. as the Kingdom of Zagwe. It was this dynasty that gave rise to the regime of Yekunno Amlak, who is credited with restoring the Solomonic line of emperors. Although it was reconstituted, the state was never firmly consolidated, and for more than seven centuries it vacillated between extreme provincialism and weak centralization. Not until the culmination of the *Zemene Mesafint* and the subsequent reign of Tewodros II was it apparent that centralizing forces were beginning to predominate.

From the twelfth century on, there is evidence that what we might call feudalism or proto-feudalism began to characterize Ethiopian society. Warrior-kings and emperors established fiefs that allowed them to extract tribute and service from a collection of vassals. This was a hierarchical system by which the dominant lord, the emperor, had as his vassals other lords or princes; they in turn had their vassals, and so on. The dominant monarch theoretically had the right, as in Medieval Europe, to assign his noble vassals to certain territories. It is important to remember that throughout this period the state remained relatively weak and dependent on a warrior class of noblemen who also served as administrators in the service of the state. For their service, they were allowed to extract from the surplus of vassals assigned to them who worked the land.

By the time the feudal tendencies of Ethiopian society began to take form, European feudalism was generally on the wane. In Ethiopia feudalism developed slowly, never quite maturing to the extent that it resembled classical feudalism in all respects. Some parts of Ethiopia were more feudal than others. In some areas, particularly in parts of the north, we could only speak of *proto-feudalism*. Proto-feudalism is a term used by Coulborn, referring to the fact that some societies might become only partly feudal. This occurred when some critical elements in the feudal paradigm never matured.[40] For instance, the essential elements of classical feudalism are vassalage and the fief. If a society is not characterized by the balanced development of *both* these phenomena, this might be considered a manifestation of proto-feudalism. The Carolingian Empire and pre-Muscovite Russia are given as examples of proto-feudalism. The former had vassals but no fiefs; the latter was characterized by peasants who could change lords at will. Yet in both cases there were some elements we could consider feudal.

Although it is customary to speak of Medieval Europe as "feudal Europe," it is important to note that not all of Europe was feudal at that time.[41] Furthermore, where feudalism did exist, its pattern and degree varied from place to place. Ethiopia was no different. Although there was a wide variation in the degree of feudalism in Ethiopia, there is no doubt that feudal tendencies were present over most of the country.

In an effort to modernize Ethiopian society, rather than to destroy feudalism immediately, both Menelik and Haile Selassie attempted to harness and even propagate it to strengthen the state's capacity to consolidate itself. Fiefs in the form of *rist, gult, rist gult, balabat meurt, siso gult, samon gult,* and *maderia* land were given as incentive for aiding in the colonization of the periphery. These institutions had broad implications for the development of social relations in the process of modernization in both the north and the south.

The reintroduction of a money economy in the early twentieth century and the gradual development of a salaried military and bureaucracy were the first signs that Menelik and Haile Selassie saw the continuation of feudalism into the age of modernization only as a temporary convenience. Money was meant to undermine that system even as it appeared to coexist with it. By the early 1960s, Haile Selassie began to dismantle the feudal superstructure in earnest, partly because of external and internal pressures but mostly because he saw it as the best way to further his absolutist position. I shall return to this point in the next chapter. For the moment, however, it is important to recognize Ethiopian feudalism—as was the case with feudalism wherever it existed—as "a judicial amalgamation of economic exploitation with political authority."[42] The state utilized this method because it was convenient. Once its strength had been restored and it had consolidated itself, it could risk introducing a seemingly more efficient system of taxation and control. In the case of Ethiopia, contradictions occurred in the process of making the transition from the immature feudal mode to nascent bourgeois democratic and capitalist institutional forms that signaled the demise of the absolutist state.

Colonialism, Class, and the National Question

Along with feudalism based on variations in traditional Amhara land tenure relationships, the process of conquest and consolidation that spawned Ethiopian colonialism contributed to the evolution of certain social formations and power relationships that go a long way toward explaining the pattern of conflict during the Ethiopian Revolution. In the core of the empire the basic social relationships between lord and vassal were initially unaffected by the expansion of the state to its present limits. It was not until Haile Selassie began his efforts to dismantle feudalism and to integrate the country both economically and politically for the purpose of more effective central administration that significant alterations began to take place in the social structure and relationships of the north.

In the south, however, the very fact of conquest and the subsequent style of administration established new social classes and ethnic relations whose contradictions were among the seeds of revolution. This can be seen if we examine both the process of establishing effective control in the south and the evolution of class and ethnic relations from the time of conquest to the end of World War II.

John Markakis maintains that class distinction in the north prior to the post–World War II era had been fairly minimal.[43] The nobility was distinguished from the vast majority of the Abyssinian peasantry mainly by its mannerisms and practices of ostentation. There were limited possibilities for the accumulation of wealth in traditional society, since the economy was based on subsistence agriculture instead of capital. What accumulation there was was in terms of rights to land. This situation made for substantial vertical integration and remained virtually unchanged until after the war. In the south, however, the influx of Abyssinian conquerors immediately contributed to the formation of clear and rigid class distinctions between the conquerors and the conquered; those who "owned" land, those who cultivated it, and Amharas and non-Amharas. The exact nature of the social relations that developed was based on a complex mix of factors, the main ones being the policies of administration, control, and extraction that took form between the 1890s and early 1930s.

In the process of subduing the periphery, Menelik had encountered varying amounts of military resistance and this contributed greatly to the style of rulership introduced in given areas. Resistance was high in most areas, including Arussi, Gibe, Sidamo, Bale, Ogaden, Kaffa, Wolamo, and Borana. The type of administration introduced there tended to be much more stringent than in regions where initial resistance had been minimal (that is, Harar and parts of Wollega). In those areas of high resistance the tendency was to set up *ketemas* from which both administration and control of conquered areas could be readily maintained. The settlement of the Oromo areas of Sidamo and Arussi was particularly brutal, characterized by widespread massacre and depopulation.[44] Once such regions were brought under control they were administered by military men and re-populated in large measure by the immigration of Abyssinian peasants, who were given land for settlement according to *ye-Amhara rist* rights.[45] This eventually led to the emergence of a class of medium-scale landlords who could be distinguished from most of the indigenous population not only because they owned land but also because they were from a different ethnic group.

Consolidation required that the emperor be concerned not only with control, but also with weakening potential enemies and strengthening the effectiveness of the central bureaucracy. Therefore both Menelik and Haile Selassie attempted to coopt the *makuānnet* by involving many of them in the colonization of the south. Noblemen were generally appointed to high administrative posts in the periphery and given new titles and land. The cornerstone of the emerging bureaucratic empire, however, comprised military officers, the leadership of the Ethiopian forces of occupation. Because of their new wealth and political power, those men came to con-stitute a new class of gentry that owed its existence not to traditional values and practices, but to the modernizing state. Together, members of the traditional Abyssinian nobility and the new military gentry provided the leadership base for the development of a viable modernizing imperial bureaucracy. They were complemented in this role by a rapidly expanding cadre of lower-grade central bureaucrats and numerous indigenous *bala-bats* who took care of the day-to-day administration at the grass roots. The beginnings of a finely honed imperial bureaucracy were more or less intact by the third decade of the twentieth century.

By removing Abyssinian nobles from their home areas, the emperor was able to take them away from their potential bases of support. This could only be accomplished, however, with the incentive of more land and poten-tial power represented in land grants and administrative posts in the south. The *makuānnet* were usually granted the most prestigious positions in the administration, such as governor-general of a province. They were also granted the most land and *gult*. District governorships were generally in the hands of high-ranking military officers. Only in those areas where resistance had been low, such as Jimma and Ausa, did indigenous elites maintain their former political roles. At the lowest level of administration, the tendency was to rule indirectly through local elites who converted to Christianity and cooperated with the Crown.

In the south the top levels of the provincial administration were domi-nated by Shoans and immigrants from other core areas.[46] It was possible for non-Amharas to become integrated into the upper reaches of the provincial as well as the central bureaucracy, but this was highly dependent on the individual demonstrating that he was loyal and above all, thoroughly Amharized. Again, another important factor dictating the chances one had of being upwardly mobile in the imperial bureaucracy was where one came from. Oromos from Wollega and Shoa, for instance, were much more likely to attain high office in the Ethiopian colonial bureaucracy than those from Wollo, Bale, or some parts of Sidamo.[47] *Balabats* might be given titles and land, but rarely were they able to become politically influential outside of their home areas.[48]

Administrators in the imperial bureaucracy were primarily responsible for maintaining law and order, collecting taxes, and administering justice. To the extent that professional soldiers were a part of this bureaucracy, they were mainly responsible for suppressing or repressing internal rebellions and for protecting the peripheral areas of the empire from foreign invasion.

Initially, the pay for field bureaucrats and soldiers was poor. The Crown made up for this by allocating land and land rights to such civil servants. The extent of these privileges and remuneration depended on the rank of the individual. For example, consider the case of the soldiers who manned the *ketemas*. Common soldiers received small amounts of land and two to five peasants as *gabbars;* warrant officers received larger amounts of land and seven to ten *gabbars;* higher-ranking officers received sizable amounts of land and thirty to eighty *gabbars;* and the governor of a province had huge amounts of land and several hundred *gabbars*.[49] *Gabbars* were responsible for providing the holders of *gabbar* privileges with tribute and service, but the amount of either was not standardized. Therefore the personal security of *gabbars* was very tenuous. Similar formulas existed for civilian members of the bureaucracy. Of course, the terms of *rist gult, balabat meurt, siso gult* and other forms of tenancy determined landlord-*gabbar* relations as well.

How land was allocated in conquered areas depended in large measure on the degree of initial resistance the area mounted. For instance, in places where resistance had been stiff, about two-thirds of each piece of land was usually given to a representative of the state's central bureaucracy. The rest was given to local *balabats* as *siso gult*.[50] The *balabat* administered not only the one-third of the land he had rights to, but also the other two-thirds inhabited by his neighbors.

Peasants on the conquered land found themselves oppressed not only by new political institutions, but also by new demands placed on them for their surplus produce. They became tenants on land they had once known as their own, and often they had to pay high tribute to alien landlords. Some of the land was *hudad* land, which meant that peasants paid tribute directly to the Crown, but most of it was held as *gult, rist gult, siso gult,* and *maderia* land by various individuals and as *samon gult* by churches.[51]

Initially, it was in the interests of landlords to keep their tenants relatively content and productive. Nevertheless the terms of tenancy were not always reasonable. There were three main types of tenancy systems: *siso arash, irbo arash,* and *ekul arash*.[52] Under the terms of *siso arash* the landlord allowed a tenant to farm a piece of land, but the tenant provided all inputs. As dues he paid *asrat* (one-tenth of his harvest) and one-third of the remaining produce as tenancy rent. This meant that the tenant was allowed to keep about 60 percent of all that he produced. *Irbo arash* required that the tenant provide all farming inputs; 10 percent of his total harvest went as *asrat,* and 25 percent of the remainder for rent. In other words he kept about 65 percent of all he produced. The most demanding, and eventually most common of the three forms of tenancy, was *ekul arash.* [53] Under this system, the landowner provided all inputs, but the amount of seed provided was returned after the harvest. From what was left, one-tenth was paid to the landlord as *asrat,* and of what remained, 50 percent was paid by the tenant as rent. This meant that in most cases the peasant had less than 35 percent of his produce for family consumption.

Before World War II, as oppressive as the terms of tenancy might become, tenancy was still relatively secure, as landlords needed their land under intense manual cultivation if they were to accumulate any wealth at all. This was true even after the initial introduction of money into the economy, because the technological capacity for mechanized agricultural production was very low. Once this deficiency was overcome, however, tenancy in both the north and south became more and more insecure. I will return to this point later in the book.

As a result of this pattern of administration and settlement in the south, a highly stratified class system developed, with status being determined by political position and land ownership and use rights.[54] At the top of this system were large-scale landowners who tended to come mainly from the Amhara-Tigre nobility, the clergy, and the highest ranks of the military officer corps. Next came large-scale landowners from among the indigenous elite and their descendants. Each of the above-mentioned class levels was characterized by a landlord-tenant relationship between individual landlords and a large number of tenants. Just beneath the second highest class level came the medium and small-scale landowners, with fewer dependent peasants. This group consisted mainly of Amhara-Tigre soldiers and bureaucrats who had taken up permanent residence in the south to take advantage of economic opportunities. The fourth level in this class structure included settler-peasants who had come from core areas and been given *ye-Amhara rist* as an inducement to settle and repopulate areas abandoned by original inhabitants as they fled highland invaders. In a few limited areas there remained indigenous peasants with *rist* rights, but for the most part all southern land was at the disposal of the Crown.

The majority of the indigenous people of the south could be found in the lowest category of the class system. Most were simple tenants and sharecroppers who tilled the land but lacked autonomy in determining how surplus production would be utilized. This right was accorded in varying degrees to members of higher-ranking classes. Disproportionately this class of people tended to come from among the Oromo population, which, in numerical terms, represented the most significant group to be affected by Amhara colonization.

Most significant about this emerging class system was that it developed simultaneously with the development of a sense of ethnic consciousness among those groups being colonized. This new form of identity transcended local neighborhoods and kin groups. There emerged a broadened sense of ethnic affiliations based on the language and culture of a people juxtaposed against the language and culture of the forces of oppression.

In addition to being seen as economically exploitative and politically dominant, the colonizers were seen as distinctively different in strict ethnic terms from those they colonized.[55] When settlers and administrators from the core arrived in peripheral regions, they were accompanied by all of the elements of the Abyssinian cultural heritage. Language and religion played central roles in the process of colonization. It was theoretically possible, for example, for an Oromo to be assimilated into the dominant culture. He simply had to become Amharized—to take on the language, religion, customs, and mannerisms of the Amhara. As mentioned previously, however, the process of assimilation was extremely selective, affecting only a small segment of indigenous elites. The bulk of the colonized masses had no hope of ever ridding themselves of the colonial bond. Throughout the reign of Haile Selassie, mostly latent but ever-present resistance was common among the colonized people of the periphery.

Initially, it seemed that the alien presence in the south was motivated more by political than economic purposes. The immediate need was to establish effective control of conquered areas. Whatever surplus was extracted—except that which was earmarked for the central treasury—was for the local consumption and subsistence of field administrators, soldiers, and their families. As the state switched from a system of tribute in kind to taxation in money, the economic basis of the colonial presence became more apparent.[56] The state saw the south's agricultural and mineral wealth as a reservoir of resources that could be used to bolster the capacity of the modernizing bureaucratic empire. Although settlers and administrators originally looked on these reforms with disfavor, by the early 1960s they had come to see the value of the personal accumulation of the capital surplus yielded by the more efficient exploitation of land.[57] In the process, there emerged a complex set of class-ethnic group relationships that engendered a great deal of resentment among the colonized peoples of the south for their Amhara-Tigre overlords as well as for their local accomplices, the *balabats*.

Rather than the Amharas taking on the role of benevolent patrons, they came to be seen primarily as exploiters. They tended to be absentee landlords and agents of the state who lived in towns and *ketemas*, journeying to peasant communities only to collect tribute and taxes and to recruit common soldiers for the army. The state provided few if any social services for indigenous populations, and while it was convenient, it fostered feudalism as the most effective form of governance and economic exploitation. Peasants and tenants had very few rights. The state used its power and authority to establish and protect the rights and privileges of its agents and other northern settlers.

The practice of upholding the class and ethnic interests of nonsoutherners at the expense of local peoples, along with the pattern of compartmentalizing administration, laid the foundation for the development of latent forms of class orientations that would be activated as the revolution unfolded in the early 1970s. It also provided a justification for the claim to self-determination expressed by oppressed nationality groups. Before Ethiopian colonialism took hold, for instance, both the Somalis and the Oromos—the major ethnic groups in the south—were divided into multiple clans that rarely functioned as broad-based ethnic unities. Each group was characterized by sophisticated political and social institutions, but each clan tended to function separately from the others under usual circumstances. Perhaps the most significant bases for identifying such groups as distinct "nationalities" were certain aspects of language and custom; but even with regard to these factors, there were substantial intragroup variations. Colonialism redefined social relationships in the south, and this eventually contributed to ethnicity and group nationalism becoming viable political categories that defined political orientations and behavior in the periphery. As Haile Selassie attempted to impose modernization, economic development and national political integration from above, contradictions and conflicts based on ethnic and class identities catalyzed the society into revolutionary convulsion, and the old order collapsed.

III

POLICY AND THE POLITICS OF SURVIVAL IN THE ABSOLUTIST STATE

Ethiopia emerged from World War II and the Italian occupation in a severely weakened condition. Haile Selassie fled into exile in the spring of 1936, and he did not return until five years later, after the country had been liberated by an army led by the British, but comprised of Indian, West, East and Southern Africans, together with Sudanese and Ethiopian regular forces. Over the period of occupation, some Ethiopians had collaborated with the Fascists, but others, known as the "Patriots," had maintained a dogged guerrilla campaign against alien rule in both urban and rural areas. As a consequence, the Italians never gained complete control over the country. Among the Ethiopians who died during the occupation period were many young, educated people who had been groomed as the pillars of Haile Selassie's modernizing autocracy.

The Italians had done much in a very brief period to dismantle Ethiopia's traditional institutions and to replace them with what they considered to be more modern institutions conducive to exploiting the country's rich economic potential. Mussolini had envisioned the settlement of Italian colonists in the Ethiopian heartland who could transform the agricultural sector into the "granary of Italy" and tap its rich mineral resources.[1] Perhaps the most significant of such changes were the curbing of the power of traditional elites and the abolition of the *gabbar* system of tenure and the infusion of massive amounts of capital and developmental infrastructure into what had heretofore been a backward economy on only the extreme periphery of the world capitalist system.[2]

Depending on how he viewed the task of reconstruction, Haile Selassie could have regarded such changes as resources or constraints. He could have attempted to reimpose the proto-feudalist system that largely characterized Ethiopia before the Fascist era, or he could begin anew, constructing a modern state on new foundations.

65

Although the traditional social system had been significantly changed by the Italians, it had not been completely destroyed. In fact, the remnants of the old order presented Haile Selassie with formidable obstacles that had to be bridged if he was to modernize Ethiopia while holding fast to the principles of royal absolutism. If Ethiopia was to survive future challenges to its sovereignty, it would have to modernize. The problem became, however, how to modernize while managing traditional forces. The path Haile Selassie chose was one that emphasized the growing bureaucratization and centralization of the state on the office of the emperor while attempting to modernize society from above. In pursuing this objective, the emperor had to eliminate the privileges of some social classes, co-opt other classes, and create still other classes anew. He had constantly to assert his power in both symbolic and tangible terms. Most important, he had to strengthen the state as an autonomous political actor that could hold its own against potential challengers in both the domestic and international arenas.

In many ways the development of the Ethiopian Empire under Haile Salassie was a logical extension of the process that began shortly after Emperor Tewodros initiated his efforts at consolidation. By the early twentieth century, however, the emperor could not simply base his rulership on authoritarian control. It was not enough to gain the fealty of subject lords who collected tribute on behalf of the Crown. Instead, the emperor had to devise ingenious mechanisms aimed at insuring the survival of an increasingly absolutist state in the face of simultaneous threats to its sovereignty from external actors. He also had to develop creative responses to pressures for modernization emanating from within and without.

To a large extent, as was the case with other bureaucratic empires that confronted similar circumstances, the structural characteristics of the Ethiopian Empire at this time determined the options for change and survival open to Haile Selassie. Traditional and nontraditional forces, values, and attitudes presented Haile Selassie with competing demands in the course of his efforts to modernize Ethiopia and to maintain its sovereignty. Given this circumstance, the potential for political contradictions was inherent.[3] In order to survive, the imperial state had to suppress successfully or completely eliminate these contradictions.[4]

The forms of challenges facing the regime of Haile Selassie were the same as for numerous other historical bureaucratic empires such as the Chinese, Ottoman, and Carolingian empires. The emperor relied on religio-traditional elements for legitimacy, and yet he had to be aware that those same elements could cause his demise if left unchecked. As was the case for monarchs in earlier empires of this kind, the emperor further had to enter into strategic alliances; extend his absolute powers so that they were not perceived as mere fictions; and develop autonomous resource bases. The major difference between the Ethiopian Empire under Haile Selassie and these earlier cases was that the former survived into the twentieth century relatively untouched by endogenous pressures for change. Exogenous forces, unbuffered by a protracted period of foreign colonial rule, foisted modern ideas and methods onto Ethiopian society in such magnitude and with such suddenness that the emperor was not able to solidify sufficiently his absolutist position so as to manage the inevitable contradictions between elements of the status quo and more change-oriented social forces. Although similar in many ways to Meiji Japan, Ethiopia did not witness the emergence of an alliance between the monarchy and traditionalist elements, allowing the state to orchestrate change from above relatively smoothly.[5] Like twentieth-century Iran, the remnant of the Persian Empire, Ethiopia under Haile Selassie attempted to preserve the absolutist state through an accommodation with modernizing forces on his own terms without completely subduing traditionalists. This was not a strategy of Haile Selassie's own choosing. Instead, he was overtaken by events and forced to deal with contradictions that were from the very beginning too formidable to be managed in the long term.

Whereas Tewodros, Yohannes, and Menelik II had invested much of their time and energies toward the goals of conquest and territorial expansion, Haile Selassie was consumed more with the problems of unifying and stabilizing his polity. To be sure, he did incorporate Eritrea into the empire, but this was done relatively late and was intended more to ensure the security of the empire than anything else. Much more than his immediate predecessors, Haile Selassie was also concerned with utilizing a money economy to enrich the imperial treasury so that monetary resources might bolster the absolutist position of the state in relation to potential internal as well as external challengers. He was keenly aware that the survival of the absolutist state, as it always had been, was contingent on the monarch's ability to mobilize various forms of autonomous resources to serve the needs of the state.[6]

The key to understanding the style and pattern of rulership in historical bureaucratic empires is understanding that the monarch was necessarily engaged in a perpetual juggling act in which he attempted to balance the state's survivalist needs against demand emanating from multiple competing traditional and modern social classes. S. N. Eisenstadt has noted that rulers of historical bureaucratic empires were always torn between their desire to use the instruments of their own creation such as the state bureaucracy and other new social institutions for their own "mostly exploitative purposes" and the necessity of co-opting groups that might challenge their absolutist position.[7] In addition, as absolutist states evolved, there were inevitable pressures within the bureaucracy itself for decentralization and devolution of power. Leaders had to know when to yield and when to hold fast; they had to know when to bargain, co-opt, compromise, or to use force.

For a long time, Haile Selassie seemed to master this peculiar art of rulership. He developed the requisite facility for entering into strategic alliances with both domestic and external groups and individual actors; this facility appeared to strengthen his position in dealing with potentially troublesome situations at various points in time. On the domestic scene, for example, he utilized the new educated classes to advance and lend legitimacy to reform measures such as land taxation and administrative reform in the face of stern opposition from traditional classes. In the international arena, Haile Selassie unsuccessfully tried to guarantee the inviolability of the Ethiopian state against the Italians, who had coveted Ethiopia since the late 1800s, by joining the League of Nations in 1923. Later, Ethiopia joined the United Nations and took the lead in the establishment of the Organization of African Unity in an effort to insure the future integrity of the state. Furthermore, Ethiopia strategically allied itself with the United States in part to discourage what were feared to be the imperialist designs of Great Britain and in part to strengthen its military capacity to deal with domestic as well as external enemies. These points will be dealt with in greater detail below. For the moment, however, it is important to note that Haile Selassie exhibited some of the same patterns and styles of rulership that had characterized other leaders of historical bureaucratic empires, and ultimately these patterns and styles led to similar consequences. By analyzing how he coped with the contradictions that emerged as he attempted to pursue the primary goal of solidifying his personal power in the face of enormous centrifugal pressures of both domestic and foreign origin, I hope to shed light on the forces that led to the collapse of Haile Selassie's regime.

The Phase of Consolidation

At the end of the period of Italian occupation, Ethiopia was left with a power vacuum. Once powerful regional armies and their commanders had been either co-opted or decimated; the Church had been weakened; and a military occupational administration had been imposed that affected both the core and peripheral areas of the empire. Most significant, the Italians had initiated economic policies that had the effect of vigorously forcing Ethiopia into fuller participation in the world capitalist system. They claimed to have a civilizing mission, but, in fact, their primary mission was economic exploitation. Massive amounts of capital were pumped into Ethiopia as part of an extensive development campaign.[8] More than four thousand miles of all-weather roads were constructed in less than five years at a cost of between $160 million and $200 million.[9] These roads could be traversed by cars and trucks, and they linked the main regions of the empire as never before. Private Italian investors complemented their government's efforts with around $760 million of their own funds that were used to establish manufacturing and industrial activities.[10] The development of roads, which could be used for more efficacious exploitation of peripheral areas as well as for the rapid deployment of a central army,

proved to be a key element in facilitating the consolidation of Haile Selassie's regime after World War II. Before that time, and in spite of his
desire to do so, he had found it difficult to move the produce collected as
tithe in the periphery to a central market where it could be converted into
money income for the imperial treasury.[11] With the network of roads
bequeathed to Ethiopia by the Italians and with the military and administrative assistance provided by the British in the immediate aftermath of
the war, Haile Selassie was able systematically to begin to build an absolutist
state of his own design. The situation he confronted both at home and in
the international arena substantially influenced how he approached the
problem of state building.

Even before he went into exile, the emperor had begun to strengthen his
autonomous position by initiating certain constitutional, administrative,
and economic policy reforms, but this effort was left incomplete. Perhaps
the most significant of these reforms, and one clearly intended to
strengthen the position of the emperor in relation to religio-traditional
classes, was the proclamation of a constitutional monarchy in 1931. Haile
Selassie apparently recognized that if his bureaucratic empire was to avoid
the fate of other historical bureaucratic empires that had been transformed
by revolution and violence, he would have to establish a constitutional
instrument that would give the illusion of democracy while at the same time
legitimizing the absolutist role of the emperor under a legalistic shroud.[12]
The rights and obligations of monarch and subjects were instead interpreted and legitimized by the Church in documents such as the *Kebra
Nagast* and the *Fetha Nagast* and for all intents and purposes were vague
and ambiguous. The 1931 Constitution was intended to spell out clearly the
proper relationships between the Crown and its subjects.

Haile Selassie wanted to be recognized at home and abroad as a modernizing monarch, one who was prepared to share power in a democratic
fashion if that was what it took to bring about political and economic
development in his country. The Constitution was patterned in style and
substance after the Japanese Constitution of 1889, although there were
some differences in the two documents made necessary by the difference in
societal context.[13] The Ethiopian Constitution was a simply written document with a total of seven chapters and fifty-five articles. The first chapter,
consisting of five articles, related to the establishment of Ethiopia as a
constitutional monarchy, guided by an emperor who traced his ancestry
back to King Solomon of Jerusalem and the Queen of Sheba. The emperor
was declared divinely ordained, and his successors could come only from
the royal Solomonic line. All of this had been established in the *Kebra
Nagast,* but the significance of the references to the nature of the empire
and the procedure for imperial succession in the new constitution was that
they effectively removed the legitimizing function from the Church and
into the hands of the monarch who promulgated the document. By this act,

governance in Ethiopia became more secularly based than ever before. This trend toward secularization was hailed as a trend toward modernity.

The Constitution also provided for the secularization and centralization of the imperial bureaucracy. Rules were laid out for the establishment of a more professionalized bureaucracy, judiciary, and budgetary institutions. Perhaps the most remarkable innovation in the document was the inauguration of quasi-representative legislative institutions, the Chamber of Deputies and the Senate. Clearly this move was meant to give the illusion of a dramatic move toward democratic reform. Yet the Constitution made it clear that these were no more than quasi-representative bodies, responsible for giving advice to the Crown rather than autonomous institutions charged with responsibility for law making. Neither house was popularly elected. Senators were appointed by the emperor from among the nobility and local chiefs; deputies were chosen by the nobility and local chiefs from among their peers.[14] The Chamber of Deputies, it was envisioned, would eventually be elected by the people when they were prepared to accept this weighty participatory responsibility.[15] Publicly, Haile Selassie wanted to create the impression that he, on his own initiative, had decided to ease gradually the Ethiopian polity in the direction of modernity, but it was obvious that if his absolutist regime was to survive in the modern age, it had to change.

John Markakis suggests that rather than demonstrating his commitment to democracy in establishing the Senate and the Chamber, "Haile Selassie was really attempting to rein-in and co-opt important members of the traditional nobility, and to strengthen the legitimacy of the regime among the new-educated classes" who he expected would be critical allies in his effort to consolidate his absolutist position.[16] This was the group most disposed to change, and he hoped that by deferring to them in a way, he could insure their loyalty. A further effect of this was to set up a channel for dispensing social prestige that competed with more traditional institutions and practices.[17] Senators relied on the emperor for their appointment just as the traditional nobility had relied on him for their aristocratic titles. In this case, however, these positions were defined by legal-rational criteria instead of religio-traditional ones. As the most powerful among the traditional nobility were required to spend time at the court, senators were required to reside in the capital city during certain specified periods. This altered but did not significantly change the tradition of imperial surveillance of noblemen who might threaten the Crown.

Traditional elites opposed the new Constitution, but their fears were somewhat allayed by the fact that the emperor did not immediately threaten their traditional rights and privileges.[18] In fact, he initially appeared to be disposed to grant them more privileges in an effort to co-opt them. This could be seen in the way the emperor dispensed political and administrative positions coupled with generous grants of *gult* and *rist gult* land in the south to the traditional elite in the early days of his rule.

Through the Chamber of Deputies Haile Selassie attempted to provide an avenue for upward mobility and political prestige for young, educated commoners and self-made men in his civil service. The idea was that these individuals would attribute all they possessed and all they had become to the emperor himself and, thus, freely commit themselves to his reformist policies. Indeed, this was initially the way the Chamber functioned. It was a rubber stamp for the emperor, and it greatly influenced the way in which the Senate behaved. Senators were generally aware of the alliance that had taken place between the Crown and these new classes, and they were cautious in expressing opinions contrary to the Crown without the support of the Chamber.[19] So, at least initially, Haile Selassie could use these quasi-representative institutions as flexible resources to legitimate decisions arrived at independently in the executive branch.

Despite the trappings of democracy, the 1931 Constitution left little doubt that the authority of the Crown was absolute. Twelve of the fifty-five articles related to the "Power and Prerogatives of the Emperor," and other articles throughout referred to the emperor's ultimate discretion.[20] Chapter III, Article VI, states: "In the Ethiopian empire supreme power rests in the hands of the emperor. . . . He ensures the exercise thereof in conformity with the established law."[21] Article V stresses that "the person of the emperor is sacred, his dignity is inviolable, and his power is indisputable."[22] Although the emperor was theoretically not above the law, he ultimately made the law and could structure it to suit his own purposes.

Few rights were declared for the citizen in the Constitution. Chapter III established that citizens accused of a crime were due a trial by a legally constituted court. They were guaranteed the right to privacy in correspondence and in their homes, the right to own private property, and the right to petition the government.[23] All of these rights, however, could be suspended if the emperor or any of his agents deemed such action necessary in the interest of national security. What emerged was an increasingly complex bureaucracy in the context of an absolutist state in which all power radiated from the monarch who attempted, so far as he could, to personalize his authority. For example, in addition to his vast appointive and sanctioning powers, the emperor was the ultimate court of appeals. He was also the person the citizen went to when his delegate in the legislature or a particular member of the bureaucracy was unable or unwilling to address satisfactorily a personal problem he might have. Haile Selassie, like emperors before him, held periodic audiences in which he received the complaints and requests of even the humblest of citizens. It was significant that Haile Selassie was able to promulgate this new document only months after his coronation as emperor. He claimed that he had wanted to initiate a constitution much earlier, as regent, but resistance from the "great nobles" was too firm at the time.[24] By the time he became emperor, however, he seemed strong enough to execute his will after only token consultation with the most important nobles. It is worth noting that already the influence of the nascent educated class was being pitted by the emperor against the traditionalists for his own purposes.

As regent, Haile Selassie had begun to pursue administrative, military, and financial policies designed to strengthen the hand of central authorities, setting the stage for more vigorous activity in this direction once he became emperor. The ministerial system was reorganized and some new ministries were created. In addition, Haile Selassie recruited and began to make extensive use of foreign advisors in organizing central administration and in advising him on domestic and foreign policy matters. He encouraged experimentation in local administration to come up with the most efficient form of colonial administration for peripheral regions. He abolished slavery, at least on paper, and began a program of road building in the capital, Addis Ababa, to make it appear as a showcase of progress. Other road projects were initiated to enhance administrative penetration to the south, southeast, and southwest. The country's archaic telecommunications system was also revised as a measure for improving the control of the center over the periphery.[25]

Haile Selassie attempted to bolster the regulatory capacity of the state by further professionalizing his army. A military academy was opened in a converted palace at Holeta in 1934, and was staffed by Swedish officers who trained Ethiopian recruits. The emperor's own semiprivate military unit, the Imperial Guard, trained by Belgian officers, also benefited from these reforms. Other would-be army officers were sent abroad to France for training.[26] The result of these changes was the emergence of a relatively potent standing army capable of discouraging or defeating any moves against the Crown by the personal armies at the disposal of certain individuals among the old nobility. An added feature of the military reforms was the introduction of aircraft (flown by European mercenaries) to the arsenal of the new army. Haile Selassie was the commander-in-chief of this new force, and he could use it either to defend the country against foreign invaders or as a means for suppressing domestic disorders. In the event that the army itself threatened his authority, the emperor could turn to his own personal army—the Imperial Guard—to help him maintain power.

Whereas the army was crucial in the immediate effort to stabilize the country, the penetration and development of an expanded, modern bureaucracy required a pool of educated, trained manpower. Haile Selassie attempted to address this need by opening several schools based on European educational traditions. He also began a policy of sending young men abroad, mainly to France and Belgium for university education.[27] The idea was for these young people to be trained as specialists in such fields as medicine, agriculture, economics, and engineering and then return home to serve as high-level officials in the imperial government. By the time the Italians occupied Ethiopia, it is estimated that there were some 125 young Ethiopians in the country who had been educated abroad under the auspices of the emperor. Many of them, however, were killed during the occupation.[28] Although it is impossible to measure the true impact of this turn of events, there is little doubt that Haile Selassie's efforts to develop a cadre of educated manpower to staff the upper levels of his bureaucracy received a significant setback, particularly when one considers that no Ethiopians received advanced education during the occupation. In fact, Italian Fascist General Rodolfo Graziani, who led the occupation forces, liquidated many of the educated Ethiopians who were unable to escape into exile.[29]

The generalized effect of the Italian interlude was devastating to Ethiopian society, and many of the innovations Haile Selassie introduced—not just education—were adversely affected. But students of Ethiopian politics generally agree that, rather than making it more difficult for the emperor to reestablish his absolutist authority and his program of modernization, this actually strengthened his position on his return. He immediately began to take advantage of the weakened state of the nobility's administrative control of the provinces and to set his own centralized bureaucracy on a firmer footing. He appointed new ministers within a week after his return and issued a decree in 1942 giving the provincial administration more power. One year later the Office of the Prime Minister was created, and the responsibilities of other ministers were more clearly specified.

The situation in the provinces at the time could best be described as chaotic. Large numbers of armed bands roamed the countryside. Some had been "Patriot" contingents; some were deserters from forces that had supported the Fascists; some were simply landless or lordless peasants displaced in the struggle to recapture Ethiopia. Roads and bridges were in a bad state of repair, having been bombarded and extensively used during the most intensive phase of the struggle.[30] There was, then, the need for a central government firmly in control to hold the country together.

As he approached his task of reconstruction Haile Selassie relied heavily on the British for necessary monetary resources and administrative and military advisers. This was an uneasy relationship, but it was one the emperor could not resist in the earliest days of reconstruction. British advisers were crucial in reestablishing the central administration; in setting up a rudimentary budgetary system for the first time; and in forming the basis for a new tax system.[31] On several occasions the British Royal Air Force was called on to aid the emperor in putting down rebellions in the provinces, and the British army was instrumental in keeping order in the Ogaden in the closing days of the war.

In spite of the extent and significance of their aid in this period, Haile Selassie was never at ease with the British. Part of the reason for his suspicion was that the British considered Ethiopia, since it had been conquered by the Italians, as occupied enemy territory. However, other Allied powers, including the Soviet Union and the United States, did not recognize the Occupation as a permanent conquest. Therefore, even as he relied on the British for aid, Haile Selassie was attempting to ensure the sovereignty of his domain. In January 1942 Ethiopia and Great Britain reached an agreement that acknowledged Ethiopian independence and the legitimacy of the emperor's claim to authority and returned most of the country to his exclusive control. In return the British were allowed to continue to occupy the Ogaden for a time and were given a special status in the country vis-à-vis other countries. Even after this agreement, however, civilian advisers and soldiers from the British military mission to Ethiopia could be found in all parts of the country. The British controlled all communications and transportation systems, and they had exclusive rights in providing air service in and out of Ethiopia.

Rather than reintroduce the new Ethiopian currency to replace the Italian lire, the British were instrumental in having the East African shilling declared the official currency during this period. The British presence and influence could be seen in such mundane areas as how the traffic was organized on city streets and in the manufactured products available for purchase in retail markets.[32] In spite of the 1942 agreement, Ethiopia was on the verge of becoming a British protectorate, if not a full-fledged colony. I shall return to this point later.

In an effort to strengthen the administrative capacity of the state, Haile Selassie promulgated a decree establishing the broad outlines of a new system of local administration. The country was divided into fourteen major provinces (*teklay ghizat*), 103 subprovinces (*awraja*), 505 districts (*woreda*), and 949 subdistricts (*miktel woreda*).[33] The chief administrative office in a province, the governor-general or *enderassie,* was granted broad powers of control over all other members of the central bureaucracy operating in a given province. He was particularly responsible for the collection of taxes, monitoring the expenditure of funds issued through the central treasury, and maintaining law and order. The administrative and political style of the *enderassie* varied from one individual to the next. Some operated as mere bureaucrats and exercised their duties more or less as dictated by law; others strayed far beyond the letter of the law, sometimes becoming over-zealous in how they interpreted their centralizing mission. Still others used their powerful political positions to amass enormous fortunes.[34]

The net administrative effect of these new procedures was to deconcentrate central government and to establish a complex network of field agents representing the various ministries in the capital. Ideally, this should have led to a more efficient administrative capacity for the central government. All civil servants were appointed and paid from the center. At the upper-most level of administration, officials tended to be well trained and educated, but at the lower levels this was not the case. For example, the qualifications for *woreda* governors and *miktel woreda* heads were minimal. Appointees at these levels tended to be local patrons and *balabats* with little or no education or training. As a result, these individuals tended to be tradionalist in orientation and were frequently the source of administrative inefficiency. They were often corrupt and unpredictable in the way they approached their duties, thus doing more harm than good in the effort to broaden the base of legitimacy for the Haile Selassie regime.[35]

The most significant political effect of these administrative forms, however, was to deprive traditional elites who had previously served as provincial administrators of an enormous amount of discretionary power. From this point on, provincial officials became part of the imperial salariat: professional bureaucrats with no real personal base of political support. Traditionally, governors were given a great deal of autonomy in administering their areas. They could levy and collect taxes, arbitrate disputes among their subjects, punish criminals, and set various administrative rules. They were only responsible to the emperor himself, who generally did not interfere in local matters. Now, however, they were appointed by the emperor on the recommendation of the minister of interior, and they were to cooperate with and engage in regular consultations with other ministers when issues relevant to them arose.[36] Rather than having a direct channel to the emperor, provincial governors now had to deal with him through the Ministry of Interior. In one fell swoop, power was swept from the hands of the traditional nobility and into the hands of the central bureaucracy. The authority of regional elites was further eroded when they were forbidden to organize their own military forces or to enter independently into treaties with other states.

Although it was difficult to implement these new reforms, by the early 1950s the Haile Selassie regime was firmly in control. It could deal from a position of strength with religio-traditional elements, enhancing its ability for autonomous action. This is not to say that traditional elements were without power, but only that now their power could not have the disorienting or controlling effect for the regime as often as it might have had in the past.

At the end of World War II the Church, like the aristocracy, was extremely disoriented and weak.[37] This facilitated the emperor's efforts to bring that institution more under his direct control. In late 1942 the first law dealing with the Church, Decree Number 2 of that year, came into effect. It was promulgated under the authority vested in the emperor by the 1931 Constitution. Interestingly, however, this article made no mention of the Church, but instead gave the monarch the right to organize all "administrative departments" and to appoint and dismiss military and civil service officials.

The decree related to Church administration. It was aimed at systematizing the financial affairs of the Church and at allowing the Crown to appoint members of the clergy to their posts. Haile Selassie again simply followed on the heels of the Italians who had removed the exemption of Church lands from taxation and went further by setting up a mechanism that allowed him to confirm or reject the appointment of clerics recommended by an ecclesiastical council. More significant, the Church was stripped of any temporal jurisdiction it had in the past. Other aspects of the decree dealt with the minimum educational requirement for clergy and with the content of the curriculum for seminarians. By 1948 the way was finally open for the emperor to gain almost complete control of the Orthodox Church of Ethiopia. After lengthy negotiations, the Ethiopian Church was granted autonomy from the Church of Alexandria, thus removing any source of outside control over Church matters. The secular control of the Church was solidified in the Revised Constitution of 1955, which made Orthodox Christianity the official state religion and gave the emperor the authority to promulgate all Church regulations except for purely ecclesiastical ones. It also gave him the power to appoint all bishops including the Patriarch himself, the *Abuna*.[38] These developments came amid a wave of Ethiopian nationalism, but their broader importance rested in the implications they possessed for the growing absolutist position of the central authorities in general, and more specifically the emperor himself.

In addition to chipping away at the administrative autonomy of the aristocracy of the Church, Haile Selassie attacked another aspect of its status and power. As I noted in the previous chapter, position and power in traditional Ethiopian society were intimately intertwined with land and access to land. If he was to be effective in controlling religio-traditional elements, the emperor had to curb their economic privileges as represented in their control of land. He pursued what appeared to be a contradictory policy, doling out huge amounts of land in the immediate postwar years to noblemen he sought to co-opt or otherwise pacify, while simultaneously dispensing land to such groups as war veterans and former exiles of all classes, members of the armed forces, police, civil service, and the landless unemployed. Approximately 95 percent of the land redistributed in this way went to members of the civil service, military, police, and national or provincial elites, all of whom were seen as having a central role in establishing the absolutist position of the state.[39]

Even as Haile Selassie appeared to be bent on deepening the feudal basis of Ethiopian society, he was setting in motion policies that would ultimately lead to its destruction. Between 1930 and 1934 he issued a series of decrees relating to land measurement, land use, and taxation. Under the communal system of the north, the land belonged not to the individual but to the corporate descent group through an ancestral "first tiller." This made it impossible to identify the "owner" of the land who was responsible for paying taxes. Moreover, peasants were reluctant to cooperate with the state's efforts to measure and register land because they felt this would threaten their traditional security system.[40] In the south, landowners, anxious to reap the benefits of this newly acquired land and the labors of their subjects, also resisted the new laws, as the government required them to cultivate all the land they possessed or to pay taxes on even uncultivated land. Governors resisted because the reforms promised to deprive them of their customary discretion over a portion of the tithe they collected. The most significant land tax reforms related to taxing land according to its assessed quality. The highest quality land was assessed E$80–90(US$40–45) per *gasha* (80–90 acres, depending on geographic area of survey). Medium quality land assessed E$60 and poor quality land E$30. From this point on all land tax was to be paid in cash.[41]

Despite ambitious plans to reform land tenure relationships and the relationship between the state and those who owned or worked the land, Haile Selassie was unable to effectively implement these measures before the war. The two most important reasons for this were the resistance by northern peasants' landlords and the *makuānnets* and the inadequacy of administrative manpower and bureaucratic capacity. Under the best of circumstances, the emperor would have had to be patient as the capacity of his government's land regulation system matured. But the brief period between his coronation and his exile was simply not long enough for these plans to come to fruition.

After the war, Haile Selassie began again an attempt to harness the landed classes by introducing measures to increase the state's jurisdiction over land ownership, land use, and taxation. In March 1942 the emperor issued his first major postwar economic reform. He introduced the law relating to the taxation of land according to its quality. However, the rate of taxation was significantly reduced. High, medium, and low quality land were each assessed at rates of E$15, E$10, and E$5 per *gasha*, respectively. Stricter rules requiring land measurement, classification, and registration were also introduced.[42] Resistance to these new regulations was swift, and it was most intense in the Amhara-Tigre heartland where communal tenure predominated. Rebellions broke out in Gojjam, Tigre, and Begemdir, where tax assessors were violently prevented from assessing the land. By 1944, the emperor decided to retreat on this issue, but only in those provinces where resistance had been stern. Proclamation No. 70 of 1944 excluded Gojjam, Tigre, and Begemdir from the rules laid down in the 1942 law. This strategic retreat is evidence that Haile Selassie was politically astute enough not to jeopardize his whole program of centralization and absolutist control by pressing too hard on one issue—no matter how important—in areas that could undermine his overall position. At this stage, he still relied heavily on both the old and new classes among the Amharas and Tigres and could not afford to alienate them completely. The emperor was also forced by landlord resistance to exclude landholders of *rist gult, siso gult,* and *samon gult* from the requirements of the land tax of 1942.[43] With the exception of the Church, however, landlords were now required to forward the 10 percent tithe they collected from tenant farmers directly to the central treasury, rather than keeping a portion of it for their own personal use. The Church was allowed to keep the tithe, but as a result of the Church reforms mentioned above, its financial activities were now closely monitored by the government.

In spite of this apparent setback, the emperor was still able to initiate significant changes in the tax system in his 1944 decree. Even though the provinces of Gojjam, Tigre, and Begemdir were exempted from the requirements of the 1942 Land Tax Proclamation, new requirements were issued in place of them. A new schedule of land taxation was established, and the two separate types of tax were defined: land tax and "tax in lieu of tithe." The three basic categories for land quality were maintained, but different rates now applied to different regions. Gojjam, Begemdir, and Tigre were taxed at the full rate that was obtained before the occupation period, plus an estimated tithe of one-tenth.

Another tax Haile Selassie introduced in 1944 in an effort to enhance the financial capacity of the state was the country's first income tax. This tax applied to all classes equally and in large measure was a response to the intense resistance to a progressive income tax by the landed classes. The tax got at the wealth of the rich, but in the process the poor were also adversely affected because of the regressive nature of the tax. Income from employment, rents, and business were all taxed by this measure.

At best, Haile Selassie's early reforms were only partially successful. He was able to improve the extractive capacity of the state in the area of tax revenues and thereby enhanced the authority of the state. But he was never able to establish complete control through this mechanism. Haile Selassie realized that he would have to continue to push on the twin issues of land and taxation if he was ever going to rein-in completely the landed classes and establish his own supreme authority.

Another strategic aspect of Haile Selassie's absolutist designs after World War II related to how he used his most valuable flexible resources: the military and the new educated classes. He had to develop both a strong military to keep domestic order and to keep his borders secure and a civil service committed to modernization as he defined it.

The emperor had begun to build a professional standing army even before the war, recruiting young officers just as he recruited young civil servants. They were generally bright young people from modest backgrounds, rather than from old aristocratic families.[44] After the war, Holeta was reopened and staffed by British personnel. The Imperial Guard continued to be trained by the Swedes. In 1957 the Haile Selassie I Military Academy was opened at Harar under the direction of Indian instructors. The Harar academy recruited cadets from among the best secondary school graduates and from the student body of the newly founded University College. Holeta catered mainly to young men who had received only a primary education. Other recruits continued to go abroad for training.

As he solidified his control, the emperor became more and more concerned with developing a crack professional military completely loyal to him alone. His military was largely built in the postwar period with the assistance of military aid from foreign donors. The 1942 agreement with Britain stipulated that the British government would provide aid at its own cost for the reorganization and training of the Ethiopian army.[45] The mission was to remain in Ethiopia for as long as it was needed or until the

British themselves decided to withdraw. The emperor, of course, surrendered some sovereignty, as the mission was under the complete control of the commander-in-chief of the British forces, but he viewed this as merely a temporary necessity, and he constantly calculated ways in which he might lessen his military dependence on Great Britain. To counterbalance the revitalization of the state army under the British, the emperor revived the Imperial Guard. This unit continued to be trained in the French military tradition and had no relationship to the army being trained by the British mission. The officers in this unit, in contrast to their counterparts recruited into the regular army, generally came from aristocratic families closely allied to the emperor.

In addition to the Imperial Guard and the regular army, a territorial army was set up, comprised of former "Patriot" groups, under the direction of various regional elites.[46] These troops were not trained soldiers, but it was felt that the best way to bring them under control and prevent their engaging in disruptive criminal activities would be to give them some official status.

Until 1944, these three militaries functioned independently of one another without serious conflict, but an agreement was reached that led to the development of a closer relationship among the different units. They all came under the jurisdiction of the Ethiopian Ministry of War, and by 1947, the British role had become only advisory. The territorial army was gradually incorporated into the regular army. The Imperial Guard continued to be the best-equipped, best-trained, and best-disciplined of the armed forces and served as a form of personal security system for the emperor. This elite force grew in size until it numbered some eight thousand men.

The British government decided to withdraw its miliatry aid to Ethiopia in 1952, and Haile Selassie moved quickly to establish relations with another "big power" patron, the United States.[47] The emperor had approached President Franklin D. Roosevelt in the immediate aftermath of World War II but did not conclude official economic and military agreements with the U.S. until the early 1950s. Since the early 1940s the United States had coveted a base in Eritrea where it could establish a communications system. Haile Selassie viewed the use of such an installation by the United States as a proposition with many more benefits than costs. He could reap the benefit of being closely allied with the most powerful military power in the world, while at the same time being paid rent in the form of military aid that could strengthen the military capacity of the state. The price paid for the use of this base in Eritrea, which came to be known as Kagnew Station, was roughly US$10–12 million per year over a twenty-five-year period.[48] By 1975, the total U.S. military assistance to Ethiopia amounted to almost US$280 million. In addition to this, over the same period the Ethiopians received US$350 million in economic aid in the form of technical assistance, capital goods, and food.[49] Such aid indeed contributed significantly to the military capacity of the Ethiopian state, as well as to its efforts at economic development.

"The Mutual Defence Assistance Agreement" and an agreement entitled, "Utilization of Defense Installations within the Empire of Ethiopia," both signed in May 1953, formed the legal basis for the expanding Ethiopia-U.S. connection. These documents complemented two treaties signed in 1951 relating to diplomatic and economic cooperation issues.[50] In effect, the U.S. agreed to guarantee Ethiopia's security. This added greatly to the confidence with which Haile Selassie could approach the task of political consolidation. With U.S. military aid the emperor could step up the modernization of his military while at the same time using it as a more effective weapon of domestic control.

In addition to the arms aid Ethiopia received from the U.S. after 1951, the Ethiopian military also benefited by the presence and activity of the U.S. Military Assistance Advisory Group (MAAG) established in 1954. The purpose of this group was to work with the Ethiopian military down to the battalion level. The Eisenhower administration agreed to train and equip three six-thousand-man divisions.[51] American military personnel were eventually assigned as instructors at both Holeta and Haile Selassie I Military Academy. A large number of Ethiopians also went to the U.S. for training during this period. The activities of MAAG were largely confined to the army, although some of its personnel were involved in providing logistical and end-use functions in connection with the navy and air force.

The motivation for the heavy U.S. investment in training and equipping the Ethiopian forces was to ensure the stability of the region, particularly as this might impinge on U.S. interests there.[52] Above all, Kagnew was important to American interests at that time. They wanted a base in Eritrea because of its strategic location, far away from the north and south magnetic poles.[53] Kagnew Station seemed ideal as a communications installation that could function year-round with little or no interruption in service. Eventually the base became an integral part of the U.S. network of radio tracking stations developed after the war that stretched from Virginia to Morocco, to Ethiopia and the Philippines. The Americans saw the price tag placed on the use of the installation by Haile Selassie as worth the investment for the value it represented for the U.S. and its NATO allies in their efforts to monitor their communist enemies. There was little or no concern in official American circles for making sure that U.S. aid to Ethiopia was well used until the Carter administration voiced its concerns over violations of human rights in 1977.[54] By then, however, the U.S. government was dealing not with Haile Selassie but with the Derg, which was becoming more and more Marxist in its orientation. The cooling of American-Ethiopian relations in 1977 had more to do with Ethiopia's new radicalism than with its misuse of American aid. In fact, it was well known that U.S. aid had been used in the past as a buttress to the imperial regime's domestic repression. In 1970, for example, the U.S. Senate Foreign Relations Committee discovered that since at least 1964 the U.S. had supplied Ethiopia with counterinsurgency training and on-the-ground advisers to help suppress the resistance in Eritrea. The government of Ethiopia had also regularly used U.S. supplied arms to suppress other domestic upheavals.[55] The extent of this kind of involvement in Ethiopian affairs was considered by U.S. officials to be minimal, but it is difficult to form an accurate estimate, since the U.S. government tried to conceal its role by referring to the advisers as members of "Civic Action Teams."

What is most important to note here is that in the formative years of the absolutist state, Haile Selassie skillfully used U.S. aid to strengthen both the state's military and economic capacity. Other aid donors were involved, but none with the scope of influence that the Americans had. Haile Selassie worked hard at diversifying the sources of his foreign aid—even taking aid from such diverse donors as the U.S. and the USSR—but in the end, he became inordinately dependent on the United States. John Spencer, a former American foreign policy and economic adviser to the emperor, pictured him as a man with "heartbreaking confidence" in the United States, one who would accept whatever advice he received from his American advisers without question.[56] He could not foresee the day when American support for him would flag, and ultimately this made him supremely vulnerable. Over the first twenty years or so of the relationship between Ethiopia and the U.S., however, he used this association to help him consolidate and maintain control over his domain with a great deal of political acumen. American military aid in particular strengthened his ability to use the armed forces as a flexible resource readily at the disposal of the absolutist state.

In addition to his armed forces, the emperor relied on the new educated classes as a crucial resource to buttress his regime and to advance its policies. The nobility at first remained the major source of recruitment after the war for top-level civil servants and members of the imperial cabinet, but Haile Selassie also began to recruit individuals from non-aristocratic backgrounds to meet the demands of a rapidly expanding governmental bureaucracy. In fact, the positions of greatest influence in his government came to be occupied by men he himself had raised to high office. There was no way to avoid liberalizing the Crown's recruitment policies. As democratic ideas filtered into the country, people of humble birth, who nevertheless had been fortunate enough to receive an education, expected to be able to move up in life through government service.

As the central bureaucracy expanded, the aristocracy became less and less important in government. To the extent that its views were represented at the national level, after the mid-1950s it tended to form the opposition to the young, progressive elements in government and to the emperor himself.[57] Haile Selassie had stimulated this polarization process, first by accelerating the rate at which young commoners were allowed to go abroad for university education and then by placing a high priority on building a national education system.

In 1941 Haile Selassie created a Ministry of Education and Fine Arts and inaugurated the first secondary school in the country, Haile Selassie I Secondary School. Between 1943 and 1950, government expenditures for education grew from E$1 million to E$10 million, to E$15 million in 1957, and to about E$108 million in 1974. Most of the growth in schools and educational opportunities, however, was at the primary level. By 1973, there were about one thousand primary schools with more than 500,000 pupils. At the secondary level there were just over fifty schools, and less than 100,000 students. The literacy rate was between only 5 and 10 percent.[58] This indicates that what was emerging was an elitist form of education, geared mainly to allowing the most academically able to pass through the education system and into public service. This served the emperor's purposes of extraction and control much more than it served the needs of the country to improve the quality of life and standard of living of all citizens in this desperately poor society.

University education was introduced in 1950 when the University College of Addis Ababa was established. It was set up by a group of Canadian Jesuits who had established several other schools in the country. In 1961 the institution had grown to the extent that it was reclassified as Haile Selassie I University.[59] Over the next decade, the American government sponsored professors to fill the college's faculty ranks, and eventually American civilian instructors and administrators supplanted the Jesuits.

Between 1950 and 1968, the university granted almost two thousand baccalaureate degrees and more than two thousand diplomas and certificates (awarded after two years of study in education, health, and law).[60] Most of these graduates were absorbed into the civil service. On the eve of the revolution, the bureaucracy employed more than 100,000, and the civil service and state enterprises had reached a saturation point. Haile Selassie approached access to advanced education as well as the staffing of his civil service in a very personal way. He tried to impress upon those who succeeded in securing advanced education or a civil service job that they were successful in large measure because of his good graces. In this way he hoped to secure their allegiance to him.

What Haile Selassie had not anticipated, it seems, was divisive conflict within the new educated classes on which he had come to rely so greatly. As more and more educated young people were absorbed into the bureaucracy, the emperor's personal hold over them became less and less effective. However, the youngest of these new bureaucrats were generally not satisfied with the fact that the emperor advanced *educated* men to the top posts in government. Top civil servants tended to be from the older generation of the educated classes who had studied abroad before 1936. Christopher Clapham has described them as "the new nobility."[61] This was a political-administrative class that came to occupy the major posts in government and circulated from one post to the other. It was difficult to define membership in this class, but there were between one and six of them in each ministry, and Clapham identified a total of sixty-eight in government in 1966. They were mainly recruited from the lower ranks of the civil service. As a class, this group was extremely homogeneous because of its small size, the level of government at which it operated, and the closeness of its members to the emperor. The "new nobility" came to be seen as representing all that the "modernizing autocracy" stood for and, along with the emperor, came to be resented by younger educated elites.[62]

By the mid-1950s the newest among the educated elite generally came to see the regime as plodding, evasive, basically conservative, and more interested in keeping power than in bringing about change. This turn of events revealed a significant weakness in the flexible resources at the disposal of the emperor. If he could not rely on a cohesive bureaucracy, or more generally on the support of the modern classes, he could never achieve his objective of modernizing Ethiopia from above and establishing a viable modern absolutist state. His only hope of avoiding an early demise was to readapt the character of his regime to mute the divisive forces that had emerged and to increase his own power relative to all social groups.

The Phase of Creative Adaptation: The Domestic Arena

In the immediate postwar years, profound political changes occurred not only in Ethiopia but throughout the Third World. The "winds of change" had begun to blow with gale force, as one colonial territory after the other demanded national independence from their European colonial masters. In preparation for their departure from Africa, France and Britain, the major colonial powers in the region, introduced political and economic reforms intended to prepare their colonies for self-government, and eventually for complete independence. Although Ethiopia could boast of never having been *colonized* by a European power, it was beset by many of the same problems of political and economic underdevelopment that characterized colonized Black Africa. This situation threatened the Haile Selassie regime in a number of ways. First, the emperor had worked diligently at presenting an image of himself in the international community as a progressive, modernizing autocrat. He had introduced a written constitution in 1931 and a host of subsequent political, economic, and social reforms after his reinstatement, including a revised constitution in 1955. He had also conscientiously attempted to gain respect among the independent nation-states of the world as *one of them*. Ethiopia was the first Black African state to join the League of Nations in 1923, and subsequently it was the first to join the United Nations after the war. Furthermore, the emperor had a long history of independently entering into diplomatic agreements with the "Big Powers" and having those agreements accepted as legally binding by other states. All of this was done with the intention of preserving the territorial integrity of Ethiopia in the face of potential external aggression or in the event of domestic demands for self-determination.

By the mid-1950s, Haile Selassie came to feel that he had to do more than court the independent nation-states of the world who belonged to the United Nations. He had also to create the impression of solidarity with the states of the colonized Third World—especially those in Africa—that were currently casting off the yoke of European colonialism. In the process of devising a diplomatic strategy for achieving his foreign policy objectives, Haile Selassie had his qualities as a statesman tested to their fullest measure. A good example of this was his effort to legitimize Ethiopia's federation with Eritrea in 1952 (and subsequently Eritrean annexation in 1962) in the eyes of the rest of Africa. I shall return to this point later, but for the moment it is important to note that one of the most important reasons the emperor seemed compelled to refashion his approach to domestic leadership in the mid-1950s was a need to improve his international image to enhance his ability to create a viable, modern, autocratic state.

A second major reason Haile Selassie altered the style and substance of his leadership in the mid-1950s was a desire to anticipate domestic demand for more democratization and economic development and to meet those demands that had already emerged. Over the first ten to fifteen years after World War II, the government had expanded tremendously. There had been numerous more or less ad hoc reforms that were not clearly specified in a written constitutional form. As he had done in 1931, Haile Selassie attempted to strengthen his own autonomous position by proposing constitutional reforms designed to accomplish this. He realized that he would have to surrender some of the more visible aspects of his power, but he hoped to preserve enough of it in a latent form to allow him to proceed relatively unencumbered with his absolutist designs.

Third, the new constitution was obviously meant to be an appeal to the forces of modernization in Ethiopia and to impress external critics of the emperor's commitment to change. Richard Greenfield, for example, suggests that Haile Selassie was essentially forced to revise the constitution by the need to harmonize it with the Eritrean constitution after the federation between the two regions was concluded. The Eritrean assembly was elected, whereas both Ethiopian legislative chambers were appointed. The United Nations Commission is said to have "indirectly" encouraged the emperor to revise the 1931 Constitution.[63]

The 1955 Constitution was quite different from its predecessor. The form and the content of the new document reflected the growing influence of American advisers in the shaping of Ethiopian public policy. In fact, most of the detailed work of drafting the Constitution was performed by three American legal advisers in consultation with Ethiopian counterparts.[64] The new constitution was not a mirror image of the American Constitution, but there were definite pretensions in that direction. For instance, this could be seen in the attempt to convey the sense of a separation of power among the three branches of government: the executive, legislative, and judiciary. Also, American influences could be seen in the more careful attention given to spelling out the "Rights and Duties of the People." Twenty-eight articles addressed such matters. A large number of specific rights were granted to the citizens of the country, such as freedom of speech and assembly, due process, and freedom of religion.[65] It is important to note, however, that it was still possible for the emperor to suspend any of these rights in the interest of national security. John Spencer, one of the American drafters of the document, reports that the Crown Council forced the constitution's authors to stress the prerogatives of the crown.[66]

In total, the Constitution of 1955 comprised eight chapters and 131 articles. The most notable features of the document were the way it spelled out the relationship between the Crown and other branches of government and the fact that it introduced the idea of a popularly elected representative institution with more than advisory powers.

The responsibilities of such executive institutions as the Council of Ministers, the Crown Council, and the prime minister's office were delineated for the first time in one coherent document. The Council of Ministers was composed of the prime minister, the heads of all the departmental ministries, and ministers without portfolio. The function of the Council of Ministers was to advise the emperor on policy matters and to coordinate interministerial activities. It studied all draft legislation and recommended a course of action to the emperor, who presented the bill to the Crown Council.

The Crown Council, consisting of the *Abuna,* the president of the Senate, and other appointed notables, gave its opinion on the bill, and the emperor then forwarded the proposed legislation to the legislature. However, neither the Council of Ministers nor the Crown Council had direct policy-making authority. Once a bill had passed executive scrutiny, the legislature acted merely as a rubber stamp.[67]

The Crown Council represented the more traditional elements in society, and even though it was consulted on policy matters, it had little input into decisions. The Council did, however, provide the emperor with a valuable sounding board for the thinking of the traditionalists. The Constitution gave the Crown Council some real discretionary powers, but there was no time when it appeared to exercise them.[68]

The emperor was more concerned about the potential power of the Council of Ministers. As a result, he attempted to shield himself from becoming the tool of the "new nobility" represented in the Council. Ministers, by virtue of their expert knowledge of the affairs of their departments, could theoretically influence policy indirectly if the emperor did not have recourse to alternative information. In 1959 he founded his own private cabinet.

The organization of the cabinet appears to have been influenced by the way in which the staff of the American chief executive evolved and operated. Originally this institution included fourteen departments and was intended to expand and systematize the emperor's staff of personal advisors. The views of the "old nobility" were represented in the Crown Council, the "new nobility" in the Council of Ministers, while the Emperor's private cabinet was staffed by young Ethiopians who had just returned from being educated abroad.[69] This created a tension between these three classes of elites, and thus the emperor felt he had strengthened his own position in relation to all of them.

The private cabinet was responsible for providing the emperor with independent and alternative sources of information on policy matters. It summarized data and did research that was presented to the monarch in the form of reports. This institution, however, was not valued as an effective and reliable advisory board by the emperor for long. In December 1960 one of the private cabinet's members was involved in an attempted coup, and this seems to have damaged the emperor's faith that he could use such an instrument as an even more refined autonomous resource than the Council of Ministers.[70] From this point on, the Council of Ministers, particularly the Offices of the prime minister and minister of finance, seem to have increased in power and influence.

The 1955 Constitution, like the Constitution of 1931, imposed no formal restraints on the emperor's powers. He could set up government departments and invest them with duties and responsibilities by executive order. He had the power to appoint and dismiss all government officials. Even though parliament secured new legislative authority, the emperor still had the power to make laws through executive order without going through parliament. As before, the emperor remained in complete control of the armed forces and was the country's chief foreign policy spokesman. Only he could declare war or a state of emergency; only he could enter into treaties with foreign countries.[71] Moreover, the emperor possessed controls over the legislative and judicial branches of government that they did not hold over him. For instance, he could dissolve parliament if he felt it necessary, and he could also maintain close control over state courts. The emperor's ultimate control over Church administrative and financial matters was also officially established in this document. Rather than curbing the emperor's powers, then, Haile Selassie hoped to insulate them behind a legalistic shroud. He did not lose power. In fact, in the short term, it appears that he gained some.

The immediate social impact of the new Constitution was favorable for the emperor's image at home and abroad, due chiefly to the passages in the document relating to citizens' rights and the popularly elected legislature. Chapter IV of the Constitution provided for a Chamber of Deputies to be popularly elected every four years. Senators continued to be appointed by the emperor. In contrast to the legislature's functions as outlined in the

1931 Constitution, both houses now had the authority to propose laws and to veto laws proposed by the executive. Prior to this the legislature could only discuss matters referred to it; it had no veto power.[72] In spite of the apparent increase in power for the legislature represented in Chapter IV, these powers were limited by the vast discretionary powers of the emperor.

Perhaps the most significant new authority vested in the parliament related to the budgetary function. It now had the responsibility of approving or rejecting all budgetary items including taxes and appropriations. It could also summon various ministers for questioning, and in extraordinary circumstances, it could initiate impeachment proceedings against those who were accused of violating their oath of office.[73] Although it was not immediately realized by the emperor or the parliamentarians themselves, the new-found measure of independence the body had obtained from the emperor gave it the potential for a great deal of power. It was significant that the emperor could not control the appointment of Chamber members. They were now popularly elected. Initially, deputies continued to be chosen from among the landed classes and continued to be aligned with the traditionalist world view. Political parties were not authorized in the Constitution. Candidates had to run on the strength of their own personal appeal. Moreover, they had to meet specified property qualifications to stand for office. A candidate had to own at least E$850 in land in the constituency he proposed to represent, or he had to possess at least E$1,700 in moveable property. The cost of campaigning also acted as a control mechanism in determining who stood for a Chamber seat. A candidate could spend anywhere from E$200 to E$8,500 on his campaign. The average was between E$1,700 and E$2,000.[74] Given the fact that the per capita income in Ethiopia at the time was less than E$150 per year, it is clear that few could afford to contest a Chamber seat even if they wished to.

The first elections were held in 1957. At that time two deputies were elected from each rural constituency, and others were selected from urban areas for a total of 210. Each constituency consisted of 200,000 eligible voters (all men and women over 21). Initially, the number of candidates from aristocratic families was relatively high (26 percent), but by 1965, their numbers had dwindled significantly (14 percent).[75] By the late 1960s, former government employees, including teachers, were the best represented group among Chamber candidates.

National elections were held on schedule from 1957 until 1973. During this period, the young, educated elite benefited most and took advantage of what limited power was represented in this process. The size of the Chamber was increased by forty after the 1957–1963 session of parliament. This figure only becomes significant when we consider the amount of attrition that took place from one election to the next. In 1963 194 (almost 80 percent) of the 210 members who served in the Chamber from 1957 to 1963 were not returned or chose not to stand again. The next three elections yielded similar patterns, the turnover of deputies dropping slightly below 60 percent in the final election year of 1973.[76] In part this could have reflected the growing importance of certain political issues (i.e., land reform and taxation), or it could have represented a keener understanding by the electorate as well as would-be candidates of the value of elections and of parliament as a political institution. The rate of voter turnout over the five elections between 1957 and 1973 fluctuated between 60 and 70 percent of all registered voters. The ratio of registered voters to the voting age population grew from 30 to 60 percent over the period. Significantly, by 1973 the highest rate of turnout (66 percent) was among young people (twenty-one to thirty-five), indicating the heightened sense of political consciousness among this group.[77]

Despite the steady increase in the rate of voter turnout, it does not seem that the majority of the Ethiopian electorate ever became a significant political force. This is not to say that the legislature was unimportant and unrepresentative of popular sentiment. In fact, parliament became an arena for struggles between the new and old classes and between the emperor and the various political factions represented in the Chamber. Thus it was a barometer of popular opinion. I shall return to this point later.

The important point is that partly in reaction to and partly in anticipation of demands for radical change in Ethiopia's political system, Haile Selassie preemptively initiated constitutional reforms in 1955. The immediate effect of these measures was to enhance the emperor's standing at home and abroad as a modernizing autocrat. However, Haile Selassie realized that he could not be content with mere constitutional changes. He also had to strengthen Ethiopia's diplomatic standing in the world through an active foreign policy. Thus if we are to understand how Haile Selassie's bureaucratic empire survived, and even thrived, in the face of enormous pressure against it, we cannot simply examine the emperor's performance in the domestic policy arena. We must also examine his manipulation of foreign policy.

The Phase of Creative Adaptation: The Foreign Policy Arena

Haile Selassie continued the largely defensive, survivalist foreign policy begun by Menelik.[78] After defeating the Italians at Adowa in 1896, Menelik entered into agreements with not only Italy, but also England and France, the other European powers with colonial interests in the Horn, in effect securing Ethiopia's borders through diplomacy and occasional threats of military action.[79] There always remained, however, the threat that Ethiopia might be invaded and colonized by a European power. As a result, both Menelik and Haile Selassie devoted much of their attention in foreign affairs to devising ways to secure Ethiopia's frontiers. In part, this is what motivated the expansion and modernization of the state's military capacity.

Equally important were the activities of Menelik and Haile Selassie in the diplomatic arena. For example, Ethiopia's joining of the League of Nations was clearly instigated by the everpresent potential for invasion of the Ethiopian heartland by the Italians. After the Italians did finally invade Ethiopia in October 1935, Haile Selassie journeyed from London, his base of exile, to Geneva, Switzerland, where he addressed the General Assembly of the League of Nations, and from his remarks it was clear that he felt the League had violated its commitment to protect the sovereignty of any of its members. He stated:

> I, Haile Sellassie I, Emperor of Ethiopia, am present here today to ask for the imperial justice due to my people and for the help which fifty-two nations had undertaken to extend to it when they affirmed eight months ago, that a war of aggression, in violation of international law, was being waged against Ethiopia. . . . I ask the fifty-two nations who have given a promise to the Ethiopian people that they would come to their aid at the time of the aggression against them, in order to prevent the aggressor from defeating them. . . . I ask these fifty-two nations for their support by upholding this promise. What are you willing to do for Ethiopia?[80]

In the end, in spite of Haile Selassie's impassioned plea for immediate action by the League to liberate Ethiopia, such aid was not forthcoming, apart from selective and ineffective sanctions.

Haile Selassie appeared to view the inaction of the League as merely a temporary setback, and he continued to have faith in the ultimate value of effective diplomacy. It was such skill that enabled him to elicit the aid of the British in organizing military operations to liberate Ethiopia in 1941, re-installing him as the only legitimate rule of that country. Subsequently, the British remained in Ethiopia, in part because they felt it was strategically necessary to do so, but in part because the emperor realized he would have to depend on some powerful external agent until he could strengthen the administrative capacity of the state so that it was again capable of autonomous action.

In the immediate postwar years, Haile Selassie was extremely dependent on the military, economic, and technical assistance provided by the British. At the same time, however, he feared that they might either declare Ethiopia a protectorate or use the claim that the whole of Italian East Africa (Eritrea, Ethiopia, Somalia) was occupied enemy territory as a pretext for annexing the country. Therefore, the emperor began immediately to attempt to establish alternative relationships that ultimately might allow him to do without the British. This was a period when the Allied Powers were all jockeying for leverage in the reordered international political arena, particularly in Africa. France wanted a return to the prewar status quo; the Soviet Union wanted to block British efforts to claim too much of the African spoils; the British wanted to solidify their influence in the Horn; and the United States wanted to establish a presence in the region.[81]

Neither the United States nor the Soviet Union recognized the Fascist occupation of Ethiopia as legitimate. Realizing this, Haile Selassie adopted a strategy for keeping the British at bay based on establishing closer diplomatic relations with the Soviets and especially with the United States. He also pressed Ethiopia's territorial claims before the United Nations General Assembly.

The Italians had struck down whatever divisions existed between Ethiopia and Somaliland, and they incorporated Ethiopia, Eritrea, and Somaliland into a new colony of Italian East Africa.[82] Addis Ababa was made the capital, and prewar frontiers were abolished. Once the war was over, it had to be decided whether the Italian episode in the Horn was an opportunity for a new beginning as far as territorial divisions were concerned, or whether to return to the prewar status quo. The British position was never clear. In a speech before the House of Commons in 1941, Sir Anthony Eden, then Foreign Secretary, indicated that his country favored a return to the status quo. This would have meant a return of the emperor to his throne and recognition of Ethiopia's territorial claims, particularly as they related to the 1897 and 1908 series of agreements. In 1946, however, Foreign Secretary Ernest Bevin suggested that the British would push for the incorporation of all Somali people into a new "Greater Somalia."[83] This could only be done if the prior agreements were abrogated.

The net effect of the ambiguity and vacillation in British policy regarding the Horn had different effects on Ethiopian and Somali official attitudes. Among Ethiopian leaders, who considered the prewar frontiers inviolable, it encouraged a sense of paranoia, as they feared a loss of territory if Britain was allowed to dictate the terms of settlement in territorial disputes with the Somalis. Among the Somali leaders British thinking on territorial issues in the Horn engendered a sense of hope. The territory the Somalis claimed as their ancestral homeland had been divided into five separate colonial entities as a result of the partition of the Horn among the French, Italians, British, and Ethiopians in the late 1800s. The Somalis held that the British had neither right nor title under treaties concluded between 1884 and 1886 with Somali chiefs making part of historic Somaliland, including the Haud and the Ogaden, a protectorate of the British Empire. Therefore, Britain had illegally ceded the Haud and the Ogaden to Menelik. Once World War II was over, the Somalis saw an opportunity to reclaim the lost territory.[84]

Haile Selassie lobbied vigorously to win international support for Ethiopia's claims to not only the Haud and the Ogaden but also all former Italian colonies in the region. In 1948, under growing pressure from the United Nations, the United States, Russia, and the British public, the British government restored most of the Ogaden and all other Ethiopian territory it occupied, except the Haud, the Addis Ababa-Djibouti Railway, and other strategically "Reserved Areas," to Ethiopia. Between 1954 and 1955 Britain completely withdrew from the region. There were violent demonstrations by the Somali population in the Ogaden and Haud, and indeed the refugee problem, which was to escalate so gravely in the 1970s and 1980s, may be dated from this time.

Simultaneously with his maneuvers aimed at reestablishing control over the Ogaden, Haile Selassie was attempting to lay claim to the former Italian colony of Eritrea. He feared that an independent Somalia, which was beginning to appear inevitable, might annex the French colony of Djibouti, thus closing off Ethiopia's only reliable access to the sea. And were Italy allowed to reassume its administration of Eritrea, Ethiopia could become completely landlocked and uncomfortably dependent on potentially hostile neighbors. Control of Eritrea was also seen as being important because it was from there and from Italian Somaliland that Italy had launched its drive of conquest. Rather than emphasizing security concerns, in diplomatic circles the Ethiopians stressed the cultural homogeneity and economic interdependence of the Eritreans and Ethiopians.

Britain administered Eritrea as occupied enemy territory after the ouster of the Italian Fascists. The future of Eritrea was to be deliberated by a UN Four-Power Commission of Investigation of the Former Italian Colonies.[85] If a solution could not be agreed on by the commission, the UN General Assembly would determine Eritrea's future. Subsequently, the General Assembly did have to vote on the issue.

Haile Selassie pressed for the annexation of Eritrea, but was unsuccessful. On December 2, 1950, the UN General Assembly, however, did agree to a federation of self-governing Eritrea with Ethiopia. The resulting UN resolution provided that the official act of union would take place in September 1952.[86] Ten years later, through his political stealth and pressure tactics, the emperor succeeded in having the Eritrean Assembly and the Ethiopian Assembly vote unanimously to incorporate Eritrea fully into the Ethiopian Empire.[87]

At last, Haile Selassie's determined drive to recover what he claimed to be the historic Ethiopian Empire was completed. On the face of it, this would appear to have been a remarkable coup, a testimony to the emperor's statesmanship. Indeed, this is the way these events were viewed in many parts of the world. Yet, in realistic terms, Haile Selassie realized that if the empire was to hold together in an era of Third World nationalist ferment, he would have to engage in perpetual diplomacy aimed at reinforcing the idea of the Ethiopian state as he defined it. Opposition to the emperor's vision of Greater Ethiopia was most severe in the domestic political arena at the time. Ethnic Somalis within Ethiopia and nationalists in Somalia, Djibouti, Oromia, and Eritrea opposed what they perceived to be Ethiopian imperialism. Ethiopia's Pan African credentials were questioned by some African nationalists wary of Ethiopia's claim that it was African and therefore not colonialist. Haile Selassie's tasks then became either pacification or suppression at home, and salesmanship abroad.

In order to secure Ethiopia's frontiers domestically, Haile Selassie expanded his military and bureaucracy so that they penetrated into the periphery as never before. He also played upon the cold war fears of the United States to develop a reliable source of military and economic resources to strengthen the capacity of the state. Aid agreements were negotiated with a whole host of other bilateral and multilateral donors, all with the expressed intention of expanding the imperial government's reservoir of flexible resources, but the relationship Ethiopia had with the United States was by far the most significant in the eyes of the emperor.[88] To preempt those who might charge him with being nothing more than an African imperialist, Haile Selassie belatedly jumped to the forefront of the struggle for African liberation. Until 1958 he had remained relatively silent about European colonialism in Africa and the need for African independence throughout the continent, but in April of that year he sent his youngest son, Prince Saleh Selassie, as Ethiopia's official representative to Accra, Ghana, to participate in the first Conference of Independent African States.[89] Present at this conclave were Morocco, Sudan, Egypt, Tunisia, Libya, Liberia, Ethiopia, and Ghana, which had, only the year before, gained acclaim as the first country in Subsaharan Africa to cast off the yoke of European colonialism. Significantly, a resolution was passed by which all participating states agreed to observe each other's territorial and political integrity. This was what Haile Selassie had desired all along.[90] From this point on, he recognized the value of not only participating in a supranational organization of this kind, but also taking the lead in the interest of the voices of moderation in determining the emerging character of African unity.

By the early 1960s, African leaders like Kwame Nkrumah, Sekou Touré, and Ahmed Ben Bella envisioned a "United States of Africa" organized along socialist lines. The rhetoric of this faction was anti-Western, and Haile Selassie saw this as a threat to the alliance he had so calculably constructed. Therefore, he took it on himself to attempt to influence a more moderate posture within the group. In 1962 Haile Selassie extended an invitation to the annual meeting of the Conference of Independent African States in Lagos to meet in Addis Ababa the following year for the purpose of clearly spelling out the concept of African unity and suggesting ways in which it might be applied. In the process he co-opted the movement and began to use it more effectively for his own purposes.[91]

At the Addis Ababa meetings in 1963, Haile Selassie presented a draft charter for an organization of African unity. This document was an effort to preempt two other more radically Pan Africanist documents that had been proposed. The emperor succeeded in having a great deal of influence over the charter that was finally adopted. Thirty-two newly independent states, including Somalia, were represented at the summit, and the organization was charged with upholding the principles of the sovereign equality of member states; noninterference in the internal affairs of member states; peaceful settlement of disputes; the eradication of all forms of colonialism from the African continent; and nonalignment. Haile Selassie cultivated the image of himself as a wise African elder statesman, and he came to be seen as a conciliator who brought African states together when outside observers had doubted this was possible. The generalized perception of Haile Selassie's role in this process made it seem only right that Addis Ababa be designated the official headquarters of the Organization of African Unity.

From about the time of his growing efforts to identify with the idea of African independence, the emperor took an active role mediating intra-Africa disputes and speaking as the conscience of Black Africa. To prove his worthiness for such a place of high esteem, he would often make state visits to various African countries and throughout the world to represent a united Africa. This, of course, meant that certain aspects of Ethiopian foreign policy had to change, but Haile Selassie proved quite willing to make such sacrifices. For instance, in 1960 Ethiopia and Liberia initiated separate legal efforts to have South Africa brought before the International Court of Justice because of its illegal occupation of Southwest Africa.[92] In 1963 Ethiopia broke off diplomatic relations with Portugal. Although the emperor acknowledged that Portugal had aided the imperial government in fending off its enemies in the ancient past, he argued that Ethiopia could not tolerate modern Portugal's continued commitment to maintaining its colonial possessions in Africa.[93] These are but a few examples of Haile Selassie's moves to legitimize his regime in the international arena. By presenting the image of an advocate of African unity and independence, the emperor hoped to avoid international pressure on Ethiopia to grant the right to self-determination being demanded by disparate ethnic minorities within the empire, especially by the Eritreans and the Ogaden Somalis.

IV

THE POLITICAL ECONOMY OF A MODERNIZING BUREAUCRATIC EMPIRE

In addition to strengthening the state's capacity for administration and political control, the leaders of historical bureaucratic empires have characteristically had to expand the economic capacity of the state. A reservoir of fiscal resources readily available to the monarch greatly enhanced his personal power and increased the state's ability for autonomous action. Without them, the state could not strengthen and expand its military and bureaucracy; it could not hope to penetrate into peripheral areas for more effective control. In order to survive and prosper, then, bureaucratic empires had to complement their regulatory and coercive capabilities with effective means of economic extraction.[1]

In the case of Ethiopia under Haile Selassie, the emperor had as his primary goal the maintenance of the state. Both his political and economic policies were structured with this in mind. He wanted to neutralize potential domestic challengers while at the same time increasing the autonomous power of central authorities. Additionally, he wanted to present a diplomatic and economic posture of sufficient strength to deter would-be imperialists from dominating Ethiopia in the international arena. To achieve these ends, Haile Selassie set about structuring Ethiopia's political economy after World War II to meet the needs of the emerging bureaucratic empire.

This chapter attempts to analyze the process by which Haile Selassie approached this task. His objective was to transform Ethiopia from an isolated, basically feudal economy with a weak central authority into a vital industrial economy with a strong and active state structure. By any measure, this was a formidable challenge. Contrary to obvious indicators, Haile Selassie firmly believed that it was possible to move his country rapidly to a position of economic takeoff.[2] Rather than aggressively moving to eliminate the role of tradition in Ethiopian society, Haile Selassie attempted to manipulate and use tradition when possible. He ignored it, however, when necessary, pressing forward with plans to develop a modern industrial sector and commercialized agriculture. The key to the success of such an approach would have been a vigorous public sector capable of generating fiscal resources and investing revenues strategically as the need arose. In the end, however, the contradictions inherent in this complex and risky venture proved overwhelming, and they set in motion the forces that led to the demise of his regime. In this chapter, I concern myself only with the attempted transformation of Ethiopia's feudal economy into a hybrid modern industrial economy. The inherent contradictions and social conflicts arising from Haile Selassie's policies will be addressed in chapters 5 and 6.

The Traditional Economy and the Growth of Public Expenditures

At the close of World War II, Ethiopia, in contrast to other African countries that had experienced European colonialism, was not effectively integrated into the world capitalist system. There were few industrial enterprises, and both domestic and international commerce were extremely underdeveloped. Some trade did take place between the major urban centers in Ethiopia and the outside world, but this trade involved only a few Ethiopians. This sector was small and dominated by foreigners. Emperors, kings, princes, and the local warlords had historically traded local produce and minerals for weapons and such luxury items as salt, sugar, velvet, cotton, and other textiles, but this was not an indication of effective market penetration. Coffee was traded in the south via Gambela through the Khartoum Shipping Service, beginning in 1907, and the joint French-Ethiopian Djibouti-Addis Ababa Railway was opened ten years later, allowing the flow of commerce between Addis Ababa and the Red Sea.[3] By the 1930s, 70 percent of the import-export trade traversed the Djibouti Railway, 20 percent went through Sudan, and about 10 percent went through Eritrea. The total value of trade was estimated at no more than E$10 million at this time, a meager amount when compared to the roughly E$30–45 million realized annually by the British colonies of Sudan and the Gold Coast.[4]

Few Ethiopians were involved in commerce prior to the 1950s. In 1944, out of a total of 215 members in the Ethiopian Chamber of Commerce, more than 60 percent were either Greeks or Italians; an additional 20 percent was accounted for by Arabs and Armenians. Only seventeen members were Ethiopians.[5] Part of the reason for this was probably the aversion of the dominant Amhara to engaging in what they considered an inferior occupation.[6] What is more likely, however, is that economic exchanges on the basis of money had not become common practice for most Ethiopians. Those mostly foreign companies involved in the money economy generally retained their profits and repatriated them to their countries of origin rather than conscientiously developing local markets.[7] What hard foreign currency existed in Ethiopia by the 1940s was concentrated in the hands of the state and its agents.

After the war, all taxes had to be paid in cash, but it was some time before a stable Ethiopian currency existed. Peasants continued to pay rent and taxes in kind to landlords and agents of the central government. These goods were then converted into cash and forwarded to the central treasury. In the case of trade, however, all taxes were required to be paid in cash, and this went directly to the imperial treasury.

Widespread confidence in Ethiopia's currency and financial institutions did not exist until the 1950s and 1960s. With the growth and strengthening of the National Bank of Ethiopia and the establishment of the Development Bank of Ethiopia in 1951, the use of money and of savings and credit institutions increased dramatically. In 1963 the Commercial Bank of Ethiopia was established, assuming the credit and savings functions previously held by the National Bank of Ethiopia. The government remained the major stockholder in the Commercial Bank, but it was joined by other investors, including individual Ethiopians and such key parastatal organizations as Ethiopian Airlines, Ethiopian Light and Power Authority, and the Ethiopian Cement Corporation. This bank came to command more than four-fifths of all banking activity in the country.[8]

The 1960s also marked the establishment of other financial institutions such as the Ethiopian Investment Corporation, which provided long-term and medium-term loans, sold shares in government-sponsored development projects, and provided equity capital for such projects. Other financial institutions that emerged at this time were the Ethiopian Mortgage Share Company and the Imperial Savings and Home Ownership Public Association, both of which were government sponsored, and the privately owned Addis Ababa Bank, a subsidiary of the Banco di Roma.[9]

Even though the use of money and the incidence of saving and borrowing increased dramatically in the 1960s, as late as 1970 less than 20 percent of Ethiopia's estimated twenty-six million people were dependent on the market economy. At that time, the number of persons involved in the market was growing at a rate of 3.5 percent per year, while population grew at a rate just over 2 percent annually. Still, few Ethiopians were directly involved in the market as traders. Irving Kaplan estimates that in the mid-1960s only 160,000 persons were directly involved in "marketing and selling."[10] Most of the rural population continued to live at the subsistence level, with little or no surplus cash. Much of the rural trade continued to be conducted through traditional markets on the basis of barter.

From his days as regent, Haile Selassie had desired to increase his regime's money income, but he experienced difficulties in this effort mainly because of provincial resistance and the difficult transportation conditions that existed between the center and the periphery.[11] The road system was poorly developed, and this inhibited the transport of commodities to the railhead for export. He realized that he would have to improve the country's transportation system if he was to shore up his own position. Most road construction, however, did not begin until the Italian occupation period. The Fascists expended millions of dollars to develop a basic transportation infrastructure. This was thought to be the first and most necessary phase in Italy's effort to exploit Ethiopia's rich agricultural potential. The result was the linkage of Ethiopia's abundant possessions in the south for the first time with a relatively efficient transportation network.

The Italians were also responsible for the first infusion of foreign investment capital into Ethiopia for the development and exploitation of the country's agricultural potential. Private Italian capital accompanied the efforts of the Italian government to transform Ethiopia into a self-sufficient export economy linked to the world market. They established nascent manufacturing and commercial enterprises, investing more than US$2 million over the period of occupation. The level of private Italian capital involvement in occupied Ethiopia was, however, much below what had been hoped. This, coupled with the brief duration of the occupation period, left incomplete the integration of Ethiopia into the world market.

By the early 1950s, Haile Selassie felt confident that the administrative authority of the state was sufficiently consolidated for him to turn his attention more to economic matters. Among his first priorities in this area was to modernize Ethiopia's highway system. In 1950 Ethiopia secured a loan from the World Bank valued at some US$5 million for the purposes of repairing, reconstructing, and maintaining the country's main road network.[12] The Imperial Highway Authority was subsequently set up to administer these tasks. Over the period of twenty to twenty-five years, Ethiopia expended upwards of US$300 million on road construction and improvement. In the process, 2,300 miles of main roads and 545 miles of feeder roads were constructed. An additional 1,699 miles of existing roads were improved. This provided Ethiopia with fourteen to fifteen thousand miles of roads throughout the country.[13] Most of the costs of these projects was borne by the Ethiopian government, but at least one-third was paid for by foreign loans.[14] The World Bank was the largest aid contributor for such purposes, investing almost US$104 million. Technical assistance in these activities was provided by U.S. Agency for International Development, German, and British experts.

The stated objective of the highway program was to stimulate the expansion of market activities throughout the country. Special attention was given to creating a transportation infrastructure that would be attractive to new foreign capital investors or would open up areas of rich agricultural and mineral potential for the first time. For instance, as a result of the Second Highway Program that began in 1957, remote areas of the coffee-rich southwest were linked to the trade center of Jimma in Kaffa Province; another road connected Addis Ababa with the Lake Tana region in the northwest, an area rich in oilseeds, grain, cotton, coffee, and livestock.

Throughout the 1960s, more and more previously inaccessible parts of the country were opened up in this manner. By the 1970s, new roads were being utilized to provide the infrastructure needed to facilitate the development of mostly foreign-financed commercial agriculture in the Awash Valley region.

Roads alone would not have been sufficient to transform Ethiopia's economy from feudalism to a form of colonial capitalism. Ninety-five percent of the population was engaged in the subsistence production of corn, wheat, barley, legumes, livestock, and *teff*, the staple grain among many of the country's people. Although more than 87 percent of the gross domestic product (GDP) prior to the mid-1960s was accounted for by the agricultural sector, most of what was produced was consumed locally instead of exported for foreign exchange.[15] Production techniques, as would be expected in a predominantly feudal society, were primitive. More than half of all farmland was devoted to grain production on small family plots. Hoes and ox-drawn ploughs were generally the most sophisticated forms of farm technology available to the peasant farmer, and often cultivation was done solely by hand.

Until the mid-1950s Ethiopia was free of any serious difficulties in her balance of trade. This was in part a reflection of the country's limited involvement in the world economy. However, with the emergence of a modern sector and the growing presence of an expatriate community, Ethiopia began to experience a gradual increase in her trade deficit. Factories needed machines and materials from abroad; foreign residents demanded finished goods from home. Between 1948 and 1971 the deficit grew from just under E\$30 million to more than E\$125 million.[16] In large measure this was because Ethiopia was essentially a monoculture economy, relying inordinately on revenue generated by one crop, coffee. Coffee consistently accounted for more than 50 percent of the country's export earnings, but Ethiopia accounted for only about 2 percent of the coffee traded in the world. The country's vulnerability as a result of its dependence on a market it could not control or manipulate was obvious.

The demand for machinery and luxury consumer items was an inevitable by-product of the government's commitment to modernization. Western tastes were automatically transferred to Ethiopia, creating a heightened demand for the importation not only of industrial technology, but also for finished products from European and American markets. Left unattended, this trend could have subverted the intentions of the Haile Selassie regime to pursue a course of self-reliant, autonomous development. A central element in the modernization effort therefore was to develop the capacity for import-substitution of some of the most valued, nontechnical imports. It was felt that this could only be accomplished through calculated economic planning on the part of the state.

The first steps in this direction were taken between 1944 and 1945 when the government introduced a ten-year program for industrial development.[17] The state's capacity to plan was limited, however, due to the extreme dearth of statistical economic data and an underdeveloped bureaucratic establishment. This was not a comprehensive plan, and between 1945 and 1957 several other sectoral plans (i.e., agriculture, forestry, education, communications, and highways) were introduced. In 1954 the National Economic Council was inaugurated to serve as a coordinating body for the state's development programs. This agency served as a planning board, chaired by the emperor, and was responsible for development policy making. It had a permanent staff that devoted its attention to the drafting of plans and the setting of priorities. Through this body the government committed itself to raising the level of agricultural and industrial productivity, eradicating illiteracy and disease, and improving the quality of life for all Ethiopians.

The first comprehensive, integrated plan appeared in 1957 and was scheduled to be in effect for a period of five years. The main thrust of the plan was a commitment to the development of the country's basic infrastructure. Additionally it was geared toward the development of a cadre of indigenous skilled and semiskilled personnel to fill positions in processing industries to help reduce the country's dependence on imports. Attention was also supposed to go toward developing the agricultural sector, but this mainly referred to the promotion of commercialized agricultural ventures.

Over the plan period, the total investment approached E$835 million, 24 percent above planned levels. Sixty percent of these funds was spent on improving transportation, communication, and construction.[18] Significantly, in spite of the alleged commitment to the improvement of the quality of life of the general population, social service was the only sector where actual expenditures fell below planned levels. According to the outline of the plan about 8.5 percent of all investments were to go to social services, but in actuality less than 5 percent were invested for this purpose.[19]

It was hoped that industrial development would stimulate agricultural production by creating a demand for increased amounts of locally produced agricultural commodities and also by providing the agricultural sector with locally made farm tools and implements. But new industrial demands for certain agricultural raw materials and minerals went unmet. Over and above these technical problems, plan implementation was adversely affected by the inexperience of the Ethiopian bureaucracy in executing comprehensive plans.

The basic goal of improving Ethiopia's infrastructure went largely unfulfilled. Nevertheless, the second plan devoted most of its attention to forging ahead on the goals of rapid industrial and commercialized agricultural development. The plans to develop infrastructure were not completely abandoned, however. Instead, of more than E$2,000 million earmarked for investments during the second plan period, E$643 million was raised from foreign sources for the development of infrastructure and services. This was an increase of more than 11 percent over the amount provided by foreign sources in the first plan period. The total percentage of foreign aid utilized to implement the second plan was over 30 percent, thus indicating a growing rather than a decreasing dependence of Ethiopia on foreign capital. This level was roughly maintained in the third plan period.[20] The reliance on foreign aid for development purposes was necessitated by the meagerness of domestic capital that could be used for public finance.

The second plan (1963–1967) was delayed for about a year as planners tried to make adjustments to avoid errors of the past. But, in the end, the second plan was inhibited by some of the same factors that had short-circuited the first plan.[21] Among the chief difficulties were a limited administrative capacity, a shortage of planning personnel in operational ministries, and poor interministerial coordination. Also, in budgetary terms, the second plan appeared to be even more overly ambitious than the first. Development expenditures were 13 percent higher than had been projected, largely due to the fact that recurrent expenditures grew at a rate of 11.5 percent instead of the projected 7.5 percent.[22]

In the second plan, even heavier emphasis was placed on the development of the agricultural sector, but it was again clear that this referred to "large-scale modern farming" rather than labor-intensive peasant production.[23] The plan also called for a diversification of productive activities and the infusion of ever-increasing amounts of modern technology. The ultimate aim was to increase the growth rate of the economy. In 1961 the annual growth rate in the economy was only 4 percent, and per capita income grew at a rate of only 2 percent per year. The lag in economic growth as a whole was attributed to the poor performance of the agricultural sector, which grew at a rate of 2 to 2.5 percent per annum. This low figure was in turn blamed on inefficient *peasant* production. Commercial farms were said to have experienced dramatic gains in terms of their contribution to the overall economic growth of the country while comprising less than 1 percent of all farming activities.[24] The logical course to follow, then, seemed to be the encouragement of commercialized farms. Manufacturing was also targeted for increased efforts, as it averaged better than 16 percent annual growth.

At the end of the second plan period, foreign planning specialists persuaded the government to wait until 1968–1969 before unveiling the third plan. In the third five-year plan (1968–1973), the government again expressed a commitment to dramatically improving the country's rate of economic growth as well as the overall standard of living. As before, it was believed that these objectives could be reached only if the performance of the more productive sectors of the economy—namely manufacturing and agro-industrial activities—were improved. The third plan, however, was different from its predecessors for two basic reasons: (1) It revealed the

government's new commitment to the expansion of educational opportunity, and (2) peasant agriculture was targeted for government attention for
the first time. Wheareas education and culture together received only 1.8
percent of the total amount allocated for the second plan, in the third plan,
education alone was slated to receive 12.4 percent of the total allocation.
The government envisioned public expenditures for all levels of education
as an investment in human capital that laid the "foundations for future,
more accelerated development."[25] "It is of crucial importance," the plan
states, "that the supply of skilled labor be greatly increased. To this end, the
plan also proposes maximum targets for secondary and technical education, limited only by considerations of what is technically and organizationally possible to accomplish."[26]

As before, the government expressed doubts in the third plan about the
ability of small-scale agriculture to make significant contributions to overall
economic growth. It was fully admitted that the stagnation of the small-
scale sector was largely due to "the lack of progress in policy measures and
organizational programs" (i.e., land reform, agricultural taxation, cadastral
surveys, registration of titles, strengthening of the administration of agriculture, and the firm establishment of the Ministry of Agriculture as the
central agency responsible for agriculture).[27]

The key problems affecting the agricultural sector were viewed as "production" and "the peasantry." The most efficient manner in which to
approach the first problem, it was suggested, was to continue to press ahead
on plans for encouraging the development and expansion of commercialized agriculture. A solution to the second problem would take much
longer and be more difficult to achieve. Rather than attempting a comprehensive transformation of the peasant sector, the plan called for a
concentration of government efforts at improving the productivity of peasant holdings in more "promising areas."[28] The vehicle for these efforts
would be experimental "package programs" in strategic locations. Certain
peasant communities would be provided with all of the material and
human resources needed to stimulate and improve their ability to produce.
They would be given relatively easy access to credit, hybrid seed varieties,
expert agricultural advice, and the most appropriate fertilizers. It was
hoped that success in peasant communities such as this would have a "spill-
over" effect, diffusing innovation to the rest of the peasant sector. Nothing
beyond the initiation of a cadastral survey would be done to reform the
feudal land tenure system as a whole. Thus, Haile Selassie avoided yet
another confrontation with traditional elites over land.

The main point to be made from this discussion is that after World War
II the role played by the state in the economy increased dramatically as it
attempted to stimulate capitalist development. Not only did this trend give
rise to the expansion in foreign private investment in the Ethiopian economy; it also increased the level of public spending for development purposes. In 1955 the capital expenditures of the Ethiopian government

TABLE 4.1

Public Expenditures as Percentage of GNP for Selected Years in Millions of Ethiopian Birr

Year	1949	1954	1960	1963	1970	1974
GNP	1,770[a]	2,166[a]	2,447[b]	2,657[b]	4,461[b]	5,551[b]
Public Expenditure	145[c]	253[c]	250[d]	396[d]	738[d]	778[e]
Percent of GNP	8	11	10	15	17	14

SOURCES:
[a] *Second Five Year Development Plan, 1963–1967* (Addis Ababa: Imperial Ethiopian Government, 1962), 77.
[b] *United Nations Statistical Yearbook, 1978* (New York: United Nations, 1978), 704.
[c] *Ethiopia: Statistical Abstract* (Addis Ababa: Imperial Ethiopian Statistical Office, 1964), 128.
[d] *Ethiopia 1972: Statistical Pocketbook* (Addis Ababa: Central Statistical Office, 1972), 74.
[e] *United Nations Statistical Yearbook, 1978* (New York: United Nations, 1978), 789.

amounted to only about E$9 million; by 1973 they were almost E$180 million. Over this same period, public revenues grew from a mere E$124 to E$779 million.[29] Significantly, in 1955 foreign capital accounted for less than 1 percent of all revenues. By 1973, more than 20 percent of the government's annual revenue came from foreign sources, thus indicating a heavy reliance on external support in maintaining increased domestic governmental activities.

All of this must be viewed against the backdrop of the overall growth in the size of government between the 1940s and 1973. Prior to the postwar period, the imperial bureaucracy was not very effective, nor was it very professional. Haile Selassie's efforts to improve this situation were extremely costly: between 1944 and 1973, total government expenditures increased from roughly E$41 million to E$778 million. Although about one-fourth of all government expenditures in 1973 was for development, almost E$600 million was for salaries and recurrent operating costs. This contrasts sharply with the E$115 million it cost to run the government on a day-to-day basis in 1955. In 1944 there were no development expenditures; all of the E$41 million expended in that year went for recurrent costs.[30] Even then the meagerness of this amount is an indication of the small size of government, the immaturity of the central bureaucracy, and the government's limited capacity for manipulating Ethiopia's economy.

Public expenditures grew steadily after the war until they represented between 14 and 17 percent of the gross national product (GNP) between 1970 and 1974. (See Table 4.1.) Much of this increase was attributable to the rise in public expenditures for maintaining law and order. Between 1967 and 1974, the Ministries of Internal Order and Justice and Defense accounted on the average for about one-third of all recurrent expenditures.[31] Social services were among the most neglected sectors in either recurrent or capital expenditures.

The pattern that emerges from this discussion implies a dramatic growth in government after World War II, not only in terms of operational expenditures, but also in development expenditures. What remains to be discerned is the effect of this trend. As I have already discussed the political and administrative effects of the expansion in government in the previous chapter, the public expenditures will be addressed more fully in this chapter. The remainder of the chapter attempts to evaluate the overall effects of the growing involvement of the state in the economic activities of Ethiopian society. How was the structure of the economy, as well as society as a whole, affected by the changes that occurred between 1970 and 1974? Specifically, how did the stress on expanding the public sector, rapid industrialization, commercialized agriculture, and the "package program" in small-scale agriculture change the character of the Ethiopian economy?

The Drive Toward Economic Modernization

In order to understand the forces that propelled economic development in Ethiopia after World War II, it is necessary to analyze the pattern of government involvement in both the public and private sectors. With the term "public sector," I am essentially referring to government ownership of productive enterprises. This necessarily implies a direct governmental involvement in economic activities. The state also affects the economy in an indirect manner through legislative regulation of the economy and tax policy. In all of these activities, government spending and planning has a role to play, and, therefore, I shall not consider these functions as separate categories of public involvement in the economy. Public spending and planning is considered as an integral aspect of its regulation and stimulation of the economy as a whole.

The Public Sector

In relative terms, Ethiopia's public sector was never very large. In 1972, for example, government at all levels and state enterprises contributed less than 13 percent of the GDP and absorbed about 15 percent of total final output.[32] Yet what was remarkable about Ethiopia's public sector was the scope of government involvement in the economy and the pace at which the number of public enterprises grew. The Ethiopian government was substantially involved in what are traditional areas for the governments of less-developed countries, such as electricity and water development and transportation and communications; but it was also heavily involved in nontraditional areas of government activity, such as manufacturing, banking, and insurance. In their study of the Ethiopian public sector, William Abraham and Seilu Abraha found that in terms of the value added, public enterprises were 13 percent as large as the nonagricultural private sector in 1972 and almost 60 percent as large as central and local government.[33] Moreover, they presented evidence that state enterprises were steadily gaining on the private sector in terms of their rate of growth. In 1972 state enterprises spent more than one dollar for capital improvements for every two dollars expended by private enterprises for such purposes.

The increased spending in the public sector, however, must be considered against its costs. Even as late as 1972, domestic savings in Ethiopia were extremely low, and few indigenous entrepreneurs were involved in the private sector. Public investments in industrial activities, therefore, forced the government into deficit spending. Public investments in state corporations were at least 70 percent larger than the capital generated locally in 1972.[34] The bulk of the funds needed for this expansion, then, had to be borrowed from foreign sources.

Between 1968 and 1973 the size of the public debt increased by some 60 percent.[35] Most of the capital borrowed came in the form of foreign direct grants, loans, and credits from such multilateral agencies as the World Bank, the International Monetary Fund, the United Nations Development Program, and such bilateral donors as the United States, Sweden, West Germany, and Great Britain. Communist bloc countries were also involved, but not nearly so much as the Western countries and multilateral agencies.[36]

Until 1970 most foreign loans and credits from public sources were devoted to the development of basic infrastructure (60 percent), transportation (13 percent), industry and mining (17 percent), and banking and financial institutions (10 percent).[37] Much of this aid was used as capital input for public enterprises the government felt were critical to the achievement of its overall policy objectives. By this time, almost 70 percent of the country's capital budget was being financed through foreign assistance, and the government was spending more than 10 percent—more than E$50 million—of its annual earnings from export for debt servicing.[38]

One has to consider this trend in light of the overall economic policy objective of the Haile Selassie regime and the context in which it operated. At the end of World War II, not only was the Ethiopian economy severely underdeveloped, but also the administrative and regulatory capacity of the State was relatively limited. The achievement of rapid industrialization and economic growth required that both these deficiencies be remedied at once. Ideally, the government would have preferred to invite in foreign private investors, directing them to invest in those areas identified as most essential to lay the foundation for economic takeoff. But these very sectors proved most unattractive to foreign private investors. They shied away from investing in transportation and communications projects because of the limited return such projects promised for the invested dollar and because of the huge amounts of capital required.[39] They also shied away from import-substitution industries as a rule because of Ethiopia's underdeveloped market and the high cost of setting up such activities. This being the case, the government itself had to become directly involved in the development of certain kinds of import-substitution industries.

Roads, railways, the national airlines, dams, power plants, government offices, telephone and telegraph systems, therefore, had to be constructed with heavy public involvement. The scale of government activities in such areas, and the cost involved, necessarily led to its disappointing performance in the delivery of social services. This would eventually prove to be problematic for the regime, exposing it to a rash of criticism both at home and abroad.

The Haile Selassie regime appeared to be consumed with the idea of ensuring Ethiopia's economic as well as political independence. It played off one foreign donor against the other and provided attractive incentives for foreign nationals and multinational firms to invest in Ethiopia, often in partnership with the government itself. The willingness of the government to become involved in industrial activities is indicated in the fact that by the mid-1960s ten of the twelve top firms with capital in excess of E$12 million were primarily government-owned.[40] By 1975, there were forty firms in which the government's share of paid-up capital was over 97 percent. In the manufacturing area, where the government was involved, its share averaged over 90 percent.[41] Abraham and Abraha go so far as to assert that "without exception, all the large undertakings selling their output to the public and falling within the public sector by any definition are 100 percent government-owned."[42] The government held a dominant—if not monopoly—position in such areas as rail and air transportation industries; telecommunications, mining, and exploration; highway and road construction; the port system; power; oil refining; cement; tobacco; liquor distilling; beer brewing; pulp and paper production; banking, finance, and insurance; and the manufacture of ammunition. It held sizable shares in many other industrial areas. Significantly, all the major industries, public or private, tended to be monopolies or near monopolies. Only in textile manufacturing was there some competition.[43]

It is difficult to form a true impression of the performance of public enterprises because of the tendency toward monopoly in the industrial sector, but it seems safe to suggest that the rate of return on investment in the public sector, as compared to the private sector, tended to be extremely low. Whereas in 1970 the rate of return on equity capital for private firms was about 20 percent, in public enterprises it generally averaged less than 5 percent return on investment, and some operated at an annual deficit. In textiles, the one area where a monopoly did not exist, Abraham and Abraha found that state-owned factories recorded substantial losses in 1971 while private firms reported large profits.[44]

In strict economic terms, the decision to expand the role of public enterprises in economic development after World War II appears irrational. But given the way in which Haile Selassie viewed his role and the role of his government in the transformation of Ethiopian society, it is pointless to search for exclusively economic answers to understand the justification behind the growth in importance of public enterprises. To be sure, official pronouncements regarding this policy always emphasized the purported economic benefits, but I would suggest that the hidden political objectives were much more important.

What is most significant to note about Ethiopia's public sector is not so much its size as its scope of involvement. This was dictated by the broader economic policies of the government and by the sociopolitical and economic character of the society it was trying to transform.

State Regulation, Foreign Private Investment, and Economic Development

In contrast to the way international capital penetrated most of the rest of Black Africa, foreign capital entered Ethiopia by invitation. Foreign traders, mostly Greeks, Armenians, and Arabs, had been allowed to do business in the country for centuries, but as late as the midtwentieth century modern industrial activity with foreign or local capital had not been encouraged and therefore was not well developed.[45] What manufacturing existed was small and generally in the hands of foreign craftsmen in service to the Crown, or it was the product of small-scale traditional enterprises operated by non-Amhara minority groups such as the Gurage, Somalis, and Arabs. Even then, the items produced—ammunition, bricks, clothes, gunpowder, and milled flour—were for local consumption rather than for export. Until 1946 and the founding of Ethiopian Airlines, the largest industry in Ethiopia was the Djibouti-Addis Ababa Railway, which was held as a joint venture of the governments of France and Ethiopia. The manufacturing sector did not begin to emerge on any scale until the 1950s, and then it was characterized by the dominance of state and foreign capital.

In his vision of the most appropriate strategy for Ethiopia's economic development, Haile Selassie invested a great deal of faith in rapid industrialization. Speaking before a group of artisans in late 1946, he remarked, "The development of industry . . . will enrich our country. Secondly, it will strengthen our government and glorify its honorable name. . . . A permanent economy cannot build only on imports."[46] Ironically, in spite of the apparent strong commitment to rapid industrialization, Haile Selassie's vision incorporated only a limited role for indigenous entrepreneurs. This fact was reinforced by government policies affecting the access of would-be local investors to government loans, credits, and other venture capital and also in official public pronouncements. For example, in a speech before the Ethiopian Chamber of Commerce in 1970, amid growing pressure on the government by nationalist groups to nationalize foreign businesses, the then-president of the chamber, Ato Taffara Deguefe, echoed official policy regarding the participation of foreign capital in the Ethiopian economy, stressing the role such investments had to play in the growth of private capital accumulation locally.[47] Deguefe went on to suggest that, because of their limited investment capital and business experience, most would-be Ethiopian entrepreneurs should confine their activities to such small enterprises as commission agencies; sales or manufacturing representatives; brokerage and travel agencies; or small-scale traders and retailers.[48] One might ask: If Haile Selassie was an African nationalist who conscientiously worked toward the achievement of Ethiopia's full economic and political independence, why would he not enlist indigenous investors on a large scale in order to reach this goal? Would not inviting in massive amounts of foreign capital lessen his country's economic autonomy rather than increase it?

In answering these questions, it is again necessary to return to Haile Selassie's global view of the process of change in Ethiopia. His ultimate goal was the maintenance of the absolutist state and the role of his regime in it. Change was essential, but if it was not to threaten the survival of the absolutist state, it would have to be orchestrated from above. Above all, the emperor did not want to undermine his overall plan by encouraging the development of an autonomous, potentially powerful and antagonistic new class of elites such as indigenous business interests. Just as all other groups in society had to be carefully monitored and controlled, local entrepreneurship had also to be kept in check by the state. Haile Selassie apparently felt that by carefully manipulating the state's access prerogative and by diversifying the range of foreign investors with interests in Ethiopia, he could maintain a loose but firm check on them and prevent them from becoming too influential in local affairs. He also tried to curb the power of foreign interests by occasionally demanding shares in a given activity for the state.[49] Nonetheless, Haile Selassie vigorously attempted to attract foreign investors to stimulate industrialization. In fact, he saw foreign private capital as the linchpin of his entire economic development strategy.

The growth of the number of firms active in the manufacturing sector was dramatic between the early 1950s and 1970. By 1958, there were 220 industrial establishments throughout the country. Over the next decade, that figure increased to over three hundred, and by 1970, there were well over four hundred industrial firms. Most foreign money was concentrated in the manufacturing and trading sectors. (See Table 4.2.)

Of the top fifty-one manufacturing firms, thirty-eight were either foreign-owned or foreign-operated.[50] Between 1950 and 1965, foreign private capital was responsible for investing E$350 million into the Ethiopian economy. What is striking about this figure is its meagerness despite government efforts to attract foreign capital investments. What is most significant about the figure, however, is that only E$60 million represented

TABLE 4.2
Distribution of Private Foreign Investment in Ethiopia, 1966

Type of Activity (Sector)	Total Capital Investment in Each Sector (E$)	Percentage Share of Each Sector
Manufacturing	166,000,000	58.2
Trading Services	90,000,000	31.6
Agriculture, Forestry, and Fisheries	12,500,000	4.5
Transportation and Communications	9,500,000	3.3
Building and Construction	7,000,000	2.4

SOURCE: Mohammed Duri, "Private Foreign Investment in Ethiopia, 1950–1968," *Journal of Ethiopian Studies* (July 1969), 58.

reinvested profit. This was an indication of Ethiopia's liberal policies regarding repatriation of profits.[51]

To encourage foreign private investment, the government decided in 1950 to attempt to create the image of an attractive investment climate by utilizing investment legislation as its chief economic policy mechanism. In that year the first law regarding foreign investments was passed. The "Notice of 1950 for the Encouragement of Foreign Capital Investment" assured potential foreign investors a five-year tax holiday on profits; that they could repatriate a sizable fixed portion of earned profits; and that they could import whatever technology or machinery they needed for production on a duty-free basis.[52] Notably, however, the law provided no incentives for local capitalists.

It was not until 1963 that Ethiopia's investment code was revised. The "Investment Decree of 1963" was issued to complement the stated goals of diversifying and expanding the country's industrial capacity referred to in the second five-year plan.[53] The new law incorporated and superseded all previous laws that dealt with investments, as well as the importation of equipment, technology, and capital, and the regulation of foreign exchange. Also, for the first time, the incentives to capital investment in industrial enterprises were broadened to include both foreign and domestic entrepreneurs.[54] Investors could now remit abroad all of their share profits, dividends, interest payments, management, consulting fees, and royalties.[55] If they chose eventually to divest themselves of their holding in Ethiopia, they could repatriate the net proceed belonging to them. The expatriate employees of industrial firms also benefited from the change in investment law. They could now remit up to 35 percent of their earnings per year for the first six years of their employment in the country.

Foreign entrepreneurs were further encouraged by Ethiopia's tariff policy, which protected them and allowed them to import needed technology and equipment without weighty import taxes. This was a boon for those firms directly involved in manufacturing, but it especially benefited the foreign suppliers of industrial technology. They could sell their wares in a foreign country with fewer restrictions than in most cases they had at home.

Despite intense efforts to attract foreign capital to stimulate the modernization of the industrial sector of the economy, growth between 1950 and 1970 was slow. The total amount of foreign investments in Ethiopia over this period was small even by African standards. In the early 1950s the average annual inflow of foreign capital was in the neighborbood of E$12 million. By the end of the 1960s, this average had risen to E$25 million per annum. This is not an indication that foreign capital was inconsequential to economic development. In fact, in the decade before the Ethiopian Revolution, foreign capital (public as well as private) accounted for 30 to 60 percent of all development expenditures.[56] What these meager figures do indicate is the small size of the manufacturing sector. As late as 1965, manufacturing contributed only 2.5 percent of the export trade.[57] Ten years later, manufacturing was growing at an annual rate of 16 percent, but it still only accounted for a meager 5 percent of the GDP.[58]

One of the main reasons for the slow pace of development in the manufacturing sector was the emphasis the government placed on import-substitution. Among the major items being produced in this sector were processed foods, hard and soft beverages, tobacco products, textiles, leather goods, and building materials. The major export item was an agricultural product, coffee, which by the 1970s accounted for more than 60 percent of the total export earnings. Next in line were hides and skins, pulses, and oilseeds, that together brought in approximately an additional 25 percent of the total export earnings. Another reason for the lag in the manufacturing sector was the reluctance of foreign capital to become involved in producing export items in a country with such a poor infrastructural capacity. Some foreign firms, such as the American petroleum firms—Gulf, Sinclair, and Tenneco—were involved from time to time in oil exploration, but by 1974 no appreciable amounts of oil had been discovered. The Soviet Union was responsible for building and maintaining the Assab oil refinery, but the oil it processed had to be imported and was used for domestic consumption.

The major foreign investors operating in Ethiopia by the early 1970s were involved in textile manufacturing, food processing, and the import-export business. The main textile firms, apart from those owned by the government, were the Indo-Ethiopian Textile Factory (Indian-Ethiopian joint venture); the Cotton Company of Ethiopia (Japanese-Ethiopian joint venture); the Cottonificio Baratolo of Asmara (Italian), and Ethio Fabrics Share Company (Swiss).[59] The bulk of the investments in the textile industry was in the wholesale and distribution of textile products and had existed long before the emergence of the local textile industry. The contribution of this industry to the GDP was quite significant. It accounted for an average of 30 percent of the total GDP, but the amount of foreign exchange it brought in was negligible.

In food processing and trade, numerous foreign interests were involved. Among the more significant were British, Italian, Swiss, and Israeli investments in meat-packing and canning, and Italian investments in flour milling and liquor distilling. Indians, Italians, and Greeks dominated the import-export trade.

In the last decade of his reign, Haile Selassie allowed foreign interests to begin to share banking and insurance activities with the state. In 1964, for instance, branches of the National Grindley Bank (British) and the Banco di Roma (Italian) were permitted to begin operation in Ethiopia with British and Italian investors holding 40 percent of the equity shares in the respective enterprises.[60]

Although Ethiopia has rich agricultural potential that could well have been developed to provide much more export earnings than it did, foreign investors generally shied away from the agricultural sector. Several significant factors accounted for this. First of all, Ethiopia's feudal land tenure system and the lack of a cadastral survey, which would have aided in determining clear title to land deeds, was a potent roadblock to foreign capital investment in agriculture. The poor quality of Ethiopia's transportation system—particularly roads and railways—was an additional deterrent.

The major foreign investments in agriculture were in cotton, coffee, and sugar plantations.[61] The most significant foreign investment in cotton was at the Tendaho Plantation in the Awash Valley. The British firm, Mitchell Cotts, possessed the controlling interest (51 percent) in this firm. The Ethio-American Coffee Company was 70 percent-owned by American interest, and a Dutch company, Handels Verenigins Amsterdam (HVA), was the major shareholder in two sugarcane plantations.

Significantly, sugar and cotton were produced mainly for domestic consumption and coffee for export. Also in contrast to sugar and cotton, coffee was characterized by limited foreign investment. There was an immediate domestic market for sugar when the sugar industry emerged, and its development was a cornerstone of the government's import-substitution efforts throughout the 1960s. As Ethiopia approached self-sufficiency in sugar, domestic markets were stimulated for items that could be consumed in combination with sugar, such as coffee and tea. The domestic cotton industry never really took off, and huge amounts of cotton had to be imported to sustain the local textile industry. In the next section, I shall address the significance of coffee in the growth of the Ethiopian economy, but for now, let us briefly examine the role of sugar, which, along with textiles, was the import-substitution industry characterized by the heaviest foreign investment. By the late 1950s, these two industries represented 75 percent of the aggregate foreign investments in Ethiopia.[62]

Sugar was not extensively used in Ethiopia before World War II. Honey traditionally had been used as a sweetner, but with the taste transfer that began during the Italian occupation and the generalized effect of Ethiopia's contacts with the outside world, the demand for processed sugar increased dramatically after the war. This led to a rise in sugar imports, a trend that coincided with the collapse of the Dutch colonial empire. Having disengaged from the sugar-producing colony of Indonesia, Dutch sugar-producing firms by this time were searching for an alternative site for their sugar production technology.[63] In the early 1950s Ethiopia concluded an agreement with the Dutch firm, HVA, that called for the establishment of a major sugar plantation along the Awash River at Wonji. This was to be a joint operation with a total capital investment of E$23 million, most of which was provided by the Dutch firm. The largest portion of this initial capital went to land development and capital structure. HVA was given a sixty-year lease on 2,100 hectares of land at the nominal rate of US$40 per year, with an automatic option to renew for an additional thirty years. The firm was given income tax exemptions and allowed to import raw materials and production equipment on a duty-free basis. The company was also allowed to remit 10 percent of its investment capital and 15 percent of its profits annually.[64]

In 1958 the contract with HVA was renegotiated to include more Ethiopian capital, bringing the total capital investment in the Wonji Sugar Estate to E$28 million. Also that year, a new factory opened in Shoa Province, the Shoa Sugar Factory, with a capital outlay of E$25 million; and a third factory opened between 1966 and 1968 at Metahara in the Awash Valley with a total investment of E$56 million. By 1969, 5 percent of the investment in these three plantations and their accompanying processing plants was held by the Ethiopian government, and 15 percent was held by private individual Ethiopians of high birth.[65]

By the mid-1960s, sugar production was the single largest contributor among manufacturing industries to the GDP. It accounted for some E$40 million in 1965 out of a total of E$108 million contributed by the manufacturing sector.[66] Dutch investors were reaping huge profits on their investment by this time, 50 percent of which was repatriated between 1954 and 1966.[67] At the same time, however, these sugar operations provided more than sixteen thousand jobs annually to Ethiopians, and by the late 1960s, the country had reached self-sufficiency in sugar. In 1972 sugar exports totaled more than 760 tons and netted almost E$1 million.[68] All of this would seem to indicate great success in Ethiopia's efforts to substitute for what was formerly a valued import item while developing the capacity to export that same commodity.

Although such results seem impressive in relative terms, there is more to them than meets the eye. Take, for example, the fact that the daily wage for unskilled labor on sugar plantations averaged only E$1 (US$0.40), and the share of labor in the value added as a result of such activities was a meager 10 percent. The rent that accrued to the government for the lease of the land for sugar production was insignificant, as I have already indicated.

Another important factor to be considered is that the manufacturing sector as a whole contributed little to the GDP; even though sugar represented a large proportion of the industrial product, in real terms its contribution was small. Furthermore, despite the fact that Ethiopia achieved self-sufficiency in sugar in a relatively brief period of time, it did so at great cost. Lars Bondestam estimates that if in 1970 Ethiopia had imported all the sugar it needed, it would have saved some E$9.5 million.[69] He argues that the cost of technology and foreign expertise more than neutralized whatever foreign exchange was saved through import-substitution. In addition, although domestic sugar production increased dramatically, lower retail prices for local consumers did not follow. In fact, prices rose, putting a damper on local demand as wages and the amount of money circulating in the economy remained steady. The balance of payments improved, but state revenues actually decreased, due largely to the increased demand for other import items.

Private investments as a whole came to dominate the Ethiopian economy. It is estimated that by 1970 they exceeded the investments of the state in the economy. Most of this private capital was of foreign origin.[70] It is important to note that in spite of the provision for the entry of indigenous private investors into the market made in the 1963 investment decree, few actually did. Until the late 1960s, those that did become involved tended to come from among the most well-placed families among the landed aristocracy and members of the "new nobility" with personal ties to the emperor. Some of this has to be attributed to the traditional aversion of the Amhara to involvement in commercial enterprises, but more important, perhaps, were the disincentives provided to local entrepreneurs by the realities of the regime's economic policies. Foreign capital was favored. Indeed, it was actively encouraged, whereas local capital was not. Few potential local investors could secure the credit it would have taken to set up a business that competed with foreign-based firms, and this served to discourage them. In some cases, where local industries did exist—textiles, for example—foreign-owned enterprises that could produce better and cheaper goods displaced local businessmen.[71]

Despite the growing significance of foreign private capital in the Ethiopian economy, the country was not inordinately dependent on one foreign investor or the other.[72] Of the E$173 million direct foreign private investments that flowed into the country between 1961 and 1968, an estimated 61 percent was made by investors from Western Europe and 5 percent from U.S.-based concerns. The balance came from such countries as Israel, India, Japan, and Eastern bloc countries (including the Soviet Union and China). Daniel Teferra found that in 1970 49 percent of all capital declared was invested in joint enterprises. Of these joint ventures, 52 percent of the capital was Ethiopian-owned.[73] This is a clear indication of the nationalist ideology that always underlay Ethiopia's economic policy during this phase of modernization. On the one hand, the government wanted direct private foreign investments, and it went out of its way to encourage them by enacting liberal investment policies. On the other hand, Haile Selassie's economic policy was inherently conservative in that it attempted to balance carefully the source and extent of involvement of private foreign capital in order to protect the state's leverage. How important the poor infrastructural development and a predominantly traditional feudal system of land tenure that characterize the Ethiopian economy were in determining these tendencies is unclear. In a way, the peculiar features of the economy enhanced the state's autonomy in its dealings with potential foreign investors. None of them was keen on making the massive investments in infrastructural development that it would take to bring the Ethiopian economy to the point of industrial takeoff, and they could look only to the state to solve the land tenure problem. This reality allowed Haile Selassie to proceed with the task of modernizing the state and its political economy at his own laborious pace.

The Economics of Taxation and Development

In the foregoing chapter I discussed how Haile Selassie attempted to use tax policy as a political weapon during the phase of consolidation. In this section, I shall briefly discuss how he used tax policy during the push toward modernization as an *economic* mechanism. Taxes during this period continued to serve political functions, but they increasingly came to be valued as an instrument for broadening the state's revenue base. The Haile Selassie regime employed both indirect and direct taxes as means for generating income. The main forms of indirect tax were customs tariffs and transactions sales and excise taxes; and the major direct taxes were those on land, livestock, and income. The nature and significance of each of these will be briefly discussed below.

Customs tariffs served two basic functions: (1) they generated state revenue, and (2) they protected the emerging import-substitution industries. However, it seems safe to suggest that the former function was much more important than the latter.[74] Customs tariffs were Ethiopia's most important source of revenue. Given the country's subsistence economy, which provided a limited domestic tax base, and because of the persistent resistance of traditional elites to taxes on income, the taxing of imports and exports proved to be a convenient alternative for generating the capital needed by the state. In 1956 customs tariffs accounted for 33 percent of state revenues. From this point on, the ratio of earnings from customs duties to total revenues declined and stabilized at around 25 percent. Part of the reason for this decline was the growing importance of excise, sales, and transaction taxes levied on valued consumer items purchased in the local market. By 1974, customs tariffs and these other indirect taxes accounted for over 50 percent of all state revenues. This contrasted sharply with income from direct taxes, which averaged only 20 percent in 1974.[75]

Most of the income from tariffs derived from imports rather than exports. Certain imported items, such as machines and equipment needed for industrial development, were either not taxed or only nominally taxed, although the tariff system was not uniform. Import duties brought in on average about 60 percent more revenue than did duties on exports.

The government tended to shy away from taxing most exports heavily, since this would act as a disincentive to local production. However, the government was not completely adverse to using export tariffs as sources of revenue. The most important export item taxed was coffee. The revenues derived from this source increased steadily throughout the 1960s and into the 1970s as coffee exports increased. All exported items were subject to a 2 percent *ad valorem* tax, but coffee was an exception. It was taxed at a changing basic rate, plus a surtax based on the current world market price for coffee.[76]

Excise, sales, and transaction taxes were also levied on some imported commodities, particularly those that competed with locally produced items. The most important taxes of this kind, however, were levied on certain valued consumer items produced at home, such as manufactured goods, gasoline, perfume, sugar, textiles, alcohol, tobacco, and salt. The main objective of these taxes was to bring in revenue rather than to stimulate the domestic market for import-substitution items. Imported and domestic products were taxed at a differential rate. Imported items were taxed at a rate of 12 percent *ad valorem* and domestic products at 5 percent of the sales value at the time of sale.[77]

The important point to note about indirect taxes is that they generally only affected those individuals and businesses involved in the modern sector of the economy. This excluded more than 90 percent of the population and did not give rise to a great deal of public protest. That was not the case with direct taxes, which were a constant source of conflict. Ethiopian economists, however, worried about the wisdom of relying too heavily on such indirect taxes as those on foreign trade. Assefe Bequele and Eshetu Chole, for example, stressed that taxes on imports should be used less for their revenue-generating capacity than for the protection of import-substitution industries. Such taxes, they argued, should also be used more effectively as a mechanism for regulating the balance of payments. This could be accomplished if import duties served to restrict or lessen the demand for costly imports.[78]

As I have indicated, the feudal nature of the Ethiopian economy tended to inhibit the development of a viable money economy. This in turn limited the tax base on which the state could draw. Nevertheless, the Haile Selassie regime attempted on several occasions to broaden the tax base by implementing direct taxes on land, income, and livestock. Health and education taxes were assessed as a portion of the land tax and tithe. The most notable attempts at reforming direct taxation were in 1944, which we have already mentioned, and in 1966, when the Income Tax Law was amended.

The Land Tax Proclamation (1944), in addition to increasing the state's authority over the landed elite, was intended to specify the rate and amount of taxation the central government could command from land. The law that was finally implemented had to be altered to avoid widespread civil protest in Gojjam, Begemdir, and Tigre provinces, and therefore it was never wholly satisfactory to the government. Nor did it achieve all that was hoped for. For instance, landlords continued to collect traditional tithe, although mechanisms in the 1944 law were intended to curb this practice. Landlords tended to pass on the cost of this tax to peasant producers in their service. Rather than lessening the tax burden on the peasant class, then, the 1944 law resulted in an increased burden of taxation on them. In the end, this was a regressive tax that weighed more heavily on the poor than on the rich.

There was the additional problem of implementation with the 1944 Land Tax Law. The state bureaucracy was simply not equipped and did not have sufficient manpower to execute this law effectively. It is liberally estimated that only about 75 percent of the tax due was ever collected.[79] Logistical problems prevented tax collectors from reaching some prospective taxpayers, and some simply refused to pay.

By 1956, the proportion of the total government revenues made up by the land tax was only 3.5 percent. Over the next ten years this figure declined steadily until in 1966 the land tax was bringing in only 1.3 percent of total revenues.[80] Revenues from tithe were higher but still low, and cattle taxes brought in the least income of all. (See Table 4.3.) Clearly, the government had to do a better job of extracting taxes from those who had the ability to pay. The 1944 law was unevenly applied. Even when delinquent or recalcitrant landlords were arrested, they were not always made to pay. Some bribed their way through the legal system; others simply used their connections in high places to get them off.

In 1966 the government decided that a more progressive tax system would have to be introduced in order to obtain more revenues. It proposed the Income Tax (Amendment) Proclamation (Number 255), which was to apply not only to the agricultural sector, but also to salary income, income from business and commercial activities, and real estate.[81] The key provisions relating to agricultural activities were Schedules "B" and "D." Schedule "B" dealt with income derived from renting property of any kind, and Schedule "D" referred to income from agricultural activities. A mildly progressive tax was imposed on salaried income as well as on business or commercial activities. The agricultural income tax was a graduated tax on actual produce. The 1966 Proclamations did not totally supersede the Land Tax Law of 1944. Some provisions relating to land in use and all of the references to land not in use were to continue to apply as before.

Significantly, the new law defined agricultural income in such a manner

TABLE 4.3
State Revenues from Land Tax, Tithe, and Cattle Tax, 1956/57–1965/66, in
Millions of Ethiopian Birr

Year	Land Tax	Tithe	Cattle Tax
1956–57	5.0	9.4	0.2
1957–58	4.8	9.6	0.2
1958–59	4.8	9.3	0.3
1959–60	4.1	8.3	0.2
1960–61	5.0	10.1	0.2
1961–62	5.2	10.3	0.3
1962–63	4.4	8.9	0.4
1963–64	5.4	10.5	0.2
1964–65	5.6	10.5	0.3
1965–66	5.9	10.4	0.35

SOURCE: Patrick Gilkes, *The Dying Lion: Feudalism and Modernization in Ethiopia* (London: Julian Friedmann, 1975), 67.

as to include rent from land, but it also encompassed income derived from the harvest as opposed to land itself.[82] In other words, taxes were now to be paid by those who exploited the land (landlords or tenants), not those who merely owned land. By doing this, the government hoped to end the system of privileged exemptions that thwarted taxation efforts in the past, and it also hoped to avert conflicts in communal tenure areas over taxing land not held as private property. This was essentially a direct income tax applied to the produce from land. The quality of land was no longer relevant.

The Ministry of Finance anticipated that, once in effect, the new law would net the government up to E$100 million per year.[83] The 1966 Proclamation also called for a gradual phasing out of the tithe. Earlier in that same year, Proclamation Number 230 had, in a *de jure* sense, effectively terminated the *gult* system.[84] As a result, all tribute payers were now to pay their tribute to the Ministry of Finance rather than to a *gulteñya*. *Rist gult* and *siso gult* were abolished, but *samon gult*, which was already considered payment to the state treasury, remained intact. It was also assumed that the traditional *gult* rights that were found in Amhara and Tigre areas, where communal tenure predominated, were also abolished.

Proclamation 230 provided that those tenants who had been tribute payers now became *gabbar* payers who paid taxes directly to the state. *Gult* holders who had no tribute payers simply became the owners of the property they occupied and were obliged to pay taxes on it to the state. What happened to *gulteñyas* who had *gabbars* is not clear. However, John M. Cohen and Dov Weintraub, basing their assumptions on several case studies, speculate that they became *gabbars* on at least half the land they formerly held as *gult*.[85] In other words, they too became the owners of agricultural land on a freehold basis. Needless to say, incidents of fraud and coercion on the part of powerful lords in an attempt to deprive *gabbars* of their land was common. In the north, the fight was usually over the amounts of *rist* land due an individual. With more power and prestige, former *gult* holders were able to manipulate the system to benefit them to the detriment of powerless peasant *gabbars*. In the south, the struggle was over how much land the lord kept and how much was transferred to his former vassals. In many cases, southern peasants were quickly swindled out of their *gabbar* rights and converted back into tenants on the property now claimed by a new or former lord. The main difference after 1966 was that peasants were deprived of their security.[86]

Other significant effects of Proclamation 230 were that it reformed tax collection and simplified the land tenure system by abolishing the principle of *gult*. All land was now held as freehold *gabbar* land. The *gabbar* was treated as a tax to the state. This reform, like Proclamation 255 that followed shortly after, was intended to increase state revenues and to break down further the power of the feudal nobility. By 1974 it had largely done both.[87]

Proclamation 255, in addition to specifying various forms of income tax, called for a gradual abolition of the tithe, although the draft proclamation was not specific on how this provision would be implemented. This applied only to rural land actually under cultivation. If land was owned by an individual, but not being used for productive purposes, the 1944 law would continue to apply. Furthermore, although the tithe was abolished on productive land, the land tax itself remained in effect.

The government had high expectations that it could finally introduce a progressive set of tax laws that would enhance its own power and revenue-generating capacity, increase its legitimacy among the masses, and further weaken the traditional elite classes. What it had not envisioned, however, was the stern resistance to one of its proposals it would meet in the Chamber of Deputies for the first time.[88] The 1955 Constitution had given the Chamber the power to amend and even veto proposals made by the government. It was several years before it felt confident enough to do this, but by 1966 it was apparent that the Chamber had become more than a rubber stamp for the government.

After a bitter struggle between the Ministry of Finance and the lower house, a revised tax bill was finally forwarded to the emperor for signature. It was not so liberal a reform as the government had pushed for, nor did it greatly strengthen the Ministry of Finance's formal control over land taxation decisions. For example, the drafters of the proclamation had wanted the Ministry of Finance placed in complete control over land assessment, but the Chamber instead approved a three-man assessment committee to be elected from among the residents of the relevant locality.[89] These assessment committees would be responsible for determining the rate of taxation. Abuses could be monitored by an appeals commission, but that institution was also controlled by regional rather than central interests. The power of these traditional forces was also demonstrated when the Chamber vetoed the proposed tax on unutilized land. The government had sought to use this measure to stimulate rural production, but traditional forces saw it as a threat to their own rights over land and land use, and they balked.

Another significant development involved the timing of the phaseout of the tithe. The government had wanted this to be a gradual process, determined by the rate at which the revenues from the income tax rose. The Chamber voted for the immediate abolition of this institution.

The government got its income tax, but it suffered a grave loss in terms of its efforts to solidify absolutist control. The constitutional reforms of 1955 had clearly rendered this an ultimate impossibility. Traditionalist forces had learned how to use Ethiopia's quasi-democratic institutions to serve their own purposes. The emperor had hoped that the forces of modernization would predominate in the Chamber, but they did not.

The government's tax program was also undermined at the provincial level, as were earlier tax efforts. Loosely organized farmers' groups emerged in Gojjam almost immediately, for example, and wreaked sufficient havoc to prevent assessment in large portions of the region.[90] The army was called in to put down the rebellion and maintain order. The area remained tense, and in August 1968 the emperor was forced to declare that the effort to collect taxes in Gojjam would be abandoned.

Between 1969 and 1974, the revenue from income tax grew from E$82 million to E$123 million, while other direct tax revenues generally remained static.[91] At the same time, however, income taxes represented, on the average, only 15 percent of total revenues. Tax evasion continued to be an enormous problem, and the heaviest burden of income taxation came to fall on salaried employees, who had taxes deducted automatically from their earnings. Significantly, there was no variation in the rate at which incomes were taxed. Single persons paid at the same rate as individuals with dependents.

Even though the income tax raised government revenues, it could never provide a dominant portion of these receipts. This is explained partly by the fact that the economic base of the economy continued to be low, and money was never widely used. On the other hand, the hostility of conservative elements in society to increased taxation, and to taxes on land in particular, did the most to inhibit the effectiveness of these reforms.

Foreign Trade and Economic Development

Between 1950 and 1974, foreign trade was very significant to the development of the Ethiopian economy, although imports and exports represented only a minor proportion of the GNP.[92] Much of the expansion in foreign trade was related to Ethiopia's attempts to exploit opportunities for earning foreign exchange through the export of certain products, but perhaps as important was the growing demand for manufactured goods and modern industrial technology associated with the government's economic modernization program. Ironically, even though the aim was to secure a measure of economic independence through import-substitution, to establish import-substitution industries a great deal of foreign technology was required.

Ethiopia is essentially an agrarian society. Most of her export earnings during this period came from the export of agricultural commodities, most notably coffee, hides and skins, pulses, and oilseeds. As late as 1973, 96 percent of the country's exports by value were from the agricultural sector.[93] The most important imports in terms of their values tended to be machinery, manufactured goods, petroleum products, and chemicals. Eighty-seven percent of all imports in 1973 were in these categories.

As early as 1948, Ethiopia had begun to experience balance of trade difficulties. In that year, exports accounted for about E$83 million of income, whereas imports cost E$112 million, leaving a deficit of E$29 million.[94] This situation continued to worsen over the next 24 years. Throughout the period, the deficit fluctuated according to the price of commodities like coffee and oilseeds on the world market. (See Table 4.4.)

The decade of the 1960s was extremely costly in terms of the amounts spent on imports. This was a period when the government was emphasizing rapid industrialization at all cost. It was hoped that a large portion of this expense could be paid for from export receipts, but as Table 4.4 indicates, imports consistently amounted to more than the inflow of capital from exports. In either case, with exports averaging only about 10 percent of the GDP between 1965 and 1975, it is clear that exports alone could not bear the cost of importing machinery and technology.[95]

Ethiopia attempted to diversify the sources of its imports. This is reflected in the decreasing value of imports from the United States and Italy and the growing importance of the import trade with countries like Japan, Saudi Arabia, and West Germany. By the late 1950s, Ethiopia's imports from the United States accounted for 20 percent of all imports. By 1967, this figure had dropped to 9 percent, and by 1974, it had declined to about 5 percent.[96]

Ethiopia's import trade has consistently been more significant with European countries than with the United States, with Italy being the most important among these. However, it is important to note that the import trade with Italy declined over the 1960s and 1970s, not in real terms, but in terms of the percentage of its exports among Ethiopia's total imports. In the late 1950s Ethiopia imported more than 20 percent of all imports from Italy; by 1967 this had declined to about 19 percent, and by 1974 the figure stood at 15 percent of all Ethiopia's imports.[97] Whereas in the mid-1960s 70 percent of Ethiopia's import trade was directed toward the United States, Japan, Italy, West Germany, Great Britain, and France (see Table 4.5), by

1974 the dependence on imports from these six countries had declined to just over 53 percent. What is more significant is that by 1974, Ethiopian imports from a total of thirteen different countries amounted to more than E$10 million each.[98] Among the newer and more significant import markets were Kenya, Iran, Saudi Arabia, the People's Republic of China, and other Asian countries, which together accounted for about 20 percent of Ethiopia's imports. The largest proportion of this amount was accounted for by the import of unrefined petroleum from Iran and Saudi Arabia after Ethiopia achieved the capacity to refine its own petroleum. This significantly lessened its dependence on the United States and Italy for such products. Asian and African countries as a group accounted for one-third of all imports, a further indication of Ethiopia's conscious attempt to diversify its external trade to reduce its dependence on the world's politically powerful countries. However, given its dogged commitment to indus-

TABLE 4.4

Total Value of Imports, Exports, and Re-Exports and Visible Balance of Trade in Millions of Ethiopian Dollars

Year	Imports	Exports	Visible Balance of Trade
1951	147.4	151.9	+ 4.5
1952	161.9	131.4	− 30.5
1953	137.9	169.4	+ 31.5
1954	160.1	160.3	+ 0.2
1955	168.0	162.2	− 5.8
1956	157.1	151.4	− 5.7
1957	178.4	192.0	+ 13.6
1958	193.6	156.8	− 36.8
1959	208.9	179.2	− 29.7
1960	219.3	192.6	− 26.7
1961	235.6	188.7	− 46.9
1962	257.3	199.5	− 57.8
1963	276.1	223.4	− 52.7
1964	307.6	262.5	− 45.1
1965	375.7	289.8	− 85.9
1966	404.3	277.0	− 127.3
1967	357.4	252.7	− 104.7
1968	432.5	266.0	− 166.5
1969	388.3	298.1	− 90.2
1970	429.1	305.9	− 123.2
1971	469.5	314.4	− 155.4
1972	435.6	387.3	− 48.3
1973	448.2	499.5	+ 51.3
1974	586.0	556.2	− 29.8

SOURCE: *Ethiopia: Statistical Abstract, 1975* (Addis Ababa: Central Statistical Office, 1975), 102.

TABLE 4.5
Ethiopia's Six Most Important Import Trading Partners by Commodity, 1967

Commodities	Automative Vehicles	Industrial Machines	Clothes	Rubber Products	Petroleum Products
United States	X	X			X
Italy	X	X		X	X
Japan			X	X	
West Germany	X	X		X	
United Kingdom	X			X	
France	X	X			

SOURCE: *Ethiopia: Statistical Abstract, 1967* (Addis Ababa: Central Statistical Office, 1967), 59.

trialization and the commercialization of agriculture, there was a limit to how much Ethiopia could cut its dependence on certain foreign manufactured goods, machinery, and raw materials. On the eve of the Revolution, these commodities continued to make up the bulk of Ethiopia's imports.

In many respects, Ethiopia's dependence on the world market and on certain trading partners has historically been much more obvious in the area of exports. In 1967 just over 70 percent of the country's total export value went to six countries: the United States (43.1 percent), Italy (8.3 percent), West Germany (5.4 percent), Japan (4.3 percent), the United Kingdom (4.2 percent), and Saudi Arabia (5.5 percent).[99] By 1974, more than 60 percent of all Ethiopian exports continued to go to these six countries. The U.S., Canada, and European countries accounted for 88 percent of all Ethiopian exports in 1973 and 61 percent in 1974.[100] Again, this considerable fluctuation is largely due to the fluctuation in the value of the world market price for key agricultural export items. In 1973 Ethiopia exported a record volume of coffee, which accounted for almost 40 percent of the total export earnings in that year. In the following year, the price brought in by coffee declined, but it was somewhat made up by the returns from the sale of oilseeds and pulse.[101]

Coffee is by far Ethiopia's major export crop, and the United States has been the most important market for that product. Between 1960 and 1972, the volume of Ethiopian coffee that entered the world market increased from just over fifty thousand tons to more than eighty-two thousand tons.[102] The United States consistently imported more than 60 percent of all Ethiopian coffee exports. No other trading partner imported as much of any one commodity from Ethiopia as the United States. In fact, it could be suggested that the United States subsidized Ethiopia by importing its coffee, and its balance of trade with that country was consistently favorable. For Ethiopia's other major trading partners, except for Saudi Arabia, the balance of trade tended to be consistently negative. (See Table 4.6.)

Despite Ethiopia's heavy reliance on income from the export of coffee,

TABLE 4.6
Balance of Trade with Selected Countries, 1967 and 1972, in Millions of Ethiopian Dollars

Country	Year	Export	Import	Balance of Trade
United States	1967	108,960	33,623	+75,337
	1972	136,119	39,934	+96,185
Italy	1967	20,968	67,689	−46,721
	1972	31,903	71,303	−39,400
West Germany	1967	13,635	50,024	−36,389
	1972	28,246	46,539	−18,293
Japan	1967	10,885	48,760	−37,875
	1972	26,799	66,176	−39,377
Saudi Arabia	1967	13,909	1,736	+12,173
	1972	22,454	389	+22,065
United Kingdom	1967	10,605	27,578	−16,973
	1972	10,656	41,171	−30,415

SOURCE: *Ethiopia: Statistical Abstract, 1967* (Addis Ababa: Central Statistical Office, 1967), and *Ethiopia: Statistical Abstract, 1975* (Addis Ababa: Central Statistical Office, 1975).

until very recently the government did little to improve the quality or quantity of coffee produced. Very little foreign capital was involved in the coffee industry. By the mid-1970s only about ninety thousand hectares of agricultural land were devoted to coffee production on plantations.[103] This occurred mainly in the Sidamo and Hararge regions. The major portion of the annual coffee crop was picked from uncultivated wild coffee trees in Kaffa, Illubabor, and Wollega provinces. As the empire spread south, *neftegñyas* (soldier-colonizers) and members of the aristocracy were quick to capitalize on the emerging coffee market. At first, it followed the convenient trade routes from the coffee-rich areas of southwestern Ethiopia into the Sudan, but by 1960, with the improvement in rail and road communication between the center and periphery, more and more Ethiopian coffee began to find its way into the world market.

In spite of the growth in Ethiopia's coffee exports, its contribution to the world's supply of coffee was almost negligible. Moreover, Ethiopia was constrained by the fact that coffee prices and quotas were beyond its control. The International Coffee Organization set prices and quotas on coffee sold on the world market. Even if Ethiopia was allowed to increase its production, there was no guarantee that it could reap huge benefits because prices might fall or quotas might become more restrictive from year to year.

Despite the dangers involved in being so bound by a monoculture economy, Ethiopia attempted in a limited way to improve its income potential from the export of coffee by setting up the National Coffee Board in 1957.[104] Publicly, it was suggested that the board's functions would mainly be that of quality control, promotion of coffee research and development, and export. As it turned out, the board came to serve the promotion function much more than the others. Cooperative societies were established to improve the efficiency of the coffee extraction and marketing processes, and large amounts of capital were spent on road development to open up previously inaccessible regions to market centers and ultimately to Addis Ababa and the world market.

Even though it was recognized that Ethiopia could reap more benefit from coffee production if it could find ways of stimulating small-scale peasant production, the Haile Selassie regime chose to rely on feudal lords to extract the bulk of the crop by requiring that their tenants, along with migrant laborers, harvest the crop at a minimal level of remuneration and by promoting the development of coffee plantations.[105] There were more disincentives than there were incentives to increasing peasant production of coffee. For example, even if a peasant farmer desired to expand his coffee production capacity, he had difficulty securing the needed credit and price supports; these benefited mainly the larger producers. The government claimed it did not possess the necessary capital resources to stimulate peasant production. This led those peasants who attempted to finance increased production with private loans to do so only at a great deal of risk. Taye Gulilat describes the perils of such a venture:

> Because funds are limited and because credit institutions are inadequate, the village moneylender is the most common source of credit. . . . When they [peasants] want to borrow, most coffee growers, with too little education and substance, look not to a bank but to some individual—a relative, a more prosperous neighbor or a coffee dealer. . . . Often they go to the village moneylender who may be a shopkeeper as well. . . . He rarely charges less than 20 percent and often more than 50 percent.[106]

Given the realities of the situation, peasant crops often had to be pledged, and the prices peasants received were much lower than the market price. Most of the profits small producers earned went directly to their creditors. Borrowing from banks was almost out of the question for small producers. To begin with, there were few banks in peripheral regions, and those that did exist demanded sizable amounts of collateral. Coffee land was a valued form of collateral, but small farmers by definition did not generally have an acceptable amount of this form of property.

In essence, the regime pursued its own development strategy, utilizing the feudal structure because of the immediate income it guaranteed and disregarding the ill effects of the growing exploitation of small producers. Emergent capitalism, in other words, fed on feudalism. Feudalism began generally to weaken, but the power of the landed classes remained intact.

Peasants, Agro-Industry, and Development: The Convergence
of Feudalism and Capitalism

The Ethiopian government fully realized that in spite of the apparent need for industrial expansion, its main hope for economic takeoff lay in the agricultural sector. As I have mentioned, from the beginning of the central planning process, the emphasis was on commercial, agro-industrial enterprises capitalized by foreign money. Few foreign firms, however, ever became involved in such activity, and very little of the regime's own capital or recurrent budget was allocated to agriculture, save for partnerships involving the state and foreign capital until the late 1960s. As late as 1974, commercial farming represented only 1 percent of the total cropped area in the country.[107] By that time, the state and foreign concessionary companies had been joined by large and medium landowners who were quick to adapt to the privatization of land in the mid-1960s.

Significantly, commercialized agriculture was concentrated in only a few regions: Shoa, Hararge, Chilalo, Wollamo, Humera, and the Awash Valley. The Awash Valley was the area of the heaviest activity. In 1975 there was a total of twenty-seven large- to medium-sized commercial farming enterprises in the Awash Valley alone.[108] The commercialization of the Awash Valley was stimulated by Dutch investments in the HVA sugar plantations, but it was propelled by the development of the Awash Valley Authority (AVA).[109] The AVA was initiated in 1962 with aid from the United Nations earmarked for a full survey of the entire river valley. It became an autonomous public agency responsible for the administration and planning of development in the region. A dam built at Koka in the late 1950s supplemented the electrical power produced on the HVA Wonji Sugar Estate. Two more power plants were added later. Irrigation schemes were also developed by the AVA. Numerous private agro-industrial enterprises began to flourish as a result of this multilevel project, incorporating a ready supply of electrical power, paved roads, and irrigation. The contribution of agro-industrial enterprise to gross economic growth continued to rise at a rate of over 15 percent per annum and came to be hailed by the government as a model for future development.

Foreign aid donors, however, constantly warned that in spite of the impressive gains made by commercial farming, the agricultural sector as a whole would continue to stagnate unless something was done to dismantle feudalism and integrate the majority of the rural sector into the market economy. The World Bank estimated that only about 25 percent of Ethiopia's total agricultural production was marketed annually.[110] The basic reason for this was that the government had largely ignored reform of the peasant sector, choosing not to tamper too vigorously with feudal structures.

With the inauguration of the second five-year development plan in 1969, it seemed that this trend could be reversed. The government reluctantly committed itself to improving peasant productivity. The plan stated:

> Farmers should be assisted to produce more marketable surpluses, so as to continue to develop the subsistence sector of agriculture into a monetary one. However, the production targets in respect to industrial crops and livestock cannot be fulfilled by the subsistence sector alone. Large-scale and mechanized agricultural undertakings have to be established by private concerns, government and cooperative initiative.[111]

Toward the end of the plan period, specific projects were created aimed at identifying ways of improving peasant agricultural production. From this point on, agricultural development was to proceed on two fronts: commercialization and "package schemes" aimed at small farmers. As in the past, the former would receive the most attention.

A package project was first inaugurated in 1967 in Chilalo subprovince with Swedish development assistance.[112] The project came to be known as CADU (the Chilalo Agricultural Development Unit). It comprised 600,000 hectares of land with 400,000 inhabitants. The primary aim of this scheme was to help small farmers to help themselves and ultimately to transfer the experiences gained from this experiment throughout the country. Theoretically, peasant farmers would be provided with easy access to credit, improved seeds, fertilizers, pesticides, cheap farm implements, crossbred cattle, and improved extension and marketing services. All of this was intended to provide, in a limited area on an experimental basis, the conditions necessary for efficiently integrating small-scale producers into the market economy.

Two more package projects, both sponsored by the World Bank, were begun between 1969 and 1970. The first was in the Wolaita region in Ethiopia's southern highlands; the second project was at Humera in the northwestern Ethiopian lowlands.[113] The Wolaita Agricultural Development Unit (WADU) project was mainly intended to organize Oromo peasants for more efficient production and to provide them with needed social services. In part, this was a step toward strengthening the capacity of southern peasants and tenants to fend off the advances of avaricious landowners bent on expanding their own holdings for commercialization. The Humera region was sparsely populated but rich in agricultural potential. The package project was intended to stimulate the development of mechanized farming. A cooperative society was organized to serve the needs of small farmers. Although the resettlement of landless peasants in the area was encouraged, little was done officially to facilitate this.

By 1972 each of these package schemes had recorded notable success. Between 1967 and 1972, the level of participation in the CADU project grew from about two hundred to over 1,200,000, and participants doubled their income.[114] This represented a quarter of the total number of farmers in the unit area. The WADU and Humera projects also experienced some success.

Despite the apparent progress made in involving more peasants in the market and in increasing their productivity, even as these projects were being established they were being undermined by the abusive tendencies of large farmers. In Chilalo, for example, large-scale farmers moved in to take advantage of the benefits intended for small farmers.[115] In 1967, when the project began, there were no commercial farms in the whole of Arussi Province where CADU was located. By 1972, there were 126 commercial estates. About 56 percent of these were owner-operated, but a full 44 percent were contracted from absentee landlords. In a five-year period, almost one-fourth of the tenants living in the area had been evicted, the price of land skyrocketed to the discouragement of would-be peasant buyers, and many more felt the weight of ever-increasing rents. Even common pasture land was usurped by large farmers to expand their own holdings. The government stood by as this process unfolded, being more committed in the first place to commercial than to peasant farming. This point is reinforced by the fact that in 1971 alone, the government granted 2,100 hectares of land in Chilalo district to large landowners.[116] Moreover, large landowners had easier access to credit, while peasants found credit, beyond a basic minimum, increasingly hard to come by.

It should be noted that these trends characterized only a limited area of the country. In most of the country, feudalism was barely affected by capital penetration even as late as 1974, except to the extent that the government's agricultural policy was directed at undermining the feudal basis of society by stimulating capitalist development wherever it could. This is clearly shown by the credit policies the government introduced at the end of the 1960s.

By 1970, the Agricultural and Industrial Development Bank was established by merging the Development Bank of Ethiopia and the Ethiopian Investment Corporation, and it became the government's principal agency for mobilizing and directing capital for agricultural development.[117] In 1972 it had disbursed almost half of its original E$100 million worth of capitalization. More than half of these funds had gone for agricultural development. Most of the loans for agriculture, however, were given to three large-scale farms and better-off individual farmers. Only 7 percent of the loans found their way into the hands of small farmers.

A further example of the continued bias of the government's agricultural policy toward agro-industry and large-scale farming could be seen in how it used its control over "virgin" state lands to encourage farming of this kind without considering the social impact on peasant populations throughout the country. Teffara-Worq Beshah and John W. Harbeson examine the case of the commercialization of agriculture in the Awash Valley, particularly in the area traditionally inhabited by the Afar, Gile, Kereyu, and Oromo peoples.[118] The reigning sultan of the Afar during Haile Selassie's reign was Ali Mira Hanfere. He ruled his people as a semiautonomous entity within the Ethiopian state, enriching himself in the process. When the Tendaho Cotton Plantation was opened in Wollo Province, he was granted a minor but substantial share in the company, and in return he cooperated with commercial efforts in his sphere and even served as a local administrator. With the shift in government policy regarding development in the Awash Valley in the 1960s, Ali Mira witnessed the erosion of more and more of his authority. Afari and other peasants and pastoralists were displaced to make way for ever-increasing numbers of commercial enterprises. A token effort was made to resettle those displaced, but the programs established for this purpose were inadequate for the task. Moreover, in spite of the expectation that many local residents of the region would be hired as wage laborers in the various estates that developed there, in actuality few were ever employed.

Other pastoralists were also dislocated from traditional grazing lands when the government granted a concession in 1973 to the Italian company MAESCO for the production of alfalfa for export to Japan.[119] Ironically, this occurred in a region that was soon to be characterized by widespread drought and famine, some of which could have been prevented if nomads in the area had not been restricted from what had customarily been their best grazing land. Similar impacts could be found throughout the country.

Wherever it could, the Haile Selassie regime pushed commercial agriculture not only at the expense of feudal relationships and structures, but also in spite of the negative social impact it might have on peasant populations. Where feudalism was resistant to change, the emperor was generally willing to let it die by degrees. He extracted what he could from it, probably realizing that its days were numbered; but he was unprepared to smash it in one fell swoop.

Conclusion

Haile Selassie employed a multifaceted economic policy in order to orchestrate the process of development from above. He put heavy emphasis on the promotion of manufacturing industry and commercialized agriculture mostly for purposes of import-substitution. However, government revenues were primarily secured from indirect taxation and peasant agricultural produce. Not much progress was made between 1950 and 1974 in inducing economic takeoff as a result of the major thrust of the government's development strategy; nor was the government able to increase substantially the proportion of its income derived from agricultural export. It did little to reform peasant agriculture or to integrate small farmers more fully into the market economy. The most profound result of Ethiopia's development strategy during this period was the sharpening of social contradictions. Capitalist classes emerged side-by-side with feudal classes and in some cases overlapped.[120] Inequalities abounded. Traditional relationships were fractured, and Ethiopian society became increasingly exploitative and insecure for the impoverished majority. The character of these contradictions and their implications for the social revolution that began in 1974 will be addressed in the next chapter.

Part Two

The Genesis of Revolution

V

DEVELOPMENT AND SOCIAL CONTRADICTIONS

THE SEEDS OF REVOLUTION

> I must die so as to see again those who died
> before, and to tell them the seed we sowed
> has taken root.[1]
>
> —Mengistu Newaye, March 30, 1961

Haile Selassie had always tried to present the public image of a modernizing autocrat with the best interest of *all* his people at heart, a leader who
followed the development strategy he did because it was the most equitable
and practical possible. Critics inside and outside Ethiopia, however, saw
him otherwise and tried gently to prod the emperor to move faster and
more radically in the effort to modernize society. At first, modernist pressures more progressive than the emperor's own orientations came in the
form of private pleas for change from a small number of Western-educated
intellectuals and highly trained military officers. Perhaps as much as the
emperor's own disposition toward modernization, such sentiments served
as catalysts for the initial spurts of constitutional and economic reform of
the late 1940s and the 1950s. By 1960, however, the scope and intensity of
discontent among the young educated elite had broadened, and it quickly
reached crisis proportions.

Several observers of Ethiopian political history have identified 1960 as a
"watershed year" in the political development of that country.[2] It was the
year in which the spectre of revolution first became apparent in the modern state, the year in which the vulnerabilities of the anachronistic bureaucratic empire were laid bare for all to see. Until then, the emperor
seemed to have things under control despite occasional signs of civil unrest
and elite opposition. His abilities and resources allowed him to suppress or
manipulate opponents, giving him the necessary freedom to pursue the

131

development of Ethiopian society from the top down, as if by some grand design. From 1960 on, however, rather than being able to dictate comfortably the rate and direction of change, the emperor was placed ever more on the defensive, having to work harder to mediate the demands of increasingly politically significant social groupings. As he had done in the past, Haile Selassie attempted to maintain the image of a composed and strong leader. His success thus far could in large measure be attributed to his ability to rely on the critical flexible resources of the military, the bureaucracy, and a pool of educated elites who felt they owed their achievements as much to the emperor's goodwill as to their own abilities. Throughout the 1960s and early 1970s, each of these elements consistently demonstrated that their support for Haile Selassie's version of modernization was not certain.

The event that first exposed the contradictions inherent in the emperor's efforts to wed royal absolutism with modernization was an abortive coup d'etat in the closing days of 1960. The coup was important not so much for what it achieved, but because it ushered in a rising tide of protest over Ethiopia's distorted development strategy, culminating in the successful coup of 1974.

The 1960 coup was led by Girmame Newaye, a subprovincial governor from a prominent Shoan family, and his brother, Mengistu Newaye, the commander of the elite Imperial Guard. These men were joined by the commissioner of police, the commander of the security forces, some relatives, and the five-thousand-strong cadre of the Imperial Guard. The guardsmen were committed to follow unquestioningly the orders of their commander under any circumstances.[3] Significantly, the plotters had not properly secured the support of the leading officers in the regular or territorial armies; nor had they cleared their actions with religious leaders. Ultimately, this lack of attention to detail, coupled with the limited military capacity of the rebels, proved decisive.

The rebels seized the opportunity to strike at a time when the emperor was on a state visit to Brazil. On the evening of December 13, 1960, the conspirators duped several ministers and other important figures into coming to the royal palace for an emergency meeting. Once there, they were taken hostage. The next morning, units of the Imperial Guard surrounded the main army installations in Addis Ababa and took control of the radio station. Crown Prince Asfa Wossen, the emperor's son, was then required to make a public announcement over Radio Addis Ababa, declaring that the old regime had been deposed. The justification for the coup centered on Ethiopia's economic stagnation and underdevelopment compared with African states emerging from colonialism. Political elites were accused of nepotism and greed, and the regime was condemned for its neglect in the face of widespread poverty, illiteracy, and low living standards. Significantly, the emperor himself was not directly vilified, and there appears to have been a calculated effort to keep the coup as bloodless as possible.

The rebels tried to gain the support of certain strategic groups such as student radicals and the military with promises of sweeping reforms. They pledged that the new regime would ensure freedom of speech, freedom of the press, and allow political parties for the first time. A substantial increase in military pay was also announced. There were plans to introduce a constitutional monarchy and to dismantle feudalism. The new regime would concentrate its efforts on social and economic reforms to help Ethiopia catch up with African states who were then gaining their independence from European colonizers.

Several commentators on this period in Ethiopian history have attributed the coup almost solely to the revolutionary vision of Girmame Newaye.[4] Girmame has been described as a radical and a Pan-Africanist who was to some degree influenced by Marxism-Leninism. Educated in the United States, he received a master's degree in political science from Columbia University in 1954. As a student, Girmame had been fascinated by the problems of European colonialism in Africa, and for his master's thesis he wrote an essay on the impact of European colonialism in Kenya.[5]

Girmame considered pursuing the Ph.D. but was recalled by his government to serve in the Ministry of Interior. Once at home, his reformist ideas began to blossom. At first he discussed his views only with other young Ethiopians who had been educated abroad. Later, however, he was assigned to become the governor of Wellamu subprovince in Sidamo Province, and for the first time he was able to put some of his ideas into operation. The provincial governor was Dejazmatch Mesfin Selleshi, whom Harold G. Marcus describes as, "the archtypical exploiter."[6] The extent of oppression and exploitation greatly shocked Girmame.

Girmame was an activist governor who encouraged the Oromo people in Wellamu to build roads, bridges, and schools, and who vigorously attempted to secure development funds from the capital for local projects. He even went so far as to distribute uncultivated land to landless peasants. This latter act caused considerable concern among local landowners, who complained that Girmame had deprived them of a vital source of casual labor. Subsequently he was recalled to Addis Ababa to explain his actions to the emperor. Girmame responded that they were justified because the people were landless and hungry, and because he assumed the emperor favored such reforms.[7] In spite of his modernist pretensions, it became clear that Haile Selassie was not prepared to undermine feudalism completely in the 1950s. Rather than praising Girmame's actions, the emperor reassigned him to Jijiga, an area in the Ogaden inhabited by Somali pastoralists.

In Jijiga, Girmame was immediately confronted with the abject poverty and underdevelopment of the region and with obvious signs of official neglect. He discovered clinics and hospitals unoccupied and in a state of decay. On a visit to the area in the early 1950s, the emperor had promised to show his regime's concern for the welfare of Somali subjects by improving social services in the area. As a result, health facilities were built. The Ministry of Public Health, however, refused to staff or equip these facilities, allegedly preferring to concentrate its efforts in more populous areas.[8]

Girmame Newaye's experiences as a student had opened his mind to the possibility of an alternative path to development and a different form of government for Ethiopia. His experiences as an administrator in the countryside convinced him of the need for revolutionary action. Between late 1959 and early 1960, Girmame Newaye apparently persuaded his brother, Brigadier General Mengistu Newaye of the Imperial Guard, that they could plan and execute a successful coup d'etat. Mengistu's support was critical, since he commanded the Imperial Guard and had connections throughout the armed forces.

The leaders of the coup apparently expected a spontaneous demonstration of popular support for their actions that would serve to convince all branches of the military to throw their weight behind the coup. Even though the commissioner of police and the commander of the security forces did join ranks with the conspirators, widespread support from the army and territorial forces did not materialize. Rather than uniting behind the coup leaders, the nobility, the army, the territorial forces, and elements of the police force were able to reach a consensus within hours of the announcement of the coup that they were loyal to the emperor. To legitimize their impending countercoup, the loyalists enlisted the support of Abuna Basileos, the Patriarch of the Ethiopian Orthodox Church. The Abuna, in collaboration with Major General Merid Mangasha and Dejazmatch Asrate Kassa, drafted a leaflet in Amharic to be distributed to the public. The thrust of the message was that the rebels were traitors and should not be followed. Richard Greenfield claims that the rebels foreclosed any chance of success when they failed to mention "God" anywhere in the statement announcing the coup.[9] Within thirty-six hours the boundaries separating the loyalists from the rebels were clear, and the clergy stood squarely behind the loyalists.

Perhaps most decisive was the failure of the rebels either to immobilize potential opponents immediately and completely or to win the support of certain elements within the armed forces. This allowed Major General Merid to build a military coalition of his own and to enlist the support of United States military advisers in mapping a strategy for putting down the rebellion.[10] Fighting broke out between the army and the Imperial Guard on December 16. Three days later the uprising was completely suppressed. Four hundred and seventy-four members of the Imperial Guard had been killed or wounded during the fighting, and two thousand had been taken prisoner. Seventy-two loyalist soldiers were killed or wounded. In addition, fifteen of the twenty-one notables who had been taken hostage in the early stages of the coup were executed by the conspirators when it was apparent that their plot had failed.[11]

Mengistu and Girmame Newaye succeeded in escaping immediate capture. They remained at large until December 24 when they were cornered by the army near Mojo, fifty miles south of Addis Ababa. Girmame chose to commit suicide rather than suffer the fate of a trial and public execution. Mengistu, on the other hand, was captured, tried, and hanged on March 30, 1961.

Even in its failure, the coup had a profound effect on the course of developments in Ethiopia after 1960. Whereas Haile Selassie had been insulated from the grievances of various groups in society prior to this time, afterwards, protests from student groups, ethnic and self-help associations, and other corporate groups became commonplace. The issues that formed the basis for these protests were remarkably similar to those the conspirators had championed in 1960: the need for land and tax reform, administrative decentralization, and the establishment of a genuine parliamentary democracy.

As I have suggested in the previous two chapters, the emperor had his own vision of society, and even though he was now forced to devote more attention to placating a wider number of social groupings, he would not be deterred from his basic course. This proved a fatal flaw, as over the next fourteen years he engaged in political, economic, and social policies that served to sharpen rather than ameliorate social contradictions. As a result, groups such as students, workers, and ethnic minorities became more and more alienated and were involved in ever-increasing incidents of social protest and even outright rebellion. What is more significant, these groups began to organize their activities in a much more sophisticated manner than ever before. In 1965, for example, what came to be known as the "student movement" engaged in its first mass demonstration before parliament, and from this point on, such incidents became commonplace. Four years later, the movement was responsible for the all but unprecedented act of distributing pamphlets attacking the emperor directly. Peter Koehn and Louis D. Hayes suggest that throughout this period, students were the only organized group openly critical of the monarchy and its policies.[12] This contention, I feel, must be qualified, because it was also over this period that such ethnic groups as the Oromo, Ogaden Somalis, Eritreans, and Tigreans began to form nationalist organizations in opposition to the regime of Haile Selassie for the first time. These pockets of opposition might never have emerged if the emperor's policies had been more sensitively directed at building legitimacy among the masses rather than simply at securing compliance or acquiescence to laws and policies. He erroneously assumed that the charisma of his office would serve as an effective check on those who advocated revolutionary changes. Instead, the social impacts of his development policies undermined rather than bolstered the authority of his regime.

The previous two chapters have touched on the unintended adverse consequences of the emperor's political and economic policies. This chapter attempts to examine more specifically the effects of social policies over the same period and to identify the cumulative social contradiction resulting from Haile Selassie's development strategy to gain a clear and more focused understanding of the underlying causes of the Revolution.

The Global Impact of Social Policy

Perhaps the most striking aspect of Haïl Selassie's attitude toward dealing with the multiplicity of social groupings in society was the low priority he apparently assigned to national political integration. In part this could be attributed to the emperor himself, but in large measure it was a reflection of the countervailing power possessed by traditional classes even to the last days of the empire. Until the 1960s, the regime viewed peripheral peoples as "subjects" and "dependents" to be pacified rather than satisfied. According to this view, the state was more interested in control than integration. The emperor attempted to disassociate himself, however, from the corruption, oppression, and other excesses of local administration, cultivating the image of a benevolent father-figure.[13]

No specific policy of national political integration ever existed except for the tendency to integrate selected members of certain Amharized minorities into the ruling class. John Markakis notes that the government conscientiously avoided any reference to ethnic, linguistic, and religious diversity and eschewed mentioning such matters in official documents.[14] Most of the government's efforts in this regard were devoted toward discouraging or destroying the culture, language, and religions of subject groups.

Even when one considers the integration of certain members of non-Amhara groups into the upper echelons of the ruling class and the imperial bureaucracy, what stands out is the small numbers of such groups represented.[15] The emperor himself encouraged the marriage of Amharas, particularly the nobility, with important Oromo families, but in practice this had a negligible integrative effect. Even though the Oromos are the largest single ethnic group in the country, except for the Wollega Oromos and some Shoan Oromos, few of that group ever occupied very high positions in the imperial bureaucracy or the army. Christopher Clapham presents statistics showing that of 156 high-ranking officials recruited into the central bureaucracy between 1944 and 1967, only three came from the six southern provinces where Oromos predominate (Arussi, Bale, Sidamo, Gemu-Gofa, Kaffa, Illubabor), and only two were Somalis.[16] Even more striking was the fact that Shoan Amharas tended to dominate at all levels of administration down to the district level. In 1967 two of the six provincial governors were military officers, and the remainder were Shoan aristocrats.[17] The tendency toward Shoan dominance caused considerable resentment among Amharas and Tigres from other areas.

Certain ethnic minorities came to be more represented in the imperial bureaucracy during the 1960s. This move on the part of the emperor was regarded as a strategic necessity aimed at "buying" the support of ethnic minority patrons. The growth of Somali and Oromo nationalism in this period, for example, appears to have forced the emperor to recognize certain of their leaders and to give them titles. Discontent in Eritrea over the annexation of that region resulted in a similar response.

In spite of Haile Selassie's efforts to systematically co-opt disgruntled ethnic groups through their leaders, this policy was doomed to fail. The core of his strategy remained the gradual Amharization of these groups without integrating them as equals or allowing them to share power in any meaningful way. Even if the emperor had wanted to share power—and it is not clear that he did—traditional Amhara elements were sufficiently strong to block any serious efforts at national integration.

With the encouragement of young bureaucrats, the government attempted in May 1962 to introduce broad local government reforms that would have given a measure of autonomy to the subprovinces in such matters as education, road construction, and health care administration. Representatives were to be elected at the subprovince and district levels to serve on development and administrative councils. The draft proclamation to "Establish Self-Government in the Empire of Ethiopia" even went so far as to delineate conditions under which these local councils could levy additional taxes and remove provincial governors.[18] The measure was debated for almost four years, and in the end it appeared as "Local Self-Administration Order No. 43," a severely emasculated version of the original draft. An effort was made to remove all provisions that were offensive to the traditional elite. Even this version of the law was defeated in parliament. The "Dissenting Group in the Joint Committee of the Chamber of Deputies and the Senate," attempting to reach a compromise on the measure, perhaps spoke for the majority of the landed classes when it stated:

> While it is clear that Ethiopia has existed for the last 3000 years . . . it is also known that [Ethiopia] is comprised of different tribal groups which were far from regarding one another as members of the same nation, viewing each other as outsiders, having different outlooks and with no free intermingling; and to create separate and autonomous *awrajas* [districts] before the people know one another . . . would be encouraging separatist tendencies.[19]

Clearly, the dominant classes in Ethiopia at the time were not about to alter the status quo, even in the interest of national political integration. What was also clear was that in spite of Haile Selassie's efforts to secularize and strengthen his own personal authority, to a considerable measure he was unable to do so. In fact, these classes adapted to the alterations in the arena of conflict and now used effectively the new parliamentary institution to serve their own interests. Moreover, traditionalist sentiments continued to stymie central government reforms at the grassroots level in the highland core and among landlords in the periphery. This was clearly demonstrated in the protests, particularly in Gojjam and Sidamo, surrounding the government's attempt to implement the agricultural income tax of 1967.[20]

That national political integration was considered by the Haile Selassie regime as not deserving special public concern was further apparent in the way the government approached the problem of regional underdevelopment. In the 1963–1967 development plan, regional development constituted an integral part of the overall development strategy. But instead of defining "development" in terms of improving the living standards and life chances of the people in peripheral areas, it was seen as the efficient exploitation of the economic potential of each region.[21] Integration was considered a natural by-product of the process of centralization and modernization and thus undeserving of any special concern. In keeping with this view, economic growth under Haile Selassie was stressed at the expense of social reforms.

It is conceivable that economic development could indeed have led to the betterment of social conditions in peripheral areas if a conscious attempt had been made to disperse modern economic activities evenly throughout the country. However, this was not done. In fact, on the eve of the Revolution, 70 percent of Ethiopia's industrial activities were clustered in Addis Ababa and Asmara.[22] Interestingly, the concentration of industries increased after the annexation of Eritrea, as several firms operating in Eritrea either ceased to function or moved to Addis Ababa. What rural industries there were tended to be concentrated in Shoa Province and the Awash Valley and were more capital- than labor-intensive.

In spite of the enormous poverty, illiteracy, and poor health in the Ethiopian countryside, the Haile Selassie regime accorded a limited role for the central government in the provision of social services. Between 1964 and 1974, government expenditure on education did increase dramatically when compared to earlier spending patterns, but illiteracy still remained as high as 90 percent. Other social services such as health care, housing, sanitation, and water development were also extremely neglected.[23] The enormity of the social neglect under Haile Selassie could be seen in a brief analysis of the impact of his regime's policies on the provision of formal education and health care.

By 1973, less than one million young people were formally enrolled in school from the elementary to the university level. This figure represented only 3 percent of the total population.[24] At the same time, it was estimated that 45 percent of the total population was under fifteen years of age. Only 8 percent of all students were in high school, and less than 1 percent were enrolled in the university.

TABLE 5.1

Students Enrolled in Primary and Academic Secondary Schools by Province and as a Percentage of Total Population, 1972–73

Province	Total Population	Percent of Population	Students Enrolled	Percent of Total Enrolled
Arussi	892,700	3.1	37,792	4.1
Bale	739,600	2.5	16,826	1.8
Begemdir	1,418,700	4.9	42,542	4.6
Eritrea	2,070,100	7.1	107,948	11.7
Gemu-Gofa	730,700	2.5	22,098	2.4
Gojjam	1,829,600	6.3	41,991	4.5
Hararge	3,510,000	12.1	54,035	5.8
Illubabor	719,400	2.4	24,273	2.6
Kaffa	1,768,700	6.1	30,996	3.4
Shoa	5,712,100	19.8	155,295	16.8
Sidamo	2,595,600	9.0	57,632	6.2
Tigre	1,916,600	6.7	45,935	4.9
Wollega	1,326,800	4.6	86,661	9.3
Wollo	2,570,200	8.9	44,944	4.9
Addis Ababa	976,870	3.4	151,859	16.4
Totals	28,777,670	100.0	923,827	100.0

SOURCE: *Ethiopia: Statistical Abstract, 1975* (Addis Ababa: Central Statistical Office, 1975), 217.

As in the provision of economic opportunities, educational opportunities tended to be heavily biased toward the center and toward the Amhara ethnic group. While accounting for only 3.4 percent of the total population, Addis Ababa possessed over 16 percent of the primary and secondary schools in the country by the end of 1972. (See Table 5.1.) More than 40 percent of the student population was concentrated in the predominantly Amhara provinces of Shoa, Begemdir, Gojjam, and Addis Ababa, although these areas accounted for only 28 percent of the total population.

Ethnic and regional inequalities are most noticeable when education beyond the primary level is considered. Both Markakis and P. T. W. Baxter note that even where there were schools in the south, above the elementary level they tended to be filled with the sons and daughters of northern settlers, soldiers, and bureaucrats who resided in the towns and *ketemas* of the periphery.[25] In 1972 there were only sixty-one secondary schools in the entire country. Twenty-five were in Shoa Province, including Addis Ababa. The pattern of Amhara dominance carried over to the university level. In 1966, for example, Amharas accounted for 55 percent of the first-year class at Haile Sellassie I University.[26]

Other problems related to education included teacher placement, teacher nationality, and the language of instruction. The best teachers tended to be concentrated in Amhara areas and Eritrea. This tendency contributed further to the economic disadvantages of certain ethnic groups from peripheral areas. With regard to the nationality of teachers, until just before the Revolution a large proportion of Ethiopia's teachers, particularly at the secondary level, were foreigners, mainly Indians and American Peace Corps volunteers, accounting for almost 70 percent of all teachers at that level in 1970.[27] This foreign influence was the cause of considerable unrest among students throughout the 1960s. Also the source of marked resentment in peripheral areas was that students were forced to learn in languages other than their own. Primary education was taught in the Amharic language, and secondary and university education in English. This policy was despised by such groups as the Oromo, Somali, and Eritreans, not only because it disadvantaged them in the competition for university places, but also because of the implications it had for the destruction of their own languages and cultures. In many cases, then, rather than education serving as an agent of national integration, it contributed to the alienation of ethnic minorities from the Ethiopian state.

The pattern of neglect and inequalities in peripheral areas exhibited in the educational sector could also be found in the health care area. As late as 1970, for example, a full 80 percent of Ethiopia's population did not have access to modern medical services, although the government had expressed a commitment to improving its capacity in this area. Between 1947 and 1972, the number of hospitals in the country only grew from thirty-eight to eighty-five. While the number of doctors grew by over 200 percent, nurses by 1,000 percent, and health assistants by almost 700 percent during this period, Ethiopia's medical system was still far below the level needed to address health care demands. Although disease was widespread in Ethiopia at the time of the 1974 coup, it was estimated that 75 percent of all reported cases were preventable.[28] The government was guilty of placing a very low priority on preventive medicine and thus allocated very little money or manpower for such purposes. Certain diseases (smallpox and malaria) received special attention but mainly because of the availability of external development funds for such purposes.

As with education, the best and largest number of health care services were clustered in Addis Ababa and other urban areas. By the end of 1973, there were only eighty-five hospitals in the entire country (see Table 5.2); twenty-five were in Shoa Province, and more than half that number were in Addis Ababa. If we add the hospitals in Eritrea and Hararge, which include the second and third largest areas respectively, we can account for 60 percent of all hospitals in the country. Significantly, the six southern provinces of Bale, Arussi, Gemu-Gofa, Illubabor, Kaffa, and Sidamo contained only 9 percent of the hospitals available in 1973, although they accounted for more than one-fourth of the country's total population. What is even more striking is the disparity in the population/doctor ratio. Whereas the ratio in 1973 in Addis Ababa was about 5,800:1, and 30,000:1 in Eritrea, the ratio in Illubabor was 80,000:1; 127,500:1 in Arussi; 365,400:1

TABLE 5.2

Distribution of Health Services by Province, 1973–74

Province	Total Population	Percent of Population	Hospitals	Beds	Clinics	Doctors	Pharmacists	Nurses
Arussi	892,700	3.1	3	130	27	7		33
Bale	739,600	2.5	1	23	14	1		13
Begemdir	1,418,700	4.9	2	217	33	14		37
Eritrea	2,070,100	7.1	17	2,240	117	69	23	158
Gemu-Gofa	730,700	2.5	2	73	21	2		18
Gojjam	1,829,600	6.3	3	232	37	13		34
Hararge	3,510,000	12.1	10	855	55	28		58
Illubabor	719,400	2.4	2	70	15	9		22
Kaffa	1,768,700	6.1	3	227	24	9		36
Shoa	5,712,100	19.8	12	533	81	19		93
Sidamo	2,595,600	9.0	5	417	47	9		53
Tigre	1,916,600	6.7	4	243	41	9	1	43
Wollega	1,326,800	4.6	4	285	37	10		50
Wollo	2,570,200	8.9	4	206	40	8	1	31
Addis Ababa	976,870	3.4	13	2,664	60	167	87	483
Totals	28,777,670	100.0	85	8,415	649	374	112	1,162

SOURCE: *Ethiopia: Statistical Abstract, 1975* (Addis Ababa: Central Statistical Office, 1975), 237–38.

in Gemu-Gofa; 288,400:1 in Sidamo; 196,500:1 in Kaffa; and 739,600:1 in Bale.

Part of Ethiopia's health care system's problems under Haile Selassie was its lack of qualified indigenous personnel. In 1970, for example, only 16 percent of the 350 doctors in the country were Ethiopians. In the 1950s the government did embark on programs designed to expand the pool of medical service personnel, but as late as 1972, only 48 doctors, 917 nurses, and 51 pharmacists had been trained locally.[29] This slow rate of growth in the training of local medical personnel and the concentration of services served to generate discontent among certain groups as demands for modern health care far outstripped the capacity or the desire of the government to expand and to distribute more equitably health care.

Land, Agricultural Policy, and the Sharpening of Class Contradictions

From the discussion of agricultural and land policy in the foregoing chapter, it would seem that social conditions in the immediate postwar period in Ethiopia favored the emergence of class antagonisms. In reality, however, this did not occur, mainly because of the dominance of national divisions. The Amhara and, to a certain extent, Tigres and Amharized ethnics were seen as "ethnic chauvinists" or "colonialist oppressors," and this, more than class, tended to shape the political consciousness of oppressed groups until the very dawn of the Revolution.[30] This is not to say that classes did not exist or were not important. In fact, the class composition of Ethiopian society experienced dramatic and significant change during the reign of Haile Salassie as feudalism and nascent capitalism coexisted in time and space. Moreover, for a short period, feudalism nurtured capitalist development. The pace of capitalist penetration quickened in the 1960s, generating a rapid sharpening of class contradictions in both cities and the countryside. Although I have touched on this process above, in this section I would like to speak more directly about class formation in rural areas between 1960 and 1974. This is important because it focuses attention on the role played by emerging rural class formations in setting the stage for the ouster of the Haile Selassie regime. Peasants were not necessarily moved by righteous indignation to storm the gates of the Grand Palace and seize the reigns of power. However, the relentless worsening of the peasant condition greatly stimulated the revolutionary cause. Here, I address more specifically the character of class relations that grew out of Haile Selassie's rural development strategy just prior to the Revolution. In the next section, I discuss the character and significance of urban class formation.

The mere "fact of conquest" in the south in the late 1800s and early 1900s began the process of modern class formation in Ethiopia even as it laid the foundation for a politicization of the national question.[31] Land in conquered areas was usurped by the state, and those who occupied it were made tribute payers. At first, this process simply made the feudal nature of society more pronounced. The agents of the state, who were mainly Amhara, Tigre, or Amharized Oromo bureaucrats in the service of the Crown, or *neftegñyas* of similar origin who manned garrisons in peripheral areas, became the landlord class in the south. This landed class was differentiated and included multiple levels of elites that could be grouped by the amount of land and the number of tribute payers they controlled. Initially, the private ownership of land was not widespread in the north or the south. The *gult* system gave individuals control over *gabbars,* thus enabling them to command fixed amounts of the surplus production of peasant families. Until the abolition of the *gult* system, it is safe to say that even though in some cases the tribute peasants were required to remit to the *gulteñya* might seem excessive to the outside observer, there were unwritten laws at work—a moral economy, if you will—that set the parameters governing the proper relationship between *gabbar* and *gulteñya*.[32] Each had a sense of what was fair and what was exploitative. As long as traditional structures and patterns of relationships remained relatively predictable, there was no cause for righteous indignation on the part of the peasantry.

Postwar economic reforms affecting the rural areas, however, caused instability in traditional society. Haile Selassie had on several occasions tried to break down the power of the traditional authority system in the north as well as the power of the feudalistic classes of a more recent vintage in the south. On each occasion he had failed to secure a complete victory. Nevertheless, he continued to pursue his plans for modernizing the economy. The fact that he could not completely subdue or eliminate the old landed classes forced him to attempt to undermine them by creating a new class of landed gentry. Rather than facilitating the implementation of his grand design, the emperor's political and economic policies were contradictory and caused problems of unmanageable proportions.

On the face of it, Haile Selassie's rural development policy throughout the 1950s and 1960s seemed to have something for everyone. For the peasantry it held out hopes for land reform, and the abolition of the *gult* system was intended to alleviate substantially the demand of the state and its local agents on increasing amounts of the surplus produce of peasants. In addition, a law offered landless and unemployed people the opportunity to petition the government for land grants up to 20 hectares. Few of the neediest people in society, however, knew about this policy or were sophisticated enough to negotiate the bureaucratic obstacles that impeded claiming such land. The "green revolution" and "package programs" were also intended to signal the government's resolve to uplift the peasantry. Even though these schemes were still at the experimental stage, by 1974 the long-range objective was to spread the benefits of such projects to the majority of Ethiopia's poor peasant communities, particularly where tractor cultivation was possible.

All of the measures in Haile Selassie's rural development strategy required significant involvement by the state for promotion and implementation. For the most part, such support was not forthcoming. The emperor solicited aid from such donors as the Swedish government and the World Bank, which had developed schemes like the Chilalo Agricultural Development Unit (CADU) and the Wolaita Agricultural Development Unit (WADU), on the promise that land reform would be forthcoming, but as late as 1972, no meaningful progress had been made in this direction. When the Swedes considered withdrawing support for the second phase of the CADU scheme, the emperor pleaded with them to understand that his own good intentions were being forestalled by a noncompliant parliament. Ultimately, in spite of the slow progress toward land reform, Swedish support for the project continued, as did the aid from other donors for similar projects.[33]

To be sure, resistance from the old landed classes was a serious obstacle to any efforts by the state to alter significantly the peasant condition. There are those, however, who argue that land reform was less important than the need to develop transportation infrastructure and the enforcement of laws stripping the landed classes of their *gult* privileges.[34] Given the fact that the land tenure systems in the north and south were substantially different, it seems logical that even this strategy would only have exacerbated regional, if not class, inequalities. Needless to say, this approach was never tried; thus the issue is moot.

In contrast to the peasantry, the politico-administrative classes created by the expansion and centralization of the state benefited immensely from Haile Selassie's land grant and rural development policies. Grants of government land had always been an important flexible resource at the disposal of Ethiopian monarchs. With the drive toward centralization and modernization between 1961 and 1971, however, this practice accelerated. Land grants were seen as a way of winning political support among the new and increasingly entrepreneurial classes while at the same time promoting the commercialization of agriculture. Between 1941 and 1960, imperial land grants averaged between 60,000 and 70,000 hectares per year; between 1960 and 1974, the annual average was almost 175,000 hectares.[35] The reasons for this trend, it must be noted, were more political than developmental. In economic terms the policy was irrational for many reasons.

Grantees were often given land well in excess of their capacity to develop it. This practice was particularly detrimental in such areas as Arussi where land was concentrated in the hands of wealthy individuals hoping to cash in on the availability of "green revolution" technology. Thus they were able to compete at an advantage against poor peasants for land as well as farm inputs.

In some cases land was granted without regard for those who currently occupied it. New landowners simply arrived on the scene, without warning, with tractors and surveyors, and evicted the occupants. Rather than being resettled in a systematic, humane way, peasants were left to fend for themselves. Leases or deeds were uncommon, thus leaving the peasantry helpless in the face of an alliance between the state and the new gentry.

There were signs that the old landed classes were not monolithic in their opposition to rural modernization and support for feudalism. In a study conducted in the late 1960s, John W. Cohen found that more than 30 percent of traditional landholding elites in Arussi Province said they would remove tenants and mechanize their production if they could be sure of more profits.[36] This seems to indicate that traditional relationships between lord and peasants were beginning to weaken. By 1972, in the CADU area alone, more than five thousand peasant families had been evicted.

The transition to freehold tenure, coupled with the government's land grant policy and its emphasis on the mechanization of agriculture, all served to destabilize traditional social systems in both the north and the south, since communal tenure practices remained relatively intact even after the abolition of the *gult* system. To the extent that a tenant class did

TABLE 5.3

Distribution of Total Cultivated Area between Owners and Tenants in Private Tenure and Communal Areas (1963–67) by Percentage[a]

Province	Private Tenure Areas		
	Owned	Rented	Partially Owned/ Rented
Arussi	38	51	11
Gemu-Gofa	48	46	6
Hararge	39	46	15
Illubabor	34	62	4
Kaffa	29	67	4
Shoa	28	55	17
Sidamo	64	35	1
Wollega	46	49	5
Wollo	61	14	25

	Communal Tenure Areas		
	Private or Communally Owned	Rented	Partially Owned/ Rented
Begemdir	85	9	6
Gojjam	80	13	7
Tigre	75	7	18

SOURCE: John M. Cohen and Dov Weintraub, *Land and Peasants in Imperial Ethiopia* (The Hague: Van Gorcum, 1975), 52.
[a] Eritrea is not included.

exist there, it comprised mainly religious and ethnic minorities. In the south, Haile Selassie's liberal land grant and commercialization policies led to a dramatic increase in both tenancy and absentee landlordism. Whereas even under the *gult* system the tenure of southern peasants was relatively stable and secure, amid the rush to acquire state land and to commercialize agriculture, peasant insecurity became a fact of life. By 1974 one out of every two farm families in the southern provinces were tenants who occupied well under one-half of all cultivated land.[37] (See Table 5.3.) In contrast to the total tenant/population ratio in the northern provinces of Begemdir, Gojjam, and Tigre, where it averaged 1:5, the ratio in the south was often more than 3:2.

Northerners, both peasants and elites, had always resented the centralizing efforts of the Crown, but they had acquiesced in a system that allowed the traditional land tenure system to survive. However, with the drive toward modernization and the introduction of the concepts of "private ownership of land" and "capitalist agricultural development," the traditional system was severely challenged. In response, traditionalists, as they had always done, resisted the efforts of outsiders to change their way of life. Although some gains were made by the state and other modernist forces in the north in reforming the northern system of production, these efforts were as much the source of resentment as they were of readily accepted change. The state and its agents came to be seen as enemies of local culture and values, and elites and peasants alike were often locked in conflict with these forces. However, it seems safe to say that in rural areas of the north, the process of class formation organized around a capitalist mode of production was not so well developed as in the south. The homogenizing effects of a common culture, religion, and ethnic heritage, in conjunction with the lack of progress in dismantling the communal land tenure system, all served to inhibit the process of capitalist class formation.

In the south, not only were classes formed during this period, but they multiplied and became more differentiated. With the abolition of the *gult* system and the privatization of land, *gabbars* were transformed into landless peasants, tenants, sharecroppers, and poor peasants with subproductive landholdings. *Balabats,* low-ranking soldiers, and bureaucrats lost their *gulteñya* status and became poor and middle peasants. Consequently, they now had to hire labor to help work their land. High-ranking officials in the police, military, or central bureaucracy became middle-sized to rich landowners who began to produce more and more for the market with the aid of hired wage laborers or sharecroppers—and tractors.[38]

The social distance between the landlord class and the tenant class grew wider as Haile Selassie's political and economic policies came to overlap, giving rise to a sharpening of contradictions. Southern peasants had never liked their colonizers for the most part, but with the changes of the 1960s and early 1970s, ethnic and class antagonisms began to blossom as never before. Amharas, along with Christian Tigreans and local *balabats,* represented not only a dominant culture in the political sense for the people of the south, but also now an increasingly exploitative and insecure economic system.

By the time of the revolution class contradictions had not yet led to a widespread sense of class consciousness among the southern peasantry. Feelings of nationalism, as we shall see below, were more common but still not of sufficient scope or intensity to challenge the hegemony of central authorities.

Industrialization, Class Formation, and Social Contradictions

The increased emphasis on the development of the industrial sector and the central bureaucracy after 1960 led to an expansion of new urban classes. These classes were comprised of the young educated elite, most of whom were readily absorbed into the burgeoning central bureaucracy, and a small, relatively ununified working class. Included in the former class were teachers who staffed formal educational institutions at all levels, and in the latter group rural wage laborers on plantations.

To an extent, employees of the central bureaucracy and white-collar workers in the private sector could be considered a "labor aristocracy." They tended to command much higher salaries than the average industrial worker. White-collar workers in administrative and technical positions earned salaries ranging from E$450 to E$1,000 per month. This contrasted sharply with the salaries of clerical employees of the state who received from E$40 to E$375 per month, and custodial and menial workers employed by the state who earned from E$30 to E$125 per month. Even more striking was the contrast between the earning potential of skilled, semi-skilled, and unskilled government workers and that of nongovernment workers in the modern sector and in capitalized agricultural enterprises. As late as 1970 skilled factory laborers earned a meager E$50 to E$80 per month. Semiskilled laborers averaged E$40 per month, and unskilled day laborers E$1 to E$5 a day. In the case of wage laborers in the rural sectors, the record was even more dismal. In coffee-growing areas, for example, wage laborers received only E$0.75 per day, but even this was high when compared to the plight of agricultural workers involved in harvesting sugar cane, cotton, and tomatoes, or in the timber industry. In these cases the average daily wage ranged from E$0.30 to E$0.70.[39] The disparity in wages and conditions of service tended to inhibit the possibility of a unified movement involving all the working classes in the modern sector. Just as important, however, was the government's prohibition on any form of union activity until 1962. Even when this ban was lifted, the change benefited only nongovernment employees. Government employees were forbidden to strike, and it was not until the early 1970s that some of them, namely teachers, began to protest about salaries and working conditions.

The growth in the industrial working class over the 1960s was dramatic. In 1957 it was estimated that the total number of Ethiopian workers in the industrial sector was 15,583; by 1970 this figure had jumped to about 60,000.[40] To the latter figure must be added 100,000 in the building and construction industry; 30,000 in transportation and communications; and 2,500 in electrical power.[41] In all sectors, however, most employees were unskilled laborers with little or no education and only tenuous urban roots.

Despite the fact that wages tended to be low and relatively static throughout the period of Ethiopia's drive to modernize its economy, an organized labor movement was slow to develop. In part, this was due to the fact that the government viewed any type of organized protest as a form of insurrection. When the Railroad Workers' Syndicate of Dire Dawa tried to strike in 1949, for example, it was brutally suppressed by government troops.[42] Strikes of this kind were uncommon even for the Railroad Workers' Syndicate. Like other such organizations that existed in the Ethiopian core prior to 1962, it was primarily a self-help association that generally cooperated with, rather than opposed, the government. To the extent that there was a labor movement at this time, it was amorphous, consisting of several mutual aid associations that generally functioned as autonomous units at the factory level. There were attempts to organize genuine trade unions, but prior to the abortive coup of 1960, the emperor kept such efforts in check either with legal restrictions or by force.

Given the small size and precariousness of Ethiopia's industrial sector at this time, it is understandable why Haile Selassie refused to tolerate organized labor. If the state was to protect its own interests and the interests of foreign capital in the emerging industrial sector, it had to be able to rely on cheap, docile labor.

In the wake of the 1960 coup, the demand for an officially recognized labor movement intensified. Workers' associations were successful in securing the support of progressive elements in the "new nobility" and some of their expatriate advisers. Buoyed by this in 1961 and 1962, workers' associations in Addis Ababa began to press openly for legislation legitimizing labor unions and their activities. These efforts reached fruition in the summer of 1962 with the enactment of the Labor Relations Decree of 1962.[43] This act gave workers the right to organize and to engage in collective bargaining. The government, however, retained ultimate powers in registering labor organizations, monitoring their activities, and settling labor disputes. A Labor Department was set up within the Ministry of Commerce and charged with registering and supervising the activities of labor groups. The Labor Relations Board (LRB) was made responsible for the conciliation and arbitration of all labor disputes. Its decisions were legally binding except for limited rights of appeal to the Supreme Court.[44] Labor unions now had the right to strike after observing a sixty-day moratorium during which the LRB considered the merits of the case. If no satisfactory resolution of the dispute materialized, striking was a legitimate alternative.

Within a year of the promulgation of the Labor Relations Decree, the formation of the Confederation of Ethiopian Labor Unions (CELU) was announced. This was an umbrella organization representing some twenty-two former self-help clubs of industrial laborers. By 1973 there were 167 affiliates with eighty thousand members. This figure represented only about 30 pecent of all eligible workers.[45]

CELU never developed into a national federation of unions. It continued to be simply an affiliation of labor groups organized at the plant level. There was some coordination of union activities through CELU's regional offices, but even by 1974 there was no cohesive, disciplined national labor movement. In addition, despite legislation legitimizing unions and their activities, both management and government treated them with contempt. The government was slow to revise archaic labor laws such as those that dealt with child labor and the minimum wage. Union leaders were harassed, and when unions threatened to strike, they were "locked out."[46]

The labor movement was constantly beset by internal organizational problems. Leaders tended to come from elite class backgrounds rather than worker or peasant backgrounds. This sometimes blinded them to the problems the rank and file felt were most important. There were also divisions of some consequences within the rank and file. A significant proportion of the membership were white-collar workers whose problems were different from those of unskilled laborers. They comprised a labor aristocracy motivated mainly by job-related concerns. They viewed union activities as being especially for *their* benefit. The Ottaways suggest that this largely explains why CELU never seriously pressed for minimum wage legislation.[47] Another factor explaining white-collar workers' economism is their privileged position in the society's wage structure. The wide disparity in wages between white-collar workers and others in the working class has already been discussed above.

Other persistent organizational problems included corruption, embezzlement, election fraud, ethnic and regional discrimination, and insufficient finances. Seleshi Sisaye indicates that less than 40 percent of CELU's regular members paid dues. Annual revenues from dues averaged less than US$3,000. This forced CELU to rely on contributions from such international labor organizations as the International Confederation of Free Trade Unions, the All-African Labor Congress, and the International Labor Organization to finance its operations.[48]

Although CELU was involved in several labor protests and strikes over the first ten years of its existence, it was never able to present a serious militant challenge to the status quo in the industrial sector. This was due partly to the obstacles presented by government and management opposition, partly to the union's own organizational problems, and partly to the economic crisis that ensued for unskilled labor as the industrial sector became more and more capital intensive but its absorptive capacity expanded at a much slower rate than the availability of unskilled labor.[49] Wages remained low, while inflation ate away at the buying power of workers at all levels. Rather than markedly improving, in real terms the plight of workers appeared to worsen after the 1962 labor reform.

The economic crisis became acute beginning in 1972, when the effects of drought and food shortages began to take their inevitable toll. From this point on, workers became more politicized and militant. In response, the government stepped up its war against organized labor in defense of management, crushing protests with brutal measures. By 1974 white-collar and unskilled laborers had reached an instrumental meeting of the minds and joined in mass protest, exposing the faltering imperial regime's inability to manage ever-increasing contradictions. The significance of these developments will be discussed further in the next chapter.

The State and the National Question

In addition to contributing to the formation of new social classes and relationships, the sociopolitical policies of Haile Selassie sowed the seeds of ethnic conflict. In part, this could be attributed to the fact that the emperor had no policy of national political integration except for the selective incorporation of ethnic elites into the ruling class through Amharization. This policy promoted the Amhara culture and Orthodox Christianity and denigrated all other cultures and religions. Whatever social benefit was dispensed in non-Amhara regions was aimed at bolstering the agents of the state in those regions as well as various Amhara-Tigre settlers and *balabats*. The net effects of such practices were the development of deep-seated resentment for the dominant culture and the state among subordinate groups and the emergence among them of a sense of their individual national consciousness within the context of the Ethiopian Empire.[50] These tendencies were most pronounced among the Eritreans, Ogaden Somalis, and certain elements of the numerically superior Oromo group. Other groups harbored similar attitudes, but these groups were particularly significant because of their sustained efforts to resist Amhara dominance and because ultimately they formed themselves into nationally based military organizations in opposition to the centralizing efforts of the state. The remainder of this chapter will assess the factors that led to the politicization of the national question among the Eritreans, Ogaden Somalis, and Oromos, as well as the development of nationalist movements in each of these groups.

Eritrea: Late Colonialism

Both Menelik and Haile Selassie attempted to establish the legitimacy of Ethiopia's claim to Eritrea in the international community. Menelik conceded Italian hegemony over the region as a matter of convenience in the late 1800s. Any efforts to hold the territory would have been costly in military terms and would almost certainly have jeopardized the security of the highland core as well as the newly incorporated areas to the south and east. With the defeat of the Italian Fascists in World War II, Haile Selassie sought to secure international support for the unification of Eritrea and Ethiopia.

The official claim that ties between Ethiopia and Eritrea go back to antiquity, however, was disputed by Eritrean nationalists who asserted that most of what was considered the Italian colony of Eritrea had never been firmly under modern-day Ethiopian control.[51] They argue that, although Eritrea was part of the ancient Aksumite Empire, no territorial connection had existed between Eritrea and the Ethiopian core since that time. Furthermore, they argue, almost all of Eritrea was independent or subject only to tribute payment to non-Ethiopian empires (i.e., the Funj, the Ottomans, the Egyptians) after the fall of Aksum.[52]

The Italian defeat at Adowa at the hands of Menelik's forces in 1896, and the subsequent signing of the Treaty of Addis Ababa, clearly established the boundaries of the colony of Eritrea. Significantly, the colony included territory in the highlands as well as the lowlands. From this point on, the Italians set about building Eritrea into a viable economic entity that could serve the interests of the Italian metropole. Italian settlers were encouraged to settle in the colony and to develop its agricultural and industrial capacity. As a matter of administrative convenience, the colony was divided into governmental units based on ethnic considerations. Some indigenous people were educated and groomed for administrative service, but this was not a common practice. Few Africans were encouraged to go beyond a minimal education. Many, however, were forced into proletarian status as a result of the need for a ready supply of cheap labor in new industries and commercial agricultural enterprises.

By the 1930s Italy was ruled by the Fascist dictator Benito Mussolini, who considered avenging the humiliating defeat of the Italians at Adowa as his sacred duty along with civilizing the Abyssinians. His troops succeeded in conquering Ethiopia in 1936, driving the emperor into exile. This was a brief period of control, however, as the Italians were routed in 1941 by British-led Commonwealth forces along with what Harold G. Marcus describes as "a ragtag force of Ethiopian exiles, European misfits and eccentrics, and the dross of the Sudanese Army [and] strong guerrilla forces [already operating in occupied Ethiopia]."[53] The emperor was reinstalled, but the British maintained administrative control over Eritrea and other territory in the region that had been occupied by the Italians, and over the controversial Haud and Ogaden.

The British had tried to enlist the support of the Eritreans against the Fascists even before World War II. They pledged to push for Eritrean self-determination if the Eritreans would turn against their colonial masters. During the Fascist occupation of the Horn, the British further raised hopes for a changed situation by bombarding the region with leaflets that appeared to support self-determination for Eritrea.[54] Once the fighting was over, it was quickly apparent that Eritrean self-determination was not a foregone conclusion.

At the Paris Peace Conference between 1946 and 1947, a formula was worked out for the disposal of former Italian colonies in Africa. Italy renounced all rights and title to Italian Somaliland, Libya, and Eritrea, and the Big Four (France, Britain, the United States, and the Soviet Union) accepted the responsibility for determining the ultimate fate of these territories. If the matter was not settled within a year of the peace treaty, the problem would be referred to the UN General Assembly for a binding resolution. Subsequently, the Big Four appointed the Four Power Commission that journeyed to Eritrea to study the situation in September 1947. The commission proved to be ineffective, as members could not work together. It was unable to resolve the Eritrean issue and referred the matter to the UN General Assembly on September 15, 1948. The Assembly set up its own Eritrean study commission made up of Burma, Guatemala, Norway, Pakistan, and South Africa.

On June 28, 1949, the UN commission submitted its findings. The majority (Burma, Norway, and South Africa) supported some sort of union between Ethiopia and Eritrea. Norway called for unconditional union, while South Africa and Burma advocated federation. Guatemala and Pakistan favored Eritrean independence preceded by a ten-year period of direct United Nations trusteeship.[55] Italy, supported by eight other states including the Soviet Union, lobbied in the UN for immediate and total independence. The United States and its allies, however, pressed for a federal solution, and this was finally agreed on.

The terms of this federation were sketched in UN Resolution 390A(V) passed on December 2, 1950. The resolution called for an autonomous Eritrean government consisting of legislative, judicial, and executive branches. This government was to have responsibility over domestic affairs; foreign affairs, external trade, defense, communications, and currency were deemed in the "federal" (Ethiopian) domain. An Imperial Federal Council composed of equal numbers of Ethiopian and Eritrean representatives was to govern and supervise the drawing up of a constitution during a transitional period not to last beyond September 15, 1952.[56] Significantly, there was no provision for the drafting of a genuinely federal constitution.

Eritrean political organizations on one side of the issue or the other emerged as early as 1944. The Unionist party, for example, came into existence in that year. It claimed that Eritrea had been "stolen" from Ethiopia and should be returned at once. The Muslim League and several smaller Islamic parties favoring independence appeared between 1946 and 1947; and in early 1948 the Liberal Progressive party, a predominantly Christian group, was established. By 1949 splinter groups from each of these initial parties joined together to form the independence-minded Independence Bloc.[57] Over the next two years, there was further fragmentation among Eritrean political organizations, and by 1952 only three were formidable enough to command significant support: the Unionist Bloc, comprised mainly of Christian Eritreans; the Democratic party, which had formally been the Independence Bloc and which was mostly Christian with some Muslim members; and the Muslim League of the Western Province.

These groups engaged in a vigorous campaign to see who would dominate the legislative assembly. Sixty-eight seats were being contested in the election that took place in March 1952. The Unionists won thirty-two seats, the Democratic party eighteen, and the Muslim League fifteen. Three seats went to splinter groups.[58] Subsequently, a ruling coalition emerged involving the Unionists and the Muslim League. On the assumption that Eritrean autonomy was protected, the new Assembly ratified the new constitution. In addition to having the authority to govern themselves, the Eritreans were allowed to fly their own flag and to retain Tigrinya and Arabic as their national languages, rather than Amharic.

Throughout the constitutional discussions, Haile Selassie had vigorously lobbied to ensure that Unionists he could influence would secure the most important positions in the new government. Those efforts continued throughout the period of federation. This facilitated the emperor's efforts to undermine and erode Eritrean autonomy.

The systematic destruction of the federal relationship was subtle but calculated. Haile Selassie smashed autonomous institutions and instituted policies that pulled Eritrea closer and closer into the central orbit. Among his first moves in this direction was to force some Eritrean industries to close down or to move their operations to Addis Ababa.[59]

The year 1952 was a watershed, not only because it marked the beginning of federation, but also because it was the year in which the Eritrean constitution was suspended. A year later all trade unions were banned, and four years later political parties were banned and the National Assembly "temporarily" suspended. Simultaneously, the Haile Selassie regime replaced Arabic and Tigrinya as the languages of instruction in schools with Amharic. In 1958 the Ethiopianization of Eritrea went one step further when a blatantly unrepresentative assembly voted to eliminate the requirement that both the Eritrean and Ethiopian flags fly in public places, opting for only the latter. The next year, the Eritrean code of laws was voted out of existence and replaced by the Ethiopian code. The final act in the *de facto* dissolution of the federation occured in 1960 when the Assembly voted to change the name of the government from the Eritrean Government to the Eritrean Administration.[60] By this act, the formal annexation of Eritrea by Ethiopia in 1962 was rendered anticlimactic.

There is some question as to whether the Assembly was coerced into accepting the dissolution of the federation. What is clear is that Haile Selassie used a combination of political skill and coercion to effect his claim over Eritrea and to incorporate it as the last colony in the modern Ethiopian Empire.[61]

On November 14, 1962, under duress, the Eritrean Assembly voted overwhelmingly to make Eritrea Ethiopia's fourteenth province. Tesfatsion Medhanie notes:

> From November 13, the Ethiopian army displayed a show of force in Asmara. Thousands of soldiers encircled the city. Others marched through the streets with tanks and ammunition declaring in war chants, "kill anyone who does not comply with our wishes."[62]

At the morning session of the Assembly on November 14, 1962, Asfaha Woldemichael, the chief administrator of Eritrea, read a statement requesting the members to pass a resolution dissolving the federation and uniting Eritrea with "motherland Ethiopia." Outside, an armed detachment of soldiers stood ready if necessary to use force to impose the emperor's mandate. Although some members of the Assembly opposed dissolution of the federation, eye witnesses confirm that a substantial majority supported the resolution, albeit meekly. Some Eritreans continue, however, to deny that such a vote took place. They argue that when Haile Selassie issued

Order No. 27 on November 15, 1962, and indicated that the Eritrean Assembly had "unanimously adopted" the resolution terminating the federation, he was merely seeking to legitimize what he had already independently decided to do.[63] Whether the vote took place or not seems less important than the fact of annexation. In either case, the act was illegal. If the vote of the assembly did take place, it violated the Federal Act, which prohibited it from jeopardizing Eritrea's autonomy. Armed with the fiction of a vote on the part of the Eritrean Assembly to abandon federation in favor of union with Ethiopia, the emperor could ward off criticism at home and abroad that he was an imperialist. The silence of the United Nations during these developments further conveyed an aura of legitimacy to what Haile Selassie had already effected.

Radical Eritrean opposition to the colonial incorporation of Eritrea into Ethiopia had begun as early as 1958 with the founding of the Eritrean Liberation Movement (ELM). This was an organization made up mainly of students, intellectuals, and urban wage laborers. The group engaged in clandestine political activities intended to cultivate resistance to the centralizing policies of the Haile Selassie regime. It collected money and published and disseminated literature directed at raising the sense of national consciousness among Eritreans. By 1962, however, the ELM had been discovered and destroyed by the authorities.[64] Like so many other radical, urban-based resistance movements, it was easy prey for the organized coercive power of the state.

Even as the ELM was being decimated, a new organization of Eritrean nationalists was coming into being. In 1960 the Eritrean Liberation Front (ELF) was founded in Cairo, Egypt, by exiles residing there. In contrast to the ELM, the ELF formed itself into an exile liberation army and began preparations for a protracted war of national liberation. The ELF comprised mainly, but not exclusively, Muslim Eritreans from the rural western, lowland border areas of the territory. At this time, the political character of the ELF was not clear, but radical Arab states such as Syria identified with Eritrea as a predominantly Muslim state attempting to escape from the colonialism of infidels.

The first several years of guerrilla activity inside Eritrea were characterized by poor preparation, poor leadership, and poor military performance. By 1967, however, the ELF had gained considerable support among peasants, particularly in the northern and western part of the territory around the port city of Massawa. Characteristically, Haile Selassie attempted to stem the tide of protest in the region by making a personal visit to reassure the Eritreans that they would be treated as equals under the new arrangements. He doled out offices, money, and titles in early 1967, hoping to buy off would-be elite opponents, but to no avail. The resistance only intensified.[65]

It is important to note that the Eritrean rebels' claim to national self-determination is not based on the assumed existence of a common national culture that can be traced to antiquity. The movement that developed at this time was multiethnic, involving individuals from Eritrea's nine major ethnic groups. It is suggested that the tie that binds these groups is a common history of colonial oppression within the territorial boundaries of Eritrea. The birth of the Eritrean "nation" can be traced only to the beginnings of Italian colonialism in the late nineteenth century.[66]

The most serious problem confronting the movement of national liberation from the very beginning was to develop a base of popular support and a cohesive military wing. The ELF divided Eritrea into five military regions, giving regional commanders a great deal of latitude in carrying out the struggle in their respective zones. The Haile Selassie regime, recognizing by 1967 that it was pitted against an increasingly sophisticated revolutionary movement with U. S. and Israeli assistance, unleashed a massive military offensive that not only devastated guerrilla units but also uprooted civilians, who fled as refugees to Sudan.

Internal disputes within the ELF over strategy and tactics led to its fragmentation and the founding of another independent movement, the Eritrean People's Liberation Front (EPLF), in 1970. Sporadic armed conflict ensued between the two groups even as they fought the Ethiopian forces. In 1976 Osman Saleh Sabbe, an Eritrean elder statesman who had indeed sent several of the younger, now independent leaders on training courses abroad, attempted to reconcile the two groups in order to form a united front. He was unable to do so, however, and resorted to forming a "third front," the Eritrean Liberation Front (ELF/PLF). Sabbe, a consummate diplomat who had been a member of the ELF, continued to secure considerable financial and military support from conservative Arab supporters such as Sudan, Egypt, Saudi Arabia, and the Gulf states.

Divisiveness among the various Eritrean resistance movements characterized their struggle throughout the 1970s and into the 1980s. Differences were partly but not exclusively ideological. At the time both the EPLF and the ELF could best be described in ideological terms as leftist-nationalist. The ELF/PLF was a moderate nationalist group. The EPLF and ELF/PLF have always demanded total independence for Eritrea. The ELF (now the ELF Central Command [CC]) has never closed the door to the possibility of an equitable federal union. As subtle as the differences among the groups appeared, they were enough to inhibit a sustained united front against Ethiopian forces throughout the 1960s. However, by 1971 the various Eritrean organizations by waging separate guerrilla campaigns had become such a serious threat that the emperor declared martial law in the region. Moreover, he was forced to deploy about half of his army to contain the struggle. In January 1974 the EPLF handed Haile Selassie's forces a crushing defeat, thus severely affecting morale within the army and exposing the ever-weakening position of the Crown.[67]

Ogaden: Nation versus State

The basis for Ogaden Somali resistance to Ethiopian colonization dates back to the incorporation of the region into the Ethiopian state between 1887 and 1955. As has been mentioned, Ethiopia secured recognition of its claims over the Ogaden through a series of treaties with Britain, France, and Italy. Until then, the area had never been under Ethiopian control except perhaps partially for brief periods during ancient wars of conquest. Even with the international recognition of its claim to the Ogaden, Ethiopia was only able to establish tenuous control over the territory. Military garrisons were posted in the few townships in this harsh desert territory; their main purpose was to maintain law and order and to protect Ethiopia's sometimes vaguely defined borders. They also bolstered the efforts of the state to collect cattle-head taxes from the nomads who inhabited the area. The full impact of Ethiopian colonialism in the region, however, was not evident until the late 1940s and early 1950s.

In contrast to Eritrean "nationhood," Somalis trace their origins as a "nation" to antiquity. Rather than being based merely on a common history of oppression, as is the case with the concept of an Eritrean "nation," Somalis in the Republic of Somalia, as well as Djibouti, Kenya's northeastern province, and Ethiopia's Ogaden all claim a common heritage. In addition, the Somali are bound together by language, religion, custom, and sociopolitical organization. Their nation was divided during the process of colonization among Ethiopia, Britain, France, and Italy.[68]

Modern Somali nationalism can be traced to the resistance led by Seyyid Mohammad Abdille Hassan, the so-called "Mad Mullah," against the forces of Menelik II, who attempted to establish control over the Ogaden in the 1890s. For twenty-one years, Mohammad Abdille Hassan fought the consolidation efforts of the claimants to Somali territory.[69] The myth of the "Somali nation," Islam, and the legend of Ahmed Guray and Mohammad Abdille Hassan all served to intensify the development of the modern idea of Somali nationalism.

The fires of nationalism among the Somalis were constantly stoked throughout the colonial period, not only by Somali nationalists but also by various colonial powers who through words and deeds seemed to legitimize the concept of "Greater Somalia." Mussolini, for example, saw "La Grande Somalia" as the "jewel" of Italian East Africa, thus justifying Italy's invasion of Ethiopia and the liberation of the Somalis.[70] During the British administrative period after World War II, British Foreign Secretary Ernest Bevin was authorized by the cabinet to present a plan for a unified Somali trust territory, but this move was dropped in the face of opposition at the Council of Ministers of the Four Power Commission. Bevin's plan was seen, particularly by the Russians, as a veil for British imperialism, and it aroused some domestic as well as international opposition.[71]

The Italian design was short-lived, as Italian East Africa was dismantled within five years of the defeat of Mussolini's troops by British Commonwealth and Ethiopian patriot forces. Rather than maintain Italian East Africa or revert to former arrangements, the British retained military administrative control over most of the Horn. Since the UN General

Assembly did not decide on the ten year United Nations trusteeship—awarded to Italy over intense Ethiopian protest—until 1949, a provisional military line suggested by the British on March 1, 1950, was to separate the territory from Ethiopia, pending a final settlement.[72]

Through diplomatic maneuvering at the United Nations, Ethiopia, with the support of the United States, was eventually able to have its claims over the Ogaden and the Haud accepted, and it formally retook control of these areas in 1948 and 1955, respectively. Somali resistance was immediate, and it mounted as Ethiopia attempted to reassert its authority by collecting taxes around Harar.[73] Effective occupation of the Ogaden by the Ethiopians thus did not occur until 1954–55.

Between 1954 and 1960, Haile Selassie made sporadic attempts to "integrate" subject Somalis into the empire. Urban administrative centers, schools, and hospitals were established to present the trappings of effective administration and allegedly to avail the Ogaden Somalis of the same opportunities as other Ethiopians. An effort was also made to absorb Somali elites gradually into the colonial administration. Nevertheless, resistance continued.

Attempting to consolidate control over the region and to establish his regime's legitimacy among the Ogaden Somalis, Haile Selassie journeyed to the region in August 1956 and delivered a speech intended to assure the Somalis that they were equal members, not of the "Somali nation" but of the "Ethiopian nation-state."[74] He pointed out all that his regime had done in the provision of social services and security for his Somali subjects and promised to do much more. These actions were justified on the basis of the fact that all Somalis were related to all Ethiopians by blood and custom. "We remind you," the emperor stated, "that all of you are by race, colour, blood, and custom, members of the Ethiopian family. Although there may be local dialects, we must always strive to preserve our unity and our freedom."[75]

As in the case of Eritrea, Haile Selassie considered that such a union was necessary not only on spiritual grounds, but also on practical grounds, as "Greater Somalia" was deemed to be an economically unpromising enterprise. This line of thinking was reiterated in an official press release in late 1963 that asserted, "Ethiopia will not part with one of her children because of any alleged linguistic, religious, or tribal affinity, nor will Ethiopia permit one single inch of Ethiopian soil to be separated from the motherland on such specious grounds."[76]

Despite token attempts to develop modern infrastructure in the Ogaden as in other regions, Haile Selassie equated Somali integration with nothing more than economic domination and Amharization. He encouraged interethnic marriages not so much to merge the two cultures, but to have the Somalis accept Ethiopian hegemony.

In 1960 former British Somaliland and Italian Somaliland achieved independence and were quickly united. From this point on, Somali nationalists, particularly through the many branch offices of the Somali Youth

League, began to press the "Greater Somalia" issue more seriously. A major border clash occurred in 1961, and a minor war in 1964. Both, however, resulted in Somali defeat. Even so, throughout the 1960s, Somali irredentists in the Ogaden, with the aid and council of their kinsmen in the Somali Republic, engaged the Ethiopians in guerrilla warfare in the Ogaden and in Borana and Bale.

The major impetus to militaristic irredentism in the Ogaden was the founding of the Western Somali Liberation Front (WSLF) in 1960. Headquartered in Mogadishu in independent Somalia, it consisted mainly of young Somali youth recruited in the Ogaden, as well as some Oromo who cohabit Bale and Borana with Ogaden Somalis. The aim of the movement was to separate Hararge, Arussi, Bale, and Galla Sidamo from Ethiopia. Once liberated, this area was to be joined with the Republic of Somalia.[77] The WSLF relied heavily on Somalia for military and logistical support until the October 1969 coup that brought Mohamed Siad Barre to power. At first, Siad Barre attempted to reverse his government's policies toward the WSLF, withdrawing military support and jailing several of its leaders. He preferred to modernize his own regular army with assistance from the Soviet Union, always keeping the goal of "Greater Somalia" clearly in sight. WSLF leaders retreated to Aden where they maintained an office in exile and attempted to pursue the guerrilla struggle from abroad. When Aden and Addis Ababa concluded a treaty of alliance in 1976, however, the WSLF was forced to turn to Somalia once again.[78] By this time Siad Barre was more receptive to a relationship between the WSLF and his government. The Ethiopian Revolution had entered a "reign of terror," as competing political groupings struggled to define Ethiopia's new social myth.[79] Several other groups within Ethiopia openly advocated a more "progressive" approach to the "nationalities question," especially with regard to the Eritrean ethnic problem, and the ensuing violence rendered Ethiopia vulnerable to significant, externally inspired change. Siad Barre attempted to take advantage of the opportunity, a point that will be discussed later.

Oromo: From Rebellion to Revolution

The Oromo people are the single largest ethnic group in Ethiopia, numbering somewhere between sixteen and twenty-two million. They are disproportionately represented in the southern areas that were the object of the colonial expansion of the Ethiopian empire in the middle and late nineteenth century.

The Oromo and Amhara have a long history of contact. Intermarriage and assimilation, especially among elite groups, were not uncommon. However, according to the Oromo, beginning with the reign of Emperor Tewodros, there was a systematic effort to destroy Oromo culture and social institutions and to establish the dominance of Amhara culture once and for all.[80]

Prior to this time, the Oromo had existed in relative autonomy as a loose

TABLE 5.4

Organization of *Gada* **among the Oromo according to Number of Years in the System and Age of Individuals**

Level	Years in System	Age of Individuals
I. Iti Mako	0–8	8–16
II. Daballe	8–16	16–24
III. Folle	16–24	24–32
IV. Qondala	24–32	32–40
V. Luba	32–40	40–48

SOURCE: "Toward Understanding the *Gada* System," *Waldaansso*, 4 (1980), p. 11.

confederation of clans who shared a common language and culture and were believed to be the descendants of a common ancestor. There emerged among this pastoral people a unique administrative system known as *Gada*. This system is said to have formed the basis of the Oromo "nation."[81] *Gada* is often described as a classic example of a traditional African form of democratic government. Legislative, executive, and judicial functions were independent of one another but were integral components of a "nation-wide" bureaucracy. *Gada* is also claimed to have been a system through which the Oromo people secured spiritual direction.

The *Gada* was a generation-grade system based on a sequence of eight calendar year periods.[82] At any one time, there existed five *Gada* "parties" or generational groups. Once in the system, it took individuals forty years to complete the cycle. Every eight years, "party" members moved from one *Gada* level to the next until they completed service at the *Luba* level. (See Table 5.4.) The *Luba* were responsible for the actual governance of the Oromo people.

At each stage, *Gada* members were educated in Oromo history, military strategy, law, and governance. Every eight years, a nine-member presidium of the *Gada* party entering the *Luba* level was elected on the basis of adult male suffrage. After serving as leaders, individuals were retired but continued to act as advisers to ascendant leaders.

This system of government is thought to date as far back as five hundred years, but by the mid-nineteenth century it had begun to break down.[83] Some suggest that the system had simply become outmoded, but there are several more plausible explanations for the demise of *Gada* as a viable institution, including the replacement of pastoralism by sedentary agriculture, the replacement of traditional religions with Islam or Christianity, and prohibitions imposed by the colonizing Amharas. I would suggest that all of these factors are interrelated. They all are by-products of the Ethiopian colonial penetration of the Oromo heartland. As a result of colonialism and its requirements, the nomadic practices of the Oromo were curbed, and they were increasingly encouraged to engage in peasant agriculture. Rather than conserving the surplus of their production for use exclusively within their own communities, they were required to share their produce with alien feudal landlords and local operatives of the state. In some cases they were forced to adopt the Christian religion; in others they turned to Islam often as a reaction to the culture of their oppressors. The vast majority of the Oromo came to see the Amhara and the state they represented as colonialists, bent on exploiting them and stripping them of their culture.

Haile Selassie maintained a policy of attempting to secure Oromo fealty through the development of alliances with certain Oromo leaders. The most favored among the Oromo were those who chose to become totally assimilated or Amharized, often adopting Christian names. Historically, the Wollega and Shoan Oromos were the most receptive to this approach, but as Haile Selassie became more concerned with firming up the boundaries of the modern state and its bureaucratic authority in the periphery, other Oromo were assimilated. From the Ethiopian perspective, at least, the Oromos were fortunate when compared to the Nilotic or Negro groups in the southwest. Oromos were viewed as pagans or as Muslims and thus legitimate objects of Amhara exploitation, and indeed they were often taken as slaves. Yet they were also seen as civilizable, capable of being Amharized. Nilots and Negroes, on the other hand, were viewed as *Shakilla,* a pariah group whose only fate in life was forever to remain as "baria" or slaves.[84]

There was hope that Oromos could become "first-class" citizens in Ethiopian society, but only if they succumbed to pressures for their "cultural suicide" and to the dominance of the Amhara over non-Amharized people in all aspects of life. The destruction of Oromo culture, as that of other non-Amhara groups, was systematic. Oromo culture was degraded. It was illegal to write, preach, or broadcast in any Oromo dialect.[85] In elementary school the language of instruction was Amharic. At the upper levels English became the medium of instruction. Over the brief period of Italian occupation, the Oromo language was promoted, but on reassuming power, Haile Selassie again banned the Oromo language from public use. Traditional Oromo shrines were destroyed, and Christian churches were substituted. In sermons, pastors preached in Amharic, and interpreters translated their sermons into the local dialect. Traditional religious institutions continued to exist, but the effects of colonialism relegated them to nothing more than ritual status.

The state was represented by central bureaucrats in the field, *balabats,* and *neftegñyas.* The majority of the Oromo were viewed as mere subjects. They were regularly victims of corrupt bureaucrats and judges, all of whom invariably tended to be Christian northerners. In the distribution of scarce resources, Oromo needs were considered secondary to those of the dominant Amhara group as a matter of course, and as I demonstrated earlier in the chapter, they received proportionately less of the fruits of modernization.

The inferior status accorded Oromos and their culture must be considered along with the fact that Oromo areas were the backbone of the Ethiopian economy. These areas were the main source of the country's chief export crops (coffee, oil seeds, hides, and skins). The Oromo areas also provided the emperor with his primary distributable resource, land, at the expense of those who lived there.[86] Bale, Sidamo, Arussi, and Kaffa provide prime examples of the sad consequences of the alienation of Oromo land and the contradictions inherent in the dominance and exploitation of Oromo peasants by Amhara overlords and an Amhara-based state. Amhara settlers and bureaucrats generally owned the land and reaped the fruits of its cultivation by Oromo peasants. Moreover, Oromo, whether peasants or pastoralists, were saddled with a heavy cash tax burden in an economy that had yet to become market-oriented.[87]

It is often argued that as a people the Oromo never possessed a sense of "Oromoness" sufficient to guarantee collective action against a common enemy, that they would just as soon fight among themselves as fight their enemies. But the Oromo did not always passively accept Amhara hegemony. There is evidence that the "fact of conquest" during the age of European colonial expansion in Africa and the simultaneous development of the concept of the modern nation-state served as a catalyst for the development of genuine Oromo nationalism.[88] Sporadic local Revolts were endemic throughout the period of Ethiopian colonialism. Several major incidents, however, stand out: the Azebo-Raya revolt, 1928–1930; the Oromo Independence Movement of 1936; and the Bale Revolt, 1964–1970.[89] There is some question as to whether the 1928 and 1964 revolts constituted struggles for national liberation, but about the 1936 incident there is no doubt. In that year emerged a confederation of Oromos from Hararge, Shoa, Jimma, and Illubabor, calling itself the Western Oromo Confederation. This association appealed to the League of Nations in 1936, and subsequently to the British government after the collapse of Italian East Africa, for recognition of the Oromos' right to self-determination.[90] The aim was to establish an independent Oromo republic, but the idea was ignored by the League as well as by the British.

Signs of Oromo nationalism did not again become apparent until the mid-1960s when the Oromo self-help association, Mecha-Tulema, was founded. The organization, named after two of the major Oromos clans, was established in 1965 as a self-help club dedicated to promoting Oromo self-identity and improving the lot of the Oromo. Since political parties were not allowed, associations such as Mecha-Tulema often took on political roles.

The organization attempted to involve Oromo in both cities and the countryside. It was most successful in the south, Arussi in particular, where Oromos had been relegated to the status of tenants on land that was once theirs. At the height of its development, Mecha-Tulema claimed as many as 300,000 members.[91] The leadership comprised educated Oromos who had been Amharized but subsequently rediscovered their culture, deciding to fight for a fair share of the spoils of modernization.

The most prominent leader of Mecha-Tulema was Tadesse Biru, a former general in the Ethiopian police force and the territorial army. He was from a Shoan Oromo family and had established himself firmly in Amhara culture. In fact, his Oromo origins were not apparent to many until he began to champion the cause of his people. Tadesse Biru appeared at organizational rallies in southern towns, delivering speeches critical of the government's policies toward Oromo areas and encouraging the people to demand their just due. He carefully linked his appeal to the dignity of Oromo culture, a culture that, he emphasized, was being destroyed at the hands of the Amhara.

By November 1966 the Haile Selassie regime became sufficiently alarmed at the growth in the movement's popularity to arrest its top leadership including Tadesse Biru. The pretext for this arrest was a bomb explosion in an Addis Ababa movie house that was attributed to him. The Mecha-Tulema was banned shortly thereafter. Tadesse Biru was brought to trial in 1968 and condemned to death, a sentence later commuted to life in prison.[92]

Mecha-Tulema was significant for several reasons. From the perspective of the government, it was a clear indication that the commitment of assimilated ethnic elites was not assured. Ethnic affinities were often much stronger than class attachments. It was also an indication that political sentiments could not be suppressed merely by forbidding political parties. The movement sensitized the Oromo to the importance of their own national culture and to the contradictions inherent in the emerging politico-economic system.

Another example of Oromo disaffection with the status quo was a rebellion that developed among the Oromo of Bale Province in 1964. This revolt followed a similar revolt among Somalis in Bale. Between 1964 and 1970, separate groups of Oromo rebels in the region conducted guerrilla campaigns against government forces, attacking military garrisons and police stations in Bale and Borana.[93]

The most prominent leader to emerge in this revolt was Wako Gutu, a local leader of great influence. There appears to have been some effort to coordinate the efforts of Wako Gutu's guerrillas with the activities of the WSLF, and between 1964 and 1969 the Oromo rebels relied on the Somali government for both material and moral support. The Oromos, however, appear to have functioned autonomously. Their grievances at this time were local, relating to perceived injustices by the government.[94]

With the change of government in Somalia in 1969 and the withdrawal of official Somali support for guerrilla campaigns in southeastern Ethiopia, it became more difficult for the Oromo rebels to sustain their struggle. Subsequently, in 1970 Wako Gutu and other rebel leaders agreed to a truce with the Ethiopian government. The most prominent of these leaders were given titles and pardoned by the emperor. Some rebels went into exile, reconstituting themselves as the Ethiopian National Liberation Front and the United Front for the Liberation of Western Somalia.[95] To the extent that guerrilla activity continued to exist in the early 1970s, it was on a severely reduced scale. Some support was funneled through the liberated zones of the ELF, but for the most part, guerrilla activities in the south and east ceased in the early 1970s. Significantly, the group that went into exile came to take on a more radical ideological character than the guerrilla bands that thrived among the Oromo in the periphery between 1964 and 1970, but it was never able to make itself felt militarily.

Serious Oromo militancy did not emerge again until the Oromo Liberation Front (OLF) was founded in 1973, dedicated to the "total liberation of the entire Oromo nation from Ethiopian colonialism."[96] This organization claimed to be more a prodigy of the primary proto-nationalist resistance of the Oromo people than of Mecha-Tulema or the Bale rebellion. The OLF began an offensive against the Ethiopian government in Hararge Province in 1974, but sustained activities did not occur until 1976, after the collapse of the Haile Selassie regime. It subsequently spread its activities to Wollega.

The leadership of the OLF initially was comprised of young, educated Oromos from Arussi Province, but by 1976 it claimed a broad-based leadership with a following from all Oromo areas. Beyond national liberation, the OLF's program calls for the establishment of the independent Democratic Republic of Oromia.[97]

VI

POLITICS, ECONOMICS, AND CLASS CONFLICT

THE PRECIPITATING CAUSES OF REVOLUTION

> Ethiopia rise. Crush the government that benefits only the few.
>
> —Voice of the Oppressed to the
> Armed Forces
> February 17, 1974

> Beautiful Ethiopia has been deflowered and she is never again going to be intact. The changes at the top have not affected the lives of the masses at the bottom.
>
> —Tegegne Yetashework,
> Vice Information Minister
> March 16, 1974

Explaining the cause of revolution in general, or even a single revolution for that matter, is never a simple exercise. The factors that give rise to revolution are many, and they vary from one context to the next. In general, however, we can identify two fundamental classes of causes that underlie all incidents of revolutionary change: long-term causes and precipitant causes. Both classes of causes are necessary before revolution can come about, but neither in or of itself is sufficient. Together, they are both necessary and sufficient when such factors intersect at the proper historical moment. Oppression and exploitation, for example, do not always lead to revolution. Some people have remained oppressed and exploited for centuries without engaging in revolutionary activity. Yet there are others who have been able to throw off the yoke of oppression after having achieved revolutionary consciousness in combination with the means to seize control of the state apparatus.[1]

The long-term causes of revolution include such factors as rapid economic growth, causing contradictions between the old and the emerging new orders; technological innovations that disrupt old societies; political modernization or democratization; secularization of authority; the efforts of the modern state to enhance its own autonomy; and long-standing inequalities based on ethnic and/or class domination.[2] All of these factors to one degree or another could be found in postwar Ethiopia. They all contributed to the cumulation of social contradictions inherent in Haile Selassie's attempt to modernize royal absolutism.

Through his manipulation of flexible resources such as a loyal bureaucracy and military, a substantial, imperial coffer, a compliant if not supportive traditional nobility and clergy, and a reservoir of new elites with which to staff and strengthen the emerging modern bureaucracy, the emperor had been able to assert his authority rather effectively. His efforts were bolstered by astute personal leadership that enabled him to secure diplomatic, financial, technological, and military support in the international community for the kind of state he was attempting to build. Haile Selassie's personal survival as well as that of his regime relied heavily on his ability to manage the domestic and international political environments in an effective manner. This being the case, any factors that eroded his command over some or all of his flexible resources might seriously jeopardize his position. Economic, political, and/or social crises invariably are the causes and/or the consequences of a regime's inability to use effectively flexible resources to maintain social order and perpetuate its own existence. In some cases a regime might have become too weak to respond effectively to serious, short-term crises, or these problems might simply be overwhelming. Such crises are examples of what I consider the potential, immediate precipitants of revolution. In this group of causes are such factors as economic depression or inflation, fiscal crises, elite fragmentation, intellectual alienation, defeat or demoralizing setbacks in war, and natural catastrophe.[3] Each of these factors tends to give rise to psychological responses of rebellion against the existing order. These responses might be passive and nonpolitical, but they also can be expressive and explicitly political. Psychological responses of this kind become relevant for our purposes only when they are channeled in a revolutionary direction. They are never uniform in character, the same for all groups and individuals in society, but they all have the potential, given the proper circumstances, to result in a revolutionary outcome. Factors such as simple frustration, anger, relative deprivation, and righteous indignation generally comprise the psychological causes of revolution.[4] Coupled with appropriate leadership and a revolutionary ideal, they can lead to a radical alteration of the course of human history in societies in which deep-seated contradictions converge with short-term precipitant crises.

The underlying causes of the Ethiopian Revolution have been extensively detailed in the preceding pages. The intention of this chapter is to analyze how these factors converged and interacted with precipitating elements to create a radical movement for the fundamental alteration of Ethiopian society. This was a complex process—as one observer put it, "indescribable chaos"—but one that must be understood in order to grasp the essence of the problems that confronted the new regime in its efforts to consolidate the revolution and establish society on new foundations.[5]

The Political Economy of Drought and Famine

The course of events that led to the unraveling of Ethiopia's bureaucratic empire began almost unnoticed in 1972, when the main rains failed in the northeastern areas of the country. Drought ensued, and drought led to famine. By 1973 between 100,000 and 200,000 people had died from starvation and malnutrition. Such natural catastrophes are not new to this area. Peasants and pastoralists living on the margins of subsistence have had to cope with such phenomena from time immemorial. As a result of the process of modernization and the centralization efforts of the state, however, the lives of poor rural inhabitants had been unalterably changed. More and more of their surplus production was either being demanded directly by landlords and the state, or being translated into cash in order to meet tax obligations. Their freedom of movement and their access to land was also now inhibited by state regulation or by a complex and aggressive burgeoning market economy. Traditional survival mechanisms were either gravely weakened or completely inoperable. Rural people unwittingly had become extremely dependent on the state. For its part, the state was more concerned with economic growth and political survival than it was with meeting its inherited social responsibilities. This is clearly demonstrated in the way in which Haile Selassie's regime responded to the drought.

As soon as the main rains failed in mid-1972, the Ministry of Agriculture conducted a qualitative survey to assess the potential impact of this failure.[6] That protracted drought might result was already suspected, as the Sahelian countries to the west of Ethiopia had already begun to wither from devastating drought. The findings of the ministry's survey were submitted to the Council of Ministers in November 1972, but instead of acting immediately to avert the impending catastrophe, a decision was made to do nothing. More important, the report was not made available to the public. Thus began an official cover-up that was to contribute greatly to the demise of the Haile Selassie regime.

By August 1973 relief camps, administered mainly by the Ethiopian Red Cross, had been set up and were catering to upwards of sixty thousand famine victims. The most severely affected areas were in Wollo and Tigre provinces. It is estimated that 20 percent of the human population and 90 percent of the animals in Wollo (the worst affected area) had died. Eighty percent of the crop had been lost.[7] Before the drought, Wollo and Tigre had supplied 40 percent of Ethiopia's total food crop production. A brisk trade in food crops continued, but the exchange involved fewer people. At the height of the drought, grain prices in Dessie, the capital of Wollo, had doubled, and shipments of grain continued to flow from the province to the major urban centers.[8]

The drought was a localized phenomenon. It did not affect all areas in the same way at the same time. In all, only seven of the country's fourteen provinces (Wollo, Tigre, Hararge, Shoa, Bale, Sidamo, and Gamu-Gofa) were markedly affected. In fact, in 80 percent of the provinces that provide this crop, the production of *teff,* the staple grain, was either average or above average.[9] Surpluses could have been moved from an area with surplus yield to an area experiencing shortages to alleviate the suffering. Even within drought-stricken provinces private entrepreneurs sometimes hoarded grain, holding out for higher prices.[10]

Ironically, the hardest hit areas were not the feudal and tenant-based economies in the south, but northern areas where the traditional land tenure system still predominated. This enabled the government, when it finally admitted that there was drought and famine in 1974, to suggest that the catastrophe was caused by bad land use, overpopulation, and the fragmentation of holdings.[11] There is little doubt that these were significant contributing factors, but they were not the sole reasons for drought and catastrophic famine. Equally important were government policies relating not only to drought relief but also to the official economic development strategy.

The Ethiopian government emphasized the ever-increasing production of crops like coffee and oil seeds so that it might acquire foreign exchange from the export of such commodities. Having achieved just about all it could through its import-substitution policies, and faced with a need for more and more foreign exchange, the government was now exporting items that heretofore had been produced almost exclusively for local consumption. By 1973 it was even exporting limited but significant quantities of grain, sugar, and other agricultural produce. Not only did grain export continue during the drought, it increased.[12] Even some of the grain that entered the country as relief supplies was rebagged and exported. It is not clear that this was done with government complicity, but it is certainly an indication of bureaucratic corruption and avaricious speculators.

Another aspect of Haile Selassie's misguided economic development strategy was the privatization of land and the consequent encouragement of prodution for the market without instituting meaningful land reform. In this time of crisis, the contradictions of superimposing such a strategy on a traditional socioeconomic system without instituting the necessary corrective measures were clearly apparent. For example, although feudalism was not widespread in Wollo or Tigre, peasants were not always autonomous producers either. It is estimated that 150,000 to 375,000 out of three million residents of Wollo were tenants or landless peasants in 1973.[13]

Famine victims were often exploited by speculators, traders, and moneylenders and forced to sell crops, animals, and even land at extremely low prices in order to buy needed grain at inflated prices. The price of grain on the retail market increased by over 20 percent in this period. Some unscrupulous officials responsible for famine relief even went so far as to sell food ration cards to the starving.[14]

By 1973 the emphasis on agricultural production for the market had begun to contribute to widespread tenant eviction throughout the country. Speculators either farmed their land on their own with the aid of a limited number of hired laborers, or they sold the land at high prices to others who utilized it in similar ways. In the case of grazing lands, the tendency was also for speculators to try to make a profit. Rather than making the land available to nomads at reasonable prices, the practice was to lease pasturage to entrepreneurs.[15] Peasants were not only being driven off the land because of drought, then, they were also being pressured by market forces over which they had no control or defense.

In April 1973 the government activated the National Emergency Relief Committee, an agency established in 1971, in order to deal with famine and a cholera outbreak. Private volunteer organizations like the Red Cross had been until then the most active in famine relief. Still, public officials refused to acknowledge that the problem had gotten out of hand. In fact, they consciously attempted to suppress the extent of the catastrophe from becoming public. Junior officials in the bureaucracy tried to approach bilateral and multilateral agencies informally to encourage them to do something in view of the fact that the government was dragging its feet. Such pleas were largely ignored, however, because those making the requests did not represent the views of the highest authorities.[16]

In *The Politics of Starvation,* Jack Shepard argues that not only was the Ethiopian government guilty of suppressing information about the true scope and impact of the drought, but that multilateral and bilateral agencies that might have pressured the government into action instead went along with the cover-up. Multilateral agencies seem to have been more concerned with maintaining good "working relations" with the host government and refrained from doing anything that might embarrass it. Shepard quotes an Ethiopian minister as telling a UNICEF official: "If it is a choice between making this public and not receiving aid, then we can do without the aid."[17]

By mid-1973 it was clear that the government wanted and needed aid, but it wanted it on the quiet. Officials approached prospective donors such as the World Food Program, UNICEF, the Food and Agricultural Organization, the United Nations Development Program, and the U. S. Agency for International Development (USAID) privately and convinced them to begin shipping aid quietly so as not to cause the government undue embarrassment. The appearance of a major crisis might have led to civil unrest at home and to a disruption in the flow of capital into the country from trade and tourism. Such organizations went along with the government's request and began shipping in limited food aid without publicly commenting about the seriousness of the problem.[18]

Hearing of the massive starvation in April 1973, three professors from Haile Sellassie I University had gone to Wollo to conduct their own survey. They brought back pictures of the starving thousands and submitted a report on conditions there to the university community. At a gathering on the campus they severely criticized the government's inadequate response to the problem and encouraged more drastic measures to be taken. The student body responded first by fasting, asking that the savings be used for drought relief.[19] Then the students organized a campaign to collect food to send to drought-stricken areas and a pictorial exhibition of conditions in these areas. The most threatening aspects of the student mobilization, however, were their demonstrations in solidarity with the starving peasantry. In late April a mass meeting was held on the campus of Haile Sellassie I University aimed at pressuring the government into declaring a state of emergency. The authorities responded by sending in police who unleashed three days of violence on the campus, prompting university officials to plead that the students curb their activities. The government was intent on resisting such pressures by any means necessary, but they continued to mount. In May a group of students journeyed to Dessie in hopes of prompting the governor-general to take more urgent measures in responding to the problem. Troops were sent in, dispersing the demonstration with gunfire and leaving several young people dead. The lecturers who exposed the deplorable response to the famine were relieved of their posts, and attempts were made to appoint them to positions in the imperial bureaucracy far from the capital city and thus to deprive them of their constituency. However, they remained in Addis Ababa throughout this crisis that ultimately led to the fall of the imperial regime.

In the summer of 1973 UNICEF conducted an independent survey and attempted to discuss its findings with the Planning Ministry. In spite of the fact that there were over one million people starving in Wollo and Tigre alone by this time, the vice minister of planning made it known in no uncertain terms that the government could not risk having this report made public.[20] The UNICEF report was leaked to a London newspaper, however, prompting a British television journalist, Jonathan Dimbleby, to seek official clearance to do a documentary on the famine relief program. After much discussion, the government agreed to let the British film crew into the country. An effort was made to structure their visit so that they filmed conditions in only the best organized and administered camps along the main highway in Wollo.

The documentary aired in London in the fall of 1973, and what it revealed shocked European audiences. Even the camps Dimbleby was allowed to film were disastrous. Moreover, the problem was compounded by the fact that cholera and typhoid had begun to affect the camps. This prompted the setting up of efforts to secure donations in Europe for relief by such relief organizations as Oxfam, the British Save the Children Fund, and others.[21]

The emperor himself was finally moved enough to journey to the drought-stricken area in November 1973 to conduct a personal assessment of conditions there. He came away genuinely appalled at what he saw. However, he offered no realistic solution to the problem. He simply uttered words of sympathy to the starving peasantry, suggesting that such catastrophes had to be endured, since they were beyond human control.[22] The government continued to conduct a limited relief effort, but a state of emergency was not declared until a year later.

Relief supplies trickled in from private, bilateral, and multilateral sources. The level of aid, however, was much below what was required. In the meantime, the relief program continued to be characterized by corruption and inefficiency as the drought expanded to the south. Bureaucratic red tape and bottlenecks hampered delivery of relief supplies to the needed locations, and as the problems of famine and disease multiplied, the limited administrative and technical capacity of the relief apparatus became all the more apparent.

Foreign donors became increasingly critical of what was perceived to be the limited and largely wasted efforts on the part of the Ethiopians. Private citizens appeared to be more concerned than the government or the Orthodox Church. For example, in spite of the vigorous efforts of foreign-based missionary groups in late 1973 and 1974, the Orthodox Church said and did nothing.[23] A 1975 report by the U.S. Inspector General of Foreign Assistance to the U. S. House Subcommittee on International Resources, Food, and Energy revealed that in February 1974 the United States and other foreign donors spent about $25 million for food relief while the Ethiopian government spent nothing—and this at a time when the Imperial regime had sufficient reserves to purchase large quantities of commercial imports and possessed enough domestic grain surpluses to alleviate immediately the burden of famine.[24]

Perhaps the most devastating aspect of the growth of this crisis was the fact that Ethiopia, like most countries throughout the world, was undergoing a severe economic crisis as a result of the rise in oil prices following the OPEC oil embargo in 1973, the declining price of coffee on the international market, and severe inflation.[25] This gave rise to domestic discontent and severely taxed the regime's ability to respond effectively. The emperor tried to get protesting groups to temper their demands, claiming that the government simply did not have the resources to do more than it was already doing. But as the drought worsened, charges of corruption and exploitation mounted. The emperor himself came to be portrayed as the worst sort of capitalist, who had amassed a personal fortune of more than $1.6 billion at the expense of the Ethiopian people and stashed it away in Swiss bank accounts.[26]

Economic Crisis and Sociopolitical Conflict

The worldwide economic crisis triggered by the OPEC oil embargo in 1973 had dire consequences for Ethiopia's fragile political economy. Faced with an oil shortage and inflated prices for imported goods, the Haile Selassie regime felt that it had to institute measures to protect and even to increase its supply of liquid capital. This was one of the most valued of the emperor's flexible resources. The policies instituted at this time had wide-ranging implications. Two of the most important ones related to the price of retail gasoline and to the country's education system.

At the end of 1973 Arab oil producers raised the price they charged for oil by nine cents per gallon. Rather than absorb the loss, the Ethiopian government decided to introduce a rationing system and to raise the price of gas at the pump by twenty-five cents per gallon. The idea was to slow the consumption of oil and gasoline and increase government revenue from the sale of petroleum products. This was designed to create capital to aid in the maintenance of the unprofitable Assab oil refinery. These measures had a devastating impact not only on the urban middle class, which predominated among the country's automobile-owning population, but also on the taxi drivers who made a living transporting the urban poor from point to point in cities and towns in small, old Fiat sedans at the meager rate of twenty-five cents (US $0.10) per person. This was a valuable complement to the public transportation system. In spite of the increase in the price of gasoline, taxi drivers were forbidden to raise their own rates.[27] This inevitably led to a strike by taxi drivers in late February 1974 that shut down the public transportation system as well. Taxi drivers were joined in their protests by students who had simultaneously risen to protest the government's handling of drought relief as well as proposed educational reforms. Sometimes violent confrontations erupted between protesters and the authorities.

In 1972 the government had authorized a study of Ethiopia's educational system in hopes that recommendations could be made for educational reform. The study was supported by international organizations such as UNESCO, the ILO, the World Bank, USAID, and the Ford Foundation, all of whom were involved in a worldwide discussion about the most appropriate educational strategy for the poor countries of the Third World.[28] The watchwords had now become "basic education," "education for self-reliance," "life-long education," and "non-formal education." These were seen as the most appropriate approaches to attacking rural poverty immediately. To achieve these ends, however, formal education would have to undergo a drastic change. Nowhere was this more evident than in Ethiopia.

Even though the formal education system catered to an extremely small number of the school age population, educational output had already superseded the ability of the modern sector of the economy to absorb that output. The Ethiopian government appears to have felt that by jumping, so to speak, on the nonformal or practical educational "bandwagon," it could diffuse a potential area of social discontent. Young people would be provided with skills that enabled them to become involved in economic activities in their own rural communities, instead of expecting that urban employment was the only alternative for a secure future. What was not anticipated was the fact that the commitment to formal education was already so strong among students, parents, and teachers that this trend could not simply be slowed or halted by imperial fiat.

Even as the so-called Educational Sector Review was being conducted, teachers were making demands on the government for increases in salary and better working conditions. Salary schedules for teachers had been under review since 1968, but as late as December 1973, the issue had not been resolved. This prompted a threatened strike by primary and secondary teachers.[29]

Almost as if in contempt, the government introduced its plans for radical educational reform in early February 1974. It proposed that education be oriented to emphasize practical, as opposed to academic, education. The primary level was to become the terminal level of education for most young people. Secondary education, rather than expanding, would remain at the current level, and university education would grow only slightly. Curriculum at the post-primary level was to be explicitly tied to the country's manpower needs. Moreover, the financing of education beyond the primary level would cease to be the responsibility of the government. Students themselves would have to assume this burden.

The Educational Sector Review went further to make drastic recommendations affecting teachers, their pay, and their qualifications. Rather than providing for the upgrading of the quality of education in the system and better pay and working conditions, it proposed that qualifications and pay be downgraded. In addition, a forty-eight week work year, double shift teaching, and a minimum class size of sixty-seven students were proposed.[30] The government was most interested in reducing the cost per pupil and forcing people to alter the values they held about the relationship between formal education and economic opportunity. Public officials seem not to have anticipated the crystallization of popular discontent over this proposed policy. By 1974 the 17,500 teachers, organized in the Ethiopian Teachers' Association, and mobilized along with hundreds of thousands of their students, presented a formidable challenge to the regime in conjunction with the host of other challenges besetting the Haile Selassie government.

The Educational Sector Review was introduced on February 8, 1973. By February 22 it had been officially decided to suspend the proposed reforms, as well as to institute price controls and to cut the increase in gasoline by 40 percent. Most important, Haile Selassie met with teachers— something the minister of education had refused to do—and promised a decision on teachers' salaries by the end of March, thus undermining the position of then-Prime Minister Akilu Habte Wolde. This was one of the first signs of a severe weakening of imperial authority. The regime was becoming divided against itself, and this was apparent to even the most casual observers, prompting not only teachers but other groups as well to pressure the government for economic measures favorable to their own (and sometimes other) corporate groups. The severity of this crisis was accentuated and made more ominous for the regime by a crisis within the military that began at roughly the same time.

As the drought worsened and the economic crisis deepened, Haile Selassie began visibly to lose the support of some of his more critical flexible resources. Unrest among teachers was a demonstration of a loss of support among a significant element of the new educated class that was so important in the secularization and centralization efforts of the state. What was fatal, however, was the regime's growing inability to rely on the military as an instrument of coercion. In fact, the military came to associate itself with the ideals of those who advocated a revolutionary transformation of Ethiopian society. Being the most organized and well-equipped agent of coercive state authority, the prospects of the army—or significant parts of it—abandoning the Crown seriously jeopardized the regime's chances of survival.[31]

A wavering in military support for the regime first became apparent on January 12, 1974, when a mutiny of noncommissioned officers and enlisted men occurred in a unit of the army's Fourth Division at Neghele in Sidamo Province. Since the abortive coup of 1960, Haile Selassie had become particularly sensitive to the morale and conditions of service in the military. He had agreed to pay increases in 1961 and 1964 to avert military crises that threatened to weaken the authoritative posture of the state. In the process, a military pension plan was established, as well as survivors' benefits for the families of soldiers who died in the line of duty.[32] Care was also taken to provide troops with decent, if not always first class, living accommodations. Ironically, the Neghele mutiny was based specifically on grievances relating not only to salaries, but also to poor living conditions.

The event that triggered the revolt involved the fact that a water pump designated for use by enlisted men had remained broken for several months, and they were forbidden to draw water from the officers' pump.[33] In protest, NCO's and enlisted men seized their superiors and issued a list of demands ranging from better food to a salary increase. The men complained that in addition to salaries that did not keep pace with rising consumer prices, horrible food, a shortage of potable water, and the inhumane treatment they received from the officer corps also contributed to their most heartfelt grievances. They demanded that Prime Minister Aklilu Habte Wolde, the minister of defense, and the commander of the territorial army come to Neghele to see personally the conditions they lived in and to hear their grievances.

Faced with mounting pressures in other sectors, the emperor appeared determined to stem an impending military revolt by demonstrating his regime's genuine concern with the plight of the soldiery. He did not completely comply with the mutineers' demand for an audience with a high-level delegation, but he did send Lieutenant General Deresse Dubale, the commander of the territorial army, to negotiate with them. When he arrived, Deresse was immediately taken prisoner and forced to live in the same quarters as enlisted men, to eat the same food, and to drink the same water for a week—an ordeal alleged to have made him extremely uncomfortable and ill.[34]

The negotiations on the grievances of the Neghele mutineers went on for several weeks. Soldiers in other parts of the country were able to monitor developments in Neghele through radio dispatches from the Neghele unit. In this way, what had begun as a set of purely economic concerns of local importance became more and more political and of nationwide significance.

The scope of military discontent was spreading like a deadly communicable disease by early February and only served to compound already existing pressures on the regime. Significantly, however, between January and early February, the complaints of soldiers were strictly professional in character. To the extent that grievances were political at this time, they related to the organizational politics of the armed forces and not to society as a whole. The earliest public political act by military people seems to have been the participation of some air force personnel in a march on February 22 led by parents of students jailed for involvement in riots in Debre Zeit.[35] Leaflets critical of the government and attributed to airmen had appeared a week earlier.

The government of Prime Minister Aklilu finally acceded to the soldiers' demands on February 23, approving a salary increase amounting to about E$18 for privates and bringing their base salary to E$100 per month. This concession came on the heels of the government's decision two days earlier to suspend plans for education reform, to impose price controls, and to roll back gasoline prices.[36] In retrospect, the timing of this cluster of official responses was unfortunately fateful, as it conveyed the image of a weak and indecisive state. Past military pay increases had been funded from nonmilitary budgets, but this time, with the convergence of demands from significant nonmilitary as well as military groups, it was not clear how the government would pay for these new commitments. When the salary increases were announced, Haile Selassie himself cautioned that this gesture was a great sacrifice on the part of the government, as it had severely taxed the imperial treasury.

Nevertheless, unrest in the military continued. Just two days after the announcement of the new military pay scale, a mutiny erupted in the Second Division headquarters at Asmara. NCO's and enlisted men, in what was now characteristic fashion, arrested their superiors, but this time they went further, closing down the airport, setting up roadblocks across roads leading in and out of the city, and taking control of the radio station.[37] They used radio facilities to broadcast a list of two dozen demands, the same kinds of grievances that came out of the Neghele revolt but with one exception, an essentially political demand that indicated a sense of relative deprivation among soldiers who resented the ostentation and conspicuous consumption associated with the politico-administrative class or new nobility: they objected to the routine issuance of Mercedes-Benz cars and operators' allowances to high government officials.

The emperor responded by sending a high-level delegation to attempt to find a negotiated way out of this continuing crisis. The mutineers were determined not to allow their grievances to be treated as purely local, and they requested demonstrations of support from other units. Immediately, mutinies occurred among some units of the Fourth Division in Addis Ababa, at the Debre Zeit air force installation, and in several specialized units (i.e., signal corps, musician corps, and the engineering and transport sections).[38] The emperor was forced into emergency consultation with his closest advisers in an effort to resolve this crisis. Rumors abounded that the military branches had agreed to go beyond the demand for more pay, and to demand the resignation of the Aklilu government. The panic escalated when virtually the whole Fourth Division in the capital threw its weight behind the rebellion. This rumor had no basis in fact, but it seems to have been decisive in forcing the government to give in to these latest demands and ultimately in forcing the entire cabinet to resign on February 28.

The military position must be seen in the context of the political mood that had gripped the country. To even the casual observer, significant changes loomed on the horizon for Ethiopia. Not only were occupational groups calling for economic relief, but students and intellectuals were demanding constitutional reforms. One of the surest signs of an impending revolution is "when the state becomes increasingly discredited in the eyes of either the population as a whole or certain key sections of it."[39] The Aklilu government was under fire for a whole host of ill-advised policies, corruption, and ineptness. The most significant attacks emanated from the ranks of the new middle class, intensifying political debate that raged in Ethiopia in early 1974. But this was not decisive. What appears to have been most important was the protracted nature of public protest, which contributed to the forging of critical alliances among aggrieved groups. Except for the students, each group initially protested because of specific, group-based grievances, but as time progressed and discussion continued, common points of grievance emerged to politicize and expand the scope of mass protest.

The emperor decided to accept the resignation of Aklilu Habte Wolde's government and asked Lij Endelkatchew Makonnen, an experienced minister and ambassador from a Shoan aristocratic family, to form a new government. On March 5, after receiving a proposal from Endelkatchew and after a lengthy discussion with advisers, Haile Selassie announced that he had agreed to constitutional reforms. He communicated his decision to the public by radio. His hope was that this announcement would stem once and for all the rising tide of politically based protest. A new constitution was to be drafted within six months. A real system of checks and balances among the various branches of government would be instituted; the judicial system would be reformed and made more equitable; measures would be taken to safeguard the rights of the general population; and, most important, in the new constitution the prime minister would be made responsible to parliament rather than to the emperor.[40] If this latter measure were to go into effect, it would result in a real diminution in the power and authority of the Crown. The extent to which the emperor could manage the rate and direction of change would certainly be drastically reduced.

After his appointment, Endelkatchew set about attempting to restore order and to reestablish the regime's legitimacy among the general population. Given the political climate in the country, this would have been difficult in the best of circumstances. Although some of the older, well-connected members of the military favored the appointment of Endelkatchew and were now prepared to serve him, young radical elements within the armed forces began to discredit him as soon as his appointment was announced. They were joined in this chorus by students who throughout the period of civil unrest had bombarded sympathizers in the military with radical analyses of the Ethiopian situation through student publications such as *Struggle* and *The Voice of the Masses,* and via personal friends in the armed forces.[41]

University students had been a source of constant headaches for the government since 1965. By 1970 student radicalism had spread to high schools and the military academies, particularly Holeta. L. Hayes and Peter Koehn suggest that it was the radicalism of foreign African students from newly independent sub-Saharan countries that first kindled the radicalism of Ethiopian students.[42] Such an interpretation, however, would seem to minimize the effects of objective conditions on Ethiopian student consciousness. No doubt, the mere fact of interacting with students from independent African countries with all the trappings of political and economic development forced many Ethiopian students to recognize contradictions in their own society. But this does not necessarily imply that it was the radicalism of non-Ethiopian Africans that made Ethiopian students radical. Two other possible radicalizing elements have been suggested: Peace Corps teachers and the Ethiopian University Service Program (EUSP).[43] American Peace Corps volunteers began coming to Ethiopia in the early 1960s. With them they brought American-derived concepts of participatory democracy and basic civil and human rights. It was through such volunteers that many young Ethiopians acquired a vision of what Ethiopia might become.

Generally, after their third year in college, students were required to live and work in the countryside as part of the EUSP. Many students doing their national service were shocked by the rural poverty and the official neglect they witnessed. As a result, some became extremely politicized. On completion of college, many of these young people ended up as teachers in the rural areas and thus had a vehicle through which to influence would-be college students. The sum of these developments was the radicalization of a whole generation of young people. Interestingly, most of them were destined to join the new middle class, but in diverse capacities. Some of them would even become soldiers, soldiers who were sensitive to the grievances of this generation of radical intellectuals because they had come from similar backgrounds and had shared similar ideas as high school students. This fact was to become critical as the Ethiopian Revolution unfolded.

One of the most significant accomplishments of the *Yekatit* or February uprisings was that student and intellectuals' demands for the lifting of press censorship and the release of political prisoners came to be supported by radicals in the military. The government agreed to allow the free expression of political ideas in newspapers and pamphlets in the same week that the Endelkatchew appointment came into effect. From this point on, Ethiopia was deluged with a torrent of political writing through the official press as well as through leaflets printed and disseminated by various groups critical of the regime and its policies.[44] Issues such as bureaucratic corruption, fraud, exploitation, and official neglect appeared again and again in a host of pamphlets and newspaper articles. People for the first time were publicly considering alternatives to imperial rule, revealing a broad-based discontent that spread across the new middle class and ultimately began to bridge the gap between this group and the working class.

The Ethiopian working class had historically been poorly organized and constrained by government regulation. It had attempted general strikes in 1964 and 1970 but on each occasion was unable to secure the necessary widespread support. In the turmoil of early 1974, Confederation of Ethiopian Labor Unions (CELU) leaders felt the time was right to petition the government for economic justice from a position of strength. The organization presented Endelkatchew with a list of demands that encompassed the following points:

1) Minimum wages, starting salary scales, salary adjustments, immunity from income tax on labor pension funds, pension schemes, alterations in provisions dealing with the firing of employees without adequate reason, strikes, and labor publications.
2) Support for student demands.
3) Price controls, free education, temporary employment, job opportunities, and priority formation of new unions in the government bureaus and parastatals.[45]

CELU threatened that if these demands were not met in forty-eight hours, it would call a general strike. The government said it needed three to six months to address these issues.

The CELU announcement coincided with a treatise issued by the Ethiopian University Teachers' Association demanding not only economic reform, but fundamental political changes as well. CELU made a conscious effort to try to link its grievances with those of other groups—a remarkable step, since CELU for the first time allowed itself to be associated with political issues as opposed to purely economic ones.

The General Strike began on March 7 and continued through March 11, paralyzing the country's economic system. Factories were closed or operated at severely reduced capacity, public transportation was disrupted, and hotels were shut down. The success of the strike led to a rash of wildcat strikes, some involving public employees who heretofore had been forbidden from forming unions or participating in strikes. Over the next several weeks public employees of the Civil Aviation Authority, the Post Office, the Ministry of Finance, the university, and municipalities throughout the country, including the Addis Ababa Municipality, all struck in support of the goals of CELU and specific demands of their own.[46] The strikes by government employees, in violation of the law, were significant in that they were a clear indication of how discredited Haile Selassie's regime had become. Unless it was able to regain the loyalty of such critical groups as the civil service and the military, it was doomed to failure. The government quickly gave in to the salary demands of most of these workers, approving salary increases to about 42 percent of the civil service, as well as pension increases.

The true dimensions of the mounting protest could be seen in the fact that groups which, though downtrodden, would have been the least likely to contemplate protesting against public authority also took to the streets. Some five hundred village priests, claiming to speak for two thousand of their colleagues, demonstrated because of their low wages and the excessive wealth of the upper echelons of the clergy.[47] Also, in some instances, the generally passive peasantry rose to support the demands of students for more efficient drought relief, an end to bureaucratic corruption, and land reform.[48] In some cases, peasants came into open conflict with the public authorities and landlords. On occasion they confiscated land, refused to pay taxes, or violently set upon local representatives of the central government. By late April even Ethiopia's minority Muslim community felt confident that the time was right to register its demands, as it was apparent that significant changes were afoot. One hundred thousand Muslims and their sympathizers demonstrated in Addis Ababa, requesting that the state recognize their religion and give it financial support.[49]

The causes of various protesters were taken up by some members of parliament who wanted to set a clear distance between themselves and the discredited regime. They pressured the government vigorously to bring the former members of the Aklilu government and corrupt provincial officials to justice. Endelkatchew labored feverishly to win the support of critical allies in the military and the bureaucracy. Forty days after he took office, he issued a policy statement that was supposed to outline the reforms his government would pursue. In vague language, the statement pledged the regime to tackle Ethiopia's fiscal problems forthrightly, to press for speedy constitutional reform, and to ensure national security. On the issue of land, it pledged to halt indiscriminate land grants and to institute land reform beneficial to the neediest cultivators.[50]

By this time, however, the regime's opposition, though disorganized, was too powerful and confident to be curbed by such measures. The military had been politicized, and civilian occupational groups, without a clear sense of class consciousness, had reached a symbolic meeting of minds. Some groups in the new middle class and intelligentsia interpreted Ethiopia's problems in class terms, but those groups appear to have been few in number. What was important, though, was that these critics found ready allies among groups who were protesting on fairly specific social and economic grounds.

The class divisions that existed at the time were clearly identified in a sample survey of six hundred workers in thirty-one businesses conducted in Addis Ababa in the aftermath of the 1974 general strike by a team of Ethiopian sociologists.[51] The study stratified respondents according to income, occupation, and ethnicity. The most revealing interview items related to perceptions of the reasons for the strike and its benefits. It was found that low income groups were much more likely to perceive the causes of the strike as being economic in nature (i.e., salaries, low salary increments, and inflation) than were high income groups. High income groups were more likely to cite political factors (i.e., corruption, poor administration, exploitation). High status occupational groups by a ratio of 3:1 viewed political factors as being most important, while low status occupational groups explained their problems in economic terms by a 3:2 ratio. Interestingly, respondents from nondominant (non-Amhara and non-Tigre) groups explained the strike in economic terms three times more frequently (48 percent) than those from the dominant group.[52] Moreover, high income, high status respondents from the dominant groups were more likely to have seen the strike as a failure than were low income, low status respondents from minority groups.

What is clear from all this is that common workers and middle-class workers alike tended to possess a sense of relative deprivation, although they did differ somewhat in their perceptions of the basis for this deprivation. The lower echelons of the workforce and members of minority ethnic groups perceived their problems in economic terms. Relative to what they thought their economic station in life should be, they felt deprived. This seems to have been an indication of what Ted R. Gurr describes as decremental deprivation, a condition that generally emerges when a group whose members do not expect much out of life in material terms witness a sharp decrease in their ability to meet basic needs.[53] The usual outcome of such a situation is a simple protest, but given the presence of revolutionary elites, decremental deprivation could lead to a relatively deprived group becoming involved in a revolution.

The nonprofessional, limited-skilled working class, at least those in this study, seem not to have drawn the critical link between economics and politics that would have been necessary to make them a self-conscious revolutionary force. They no doubt allied with other groups, mostly in hopes that this would enhance their chances of having their economic grievances resolved satisfactorily.

Many of the better educated, more highly paid, higher status workers in this study, however, had clearly come to see the political basis of the country's economic woes. As a group they seem to have felt aspirational deprivation in addition to decremental deprivation.[54] Their perception was that they and society as a whole were not realizing their potential because of flaws and excesses among the ruling elite. They expected more in both political and economic terms than the existing political economic system was able or prepared to provide. It is understandable why, holding this view, they would seem to feel that the strike had accomplished little. After all, it had not led immediately to a change of regime, economic justice, or even constitutional reforms. Such sentiments might well have been a reflection of the attitudes of the new middle class at large, judging from their actions and the character of their ideas during this period.

Without acting as a systematic, organized faction of the petit bourgeoisie, middle-class workers and members of the intelligentsia maintained steady political pressure on the regime. They recognized the failings of the ruling class, but as a collectivity, they did not act as a self-conscious class in opposition to dominant elites. This is not to say that there were no class-conscious, politically motivated and goal-directed individuals in this group. There were, but there was no specific revolutionary class movement, straining to engage the ruling class in all-out class war.

All of this notwithstanding, class alliances, however tenuous and unclear, did emerge in the first eight months of 1974 and had a decisive effect on the onset of revolution. This occurred only when elements within the military became strong enough and organized enough, clarified their political views to some degree, and seized upon a revolutionary ideal. It was only then that revolution seemed imminent.

The Act of Revolution

Revolution is not an event. It is a process, a series of interrelated actions initiated by organized opponents of a given regime, designed to sweep out the old order and usher in the new. The first definitive act in any revolution is the forceful, unconstitutional removal and replacement of one set of powerholders by another.[55] This event is always preceded by the cumulation of deep-seated contradictions and short-term crises. It is followed by the introduction of policies and programs intended to replace the old institutions, values, and relationships with new ones based on a new concept of how society should be organized and administered, a new social myth.

The level of violence that accompanies the initial act of revolution as well as the level of violence that follows it varies from one case to the next. Also, the method used to depose the old regime has many forms ranging from conventional war, to peasant-based guerrilla warfare, to a conspiratorial coup d'etat.[56] The objective conditions existing in a given society at a given moment in history are significant in determing the form a particular revolution assumes. The makers of revolution must be conscious of a society's objective conditions when attempting to arrive at the optimal revolutionary strategy. History is replete with revolutions that failed because leaders did not anticipate their own or their enemy's strength or the disposition of critical masses toward the revolutionary alternative.[57] In fact, the failure of the 1960 coup by Girmame and Mengistu Newaye is a classic example of this. Once the revolutionary ideal took hold among the men in uniform in 1974, they seemed determined to avoid the mistakes of the past.

The Ethiopian armed forces were far from monolithic or political in opinion at the beginning of 1974. Between January and June, however, this changed as a certain amount of cohesion and significant politicization occurred among some elements of the armed forces. In part, this was facilitated by the availability of modern communications, such as shortwave radios and telephones, that enabled military rebels to seek each other out and to identify the basis for forming a radical coalition. This transformation was also greatly influenced by the open climate of political discussion that flourished in Ethiopia beginning with the *Yekatit* uprisings. Radical political exiles and students who had been studying abroad flocked back to the "motherland" and added their voices to the intense discussion of the future of Ethiopia. These factors, along with the ideas conveyed in the official press and through the pamphlets and newspapers produced by civilian and military radicals, sensitized radicals in the military to the political mood of the country.

Between January and July 1974, at least six separate military groups claimed to represent the armed forces.[58] The most important ones proved to be two that developed in the Fourth Division headquarters at Addis Ababa and another group of radical airmen at Debre Zeit. The first Addis group to demonstrate its political disposition was a group of thirty NCO's who claimed to represent every military unit except the navy.[59] The group appeared sometime between January and February 1974 and quickly came under the influence of a second group comprised of officers of intermediate rank. The officers' group was a collection of politically oriented and well-connected moderates and radicals. The most important among them were the moderate Colonel Alem Zewde Tessema, the commander of the Fourth Division's airborne brigade, and the radical Colonel Atnafu Abate. The first signs that there was a military group prepared to take independent action against civilian leaders came on February 26, when the committee sent troops to arrest eight members of Aklilu Habte Wolde's cabinet on charges of corruption. These individuals were released, however, after the emperor personally intervened and promised that they would be investigated and brought to trial if they were found to be culpable.

In spite of the first signs of coordinated action on the part of a politicized military, the level of politicization within the armed forces had not reached a level capable of successfully challenging civilian authority. In fact, when Endelkatchew Makonnen assumed office, he immediately attempted to co-opt the army by boosting military pay to a much higher level than had been approved by Aklilu and by increasing fringe benefits.[60] As a result, some units dispatched messages to Addis Ababa expressing loyalty to the emperor.

Endelkatchew also tried to diffuse the potential influence of the radicals in the military by entering into alliances with moderate officers who had bases of support in the armed forces. It has been suggested that this was what he had in mind when he supported Alem Zewde Tessema's efforts to organize the officers' committee in the Fourth Division.[61] He had hoped that Alem Zewde's committee would reestablish support for the regime in the military and help weed out radicals in its ranks. For a time, this alliance succeeded. The armed forces were divided on whether or not they had a political role to play. Alem Zewde's paratroopers were solidly behind Endelkatchew throughout the spring. His support was also strong in Harar. But in Eritrea's Second Division, in parts of the Fourth Division, at Harar and Holeta military academies, and at Debre Zeit air force base, there did exist some rebellious sentiment.[62] Yet there was no radical armed forces movement.

Alem Zewde became the chair of what came to be known as the Armed Forces Coordinating Committee (AFCC) on March 23. Two days later he ordered the arrest of sixty radical airmen at Debre Zeit.[63] This act neutralized some of the more vocal and visible military radicals, but it did not completely stifle radicalism. Nevertheless, it did buoy the regime's confidence that it was succeeding in bringing matters under control.

In late April Endelkatchew attempted to broaden his legitimacy and gain support for tough measures against public dissidents. On April 30 the cabinet appointed a thirty-man National Security Commission.[64] Its members were drawn from the military, the police, and other security agencies, and from various government ministries. The commission was supposed to coordinate the suppression of strikes and demonstrations by the most expedient means. As if consciously using a carrot-and-stick approach to recapture public support, Endelkatchew authorized the arrest of former ministers in the Aklilu government (his former colleagues) even though the commission of inquiry set up to investigate their misdeeds had not completed its work.

Even as Endelkatchew made move after move aimed at curbing the spread of antiregime sentiment, radicalism grew virtually unchecked both in society at large and within the military. By late spring 1974 radicalism had even engulfed the Alem Zewde–led AFCC. Some members had come to question the wisdom of the military being used as an agent of repression by a regime that had not proved it was committed to major reforms. The feeling was that Alem Zewde himself had not pressed the prime minister enough by using his position in the military as a political lever. By early June Alem Zewde had become discredited within the AFCC and in the military at large.[65] On June 22 he even lost control of his own paratrooper battalion, which had been defeated in a violent conflict with radicals at Debre Zeit, and fled to Gojjam in an effort to escape harsh reprisals.

In early June 1974 twelve to sixteen radical members of the AFCC, led by Colonel Atnafu Abate, broke away from the parent group. They had apparently decided to take matters into their own hands and to exert more direct pressures on Ethiopia's civilian leaders.[66] The group comprised mainly Holeta graduates, although there were about a half-dozen members who had gone to Harar Academy. This appears to have been significant, because Harar was generally viewed as an elite institution catering to the sons of the aristocracy. By contrast, Holeta tended to attract cadets from poor and minority groups. The resentment of Holeta men for their Harar counterparts had become legend. To the extent that there were Harar graduates on the committee, they tended to be younger men less bound to the status quo.

The splinter committee used the early part of June to begin setting up a framework for an organized entry of the military into politics. Telegrams were sent to all battalions around the country, to the military academies, the territorial army, and the police—forty-two units in all. Each was requested to send delegations of three men to a meeting to be held at the Fourth Division headquarters later in the month. In some cases delegates were elected, in others they were simply appointed. By June 28 125 delegates had converged on Addis Ababa to begin deliberating how they could dictate the tenor of politics in the country.[67]

Even before all the members of this new committee had arrived in Addis Ababa, the die had been cast. The critical event seems to have been a visit to the Grand Palace by a group of conservative members of the Chamber of Deputies on June 26 to request that the emperor order the release of twenty-five of the political prisoners the soldiers had jailed.[68] This was seen as a clear indication that ruling politicians had no intentions of bringing these individuals to justice. The committee's response was definitive. Two days later, troops were sent to take command of the national radio and television stations and the missionary-run Radio Voice of the Gospel. Rather than releasing the political prisoners as the conservative deputies had desired, the committee asserted its own power and independence by arresting fifty more alleged culprits from the ruling class on June 30. Within the next two weeks, an additional 150 were jailed. In this group were not only members of the former government, but also members of the ruling government (the minister of defense), the royal family (Lij Iskender Desta, the emperor's grandson), the nobility, and the provincial administration.[69] So sweeping was this series of arrests that it amounted to a coup d'etat. The committee had served notice that it was prepared to hold politicians personally accountable for their actions. Endelkatchew continued, however briefly, to hold the reins of governance, but he was no longer able to rely on the military as a flexible resource to do his bidding. In fact, even though these soldiers continued to disdain public involvement in politics, they had clearly decided to control the actions of the government very directly.

In the closing days of June the committee chose its leadership and organized itself into subcommittees paralleling the major governmental ministries. Given that the group reflected the country's diverse ethnic and class character and that no clear idea had emerged as to how the existing order should be changed, the way was open for the emergence of an individual who seemed to best represent the broad masses of the oppressed. Atnafu Abate had been instrumental in forming the group, but he was a Gojjami from the Amhara heartland. Other members in the original organizing group were also Amharas and not likely to be able to command a broad base of support.

During the deliberations in the initial meetings, attention turned to a newly arrived major from the Third Division, Mengistu Haile Mariam. There are conflicting accounts of Mengistu's ethnic origins, as well as his date of birth. He is variously reported to have been born between 1939 and 1942 of either a Sidama or Konso mother from either Wellamu or Gemu-Gofa, who was married to either an Amhara or Gurarge from Shoa.[70] He studied at Holeta and in the United States and later became an ordnance officer in the Ethiopian army. Mengistu had gained the reputation of being a tough, pragmatic, ruthless leader who was not afraid to make decisions. This, along with his rather heterogeneous ethnic origins and an impassioned, patriotic speech, won him the support needed to be elected chairman of the coordinating committee, or *Derg* (a group of equals), as it came to be known. Haggar Erlich notes:

> Mengistu seemed to symbolize the revolution. He was the baria, the slave who overthrew the master, the member of the conquered tribe who got even with the conquerors, the poorly educated son of a servant who rose against the intellectual elite.[71]

In his address to his colleagues, Mengistu had stressed the importance of the committee to Ethiopia's survival and to the unity of the country. This was perhaps the first time the phrase that became the motto of the revolution, *Ethiopia Tikdem* (Ethiopia First), was used.[72]

Mengistu, then, appeared to be a conciliator—the ideal man for the job of welding these disparate representatives of the rank and file of the armed forces into a viable political force. Even he realized, however, that his national stature would not command immediate widespread public legitimacy. With this in mind, Mengistu supported the invitation of the Eritrean general, Aman Andom, to the group's discussions. General Aman was renowned for having led troops in successful operations on the empire's southeastern frontier—his troops called him "Lion of the Ogaden"—in 1960–1961 against an invading Somali force. Initially the Derg insisted on having Aman appointed to the government as chief of staff, and subsequently he was its choice to head the Provisional Military Administrative Council when the Derg seized power in September.

Between July and September, Mengistu became the most instrumental member of the still largely anonymous Derg. The Derg did indicate on July 2 that it had become institutionalized when it issued a statement in a radio broadcast in the name of the "Armed Forces Coordinating Committee," but nothing was revealed about its membership.[73] The Derg spelled out its demands of the Haile Selassie regime:

1) The release of all political prisoners other than those the Derg itself had jailed.
2) The granting of amnesty to all political refugees.
3) Passage and implementation of a new constitution in which true democracy would be guaranteed.
4) The extension of the current session of parliament to step up work on the new constitution and a variety of social measures.
5) Close cooperation between the civilian government and the Derg.[74]

The emperor acceded to all five demands.

This was a watershed for Ethiopian politics over the next several months. The government of Endelkatchew was under extreme pressure with the Derg now clearly watching its every move and even on occasion intervening in matters of policy. The real political power in Ethiopia had now become the Derg, which paralleled and controlled a nominal civilian cabinet. It became clear that while the "men in uniform" had no desire to govern directly, they would not return to their barracks until major reforms had been set in motion.

The events of early July were significant also because the radicalization of politics was legitimized. Radical airmen who had been jailed in March were released and began to exert their influence over the Derg's thinking. Civilian radicals in exile or underground now appeared to make their contribution to the public discussion taking place. The Derg actively solicited suggestions as to what problems needed addressing and how. It even went so far as to set up a post office box to which ideas could be mailed.[75]

Informal contacts between soldiers and intellectuals also became important. The airmen had begun this practice in March when they went to the university to enlist student support for military reform and to declare their solidarity with students on issues they considered important. They had even cooperated with civilian groups in the dissemination of antigovernment literature. Now, however, contacts were made between Derg members who had studied at the university and their former professors and fellow students. They sought advice from radical intellectuals on reform priorities and strategies.[76] Over time, the notion of a civilian advisory group to the Derg became institutionalized as the Politbureau.

The Derg forced Endelkatchew out of office on July 22, suspecting him not only of footdragging on the matter of reform, but also of plotting against the Derg. He was replaced by Mikael Imru, also a Shoan nobleman, who had a reputation as a progressive. Aman Andom, who had been named chief of staff on July 1, now also became minister of defense. Ten days later Endelkatchew was arrested, along with nine of his supporters, and charged with a series of misdeeds including "a lack of enthusiasm" for the ideal of Ethiopia Tikdem.[77] There was also some question as to where the prime minister stood on the matter of constitutional reforms. During the period of the most intense debate on the constitutional commission, Endelkatchew had outlined a position that seemed unprogressive to many. In contrast to the wishes of parliament and liberals on the commission, for example, Endelkatchew proposed that parliament should suggest a list of possible candidates for prime minster from which the constitutional monarch would choose one, rather than parliament itself making the selection.[78] Endelkatchew was further accused of trying to foment dissension within the Derg. He created internal conflicts in the committee when he offered it six cabinet posts in early July, allegedly realizing that a debate might ensue among the committee members over who should serve in these positions.[79]

In August the pace of the "creeping revolution" quickened. The Derg began a systematic publicity campaign to discredit the regime. Not only were the governments of Aklilu and Endelkatchew more vigorously attacked, but the emperor himself was accused of numerous excesses. He was portrayed as an avaricious "merchant" and a "thief" who had amassed a private fortune on the sweat and blood of the "toiling masses." The emperor was further accused of squandering the country's wealth on lavish trips abroad designed to enhance his international reputation. Two weeks before he was formally deposed he was even accused of being personally involved in the cover-up of the Wollo famine. All of this was intended to prepare the populace for his dethronement.[80]

One public institution after the other was dismantled. The crown council, the court of justice, the minister of the pen, and the military council were unilaterally abolished by the Derg. The commander of the Imperial Guard was arrested.[81] Thus the emperor was stripped of the remaining vestiges of his power. His land, along with that of other members of the nobility, and various businesses owned by the royal family and the nobility were nationalized, and the emperor was placed under virtual house arrest.

Despite severely weakening the civilian government and chipping away at the institutional establishment, the Derg could not agree on formally removing the emperor. Even the increasingly powerful Major Mengistu is said to have felt that it would make good tactical sense not to dethrone him.[82] After four days of deliberation in early September, however, the Derg reached agreement that Haile Selassie should go. As if still in doubt about the prudence of the decision, the final act was delayed by three days. In the meantime, the case against the emperor was further clarified. The Derg accused him of "building statues to dead dogs and feeding live ones while hundreds of thousands of people were starving."[83] They produced a picture of a headstone for the Emperor's deceased pet Lulu, a Chihuahua, that read: "To Lulu—Our Beloved dog. He has been with us to Europe, Latin America, and Asia."

The crowning act of the desecration and destruction of the imperial myth came on September 11, when Ethiopian television aired "Hidden Famine," Jonathan Dimbleby's film on the Wollo famine. The film was interjected with scenes of the emperor and his guests eating expensive food, drinking champagne, and feeding meat to his dogs from a silver tray. The emperor himself is alleged to have been forced to watch the film.[84]

The next day the emperor was formally deposed. The end of Haile Selassie's reign on September 12, 1974, appeared anticlimactic given the events that had unfolded since July. The Derg formally assumed power, changing its name from the Armed Forces Coordinating Committee to the Provisional Military Administrative Council (PMAC) and setting up a provisional military government. Both parliament and the newly prepared constitution were suspended. Lieutenant General Aman Andom assumed the position of head of state, chairman of the PMAC, as well as the chairmanship of the Council of Ministers and minister of defense. Even though Aman was not a member of the Derg—save for departures, its membership never changed after it was established—he became its chairman. This was an obvious move to legitimate the Derg in the eyes of the people by demonstrating its association with a heroic figure.

Part Three

Revolution in the Revolution:
The Dilemmas of the New Order

VII

THE QUEST FOR A NEW
SOCIAL MYTH

The act of displacing the Haile Selassie regime was an essential but nevertheless only an initial step in the revolutionary transformation of Ethiopian society. The larger task was to reconstitute society on the foundations of new social, economic, and political institutions and a new social myth. Under the best of circumstances this would have been no easy task. But given the fragility of the state apparatus and the uncertainty of the Derg's unity and power, this process would prove to be particularly difficult.

The Derg realized that it lacked the legitimacy that once surrounded the imperial throne and that it would therefore have to fashion new symbols of authority to replace the old social myth. It was clear that at the crucial moment of seizing power, there was no consensus in the ranks of the Derg about a new social myth. Few in society at large, except for young radical intellectuals, had given much thought to anything different from the monarchy.

As the revolutionary forces in society moved toward their destiny between 1973 and 1974, the climate for political discourse was liberalized. Criticism of the old regime on ideological grounds became commonplace, particularly in the capital city. In the countryside, among groups incorporated into the Ethiopian state in the nineteenth and twentieth centuries—the Oromos, Afar, Somali, Eritreans, and others—the emphasis was most often on criticizing the ethnic chauvinism that had inspired and undergirded the imperial state. Many among those groups saw the Ethiopian state itself as illegitimate. The Derg faced the challenge of introducing a new ideology, a new social myth, that would at once provide the basis for its legitimacy among the general population and serve as a guide for policy and political action. This would involve winning the widespread acceptance of a military-based regime and its program and of the concept of a multiethnic society based on the territorial configuration that existed at the time the emperor was deposed. In other words, in the course of building the new state, the Derg had to create a new social myth *and* resolve the national question.

This chapter considers how the Derg addressed these twin challenges in its thirteen years of rule. Without a satisfactory approach to dealing with these issues, the road to revolutionary transformation is destined to be not only long and hard but also perilous. Opposition groups who objected to the social myth articulated by the Derg or to alleged continued "Abyssinian" chauvinism on the part of the ruling class acted as a drag on revolutionary consolidation. Policies and institutions introduced by the Derg between 1975 and 1987 were conscious attempts to find a formula that would provide the legitimacy necessary for unchallenged rule.

Socialist Revolution by the Back Door

The establishment of the Provisional Military Administrative Council (PMAC), under the leadership of General Aman Andom, was announced by the Derg on September 15, 1974. From this point on the programs and policies of the Derg began to take form and to become more radical. At the time, the government's ideological orientation could not be definitively described. It appeared to be nothing more than a radical-nationalist military dictatorship. The Derg continued to operate as a secret committee of about 120 with anonymous membership, entrusting the day-to-day operation of the government to those of its members appointed to the PMAC, some of whom, like Aman Andom, were not originally involved in the revolutionary movement.

Even as it organized itself and prepared to make its decisive move, the Derg, and by extension the military, was being criticized by civilian leftists, who favored the revolution but opposed military rule, and by radicals within its own ranks. Nevertheless, when the PMAC took power, conservative elements within the Derg held sway. Interestingly, even Major Mengistu Haile Mariam, who was to become the ruthless leader of the Ethiopian Revolution, demonstrated conservative caution in the Derg's deliberations over social reconstruction. He initially opposed, for instance, deposing the emperor on "tactical" grounds, but acceded to the compromise involving the maintenance of the institution of the emperorship, but only as a figurehead. The dominance of a conservative or moderate mood in the Derg, however, did not last for long. No doubt this was influenced by the growing pressures from the civilian Left, pressing the Derg for a revolutionary solution to Ethiopia's problem, and the desperate search of the Derg for the popular legitimation of its actions. In late November a dispute between General Aman Andom and other members of the Derg over a solution to the Eritrean problem ended in the PMAC chairman's death while resisting arrest for the treasonable act of suggesting a negotiated settlement with the Eritrean nationalists. Hardliners in the Derg favored a military solution rather than a political one. The same night, the Derg voted to execute immediately fifty-seven of the most important political prisoners. From this point on, radicals within the Derg and PMAC apparently gained the upper hand. The clearest manifestation of this was the proclamation of December 20, *Ethiopia Tikdem* (Ethiopia First), which was the first clear-cut statement of the Derg's firm commitment to what came to be known as *hebrettesebawinet* (communalism). The essence of this new ideology appeared similar to other brands of African socialism, namely commitment to equality, justice, self-reliance, the dignity of labor, cooperativeness, cultural pride, and above all national unity. It was devoid of explicitly Marxian terminology and even appeared to look on all foreign ideologies with disdain. Commenting on the criteria for selecting *hebrettesebawinet* as its philosophy, the provisional military government (PMG) proclamation stated, "The political philosophy should spring from the culture and the soil of Ethiopia; and should, moreover, emanate from the aspirations of the broad masses; and not be imported from abroad like some decorative article of commerce."[1]

The policies that grew out of this declaration covered the structure of government, political organization, economic policy, social policy, and foreign policy. The new regime committed itself to a decentralized form of government in which the people down to the village level would have the right to govern themselves. The people would hold the government in check through popular participation via an all-embracing political party. In the economic sphere, poverty, rather than feudalism and capitalist exploitation, was seen as the most pressing problem. Like other brands of African socialism, however, *hebrettesebawinet* advocated "public ownership of economic resources." In the area of social policy, Ethiopia Tikdem emphasized the need to expand opportunities for formal education and modern health care and to encourage the full development of the country's cultural heritage. The foreign policy component of the document was simply a token reference to Ethiopia's support of the principles of African unity.

In spite of its moderate, almost mechanical tone, Ethiopia Tikdem, in the initial phase of consolidation under the PMAC, came to provide the ideological justification for the regime's policies. Within weeks, the war in Eritrea was stepped up, officials claimed, in the interest of preserving Ethiopian unity. Within days, the government announced the inauguration of the National Campaign for Development through Cooperation, the *Zemacha*. This campaign came to involve about sixty thousand university and high school students. In the absence of a vanguard party, the Zemacha was intended to explain the aims of the revolution to the "toiling masses" in the countryside. The immediate objective of the campaign was "to give all Ethiopians a uniform orientation, to organize them in a manner consistent with the spirit of the revolution so that a strong and unified democratic Ethiopia would emerge."[2]

In January 1975 the Derg spelled out more fully its economic program. Over the next several weeks all banks and insurance companies and most large-scale industries came under state control. By 1977 about two hundred industrial and commercial enterprises had been nationalized; and by

1982 the state owned 80 percent of the entire industrial sector. Significantly, however, the industrial sector (manufacturing, building, and construction) accounts for only 10 percent of the Gross Domestic Product annually.

In spite of the symbolism involved in the nationalization of the industrial sector, this action was far from revolutionary. The state under Haile Selassie had been heavily involved in the economy even though it remained essentially a free market economy. What was different and potentially revolutionary were the apparent intentions of the Derg to control and manipulate the economy more directly.

In the early stages of the revolution the most radical policy move made by the Derg was the nationalization of all rural land. On March 4, 1975, the PMG issued the "Proclamation to Provide for the Public Ownership of Rural Lands." This step went far beyond what could have been expected from Ethiopia Tikdem. The proclamation nationalized all rural land and set guidelines for the size of land holdings and conditions of land use. Moreover, it was declared that farmers could not possess more land than they themselves could reasonably farm. In other words, the practice of hiring wage labor to aid in farm cultivation was abolished. In one fell swoop the basis of feudal power was ordered swept away.

The immediate result was the abolition of most existing systems of land tenure. Rural property reverted to the state, which accepted the responsibility of equitably redistributing the land to those who would farm it. Farmers were granted usufruct rights to what was considered a fair allotment of land. Where possible, there was an attempt to standardize the amount of land given to each conjugal family at no more than ten hectares. But in some cases this was not possible because of the variability in land quality. In no case was a farm family allowed more than they themselves could cultivate. Tenancy was abolished, and wage labor was now allowed only on state farms or in institutions where the head of household was indigent or otherwise handicapped.[3]

Another important feature of the land reform proclamation was that it encouraged peasants to form themselves into peasant associations, consisting of one association for every eight hundred hectares of land. This amounted to an average of 200 to 250 farm families per association. Membership was automatically open to all former tenants and owners of less than ten hectares of land. Farmers owning larger plots of land could keep more than ten hectares and join an association, but only after all landless peasants in the area had been given an adequate share of redistributed land.

The complexity of Ethiopia's various land tenure systems, the poor quality of land registration procedures and records, the logistical problems inhibiting acceptable cadastral surveys, and a lack of sufficient manpower had all been given as excuses by the Haile Selassie regime for not attempting land reform. These same obstacles faced the Derg, but it proceeded with land reform nevertheless. The government did not possess the administrative capacity to send bureaucrats from the center to oversee land redistribution. Nor did it possess an ideologically conscious vanguard party that could aid in this process. Instead, it vested a great deal of responsibility in the newly created peasants associations under the directions of Zemacha campaigns. These youth played a major role in the early phases of peasant association development. They had been in the field even before the land reform proclamation, studying the conditions of peasant society and preparing the people for the expected land reform.[4]

It was not long, however, before the Derg realized that the lack of a clearly defined program and a trained and disciplined cadre of field administrators was sabotaging, rather than facilitating, its land reform objectives. Social leveling was taking place, but the peasantry was calculating its behavior on perceived family or local needs rather than on national needs. The Derg had been more interested in campaigners overseeing the mechanics of implementation than acting as agents of peasant mobilization. The most socially conscious of the students, on the other hand, saw their mission as that of empowering the peasantry and raising their consciousnesses.

Many of the Zemacha campaigners were much more ideologically radical than the Derg at the time. The Derg's initial ideology was essentially nationalistic rather than universalistic (i.e., Marxist-Leninist). By contrast, the students were often well versed in the tenets of Marx, Lenin, and Mao, and they attempted to use these as organizing and educating principles in their dealings with the peasantry. In many cases, this set them at odds with the Derg as well as with the traditionally cautious peasantry. Zemacha students in some cases attempted to get peasant communities to farm collectively even though the Derg had not ordered this.[5] In the climate of turmoil that preceded the fall of Haile Selassie in some areas of the south, peasants spontaneously revolted and chased Amhara landlords from their holdings.

Complicating the generally uncontrolled changes taking place among the peasantry as the land reform program unfolded, other problems forced the Derg to attempt to recapture some of the authority it had delegated to rural communities. In some cases, for example, local members of the civil service and police who were expected to help enforce the Derg's decrees were compromised by the fact that they themselves were former landlords and used their offices to protect their own class interests rather than to serve the will of the state.

Faced with enormous problems of coordination and control in its land reform program, in December 1975 the Derg issued an additional proclamation on peasant associations. The decree established the legal standing of peasant associations, defined their duties and responsibilities, and called for the establishment of agricultural cooperatives as the basis for socialist agriculture.[6] This was the first clear indication of a leftward drift in the

Derg's orientation. The main function of peasant associations was now to be the promotion of cooperative farming. A gradual evolution from service to producer cooperatives was envisioned, and these would ultimately be transformed into advanced producer cooperatives or collectives.[7]

The Derg followed the rural lands proclamations with other edicts relating to the nationalization of all urban land and houses not physically occupied by the owners. Whereas the rural lands policy had effectively led to the demise of the landed aristocracy and gentry, the urban lands policy was a decided effort to eliminate the wealth, power, and influence of a growing urban-based indigenous entrepreneurial class.

An estimated 409,000 urban houses and apartments were nationalized.[8] Most of these units were assigned to newly created urban dwellers' associations, kebeles, for administration. Urban areas were divided into administrative zones, all headed by kebeles. These organizations became new instruments of state power. The central government administered almost twenty thousand units; these were among the most attractive and expensive domiciles. The rest were managed by individual kebeles. Kebeles were also given the responsibility for neighborhood development and security.

The Derg further set in motion policies intended to improve the housing, health, education, and other aspects of the welfare needs of the vast majority of the population. Low rent housing units, for example, were built on urban land that had belonged to members of the royal family, the nobility, or urban-based indigenous entrepreneurs. Efforts were also made to make safe water and modern health care more accessible to more people; to improve the overall literacy rate; and to generally improve the quality of life throughout the country. Positive results were slow but unmistakable over the next twelve years. I shall return to this point in the next chapter.

Ideology and Social Conflict

As the Derg took its first steps to implement its program, elements of the civilian Left that had been allowed to surface during the period of the "creeping coup" vigorously challenged the legitimacy of military rule and pushed for variants of a civilian-based people's government as an alternative. The Derg's economic and social policies under the rubric of Ethiopia Tikdem were clearly intended to win the support of the civilian Left and the population at large, as well as to improve social conditions. Yet this support was not forthcoming in any significant sense. Rather than suppressing its civilian critics, the Derg at first attempted to appease them with increasingly radical policies.

When it became evident that the Derg was willing to listen to the demands of civilian groups and even to accept some of their advice, but not to hand over or share power with them, civilian opposition intensified and became more clearly articulated. The most important opposition between

1976 and 1977 came from the Ethiopian People's Revolutionary Party (EPRP), which tried to undermine the regime by disseminating political leaflets intended to discredit the Derg and by infiltrating key mass organizations like the Zemacha and the Confederation of Ethiopian Labor Unions (CELU) and eventually the Provisional Office of Mass Organizational Affairs (POMOA), an ideological arm of the regime introduced in 1976.

The climate of new freedoms that existed at the time contributed to open public debate over the future of Ethiopia and the character of the new society. The main protagonists in this debate were the EPRP and *Meison* (the All-Ethiopian Socialist Union). Meison was willing to accept the idea of military rule, at least for the moment. The EPRP, on the other hand, was diametrically opposed to such an idea. The debate between the two groups first took place in the pages of pamphlets, newspapers, and other documents and did a lot to shape the thinking of the general population on what should be the nature of the new Ethiopia. The debate also revealed the fundamental difference in the views of Meison and the EPRP. In addition to their contradicting positions on the issue of military rule, EPRP and Meison differed on the kind of democracy they envisioned. Meison favored "controlled democracy," guided by a vanguard party. The EPRP pressed uncompromisingly for an unlimited "people's democracy."

The friction between the two groups seems to have inspired the Derg to become more radical. By mid-1976 it was clear that to maintain its hold over the state, the Derg would have to alter its ideological program and either co-opt or destroy the civilian Left. It began to pursue both goals simultaneously with the announcement of the Program for the National Democratic Revolution (PNDR), the founding of POMOA and the *Yekatit 66* (February 1973) Ideological School, and the establishment of an advisory political body, the Politbureau.

The announcement of the PNDR signaled the Derg's jettisoning of Ethiopia Tikdem and its replacement with a commitment to the principles of scientific socialism as articulated by Soviet ideologists. This document attempted to outline a noncapitalist strategy for socialist development, in keeping with the way Soviet ideologists had come to rationalize the legitimacy of radical regimes in the Third World. Those who pursue this strategy are termed "revolutionary democrats," and their aim is the creation of a "people's democratic republic."[9] A noncapitalist approach to development was dictated by the fact that African states had not matured as capitalist systems but instead were characterized by "medieval survivals." This made conditions in countries like Ethiopia different from the conditions that gave rise to the Russian Revolution of 1917. Logistically, then, it was assumed that the general theory and practice of socialist transformation had to be adapted to the specific conditions of Ethiopia. Soviet ideologists justify such an approach by arguing that Lenin himself came out categorically against overemphasis on technical-economic prerequisites as well as against rigid, deterministic political preconditions for socialist revolution. The fact that Ethiopian leaders exhibited a "socialist orientation" was reason enough for the Soviets to consider embracing them as clients.

Ethiopia's PNDR couched its ideological position in terms of Marx's theory of class struggle. It divided Ethiopia's classes into two basic groups: a counterrevolutionary front comprised of the feudal class, the comprador bourgeoisie, and the bureaucratic bourgeoisie, all of which were in league with the forces of imperialism; and the broad front of revolutionary forces based on the alliance of peasants and workers along with the progressive bourgeoisie. The latter group included the military, and together with peasants, workers, other oppressed classes, and elements of the petty bourgeoisie, it is said to make up the vanguard of revolutionary democrats. In practice, however, the "men in uniform" came to occupy the position of first among equals in the so-called "progressive front."

The immediate mission of the revolution was claimed to be the liberation of Ethiopia from the vestiges of feudalism, bureaucratic capitalism, and imperialism. It was argued that this could only come about through intense political education and agitation; the strengthening of the state apparatus; the reorganization of the productive forces in society; the development of a centrally planned economy; and the establishment of a viable, all-embracing Marxist-Leninist vanguard party. By following the correct line, it would be possible to create a society free of the exploitation of man by man. Special attention was to be given to finding a just solution to Ethiopia's "national question."[10]

By endorsing Soviet-style scientific socialism as the foundation of the new social myth, the Derg was attempting to come up with a universalistic "correct line" that made nonacceptance of or opposition to its program illegitimate. In theory no one could be allowed not to learn the tenets of the new myth or to refuse to take an active part in the revolution. Anyone who disagreed was branded a "counterrevolutionary," "antipopular," "retrogressive," or "narrow nationalist." Progressives in the revolution theoretically had it as their duty to resort to immediate revolutionary justice and "liquidate" the enemies of the revolution whenever they were exposed. In fact this happened frequently during the Red Terror period between 1977 and 1978. There was no room for pluralist party competition. The Derg employed this type of reasoning to shield itself from those who objected to its self-proclaimed vanguard role in the transition to socialism.

The choice of the scientific socialist path by the Derg, it can be argued, was based more on pragmatic than ideological considerations. This approach is valued more for what it allows the regime to do than for what it is. What the Derg and its supporters seem to find convenient about the Soviet model is that it allows the ruling elite to define the normative order (under the old order this was defined in documents establishing the Solomonic myth and in politico-religious ritual); and it approves of the domination of a ruling oligarchy and a statist rather than populist development strategy. Pretensions are made toward democratic participation, but the ruling oligarchy consciously structures politics so that its values always predominate.

While it claimed to recognize the need for a vanguard party, the Derg did not announce the formation of such an institution at the time the PNDR was proclaimed; nor did it set a clear timetable for such an occurrence. It tried to create an aura of openness, conducive to the free exchange of ideas, by allowing political groups to operate in a semilegitimate fashion. They were not allowed to organize on a mass scale but served in an advisory capacity as members of the Politbureau. Among these were the EPRP, a group of young Marxist intellectuals and students (often referred to by the Derg as the "sons and daughters of the old feudal class"); Meison, led by the French-educated Oromo Marxist, Haile Fide; *Abyot Seded* (the Revolutionary Flame), founded in 1976 among members of the armed forces and led by Mengistu himself; the *Waz* League (Labor League), which claimed a working-class base and shared the EPRP's populist tendencies; and ECHAAT (the Revolutionary Struggle of the Ethiopian Masses), a largely Oromo political organization.

Bitter ideological conflicts erupted between the two most powerful civilian groups of the Politbureau, the EPRP and Meison. Meison supported the Derg while EPRP tried to undermine it. In addition to infiltrating mass organizations, the EPRP tried to consolidate its influence among elementary, high school, and university students. In 1976, around the time of the announcement of the PNDR, sporadic bloody encounters, assassinations, and counterassassinations began to occur in the streets and back alleys of Addis Ababa between Meison and the EPRP. By this time Meison had secured the position of the most influential civilian group in the Politbureau for itself. Even as this was happening, within the Politbureau and in kebele cells, Meison was being challenged by Abyot Seded. The Derg was suspicious of Meison's growing influence in all sectors of society.

Abyot Seded appeared to be systematically preparing itself to assume the role of chief adviser to the Derg on ideological, political, and organizational matters. It aspired to displace Meison in that capacity. Given its military membership, it was in a good position to do this. Also apparent was that influential members of Abyot Seded were transforming themselves into "committed communists" if they had not done so before. Several officers associated with Abyot Seded were sent to the Soviet Union, East Germany, and Cuba after 1976 to receive ideological training. They returned and set about politicizing the military rank and file with enlightened vigor.

Violent opposition to the Derg and its Meison collaborators on the part of the EPRP in urban areas escalated into a systematic terror campaign in the fall of 1976. The EPRP was responsible for the bombing of the Ideological School and for the numerous political assassinations aimed not only at Meison and Derg members, but also at public officials at all levels. The aim was to discredit totally the regime and its supporters. The EPRP's tactics came to be labeled as "White Terror" by the Derg and were countered by the regime's "Red Terror." The object of the Red Terror campaign was to liquidate the so-called enemies of the revolution by any means available. Over an eighteen- to twenty-month period between 1977 and 1978, upwards of five thousand young people were killed.

Over this period, the Derg became estranged from civilian groups one by one. By early 1979 Abyot Seded stood alone as the only officially accepted political organization. The others were branded "Trotskyites" and "anarchists" (EPRP); "opportunists" (Meison); "Maoists" (Waz League); "narrow nationalists" (ECHAAT); and "antirevolutionaries" (*Malered*, a small splinter group from Meison). The Derg eventually came to the conclusion that it could not trust the cooperation of even the Marxist-Leninist "organizations" as long as they had hidden agendas.

Growing violations of human rights in Ethiopia prompted its military ally, the United States, to encourage moderation in the Derg's policies for dealing with its mounting problems in urban and rural areas. This admonition came at a time when the Derg and Meison were actively arming peasant, worker, and student supporters of the regime's program as a counter to the White Terror. From the Derg's perspective, what was at stake in the political crisis was its very survival. It felt it could not compromise with either those who would remove it from the vanguard role in the revolution or those who would balkanize the state.

Even though it had committed itself to scientific socialism, the Derg had not severed its relations with the U.S. or unreservedly committed itself to the Soviet camp. One of the main reasons for this apparent ambivalence within the Derg was the failure to develop a workable alliance among conservative, radical, and moderate elements within the group. Several bloody internal power struggles were necessary before such an accord was reached, and Mengistu Haile Mariam emerged as the first among equals between 1977 and 1978. From the time of the announcement of the PNDR on, however, Ethiopia-U.S. relations worsened precipitously.

The decision by newly elected American President Jimmy Carter in early 1977 to curtail arms sales to Ethiopia seems to have been the proverbial straw that broke the camel's back. In April Mengistu ordered all U.S. military personnel in the country to leave within seventy-two hours and set about attempting to establish new alliances with countries such as Cuba, the Soviet Union, and other Eastern bloc countries. This move precipitated a worsening of the multiple crises being faced by the regime, almost leading to its downfall. Perhaps the most serious challenge the Derg faced were internal wars that erupted throughout the country involving ideological opponents of the Derg like the EPRP, as well as such nationalist movements as the Eritrean People's Liberation Front (EPLF), the Oromo Liberation Front (OLF), the Tigre People's Liberation (TPLF), and the Western Somali Liberation Front (WSLF). The regime appeared more vulnerable than ever before, and opponents clearly wanted to exploit this weakness. I shall return to this point in the next section. The rejection of the alliance with the U.S. and the turn to the Soviet Union and Cuba was at once a "divorce" and a "marriage of convenience." The Derg was forced into its actions not only by a felt need to survive as a class, but also by its concern for the territorial integrity of the Ethiopian state. It seems that the thought among even moderates and conservatives in the Derg was: "if survival as a ruling class and as a multiethnic state requires a more definitive public commitment to scientific socialism, this is a price worth paying for the sake of the 'motherland.'"

As soon as the embers of internal war began to cool in 1978, the Soviets began to pressure the Derg to patch up its differences with civilian leftists and to move seriously toward setting up a civilian-based vanguard party. Despite its continuing lack of consensus on the need for such a party, the Derg made a final attempt to strike a deal with civilian groups. In late June the Derg agreed that Abyot Seded, along with the factional remnants of Malered and the Waz League, would be amalgamated into one all-embracing organization called the Union of Marxist-Leninist Organizations— *Emaledeh* in Amharic. This plan to form a front of parties to facilitate the search for a "dependable proletarian leadership" ended in failure just over one year later.

On September 13, 1979, Mengistu announced that a commission to establish a framework for the long-awaited vanguard party of working people would soon be constituted. The commission was to supersede all existing political organizations (i.e., civilian parties, Abyot Seded, POMOA) and to prepare the way for the creation of a bona fide party of workers that would take over the leadership of the revolution. Mengistu became the chairman of the commission, and he chose its membership from mass organizations. As a way of appeasing the military, almost half of the commission membership came from the armed forces.[11] One of the main responsibilities of the commission was the nomination of a Politbureau that was supposed ultimately to replace the Derg.

Mengistu made the formal announcement of the Commission to Organize the Party of Working People of Ethiopia (COPWE) in a nationwide radio and television address on December 17, 1979. He explained that although there was always an awareness in the Derg that a vanguard party was necessary, until then the objective conditions of society had not dictated its formation.[12] I shall return to a discussion of the significance of party formation in the next chapter.

The main point here is that the Derg was pressured into becoming more leftist and radical by the civilian Left, but it translated this trend into an opportunity to entrench itself as a new ruling class. It consciously and systematically separated itself from civilian groups and carved out its own ideological identity, guided by its own policy objectives. The seeds of ideological opposition, however, continued to present the regime with difficulties, and the "national question" remained unaddressed.

Nationalism and the New Order

The Derg readily acknowledged that many nationalities within Ethiopia had been oppressed and exploited under the old order, and it was obliged to reverse this situation. The solution that the new regime envisioned, however, at no time included the option of secession. This was clear from the very first utterances of the Derg in Ethiopia Tikdem, which laid heavy emphasis on the need to preserve national unity.

The chaos during the months leading up to the overthrow of Haile Selassie seems to have inspired the Eritrean liberation movements. By the time the emperor actually fell, the Ethiopian forces were being seriously challenged in the region. In fact, crushing defeats of the imperial army in Eritrea between December 1973 and January 1974 were among the precipitants of the revolution.[13] Those setbacks fueled the Neghele and Asmara army mutinies and signaled that, as never before, one of the most critical of the emperor's flexible resources, the army, was not unquestionably with him.

On assuming power, the first order of business for the Derg was to solve the Eritrean "problem." Some in its ranks pressed for a decisive military solution. Others favored some form of a negotiated settlement. Among the latter was General Aman Andom, the first Derg chairman. There was a lull in the fighting in Eritrea after the September 1974 coup, as people in the region, as in others, waited in anticipation of the Derg's "new deal." Before he was deposed in a bloody palace coup in November 1974, Aman Andom made two visits to Eritrea in hopes of arranging a political solution to the conflict. For his efforts, hardliners in the Derg accused Aman Andom of having shown weakness in dealing with the Eritrean situation. Influential nationalists in the Derg continued to endorse the idea of "Greater Ethiopia" espoused by the previous regime. They continued to press for a military solution, while at the same time claiming to be supportive of the right of all Ethiopian nationalities to self-determination. The Program for the National Democratic Revolution was a first attempt to articulate the regime's position on this issue. The document asserts:

> The right to self-determination of all nationalities will be recognized and fully respected. No nationality will dominate another one since the history, culture, language and religion of each nationality will have equal recognition in accordance with the spirit of socialism. The unity of Ethiopia's nationalities will be based on their common struggle against feudalism, imperialism, bureaucratic capitalism, and all reactionary forces. This united struggle is based on the desire to construct a new life and a new society based on equality, brotherhood and mutual respect.[14]

The PNDR statement on nationalities was followed by the Nine Point Statement on Eritrea in May 1976, which in essence restated the language of the PNDR so that it more directly applied to Eritrea. Subsequently there were other attempts by the regime to deal at least rhetorically and symbolically with the Eritrean problem, including a seminar conducted in June–July 1978 to discuss the Eritrean situation; Operation Red Star in 1982, a multifaceted approach (social, economic, cultural, military) to bring Eritrea back into the Ethiopian fold; numerous secret meetings in the early to mid-1980s; the creation of the "Institute for the Study of Ethiopian Nationalities"; and Mengistu's May Day speech in 1983 when he said for the first time that "in principle" he accepted secession as a legitimate option for oppressed nationalities. Nevertheless, over the first decade the Derg never indicated it was willing to compromise on its view of how much autonomy was acceptable within a larger unity. Instead, it pressed relentlessly to neutralize nationalist opponents militarily, and through its social policies it tried to win itself widespread legitimacy.

Official publications relating to the nationalities issue tended to center their argument around the notion that "the contradictions between nationalities is one aspect of the class struggle."[15] What appear to be "ethnic" tensions, then, are reduced to "class contradictions." The land reform programs, nationalization, the National Revolutionary Literacy Campaign, programs aimed at fostering cultural and religious equality, the creation of numerous mass organizations and policies designed to improve the overall quality of life—all are said to represent the new regime's serious attempt to address age-old injustices rooted in the ethnic chauvinism of Shoan Amharas and their collaborators. The argument further suggests that because of the sensitivity of the regime to these matters, calls for secession—or even for the removal of progressives in the military from a vanguard role in the revolution—are illegitimate.

In spite of herculean efforts over its first decade of rule to create conditions for its widespread acceptance, the Derg was not able to convince significant segments of the population that it was legitimate or that its vision of the new society was correct. The most serious initial challenge to its authority came between 1976 and 1978 when civilian groups confronted the regime in both urban and rural guerrilla campaigns. As mentioned above, groups like the EPRP and Meison attempted to undermine the Derg during this period mainly because they questioned its vanguard role. This opposition occurred mainly in the cities and was accompanied by much bloodshed. Other challenges, inspired by the regime's apparent weakness and disorganization, emerged in the countryside and were more separatist and nationalist in character.

Historically, the Ethiopian state under Haile Selassie relied considerably on U.S. military and economic aid as well as on its diplomatic support to provide it with the leverage to neutralize elements within society that threatened its territorial integrity. By 1976, however, it was clear that U.S.-Ethiopian relations were on the wane. From the perspective of the Derg, this turn of events proved to have profound consequences in light of widespread civil unrest.

The Derg's determination to pursue a "military solution" to the ever-expanding political challenges it faced caused concern within the U.S. government during the last days of the Ford administration because of growing human rights violations. Although Ford and Secretary of State Henry Kissinger at first feared Ethiopia's drift to the left, the administration appeared ready to stand by its client state in its later moment of crisis. The feeling was that American credibility was at stake.

The Ford administration sought to exercise some moderating leverage on the Derg by dragging its feet on approving the delivery of requested military aid. Nevertheless, even as the U.S. Congress and American public opinion favored pulling completely out of Ethiopia, the administration was making plans to deliver $22 million worth of military aid that had already been agreed.[16] The Pentagon feared a threat to Ethiopia from Soviet-backed Somalia, given the widespread turmoil raging in the country and the Derg's obvious limited capacity to control events. The Soviet Union was believed to be stockpiling massive amounts of arms and ground-to-air missiles in Somalia. Indeed, the Soviets had pumped over $400 million into Somalia by 1977.

The Derg was desperate. The Americans had dragged their feet on delivering badly needed military aid since 1975, and with Jimmy Carter about to take office, the possibility loomed of a complete cutoff, since Carter pledged during the 1976 presidential campaign to make human rights his number one priority. Ethiopia began to turn elsewhere for military aid. The Derg sought to buy arms from Turkey, Yugoslavia, China, Vietnam, and Czechoslovakia. It even turned to Libya, striking a deal that in effect guaranteed that Libya would cease aid to Eritrean rebels and give Ethiopia aid instead if the Ethiopians would allow a coup against Sudan's President Gaafar Nimeiry to be launched from Ethiopia. And in December 1976 the Soviet Union signed an agreement with Ethiopia for the delivery of $100 million in military supplies. At the time there appeared to be no intentions of completely turning away from the United States, but merely to supplement U.S. military aid.

Events in Ethiopia, propelled by their own dynamics, moved on at a dizzying pace. If the U.S. had ever been in a position to exercise influence on these developments, by January 1977 this was surely impossible. The Derg was in the midst of a bitter power struggle that ended on February 3, 1977, with Colonel Mengistu Haile Mariam emerging victoriously from a bloody palace shootout. In the next several days there followed a series of violent encounters involving the Derg, the civilian Left, college students, and even elementary and high school students.

During November 1976, President-elect Carter had noted his displeasure with the human rights record of the Derg. Whereas the Ford administration had hesitated, only threatening to cut off military aid to Ethiopia, Carter moved swiftly to establish human rights as the centerpiece of his foreign policy when he assumed office. On February 25, 1977, the administration announced that because of continued gross violations of human rights by the governments of Ethiopia, Argentina, and Uruguay, U.S. military aid to those countries would be reduced by October 1977. In the case of Ethiopia this meant a curtailment of $6 million in military aid grants, but neither military credits nor sales were immediately affected. Simultaneously, the U.S. and other Western countries began to apply economic pressures on Ethiopia, including the restriction of trade and credit, withholding investment guarantees, and pressing for compensation for the businesses seized in 1975.

In the meantime, the Soviet Union moved into the breach, attempting to orchestrate the creation of a Marxist-Leninist federation in the Horn of African involving Ethiopia, Eritrea, South Yemen, and Somalia. Between March and April 1977, Fidel Castro and Soviet President Nikolai Podgorny attempted to negotiate a settlement to the differences between Ethiopia and Somalia and to secure agreement on the federation idea. But to no avail. Siad Barre, the president of the Republic of Somalia, rejected the notion.

These talks coincided with the arrival of the first consignment of Soviet-made tanks provided to Ethiopia by South Yemen. One month later more tanks and personnel carriers arrived.[17] These developments were enough to allow Mengistu finally to respond to the announced reduction in U.S. military aid two months earlier. In April 1977 Mengistu announced that Ethiopia was demanding that the U.S. close down Kagnew, all Military Assistance and Advisory Group operations, the Naval Medical Research Unit, and the United States Information Service. Also the personnel of the U.S. embassy and Agency for International Development were to be reduced. One hundred American officials and their families were required to leave the country within four days. Mengistu's move came less than a week after Carter is reported to have declared his intentions to move closer to Somalia in an effort to dislodge the Soviets.

The Soviets continued to supply arms to both Somalia and Ethiopia, while attempting to negotiate a peace accord between the two sides. The United States and its Western allies stepped up efforts to woo Somalia away from the Soviet Union. The strategy was two-fold: to contemplate direct military aid to Somalia and to encourage indirect aid from third party countries in the region friendly to the West.[18]

The United States encouraged countries like Egypt, Saudi Arabia, and Sudan to funnel aid to Somalia while it considered aid requests on its own.[19] These moderate Islamic regimes were themselves concerned about the growing Soviet presence in the region. The United States continued to consider the possibility of direct military aid to Somalia, and on July 26, 1977, it announced that an agreement had been reached for that purpose. The United States claimed that this aid was contingent on Somalia's rejection of Pan-Somali claims over parts of Djibouti, Ethiopia, and Kenya. It appears that remarks made by the Somali president's American physician,

Kevin Cahill, were construed by Somali officials to mean that the Carter administration had no objection to Somalia's invasion of Ethiopia. The Somalis claimed the U.S. agreed not to resupply Ethiopia if Somali regular forces invaded but would rather seriously consider a Somali request for U.S. military aid.[20]

Eight days after a military agreement was announced between Somalia and the U.S., regular Somali troops were discovered fighting alongside guerrillas of the WSLF in the Ogaden. The Somalis had built the fourth largest army in Black Africa.[21] It was well trained and well equipped, and the U.S. was aware that it was capable of penetrating well inside Ethiopia before it was halted. The U.S. denied any complicity in the invasion and suspended further talks on military aid to Somalia until regular troops were withdrawn. Although the Soviet Union continued to supply aid to Somalia after the Ogaden invasion, it began to withdraw its personnel until by September no more than four hundred were left out of a contingent of more than one thousand. Relations between the two countries deteriorated rapidly, and on November 13, Somalia announced the abrogation of the July 1974 Treaty of Friendship and Cooperation with the Soviet Union. All military and civilian advisers and technicians were asked to leave, and the Soviet Union lost its rights to use Somali bases. In addition, diplomatic relations with Cuba were suspended.

Somali actions were a response to the growing involvement of Cuban troops and advisers and the Soviet advisers to Ethiopia. On the evening of November 28, the Soviet Union launched a huge air- and sealift of arms and materials intended for Ethiopia.[22] In a very short time more than $1 billion of military equipment was pumped into Ethiopia. In addition, over the next several months more than eleven thousand Cuban and one thousand Soviet military personnel arrived in the country and were dispatched to the Ogaden to help Ethiopian troops halt the Somali advance. By the end of 1977 Somali forces had penetrated beyond the Ogaden to the gates of Dire Dawa and Harar. This aid was decisive in turning the tide in favor of Ethiopia by early 1978. Before this happened, however, Ethiopia was on the brink of balkanization, and the nationalist movements that flowered into military and guerrilla movements at this time posed (and continue to pose) major threats to the Derg's new social myth.

Regular Somali troops and guerrillas from the WSLF occupied vast tracts of the Ogaden and forced the Ethiopian army into its fortresses at Jijiga, Harar, and Dire Dawa for almost eight months beginning in June 1977. The intention was to separate the Ogaden from Ethiopia and to set the stage for ethnic Somalis in the region to decide on their own future. Although similar gains were being recorded by the EPLF, the Eritrean Liberation Front, and several splinter groups in Eritrea, the Derg appeared to view the Ogaden as its most pressing problem.

After November 1977 the Soviets provided not only massive amounts of military equipment but also Soviet advisers to fill roles ranging from training officers to pilots for combat missions in MIGs and helicopters.[23] More-over, Cuban troops, whose numbers peaked at seventeen thousand after early 1978, spearheaded the counteroffensive that began in March of that year. Combat operations during the counteroffensive were orchestrated by the National Revolutionary Operations Command consisting of two Soviet generals, one Cuban general, and Mengistu.

More than fifty-five thousand soldiers were in the field at the height of the counteroffensive. Most of these were from the People's Militia, which had been hastily enlisted as civil turmoil expanded. Although many were forced into military service, other militiamen responded willingly to the "Call of the Motherland" as Mengistu harped on the need to protect Ethiopia from foreign invaders that threatened its sovereignty. These mili-tiamen were expected to overwhelm the Somalis by their sheer numbers. They were hurriedly and poorly trained and poorly supplied.

The Somali and WSLF forces, which numbered only about ten thousand, were quickly decimated once the counteroffensive began. Many WSLF fighters simply gave up the fight and returned to their villages. The massive counteroffensive rapidly routed regular Somali forces as well. Ethiopian and Cuban troops moved in to reestablish control over the southeastern border. From this point on, ethnic Somali opposition in the Ogaden took the form of sporadic guerrilla ambushes and occasional acts of sabotage. Today, even guerrilla actions are more difficult than in 1977–1978 because of the increased Ethiopian military presence in the Ogaden. By 1985 there were thirty thousand troops stretched out along the border. Guerrilla campaigns did not completely cease, but they were less regular and effec-tive than in 1977–1978.

After 1981 the WSLF came to be characterized by internal conflict and factionalism. Cooperation with the Oromo-based Somali Abbo Liberation Front (SALF) also deteriorated after this time. Any effort by the Ogaden Somalis to present a united front was thwarted by the Derg's sponsorship of opposition groups aimed at the overthrow of the Siad Barre regime in Mogadishu. Over the next two years the WSLF seems to have abandoned its commitment to a military liberation of the territory it claimed and called for a plebiscite under UN, OAU, or Arab League supervision to allow the populace of the region to exercise their right to self-determination.

Having brought the Ogaden under military control, the Derg set about attempting to win the support of the people living there through its social policies. Schools were rebuilt, and basic literacy, health, and other forms of social services were provided by the Relief and Rehabilitation Commission. Most important for Somali nomads and Oromo peasants, a program for restocking livestock herds was introduced. In addition, settlement schemes were begun. The army came to have an important role in this process, helping to rebuild infrastructure such as roads, dams, and water systems and doing ideological work.[24]

As late as 1985–1986, the regime had not consolidated its support and legitimacy in the hinterland. This seems to have inspired the development of the nationwide villagization program designed to facilitate the delivery of social services down to the village level.

Once the Ogaden was reoccupied the Derg turned its attention and its resources to Eritrea and other regions being overrun by opposition groups. Between late 1977 and mid-1978, the Derg had lost most of Eritrea, retaining control only of the capital of Asmara, the port cities of Assab and Massawa, and some small towns. Most were enclaves under siege by Eritrean forces. While simultaneously preparing a counteroffensive, the Derg, as had been a frequent pattern, negotiated with the EPLF, the dominant Eritrean movement, but these sessions failed. In May 1978 the counteroffensive began when government forces, with Soviet, East German, and South Yemeni support, pushed their way out of their Asmara bastion.[25] Over the next year more than 120,000 regular and militia troops pressed the offensive, gradually reclaiming 95 percent of the land that had fallen to the EPLF, ELF, and the Eritrean Liberation Front (ELF/PLF). The only area remaining under Eritrean control was Sahel Province on the border with Sudan.

In spite of four major mopping-up offensives, the Derg was unable to crush the Eritrean opposition by 1982. Yet the Derg decided to launch the "Red Star Campaign" in January of that year in a concerted effort to win the hearts and minds of the general population of Eritrea.[26] The thrust of this program was twofold. First, it was supposed to provide the resources necessary for the economic reconstruction of the region: rebuild and reopen factories that had been closed, repair school buildings, transportation networks, and other infrastructure; provide jobs for the unemployed; and improve food and commodity distribution. Second, the program aimed at arming workers and peasants, giving them military training, and providing them with the political and technical education deemed essential to the development of the new Ethiopia. At the same time the national army would deal a death blow to so-called "secessionist bandits." Clearly, this was an attempt to enhance the Derg's control and legitimacy in this troubled region.

On balance the Red Star Campaign was a failure, particularly from a military perspective. The offensive ground to a halt in May 1982 after coming within three miles of the EPLF stronghold of Nakfa. The toll in human lives was extremely high. More than thirty thousand Ethiopian soldiers were killed or wounded. The EPLF casualties were around four thousand.[27] The EPLF and other opposition groups operating in the region had to be content with a return to guerrilla tactics. They were entrenched in the Sahel Province area, but they were never able to consolidate their hold over as much territory as they had in 1977–1978. They kept the Ethiopian government further off balance by helping the TPLF to become a formidable fighting force in Tigre.

Despite the unsettled political as well as military climate in Eritrea, the

TABLE 7.1
Estimated Red Star Campaign Expenditures, January 1982–September 1983, in Thousands of Ethiopian Birr

Programs	Costs
Social and Economic	113,765
Rehabilitation and Resettlement	27,413
School Reconstruction	1,585
Organizational and Political	20,700
Total	163,463

SOURCE: *Ethiopian Herald*, Sept. 3, 10, 1983.

Derg forged ahead with the Red Star reconstruction and development program. By September 1983 fifteen major industrial complexes had been either rebuilt or repaired, creating more than eleven thousand jobs. Eleven schools had been reconstructed or built anew, as well as dams, roads, reservoirs, hospitals, and other infrastructure and service facilities in those areas controlled by the government.[28] Terracing and forestation projects were begun to aid in farm soil conservation. These achievements were realized at great cost. A rough estimate would be that about 162,463,000 Birr (US$66 million) was spent over the first nineteen months of the campaign.[29] (See Table 7.1.) This was close to 10 percent of the country's total nonmilitary budget.

Much of the regime's attention was devoted to attempting to establish a political and administrative presence in the region. COPWE branches were opened and said to be functioning normally as early as January 1982, its cadre carrying out organizational and ideological work in firms throughout Eritrea.[30] There was also a drive to create mass organizations such as youth groups, women's groups, peasant associations, and kebeles. A year after the campaign had begun the regime claimed that 303 peasant associations were operating in the region with almost sixty thousand members, and that there were 149 urban dwellers associations in fourteen urban centers.[31] Significantly, no such local governmental units had been set up in Barka and Sahel provinces where the opposition was strongest.

The government did succeed in securing some compliance among the population in the parts of Eritrea it controlled, but there was little evidence that this was a result of voluntary support. In response to the Derg's promise of amnesty, some Eritreans who had gone into exile did return and were ceremoniously absorbed into the government's program, but after a year, the number of returnees was still less than one thousand. Society became more regimented, but this was no indication of legitimacy. Evidence of this could be found in the apparent lack of enthusiasm Eritreans had for joining semivoluntary organizations like cooperatives. In September 1983 there were only forty-one service cooperatives with an estimated twenty-seven thousand members and eight producer cooperatives.[32] This compared with 3,651 service and 1,006 producer cooperatives nationally. There were over three hundred peasant associations and an equal number of Revolutionary Ethiopia Youth Associations and Revolutionary Ethiopia Women's Associations, but these organizations tended to form under government auspices and encouragement more often than service or producer cooperatives did.

The various Eritrean liberation movements seemed bent on disrupting the Derg's efforts to have its ideology and its rule accepted as legitimate. Even as reconstruction proceeded under the leadership of COPWE and other agencies of the Ethiopian state, efforts were often sabotaged by guerrilla assaults. The frustrations became more profound as opposition movements in other parts of the country stepped up their own guerrilla activities.

The TPLF, for example, recovered from near decimation in 1978 to become an extremely effective fighting force of about ten thousand by the 1980s. This was largely accomplished through the support of the EPLF, which provided training, arms, equipment, and even troops to assist the TPLF in its operations in Tigre. The TPLF came to control almost 90 percent of Tigre.[33] In part this had a lot to do with the limited military, economic, and organizational capacity of the Derg.

Even though the Ethiopian national army had swollen to almost 300,000 by 1983, it was incapable of dealing effectively with extremely active guerrilla movements scattered throughout the country. When it concentrated on the Ogaden or Eritrea, the pressure was stepped up in Tigre, Wollo, Sidamo, or Bale. Moreover, large mopping-up campaigns were extremely costly and, at least until 1984, were not followed up by intense political organizational work by COPWE outside of towns. Moreover, broad gauged development projects affecting large numbers of people were few.

The EPLF and TPLF sponsored the development of movements like the Ethiopian People's Democratic Movement (EPDM) and participated in some joint operations with this splinter group, which had its origins in the EPRP in Wollo and northern Shoa regions around 1982. Other opposition groups that had been driven into exile or underground also surfaced at this time. For example, the core of the moribund, monarchist Ethiopian Democratic Union (EDU) reappeared as EDU Tahadesco (the New EDU) and established two fronts in Gondar. The EPRP, operating in the same area, also resurfaced at the same time. In the south, the OLF and the Sidamo Liberation Movement (SLM) increased their guerrilla activities to coincide with these developments in the north. Significantly, by 1984 the TPLF and the OLF claimed to be parts of a unified movement of nationalist groups struggling not necessarily for total independence of their respective peoples but for their right of self-determination. The will of the people, they claimed, like the position now being taken by the WSLF and even the EPLF, could be determined in a free and fair plebiscite.[34]

By the mid-1980s the Derg seemed to be fighting a losing battle against nationalist groups. At best, a stalemate had been reached in Eritrea, but in other regions the situation was deteriorating. There were many reasons for this. One of the main reasons was the low morale among many government troops who had begun to tire under the weight of civil turmoil that had existed constantly since 1973 and had even intensified. Even worse, in Tigre the central government was faced with subversion from members of the regional administration. This prompted the Derg to purge numerous central government representatives and local officials in Tigre because of their suspected connections with the TPLF.[35]

Another problem had to do with the inability of the regime to establish effective COPWE cells in the hinterland of dissident provinces. This was especially true in Wollo, Eritrea, Gondar, Tigre, Sidamo, and Ogaden.[36] Movements operating in these regions continued to view the Derg and its agents as "Abyssinian colonialists." Even though such nationalist organizations as the TPLF and EPLF were dominated by Marxists by 1984, they tended to hold in disdain the Soviet brand of Marxism-Leninism espoused by the Derg.[37]

In response to continuing incidents of disaffection among nationalities, the Derg attempted to intensify its social and economic efforts in all parts of the country. This was particularly difficult, not only because of the continuing civil turmoil, but also because of the onset of another catastrophic drought—rivaling the one that led to Haile Selassie's demise—that became particularly intense between 1982 and 1984. The difficulty in areas like those in the north ravaged by war, drought, and famine was profound, but the Derg tried nevertheless, with only limited and in some cases ephemeral success, to press forward with it social program.[38]

To attempt to firm up its political and ideological position in areas outside cities, the Derg established the ideological school of COPWE, which ultimately came to serve the Workers' Party of Ethiopia (WPE) after September 1984. Some cadre had been posted to perform certain tasks before, but now the process became much more systematic. In spite of this, by 1987 the WPE was far from being an effective, highly centralized and disciplined vanguard party capable of leading development.

Failing to record immediate success in military, economic, or political terms, and faced with the blustering U.S. administration of Ronald Reagan determined to halt the spread of communism in the Horn, the Derg apparently felt it had its back against the wall and moved to bolster its military capacity.[39] It did this by spending more on defense and by expanding its army. The most up-to-date statistics indicate that Ethiopia's defense expenditures grew more than tenfold between 1974 and 1982 to $381 million, not including grants.[40] The armed forces grew to approximately 300,000 by 1984. In part this was a result of the buildup during the 1977–1978 crisis that involved the re-creation of a people's militia. This trend achieved semipermanence with the Derg's decision to introduce national conscription in 1983. Article 33 of "The Proclamation on the National

Military Service, the Military Commissariat and Territorial People's Militia" mandates that every Ethiopian between the ages of 18 and 30 engage in a six-month training course and then spend two years on active duty. Those between the ages of 30 and 55 are required to participate in a six-month training period and then remain committed as reservists.[41] National military service is defined as an active and reserve service in which every Ethiopian has the opportunity to serve and thereby renew his patriotic heritage "in the spirit of socialist patriotism and proletarian internationalism." Mengistu stated, "One of the fundamental preconditions of successful socialist construction is to ensure the people's readiness to defend themselves from the ravages of probable regional or global wars on the basis of the balance of forces generating from the basic contradictions of our epoch."[42] The service was also viewed as an important revolutionary education in that it contributed to the creation of "conscious militants" essential to carrying out revolutionary purposes. Some popular dissent arose as a result of this policy, but the Derg rationalized this away and forged ahead.

A token gesture toward addressing the "national question" was made with the founding of the Institute for the Study of Ethiopian Nationalities in March 1983, but it was clear by then, as before, that the Derg's highest priority was Ethiopia's territorial integrity and its own perpetuation as a ruling class.

VIII

SOCIALISM FROM ABOVE?
POWER CONSOLIDATION IN A
"SOFT STATE"

The difficulties encountered by the Derg in establishing the ideological basis for its version of a new society were equaled and even surpassed by the problems it experienced in attempting to lay a statist foundation for social and economic development. From the first halting steps the regime took to provide some substance to *Ethiopia Tikdem*, to the bold creation of the vanguard Workers' Party of Ethiopia (WPE), to the establishment of the People's Democratic Republic, the Derg consistently attempted to ensure its own survival and shore up its capacity to rule. Symbolic political gestures were complemented by purposive, tangible programs and policies. The Derg quickly demonstrated that it wanted to dismantle feudalism once and for all, to create new authorative institutions and social relationships, and to set society on a totally new foundation.

The challenge of social, political, and economic reconstruction was formidable. The importance of introducing a new social myth and having it widely accepted notwithstanding, it was clear that power consolidation and state building should be of equal priority. Any regime's survival rests heavily on its ability to address successfully both challenges simultaneously.[1] Under such circumstances the state becomes extremely instrumental in its efforts to utilize public resources to mobilize or control the general population. In Africa over the first several decades of the postindependence era, this tendency has been true no matter what the ideological orientation of a regime. The state has been compelled to become actively involved in providing for the public welfare and for leading economic and political development. Whereas in western polities laissez-faire economic development preceded the emergence of the welfare state—and indeed made it possible—the new states of Africa have had to cope from the earliest days of political independence with widespread demands for state welfarism as well as for popular participation in politics.[2] All but a handful of African countries are among the poorest in the world. (With an annual per capita income of just over US$100, Ethiopia is among the poorest of the poor.)

213

These countries are characterized by organizationally fragile political and administrative institutions with limited resources in state coffers.

Until the 1970s Haile Selassie did an effective job of getting the most out of the imperial state apparatus in attempting to control and limit popular demands and to manipulate the course of development. His inability to continue to harness popular demand eventually led to his demise. After 1974, the Derg found itself in the position of having to construct an authoritative state apparatus in its effort to direct and control development from a position of weakness. Indeed, present-day Ethiopia, in spite of its ideological pretensions, represents a quintessential "soft state," largely incapable of predictably following through on its will in an efficient manner.

The term "soft state" was first employed by Gunnar Myrdal to describe the governments he observed in a South Asian study.[3] Myrdal found that throughout the region, governments seemed unable to promote rapid economic development because political and social conditions prevented them from implementing public policies that imposed substantial obligations on the general populace. Even in situations where rules and regulations existed, he found that the governments he studied were not able to ensure compliant popular behavior. Myrdal concluded that the reason for this condition was a widespread syndrome of social indiscipline in South Asian societies. The people, he argued, belonged more to a "primordial public realm" than to a "civic public realm." Kinship and patron-client ties commanded more respect and legitimacy in peasant communities than did the state. People strove more to keep the state at bay or to escape from its domain than to follow it.[4] This lack of discipline, Myrdal contended, resulted less from cultural "givens" than from the specific historical circumstances that characterized such societies at a particular moment. Most possessed weak, inefficient, and/or corrupt state bureaucracies.

Most African states, no matter what their ideological orientations, tend to fit the "soft state" mold. Some attempt to strengthen their capacity to rule by reorganizing bureaucratic and political institutions or by invoking ideology almost as if it were magic. In either case, however, the realities of state "softness" prevent any quick fixes. Soft states are often authoritarian, coercive institutions, but this is more a reflection of their weakness or "softness" than of their power.

In contrast to what Myrdal found in Asia, what makes the state "soft" in Africa is not so much a lack of social discipline as it is the resource constraints that confront political leaders and their tendency to make bad or misguided policy choices.[5] Under the old regime in Ethiopia, Haile Selassie had spent much time and energy cultivating, managing, and expanding his independent resource base. His regime had to do this simply to survive. The challenge facing the Derg was the same. It had to devise mechanisms to cultivate, manage, and expand its reservoir of flexible resources. Without an adequate resource base accessible to the regime, even rational planning might fail. Y. Dror has suggested that in some cases even

when the leaders of poor countries try to plan rationally, they are disap-
pointed. He contends that although planning agencies may have relatively
better rational components than other policy-making agencies, their policy
making quality is often still poor. The reason is partly that the habit of
rational policy planning is not widely accepted or understood, and partly
because the needed policy inputs are scarce.[6] Qualified manpower is
scarce; appropriate modern technology is scarce; and financial resources—
particularly foreign exchange—are scarce. All of these constraints tend to
structure the quality of policy making in such situations.

Naomi Caiden and Aaron Wildavsky have identified the problem as a lack
of resource redundancy. Such redundancy is a prime requisite for coping
with change. Caiden and Wildavsky suggest that the main difference between policy making in rich and poor countries is that:

> The rich country may stockpile resources; it may embark on a number of
> courses of action, any one of which may be jettisoned or promoted as the
> course of events unfolds; it may collect a large bank of information some of
> which, at the moment, may be of little or no interest, but with the possibility
> that it may be crucial later on; it may employ bureaucratized procedures
> which reduce uncertainties.
>
> The uncertainties facing poor countries are more numerous and more
> intense than in rich ones. The interaction of these uncertainties vastly multi-
> plies their impact. Yet governments in poor countries lack the benefits of
> redundancy—the surplus, the reserve, the overlapping networks of skill and
> data—to cushion the reverberating effects of uncertainty.[7]

The Derg's approach to development in the face of limited resource
capacity has consisted of attempting to devise a statist strategy based on a
new social myth that is radically different from what guided and justified
the old order. For this strategy to be effective, it was determined, ideology
would have to be complemented by institutional transformation as well as
by innovation. The chosen statist strategy came to be modeled on the Soviet
Union's brand of state socialism. As mentioned in chapter 7, this model was
endorsed mostly because it represented a convenient justification for the
rule of a relatively small oligarchy and because it allowed this new ruling
class the exclusive authority to define the acceptable normative order.

Soviet endorsement of Ethiopia's attempt to copy their model was facilitated by the fact that Soviet analysts now admit that they do not expect any
revolutionary, genuinely Marxist-Leninist "breakthroughs" in Africa. They
have therefore come to accept that the "science" in some African socialist
experiments can be locally defined, based on local objective conditions. All
that is required for Soviet acceptance is adherence to the Marxist-Leninist
methodology and a relatively close association with the Soviet camp. This
would imply the acceptance and propagation of a theory or ideology based
on that articulated by contemporary Soviet ideologists.[8] The Marxist-
Leninist methodology further involves the concepts of class war; the strug-

gle against imperialism, capitalism, and neocolonialism; a materialist interpretation of history; the necessity of political agitation; and the ultimate
equality of all members of society. "Narrow nationalism" is to be condemned, while the need to preserve the identity of national groups within
the context of a people's democracy is emphasized.

At an operational level, the choice of this new orientation required the
reorganization and reconstitution of the state, the redistribution of wealth
and property, the creation of a capacity for central planning, the pursuit of
a state socialist development strategy under the guidance of a vanguard
party of "revolutionary democrats," and the establishment of a constitu-
tionally based people's republic.

Since the announcement of the Program for the National Democratic
Revolution, the regime has consistently attempted to synchronize the theory and practice of its brand of scientific socialism. In the process, a new
variant of state socialism is taking hold.[9] Although what is developing in
Ethiopia proceeded from different historical circumstance from other state
socialist experiences, the basic elements of what seems to be emerging there
are similar to what is found in more established systems based on the
concepts of state socialism (e.g., the Soviet Union, East Germany, and
Yugoslavia).

The regime attempts to utilize ideology as well as new socialist institutions
to legitimize its policies. The assumption is that the people must be educated to adopt a socialist consciousness. The values defined as "correct"
must serve to harmonize all aspects of the state with society at large. Above
all, the practice of state socialism requires that the state lead and organize
the economy. Rather than withering away, as Marx predicted, the state
under socialism is viewed by the Soviets as having a critical role in leading
and structuring the pattern of economic development in society as well as
protecting the gains of the revolution.

The purpose of this chapter and the next is to assess critically the new
regime's attempt to consolidate its power through the policies it introduced
over the first decade of rule and through the institutions it created. The
present chapter concentrates on social policy and party and state building.
Chapter 9 examines the Derg's attempt to socialize the economy. Special
attention is given to the lead role played by the agricultural sector.

Social Reconstruction: A Balance Sheet

The revolution was made in the name of the "Toiling Masses," the
"Oppressed Tillers of the Soil." All of the failures of the imperial regime
were laid bare in the days leading up to the demise of Haile Selassie. When
it assumed power, the Provisional Military Government (PMG) pledged to
address immediately the social injustices that had been perpetrated by the
previous regime.

The most dramatic and indeed profound social policy introduced by the Derg was the nationalization of all rural property.[10] Almost 90 per cent of the Ethiopian populace is dependent on the land for a living, and this policy affected them all. This move was made in spite of advice to the contrary offered the Derg by the Soviet, Yugoslav, and Chinese embassies in Addis Ababa. These advisers seemed to feel that the revolution was much too fragile for such a bold step, and they predicted that this would result in a sharp downturn in agricultural production, triggering economic and political problems.[11]

This policy was not inspired by a deep-seated commitment to land tenure reform on the part of members of the Derg. Rather, it was a response to the pressure being applied by the civilian Left for such reform and to the expectancy among most peasants that the old feudal or colonial structures depending on their situation would be immediately dismantled. Beginning in the summer of 1974, some peasants in the west and south refused to pay rent and in some cases simply usurped land from landlords.[12] This tendency continued after the emperor was deposed, and the land reform proclamation in 1975 signaled the Derg's determination to retain the authority for land redistribution. As mentioned in the previous chapter, the students involved in the first *Zemacha* were expected to help the regime implement the reforms. Indeed, they did give some semblance of order to the process and helped lay the groundwork for the establishment of peasant associations that came to serve the function of the lowest level of administration. When the campaign ended and the students returned to the classroom, peasant associations assumed the responsibility of land distribution and the adjudication of land disputes.

As sweeping as the land reform proclamation was, its impact was not uniform. It was most effective in areas of the south that had been characterized by tenancy and absentee landlordism. There, land reform was greeted with great enthusiasm; but even in the south, actual redistribution took time. In Sidamo and Kaffa, for example, land was not redistributed until 1977.[13] Land reform was least effective in areas of the north characterized by *rist* tenure. For the most part, in *rist* areas the reform was often greeted with peasant intransigence, and change was slow. Not until the devastating intensification of the civil war (compounded by drought) in 1983–1985, which caused massive human dislocation in the north, was the Derg able to force some peasants in the region to settle elsewhere. The result was a disruption in the relationship between peasant and land in a sizable portion of the *rist* area. The profoundness of these developments, however, was not immediately clear. Nor was it evident what effect the growing reach of the state bureaucracy would have on the ability of northern peasants to continue their traditional practices.

Significantly, the old landed classes and the Coptic Church, which had exerted such strong influence during the imperial era, offered little effective resistance to the Derg's land reform policy. This measure has come to be viewed by most observers as the one act that guaranteed that feudalism was dead forever.

Despite the generally positive effect of land redistribution, the situation of the peasantry remained far from ideal. In some cases, there is land fragmentation.[14] A farmer may be required to cultivate several plots of land at a distance from each other because of the variability in land quality in some areas. Others must make the best of small plots of land of poor quality and are lucky to grow enough food for their families, let alone the market. Problems relating to peasant agriculture will be further discussed below.

In terms of social impact, the nationalization of urban property and extra houses was almost as profound as the nationalization of rural land. The stated purpose of this measure was to relieve the "broad masses" from exorbitant rents and to wipe out land speculators. Low rent houses were constructed on some of the nationalized urban land. In the Revolution Day speech of 1978, Mengistu claimed 111,200 houses would be built over the next five years.[15] By 1980 the government was announcing that housing construction was increasing at a rate better than 6 percent per year. In part this was stimulated by improved individual access to bank credit. Credit reforms resulted in more and more people taking loans in order to build their own homes. In spite of this building boom, the number of new houses and apartments constructed each year was barely enough to keep up with the rate of urban population growth. Ethiopia's urban population was estimated at four million in 1982 and growing at a rate of 5.5 percent annually. As a consequence, thousands of people continued to be on waiting lists for housing.[16] This is not to say that the urban land policy of the Derg was ineffective, but only that it had a limited impact on the lack of decent, affordable housing units in urban areas. Demand continues to outstrip supply, and the government can do little else but keep up with the rate of change in the market.

Workers in the modern sector of the economy, like the peasantry, expected that their plight would improve once the imperial regime was displaced, but this did not happen. Moreover, the Derg quickly declared its own preeminent role as the vanguard of the revolution, causing concern among urban workers that they were being deprived of their proper role in the revolution they had been most instrumental in creating. Between 1975 and 1976, the Confederation of Ethiopian Labor Unions (CELU) became more and more political and allied itself with elements of the radical intelligentsia, pressuring the Derg to share power. The confederation also demanded shop-floor control over production. Eventually the entire leadership of CELU was imprisoned. On several occasions white- and blue-collar workers in and around Addis Ababa defied the 1975 labor code that prohibited strikes, sometimes resulting in bloody confrontations with the military.

CELU was branded a reactionary organization and disbanded in 1976.

The Derg realized that it needed the support of labor if its "revolution" was to have any chance of being viewed as legitimate. Therefore, it immediately set about creating a "friendly" labor movement. On January 8, 1977, the PMG formally inaugurated the All-Ethiopia Trade Union, a confederation of seventeen hundred unions whose rank and file numbered over 300,000 by 1984.[17]

The Derg did not confine its labor policy to regulation; it was also concerned with unemployment. In early 1979 it was estimated that 140,000 people, or about 2 percent of the workforce, were unemployed, compared to as many as 250,000 prior to the revolution.[18] Most of the unemployed were manual laborers or unskilled youth not in school. In 1978 the Relief and Rehabilitation Commission (RRC) engaged in a campaign to round up over 1000 hard-core unemployed people, including beggars and prostitutes, who were taken to settlement sites, orphanages, and homes for the elderly. Those who could work were rehabilitated and trained for gainful employment.

The unemployment problem has been somewhat affected by the dramatic expansion of the public bureaucracy. Although it is difficult to calculate the actual size of the central bureaucracy, an idea of the dimensions of its growth can be gathered from consumption expenditures, which include wages and salaries. Between 1974 and 1980 such expenditure grew from about 5 billion to almost 8 billion Birr. About 80 percent of this amount in 1980 was for central administration and defence.[19] The military grew from 65,000 in 1974 to over 300,000 in 1987, and the central bureaucracy took on more layers and expanded horizontally. The growth in the size of the state bureaucracy, coupled with the small size of the modern sector of the economy, would tend to distort the image of the regime's actual progress in addressing the unemployment problem.

Some critics of the regime note what they perceive to be "the massive poverty the urban poor have been forced to bear."[20] A 1983 International Labor Organization report suggested that by 1982 almost 70 percent of all urban households were impoverished, as compared to 55 to 60 percent a decade before. Moreover, the minimum wage level was exceeded by the minimum cost of food alone necessary to sustain the average household. In 1986, the per capita income was only US$110, the lowest in the world. The important point is that although some social progress was made over the first decade of the revolution, there was much still to be done.

Social policies introduced by the Derg in its efforts to respond to the hopes and aspirations of the populace while enhancing its own power and legitimacy included the National Literacy Campaign; the expansion of formal educational opportunities and curricular reform; and the improvement of access to modern health care.

When the Derg assumed power, the literacy rate was estimated somewhere between 5 and 8 percent. The new regime set improving this record considerably as one of its highest priorities. In 1977 a team of 121 educators was appointed to devise a national literacy program. In the first year it was claimed that 120,000 adults successfully completed literacy classes. In 1979 this program was given new impetus and expanded into the National Literacy Campaign. By 1987 the government claimed that the rate of illiteracy had dropped to less than 40 percent.[21] This remarkable achievement won recognition of the campaign by UNESCO, which hailed Ethiopia's success in literacy training by presenting it the prestigious International Reading Association annual award in 1980.

The literacy program is organized around the concepts of functional literacy training. Participants use simply written materials designed not only to teach reading but also to provide basic information to help them improve the quality of their lives. For example, subjects such as hygiene, better farming techniques, better food preservation techniques, poultry keeping, and basic tips on nutrition are commonly the focus of reading materials. Reading materials are written in fifteen different languages, but there is evidence that in practice Amharic is most often the language of instruction throughout the country.[22] In the imperial era, the emphasis was on Amharizing all education. Although the current government publicly disdains Amharization, in practice that process has changed little since the imperial era. The publication of literacy materials in languages other than Amharic is valued more for its symbolic than for its substantive impact. Some critics have argued that the Derg is committed—as much as the imperial regime had been—to imposing Amhara language and culture on subject peoples.[23] Indeed, Amharic is enshrined as the national language in the most recent constitution.

Government officials claimed that in the first five years of the literacy campaign, some twenty million people became literate. It said this was made possible not only by good organization, but also by the mobilization of a large number of instructors at a low cost. By 1980 fifteen million copies of literacy materials had been distributed at a cost of about US$6 million (2 percent of annual government expenditures).[24] The cost of the campaign was kept low because many of the instructors were unpaid. The government claims that 90 percent of the instructors are youth from Revolutionary Ethiopia Youth Association (REYA) cells who act as literacy instructors during the summer months. Others include teachers and soldiers who do volunteer work as literacy trainers.[25]

This program is said to have had a tremendous impact on the people it has been able to reach. The initial training courses are supposed to be followed up by progressively more advanced instruction and facilitated by the access peasants have to postliteracy and vocational training at some 306 adult training centers. In 1984 it was estimated that over one-half million people were enrolled in such courses.[26] Needless to say, the program was most effective in those areas firmly in government control. There is evidence, however, that the government is having difficulty in producing and supplying literacy centers with fresh education materials.

TABLE 8.1
Students Enrolled in Primary and Secondary Schools by Region and Percentage of Total Population, 1972–73

Region	Total Population 1972–73	Percent of Population 1972–73	Students Enrolled 1972–73	Percent of all Students 1972–73
Arussi	892,700	3.1	37,792	4.1
Bale	739,600	2.5	16,826	1.5
Begemdir/Gondar[a]	1,418,700	4.9	42,542	4.6
Eritrea	2,070,100	7.1	107,948	11.7
Gemu-Gofa	730,700	2.5	22,098	2.4
Gojjam	1,829,600	6.3	41,991	4.5
Hararge	3,510,000	12.1	54,035	5.8
Illubador	719,400	2.4	24,273	2.6
Kaffa	1,768,700	6.1	30,996	3.4
Shoa	5,712,100	19.8	155,295	16.8
Sidamo	2,595,600	9.0	57,632	6.2
Tigre	1,916,600	6.7	45,935	4.9
Wollega	1,326,800	4.6	86,661	9.3
Wollo	2,570,200	8.9	44,944	4.9
Addis Ababa	976,870	3.4	151,859	16.4
Total	28,570,670		923,827	

SOURCE: *Ethiopia: Statistical Abstract, 1975* (Addis Ababa: Central Statistical Office, 1975).
[a]By 1980, Begemdir was replaced by Gondar in official publications.

Under Haile Selassie's rule, formal education was seen as more of a privilege than a right. On the eve of the revolution only about one million school-age children, about 19 percent of all young people in this category, were in school. The Derg set universal general education as a high priority goal in its education program. By 1984 there were three million students in elementary and secondary schools, almost 50 percent of those eligible. The number of teachers had climbed from almost twenty-five thousand to almost fifty-five thousand. The number of elementary and secondary schools more than doubled to 7,598 by 1984. At the postsecondary level, growth was equally impressive. The number of students at that level grew from 8,151 in 1974 to 16,117 in 1983.[27] Significantly, however, not until 1979 were schools able to remain open an entire academic year.

In spite of its proclaimed commitment to distributive justice, the Derg's efforts to eliminate inequities in educational opportunities met with mixed results. For example, the urban bias in access to formal education was noticeably altered. The percentage of young people in school living in Addis Ababa, the largest urban center, shifted from 16.4 percent in 1972–1973 to 11.8 percent in 1979–1980. In areas of the south and west, historically deprived of formal, equitable educational opportunities, the changes were dramatically positive for the most part. (See Table 8.1. and Table 8.2.)

TABLE 8.2

Students Enrolled in Primary and Secondary Schools by Region and Percentage of Total Population, 1979–80

Region	Total Population 1979–80	Percent of Population 1979–80	Students Enrolled 1979–80	Percent of all Students 1979–80
Arussi	1,119,300	3.7	115,142	4.5
Bale	856,100	2.8	58,988	2.5
Begemdir/Gondar[a]	1,999,600	6.6	89,513	3.5
Eritrea	2,362,600	7.8	94,513	3.7
Gemu-Gofa	977,100	3.2	76,652	3.0
Gojjam	1,984,400	6.6	114,744	4.5
Hararge	3,043,200	10.0	118,476	4.6
Illubador	798,500	2.6	94,527	8.7
Kaffa	1,573,000	5.0	150,974	5.8
Shoa	6,195,300	20.5	512,559	20.0
Sidamo	2,734,700	9.0	299,000	11.7
Tigre	2,105,400	7.0	66,166	2.6
Wollega	1,966,300	6.5	319,261	12.5
Wollo	2,544,100	8.4	142,973	5.6
Addis Ababa	1,216,300	4.0	301,836	11.8
Total	30,259,600		2,558,313	

SOURCE: *Ethiopia: Statistical Abstract, 1980* (Addis Ababa: Central Statistical Office, 1981).
[a] By 1980 Begemdir was replaced by Gondar in official publications.

The regions of Illubador, Kaffa, Sidamo, and Wollega recorded the most remarkable gains. However, in areas of the north and southeast characterized by rebellion against the new regime, the record was generally negative. The number of school-age children in school in Eritrea actually dropped by 8 percent; by 1.2 percent in Hararge; by 2.3 percent in Tigre; and by 1.1 percent in Gondar. It remained constant in Gojjam, and only gained by 0.5 percent in Bale. These regions were characterized by constant or intermittent turmoil and in some cases generalized resistance to any policies the regime wanted to introduce. This is further evidence of the regime's inability to ensure compliance or elicit support from significant segments of the population. Even when it had the will and the resources to introduce desired change, the Derg's lack of legitimacy in some areas prevented it from being effective.

In keeping with its goal of stamping out all vestiges of the old order, the Derg attempted to socialize the curriculum at all levels of education. A 1982 article in *Meskerem*, an official journal designed to relate Marxist-Leninist theory to Ethiopia's objective conditions, stated:

It was imperative that the educational system be devised in such a way that it become compatible with the revolutionary process, reflects and spreads the

Marxist-Leninist ideology. . . . Aimed at developing the students overall socialist personality, the change of educational system continued with the
fundamental and national motto of "Education for production, scientific
research and socialist consciousness."[28]

Some young people have been chosen to study Marxist-Leninist theory
abroad in such communist countries as the Soviet Union, Cuba, and East
Germany, but most receive political indoctrination in REYAs and the classroom. Teachers participate in seminars and workshops at specially organized ideological training institutes which introduce them to new socialist
materials and give them pointers on how to transmit this doctrine in the
classroom.[29] Whereas under the imperial regime textbooks were generally
imported from abroad, the regime now claims that over 80 percent of all
textbooks are produced locally and possess the "proper" socialist orientation.

The push for universal general education has revealed a severe shortage
of teachers and school buildings. Classes are held in many areas in three
shifts: morning, afternoon, and evening, often under less than ideal conditions. The teacher shortage is due not only to the rapid expansion of the
educational system, but also to factors such as the Ethiopianization of the
teacher corps and the voluntary phasing out of some teachers who chose to
abandon the teaching profession rather than be retrained in the new
socialist methodology. The regime admits that some defecting teachers
have chosen to join and lead armed opposition to its rule. The teachers that
remain tend to be overworked and underpaid.

The Derg's record in improving modern health care opportunities
throughout the country is difficult to interpret. The distribution of hospitals did not change between 1974 and 1980. Perhaps the most revealing
statistic is the doctor/population ratio in selected regions. (See Table 8.3.)
The doctor/population ratio improved in Addis Ababa and in historically
deprived regions like Bale, Sidamo, Gemu-Gofa, and Kaffa—and in
some cases dramatically—but it worsened substantially in government held
as well as in contested areas of Tigre and Eritrea. It is estimated that by
1987 the ratio of doctors to population for the entire country was only
eighteen doctors for every one million people.[30] Significantly, however, the
number of clinics and health centers throughout the country increased,
even in most contested areas. Eritrea seemed to be the only place where
progress was stymied.

Overall figures are impressive. Between 1974 and 1983, clinics grew
from 649 to 1,850, health centers from 93 to 130, health personnel from
6,472 to 16,220. It was estimated that by 1984 45 percent of the population
had access to decent health care as compared to only 15 percent in 1974.[31]

Drought, Famine, and the "Soft State"

The limited ability of the state to lead development, let alone respond to
periodic uncertainties that strain its resources, was dramatically demon-

TABLE 8.3
Doctor/Population Ratio in Selected Regions, 1974 and 1980

Region	1974	1980
Addis Ababa	1: 5,800	1: 5,132
Eritrea	1: 30,000	1: 76,213
Bale	1: 739,600	1: 142,683
Gemu-Gofa	1: 365,400	1: 244,275
Sidamo	1: 288,400	1: 228,642
Kaffa	1: 196,500	1: 12,100
Arussi	1: 127,500	1: 223,860
Tigre	1: 212,956	1: 300,771

SOURCE: *Ethiopia: Statistical Abstract, 1975* (Addis Ababa: Central Statistical Office, 1975); *Ethiopia: Statistical Abstract, 1980* (Addis Ababa: Central Statistical Office, 1981).

strated by Ethiopia's heavy reliance on foreign famine relief aid between 1984 and 1986. By 1983 the low intensity war taking place in the north combined with a drought that had prevailed for more than a decade contributed to mass starvation in Eritrea, Tigre, and Wollo. Drought alone had a devastating impact by the fall of 1984 on an additional nine of Ethiopia's remaining eleven provinces. This catastrophe far exceeded the one of 1973–1974. By early 1985 some 7.7 million Ethiopians were suffering from drought and food shortages. Of that number, 2.5 million were immediately at risk of starving. More than 300,000 died in 1984 alone, more than twice the number that died in the drought a decade before. By the end of 1986 the death toll from this latest disaster had climbed to one million.[32]

In response to the human tragedy, the international community responded generously once the dimensions of the unfolding crisis were understood. Aid came in the form of bilateral, multilateral, and private donations of food and other relief supplies ranging from transport trucks to antibiotics and from technical assistance to water-drilling equipment. The crisis stimulated an unprecedented outpouring from the public at large in the West, inspiring the formation of fundraising extravaganzas on the part of musicians who formed themselves into humanitarian organizations such as "BandAid" in England and "USA for Africa" in the United States. Similar events were staged by other groups ranging from church organizations to athletes. Activities such as these generated millions of dollars that were then spent on relief inside Ethiopia and in refugee camps in Somalia and Sudan. The bulk of the relief dollars and supplies, however, was provided by Western governments like Canada, the Scandinavian countries, England, Italy, and the United States. More than $2 billion in foreign assistance was needed to bring the catastrophe under control. The delivery of this assistance was coordinated by the RRC but also involved more than forty foreign nongovernmental and governmental agencies.

By 1987 the physical impact of this massive influx of aid to Ethiopia over such a short time was noticeable not only in the abatement of famine, but also in what seemed to be a permanent establishment of donor agencies prepared to assist Ethiopia in long-term famine prevention and development. The United Nations Office for Emergency Operations was closed in early 1987; many foreign relief workers returned home; and some relief agencies had closed down their operations in the country. Behind they left a large number of heavy-duty trucks, which had been used to move donated supplies, and infrastructure such as wells and grain-storage bins. Other foreign agencies, however, brought in new personnel and built compounds to house their offices and staff. Organizations like World Vision, Save the Children Fund, Oxfam (UK), Oxfam America, and other nongovernmental agencies along with bilateral aid agencies (especially from Western Europe) and multilateral agencies turned their attention to rehabilitation and long-term development.

For the first time in five years, Ethiopia appeared to be headed for normal grain harvests. In addition, only 2.5 million people remained in residual pockets of famine, down from 6.5 million in 1986. Only a few small feeding centers remained open, and Mengistu announced the goal of food self-sufficiency by 1990.[33]

The huge influx of famine relief aid between 1984 and 1986 served almost as a blessing in disguise for the Derg. The enormity of the crisis and the regime's apparent willingness to deal with it seemed to minimize in the eyes of many Western critics the fact that Ethiopia's problems were as much due to flawed or ill-timed policies as anything else. Even the United States provided millions of dollars in relief aid to Ethiopia, while consistently criticizing the policies of the Derg. Funds and other resources that might have been used to purchase food for the starving continued to be used for social, political, and military purposes. The net effect was to lessen the threat to the Derg's survival posed by the combined effects of drought, famine, and war.

The Political Economy of Resettlement

One of the most controversial of the Derg's policies during this period was the massive resettlement of drought victims. At the height of the drought and famine, the regime set in motion a resettlement policy supposed to relocate some 1.5 million people from the areas most severely affected by drought in the north to so-called virgin lands in the south that had adequate rainfall. The argument made by officials was that such a move would allow people who had been forced from barren, exhausted, and overpopulated areas to begin anew. Moreover, the government would be in a better position to provide resettled communities with needed social services. Initially, settlers were chosen from feeding centers in Wollo, Tigre, and northern Shoa and transported by trucks, buses, and cargo planes to resettlement sites in Kaffa, Gojjam, Gondar, Wollega, and Illubabor. The government was poorly prepared for the operation, and the first settlers experienced tremendous hardships in alien, disease infested, and under-developed areas. In some cases, would-be settlers resisted being moved so far from their homelands and were brutally forced to do so.[34] Once resettled, some fled their new communities into Sudan and either took shelter in refugee camps or walked thousands of miles with the ultimate goal of clandestinely reentering their old areas.

Despite the government's official position that resettlement is strictly for humanitarian reasons, critics have argued that the main purpose of the program is to depopulate areas characterized by on-going military opposition to the regime by groups such as the Eritrean People's Liberation Front (EPLF) and the Tigre People's Liberation Front (TPLF).[35] Criticism not-withstanding, the regime continued its resettlement efforts throughout the height of the drought until March of 1986. At that time the project was suspended for one year. During the initial phase of the 1984–1986 resettlement campaign only 600,000 people were relocated. The largest numbers (150,000-180,000 each) were resettled from Wollo and Tigre to Illubabor and Wollega. Less than 100,000 each were resettled in Kaffa, Gojjam, and Gondar.

After a year's "consolidation period," the government resumed the resettlement project in the spring of 1987. It was expected that 200,000-300,000 people would be moved in a year's time. The long-term goal was still to resettle a total of 1.5 million people. The authorities claimed to have learned from the mistake of the earlier phase of resettlement and pledged to implement the current phase in a more systematic and humane manner. An area is targeted for resettlement when more than 50 percent of its population is dependent on supplemental feeding.

Seemingly in response to the criticism that resettlement was for the most part forced on northerners, the RRC now attempted to "persuade" those targeted for relocation that it was in their best material interest to move. Agents of the relief agency organized village meetings to "agitate" on behalf of the program. They also took farmers from the targeted northern areas to visit model resettlement communities in the south. Several resettlement sites were expected to achieve food self-sufficiency in 1987 and were singled out as evidence that the overall concept of resettlement was a good one. The government met with limited success in securing volunteers for the newest phase of the resettlement campaign, and there is evidence that where volunteerism is not forthcoming, the authorities are prepared to force compliance.[36]

Many critics argued that the Ethiopian government disrupted the efforts of international relief agencies to bring famine under control between 1985 and 1986 by forcibly removing drought victims from northern feeding centers and moving them to the south. Moreover, critics contended that the process was a violation of the most fundamental human rights. In an open letter to the RRC in November 1985, for example, the French relief agency Médecins sans Frontières claimed:

> In Korem most people dispatched to resettlement zones are taken against their will, without regard for family ties. More than 15,000 people fled into neighboring mountains when the militia arrived in Korem on October 15 last. Our staff are categorical, the vast majority of the people were forced to leave under duress and were escorted by armed militiamen.[37]

Others portrayed the regime of Mengistu Haile Mariam as being akin to the Khmer Rouge who in the mid-1970s attempted to forcibly restructure Cambodian society.[38] Reports of upwards of 100,000 people dying in the earlier stages of resettlement proved to be unfounded, but there was ample evidence that many deaths did occur. The living conditions in the new settlements were extremely poor, and food and medical supplies were inadequate.[39] In addition, the people chosen for resettlement had their own ways of life disrupted.[40]

Despite the problems encountered in resettlement, as well as the criticism it generated, the Ethiopian government continued to pursue the project. By early 1987 it seemed to have secured the endorsement of most Western donors that on purely technical humanitarian grounds resettlement was both necessary and feasible. It only had to be done better.

No matter what the real motive for the resettlement policy—to depopulate areas of civil strife or to enhance the life chances of northern communities perennially at risk because of drought and war—the net effect of the policy has been to further improve the statist control of the regime over a significant segment of the population. In each resettlement site cadre of the WPE carry out the tasks of political education and agitation, and they attempt to monitor and stimulate production. The regime insists that its intention is not to forcibly collectivize peasants, but resettlement communities are invariably organized into producer cooperatives and are expected to farm collectively. Clearly, then, the government is able to enhance its top-down control of development.

Villagization as a Development Strategy

Another dimension of the regime's determined effort to strengthen the control of the state over the population is represented by the government's villagization policy. The notion of villagization was introduced in the land reform proclamation in 1975, but there was no immediate effort then to implement such a policy on a large scale. However, following the invasion of the southeastern part of the country in 1977 by Somali forces, most of Bale Province was villagized. The purpose of villagizing communities was, according to government officials, to cluster rural families in sparsely populated areas of Bale so that they might better take advantage of such services as education, health care, agricultural extension, and safe water. Villagization was also intended to facilitate the development of voluntary community self-help activities. By March 1983 there were 519 villagized communities formed in Bale, encompassing 106,318 families. The largest villages housed as many as seven thousand people and the smallest as few as three hundred.[41]

The Ten Year Perspective Plan envisioned villagization as an integral part of a long-term rural development strategy. The resolve of the government to extend this strategy was made clear when villagization was begun in January 1985 in the Hararge highlands. Late in that year the process was begun in Shoa and Arussi, and in 1986 small-scale villagization efforts were begun in Gojjam, Wollega, Kaffa, Sidamo, and Illubabor. The project is under the overall control of a ministerial committee, the National Villagization Coordinating Committee in the Ministry of Agriculture, and the WPE plays an active, leading role. By March 1987 there were an estimated ten thousand villagized communities throughout the country.[42] The long-term goal is to move some thirty-three million rural people into such communities by 1994.

The party produced guidelines for site selection, village layout, and other matters. At the regional level a committee plans, coordinates, and monitors the program through eight subcommittees (planning and programming; site selection and surveying; materials procurement, transportation, and logistics; construction; propaganda and training; monitoring and evaluation; and security). Coordinating committees with comparable subdivisions exist at the *awraja, woreda* and peasant association levels. Peasant associations have a particularly critical role to play in policy implementation.[43]

Old communities are disassembled by the peasants themselves, and where possible they transport the housing materials from the old domicile to the villagized area. With the aid of outsiders—in 1986 this included, among others, university students and professors on *Zemacha*—peasants reconstruct their houses in the new community. The process, like resettlement, invariably results in a good deal of social disorganization for peasant families. They must move from traditional household settlements with farming plots in close proximity into clustered villages where cultivable land is fragmented and a longer distance from the homestead.[44]

The government has experienced the most success in such areas as Shoa, Arussi, and the Hararge highlands where it is in firm control and has a reasonable amount of popular support.[45] About 33 percent of the population of the country is clustered in these regions. They are also important in that annually they provide 40 percent of all agricultural produce and 55 percent of the Agricultural Marketing Commission's cereal purchase. The regime concentrates the bulk of its agricultural inputs and credit to peasant farmers in these areas.

Attempts to villagize parts of western Shoa, the Hararge lowlands, and all of Gojjam have met with local resistance. This was countered by government force. The historic reputation of traditional conservatism in Gojjam explains in part why the government has had to proceed slowly in implementing villagization in that region. Peasants also balked in part because they were pressured to villagize during the critical planting season.[46]

Many Oromo fled from the villagization program in Hararge when it began to expand after January 1986, finding refuge in camps just inside the Somali border at Tug Wajale near Hargesia.[47] By June 1986 more than fifty thousand refugees had streamed into these camps from Ethiopia, and an estimated one thousand came across the border each day. Refugees claimed that they fled mostly for political reasons. They were being forced to abandon their traditional patterns of cultivation and to move into villages where they were expected to farm collectively and participate in food for work programs. Conditions at the Tug Wajale camps were reported to be extremely poor and difficult. The problem was not so much insufficient food as it was poor sanitation and inadequate living facilities.

Private humanitarian agencies and bilateral and multilateral development assistance agencies were cognizant of the alleged *and* real violations of human rights involved in implementing villagization; but by early 1987 many had decided to rationalize their indirect (and sometimes) direct involvement in the process. They tended to ignore the politics of villagization and to focus on the "real needs of the people." A World Vision spokesman, for example, said, "We were able to help these people when they really needed us in 1984. Our aim is to help the poorest of the poor, and here's [the villagized community] where they are. How can we just abandon them because of politics."[48] On purely technical grounds, villagization, like resettlement, seems to make sense. Its objectives are to enhance extension services and thereby improve productivity, to promote more rational land-use patterns and natural resource conservation, to improve access to social services, and to strengthen self-defense.[49] Although rhetorically collectivization of production is assigned a lesser priority, there is no doubt that the long-term goal of the program is to convert villagized communities into producer cooperatives.[50]

The politics of villagization cannot be ignored. In fact, the political underpinnings of the policy are as important, if not more important, than the economic ones. The regime is able to utilize the resources provided by foreign relief and development agencies to consolidate its phase collectivation of peasant agriculture. In addition, this scheme enhances the central control of the state over the rural population. Many critics claim that villagized communities, especially in places like Bale and Hararge, are nothing more than "strategic hamlets" designed to separate the general population from insurgent movements. Villagers, the government claims, are armed merely to protect their property from *shiftas* (bandits).

Few impact and evaluational studies of villagization were available in

1987. However, the Swedish International Development Agency (SIDA) did commission a valuable study of villagization in late 1986 to provide the Ethiopian government with needed information on the impact of villagization in Arussi and to provide SIDA data on the effects of villagization relative to its own technical support in the area. The report was prepared by John M. Cohen, an American expert on agricultural development in Ethiopia, and Nils-Ivar Isaksson, a Swedish agricultural economist.[51] The report concluded that the 1985–1986 phase of villagization was poorly timed, and that the project was unlikely to achieve its stated social goals: improve the economic well-being of peasant families and improve the overall quality of life for rural producers. The report went on to recommend that further villagization be postponed until certain technical, environmental, and marketing problems were addressed and solved, or at least until the first phase of the program had been adequately evaluated.

From the political standpoint, it is important to note two things. First, the SIDA study team recommended that the agency continue to fund projects in villagized areas of Arussi. Second, the two Ethiopian members of the four-member team were not in agreement with some of the main views contained in the report. The fact that the concept of villagization was not questioned by the SIDA team is noteworthy given the critical importance of this kind of foreign assistance in this key region. What the team did question was the method and timing of implementation. If the past record is any indication, it seems safe to assume that the regime will make changes at the margins of the policy, simply to keep technical assistance funds flowing, as long as the basic thrust of the policy remains unchallenged by donors.

Bureaucracy and Party in State Building

Creating an Authorative State Apparatus

A key element in the quest for socialist development is an effective state center. It is up to the state, in conjunction with the vanguard party, to set organizational, strategic, and policy goals and standards. The state must also be capable of providing whatever material and logistical support is necessary for the achievement of political and ideological objectives. Without an authoritative state apparatus, the revolution could well flounder.[52]

It would seem logical that one of the initial steps of the Derg would have been to dismantle the old bureaucracy and replace it with an institution of the revolutionary movement's own creation. But this did not happen in any real sense, particularly with regard to the central bureaucracy. For practical reasons this seemed to be impossible. If the decision had been taken to conduct a systematic purge of the central bureaucracy, the new regime would have been left without sufficient numbers of educated and skilled administrative personnel to conduct even the normal affairs of government. What was required was a substantial pool of skilled bureaucrats either steeped in the values of scientific socialism or at least acquiescent to the regime's goals. However, few were available.

Initially the Derg simply allowed most of the central bureaucrats who had served the emperor to remain at their posts and appointed army officers to monitor their activities in every ministry. At the same time, the Derg attempted to recruit into the civil service former high school and college students who were then serving in the *Zemacha*. As a rule, this group tended to be committed to the idea of revolutionary change but often lacked the skills required of competent bureaucrats. Moreover, although the campaigners generally favored revolution, many were opposed to military rule, and once in positions of authority they would undermine rather than promote the goals of the regime.

Another measure used to bolster the central role of the state apparatus was to require that all senior civil servants and political appointees undergo a period of intense reeducation so as to adopt a socialist orientation. Many civil servants and military personnel were sent to the Soviet Union, Eastern Europe, and Cuba for ideological indoctrination just as selected teachers and students had been. After the establishment of the *Yekatit 66* Ideological School, hundreds more were taught Marxist-Leninist doctrine.

Even as the Derg was trying to develop the central bureaucracy as an effective instrument of its authority, debates emerged among technocrats and ideologues over the most appropriate manner to reorganize the different administrative sectors. Rather than the bureaucracy serving as an effective instrument of the Derg's rulership, then, it was initially characterized by constant bickering among the various ministries and a lack of interministerial coordination.[53] This forced the Provisional Military Administrative Council (PMAC) to create a new Ministry of National Resource Development (MNRD) in 1975 to promote agricultural development and to monitor the operations of nationalized firms. The MNRD was envisioned as a possible solution to the coordination problem as well as the problem of low productivity. But by 1976 this strategy had failed, and the MNRD's functions were divided among several ministries and parastatal bodies. The creation of the Central Planning Supreme Council two years later represented a more serious, concerted attempt to coordinate bureaucratic involvement in development.

The Derg's success at reorganizing the central bureaucracy was more evident at the regional and local levels. Immediately after assuming power, the PMAC reorganized Ethiopia's fourteen provincial administrations and replaced all serving governors-general. The provinces were renamed regions *(kifle hagers)* and divided into 102 subregions *(awrajas)* and 556 districts *(woredas)*. This was seen as a major step in dismantling feudal privilege.[54] All new appointees were either military men or university-educated individuals who were deemed to be progressives. The main charge of these new administrators was to promote development. The maintenance of law and order was considered only of secondary importance. Despite this clear commitment to rural development and to the staffing of regional administrative positions with young, dynamic, educated people, not much could be done to speed up the process of change. Field bureaucrats had few resources to work with. Their staffs were small, and their budgets were committed almost entirely to salaries.

The Derg attempted to spread administrative reform even down to the lowest echelons of regional administration. The land reform proclamation of 1975 had abolished the lowest level of rural administration, the *balabats*. In their place the Derg introduced peasant associations, allegedly to devolve more and more power to the local community. They were to be guided initially by students in the *Zemacha* who would teach them the goals of the revolution and aid them in planning and implementing development in their neighborhoods. This also applied to urban dwellers associations, *kebeles*. Initially it was not clear how much power, authority, or autonomy the Derg intended to vest in these local institutions. As a result, rather than this change being an effective means for state penetration, conflict often emerged between agents of the state and neighborhood organizations under the direction of student campaigners or in groups infiltrated by leftist opponents of the Derg. The Derg eventually introduced additional laws spelling out the rights and obligations of peasant associations and kebeles.

By 1984 there were almost twenty thousand peasant associations throughout the country. They represented the lowest level of government administration, processing and interpreting policies from the center; maintaining law and order; facilitating party formation and ideological indoctrination at the local level; and leading economic development.[55] More than five million peasant families were represented in such institutions. The Derg claimed that this represented the entire farming population, except those farmers in politically unstable areas like Eritrea and Tigre. By 1984 their economic function seemed as important as their political roles.

Peasant associations are semiautonomous institutions. Leadership is elected by local populations, but the regime has systematically reduced their autonomy and tried to shape their orientations and activities. One of the main objectives of the 1975 proclamation giving peasant associations legal personalities was to enhance central control of these emerging grassroots organizations. A measure of state control was further extended in 1975 when the Derg promoted the formation of the All-Ethiopian Peasant Association. To the extent that peasant associations maintain their autonomy, they do so almost exclusively with regard to local issues. On national issues, the regime, through the party and other agencies, is able to manipulate peasant associations to suit its purposes. After 1978, for example, production and political cadre of the National Revolutionary Development Campaign played an important role in motivating peasant production and in political indoctrination. Also, as mentioned above, the trend toward villagization and resettlement increased the state's control over local populations.

In the industrial sector Working People's Control Committees (WPCCs), created in 1981, have come to serve a somewhat threatening "watchdog" role over productive activities. WPCCs are supposed to be involved in the "follow-up and supervision of the proper implementation of proclamations, regulations and directives, and auditing and causing to be audited accounts of any government institution, organization, mass organization or private individuals."[56] The regime credits these new institutions with having uncovered numerous incidents of fraud, corruption, wastefulness, and counterrevolution. The Haile Selassie regime was never able to achieve such tight surveillance. The Derg's capacity in this area is in large measure testimony to the effectiveness of the security training provided the government by Soviet and East German security advisers. Clearly, then, the central administration is acquiring the capacity to project its authority to remote corners of society, however unevenly.

In the cities, kebeles serve functions similar to peasant associations in the countryside. They have broad political, economic, and judicial powers, although not as much as they did during the period of the Red Terror. The government estimates national kebele membership at about 4.4 million.[57] Kebeles throughout the country are linked in the Urban Dwellers Association at the national level. This structure stretches, in succeeding layers that parallel the central bureaucracy, down to the neighborhood level.

At the grassroots level, these democratically elected committees are responsible for the management of their own "people's shops," housing offices, schools, and neighborhood courts. From the earliest days of their creation, kebeles were involved in housing redistribution and management and in meeting the welfare needs of their constituencies. One of their primary goals was to provide retail outlets for food at the neighborhood level to offset endemic problems of poor food distribution, food shortages, and hoarding.[58] However, they were never able to tackle this problem adequately on their own. Food shortages were beyond the control of kebeles, but they turned this in some cases into an opportunity, using this valuable commodity to elicit the compliance of the citizens. Salt or sugar, for example, might be withheld from heads-of-household who stayed away from meetings called by the kebele.

Kebeles were the Derg's first attempt to establish the state's authority at the grassroots level, and they were initially given considerable power. Soon after they were established in 1975, kebeles became battle grounds for struggles between the Derg and *Meison* and the Ethiopian People's Revolutionary Party (EPRP). When the Derg discovered the attempt of the EPRP to undermine its authority by seizing control of grassroots organizations like kebeles, it decided to fight back by arming kebele elements loyal to it so that they might root out counterrevolutionaries and squelch their urban guerrilla campaign. Neighborhood defense squads were created, numbering from 15 to 125 armed individuals, and they became ruthless neighborhood arms of the regime during the Red Terror. They patrolled their neighborhoods day and night and sometimes operated outside the control of the central authorities. Many brutal excesses were attributed to kebele defense squads between 1976 and 1978. They were responsible for a considerable amount of urban violence, torture, and intimidation. They even administered their own jails.[59] However, after the Red Terror ended and the Derg's opponents liquidated from kebele ranks, the central authorities systematically deprived them of their security functions and began to exercise tighter control over their financial and administrative matters. Kebeles continue to be responsible for neighborhood vigilance and for guarding against petty crime, but they came to be more closely supervised from higher up.

This turn of events was in keeping with the Derg's concerted efforts to strengthen its own authority relative to any possible opponent. Between 1978 and 1984 there was a proliferation of new bureaucratic institutions radiating from the center. Leadership roles in these new institutions were used as patronage to reward loyal supporters or to buy off potential adversaries in the military. This was reminiscent of the system employed by Haile Selassie. It was different, however, in that it was not rooted in feudalism but in the spoils accruing to a transitional state that controls access to wealth and power.

The expansion of the central bureaucracy was clearly an effort to shore up the coercive capacity of the state and to lay the groundwork for the establishment of the all-embracing vanguard party. For instance, in May 1983 the Derg decreed its plan for a national military service. In effect, this new scheme would institutionalize the regionally based people's militia that had been under arms since 1977 and standardize the terms of service for the armed forces. Certain military officers were promoted and rewarded by being appointed military commissars in the fourteen regions and Addis Ababa. Military commissars are charged with overseeing the political education of the military rank and file and with supervising the national military service scheme.

Another military-related institution created since 1978 is the National Defense and Security Council. This is a high-level organ manned by military people and designed not only to oversee matters of defense and security but also to deal with natural disasters and other military matters.[60] Derg and other military people also hold key positions in the Politbureau, National Planning Council, and the WPE. The state bureaucracy grew enormously in the first decade of the revolution, and the control of the "men in uniform" deepened and expanded in the process. No institution was immune from the Derg's appetite for power and its desire for self-preservation, not even the vanguard party.

Party Formation and Political Penetration

Although the Commission to Organize the Party of the Working People of Ethiopia (COPWE) was announced in 1979, the first general congress of the commission was not held until the summer of the following year. The second did not take place until 1983, and the third and final congress occurred in September 1984. At the conclusion of the third congress held in the newly constructed Hall of the People, the long awaited vanguard Workers' Party of Ethiopia was proclaimed. It was no coincidence that this event coincided with the tenth anniversary of the revolution.

Simultaneously with the creation of COPWE in 1979, the Derg set about creating new mass organizations such as REYAs, REWAs, WPCCs, and various professional associations, and strengthening already existing mass organizations such as the All-Ethiopia Peasants Association, the Urban Dwellers Association, and the All-Ethiopia Trade Union. In response to the fiasco of attempting to create a union of Marxist-Leninist organizations, the Derg determined that the WPE had to be a party of individuals and not political organizations. To the extent that individual interests were represented, this had to be done through mass organizations.

The function of mass organizations was not only to represent the interests of their membership at party congresses, but to do so on an everyday basis. They are assumed to have active educational and development roles. Individuals can belong to more than one mass organization at a time.

The two congresses that took place between 1980 and 1983 were attended by fifteen hundred and sixteen hundred carefully chosen delegates representing a wide range of mass organizations, the armed forces, and bureaucracy. The first congress was basically an organizational meeting. Not until then was the membership of the all-important COPWE central committee unveiled. The second congress deliberated resolutions that had been generated in sessions of the central committee between congresses. These resolutions dealt with such matters as programs and strategy in organizational affairs; economic priorities and strategy; social development; the appropriate timing of the actual commencement of the vanguard party; steps in drafting a party program and party rules; and, finally, preparations for the celebration of the tenth anniversary of the revolution. At the end of the second congress it was announced that Ethiopia's social and political organizations had "achieved maturity in social and ideological matters" and that the vanguard workers' party would be inaugurated in September 1984.

Delegates to the general congress were drawn from all levels of the COPWE hierarchy. By mid-1983 this structure stretched from the national center to the fourteen regions, the subregional, kebele or village, and cell levels. In all at that time there were an estimated sixty-five hundred COPWE cells. Membership in cells was composed of individuals from the various mass organizations. The total membership of COPWE at the time was not certain. One Cuban report quoted official sources as claiming that more than one million people were serving as COPWE cadre in 1983.[61] This figure seems much exaggerated, however, since when the WPE was finally declared its total membership was placed at about thirty thousand.

As late as 1987, an "educated guess" put the party's membership at no more than fifty thousand.[62]

It is important to note that party membership was not open to all. An elaborate screening process was employed to weed out so-called counter-revolutionaries. Purges at all levels were common. Mengistu, in a speech to the Second Plenary of the COPWE central committee in February 1981 counseled those in attendance that "numbers" are not as important as the ideological purity of a few "committed communists," governed by organizational discipline and prepared to do reliable organizational work.[63]

The concern for ideological purity seemed to be an effort to hide the fact that the Derg was at base trying to neutralize or preempt its opponents. In the past it was challenged by groups like the EPRP and Meison that had infiltrated key institutions like kebeles and peasant associations, labor unions, and even the Derg itself. The Derg felt that it had to be forever vigilant to guard against this happening again.

After 1978 the Derg seemingly attempted to avoid what it considered the errors of the past. It attempted, for example, to project itself into the most important sectors of the central bureaucracy. Derg members were appointed to serve as the regional administrators of twelve of the fourteen regions. An additional thirty took up influential positions in subregional administration and in central ministries. After 1978 the presence of military personnel in the bureaucracy was expanded so greatly that not only members of the Derg but also other trusted military personnel served in such roles. With the establishment of the COPWE bureaucracy, military people holding bureaucratic positions at all levels assumed similar positions in the COPWE bureaucracy that between 1982 and 1983 came to parallel the government. The process was reinforced and streamlined with the inauguration of the WPE.

Further evidence of the politicization of the military can be found in the fact that, beginning in 1978, the Derg as a matter of policy attempted to indoctrinate the military rank and file. Initially this was done by *Abyot Seded* cadre, later by COPWE subcommittees, and now by WPE cells. In announcing the establishment of COPWE and in subsequent speeches, Mengistu made a special point to praise the role of a well-disciplined and politically conscious armed forces in "dealing a death blow to the enemies of the Ethiopian Revolution."[64] Not only did he attempt to manipulate the rank and file of the military to secure their loyalty to the Derg, he also cultivated the personal support of certain elements in the officer corps to protect his own position against potential challenges within the Derg.

There was always a tension between the senior careerists in the military and more ideological junior officers. Junior officers were highly represented in the ranks of the military political commissars. Senior officers often complained about the commissars' interference in military matters. Mengistu carefully tried to keep military and political matters separate to maintain the support of senior officers.[65]

As the date for the conference to form the party approached, Mengistu systematically removed or reassigned some pro-Moscow Derg members from top administrative positions and installed officers more supportive of his predominately nationalist views. It is not that he completely stifled them, but he maneuvered to reduce their potential influence. For example, even though the Abyot Seded cadre had been instrumental in winning the support of the military rank and file for COPWE, few were awarded with key positions on COPWE. When some pro-Moscow zealots in the Derg were represented on important COPWE subcommittees, they found themselves having to work with nationalists. Pro-Moscow elements in the Derg were further neutralized after the WPE was formed.[66]

Even though there was an apparent working tension between self-styled "committed communists" and "nationalists" in the Derg, there seems to have been agreement that their collective position as a ruling class was unassailable. This could be seen clearly in the situation and distribution of power in COPWE and now in the WPE. The most important institutions in COPWE were the executive committee of seven (all Derg members) and the central committee of ninety-three standing members and thirty alternate ones. Of the 123 members of the central committee, 79 were military or police officers. There were at least twenty Derg members in this group, and others held important regional posts in the bureaucracy as well as in COPWE. At the time of the formation of the WPE, military people represented more than 50 percent of the conference participants.

An eleven-member Politbureau was named theoretically to replace the Derg when the WPE was formed, but the entire seven-man committee of the PMAC is included in that body. Of the 134 full members of the WPE central committee, 29 are members of the armed forces and at least another 44 are ex-soldiers. This contrasts with only twenty-two positions held by representatives of mass organizations. Counting full and alternate members of the WPE central committee, military people make up over 60 percent, and most commissars are on the full WPE central committee.[67]

Because of the overlap in the most important positions in the Derg and the WPE (and COPWE before it), individuals who occupied these roles after 1984 seemed to be contributing to a fusion of the two institutions. Mengistu and others in the ruling group suggested that this was the way it should be; ultimately this fusion would lend to a withering away of the Derg's influence and the emergence of a preeminent vanguard party. By this time, the Politbureau was considered *the* most authorative political institution. Regional and district party secretaries displaced chief bureaucratic representatives of the state at those levels as the most authoritative officials. In some cases they controlled and coordinated matters in their domains like petty dictators.

The four civilian members on the Politbureau became responsible for the day-to-day direction of party matters and evidently had Mengistu's confidence. Chief among this group were Shemelis Mazengia, the former editor of the party newsletter, *Serto Ader,* and by 1985 the head of the WPE's ideological commission; Alemu Abebe, head of the Commission on Worker's Committees in Places of Work; Fassika Sidell, head of the WPE Economic Commission; and Shewandagne Abebe, head of the Institute for the Study of Nationalities.[68] In spite of the high profile of civilian members of the Politbureau, the primacy of the Derg was still evident after the founding of the WPE.

More significant and striking than the predominance of Derg members in the Politbureau and WPE central committee is the fact that the party is far from being democratic in its representation. Although mass organizations such as labor unions and peasant associations are represented at party congresses, few of their representatives are on the WPE central committee. In fact, fewer than 35 percent of the central committee is civilian. One in five civilians is a technocrat.

The dominance of military elements and members of the bureaucratic class who support this hegemony could be seen in the composition of the delegates to the conference to found the party. Eighteen hundred delegates attended; among them only 12 percent were peasants, and 19 percent were workers. Most of the remainder were members of the armed forces and government bureaucrats. Only 6 percent of the delegates were female. Although three-quarters of the delegates were from peasant or working-class backgrounds, they tended to be educated professionals.[69]

The WPE's commitment to people's democracy and broad participation in party affairs could be further brought into question by the party's apparent lack of immediate attention to the "national question." At the time the party was formed there were no mass organizations that represented ethnic nationalities. The Derg did create the Institute for the Study of Nationalities in 1983.[70] Its principal tasks were to analyze the social plight of the more than eighty separate nationalities in the country and to draw up plans for autonomous regions.[71] Three years after its creation, however, the institute had come forth with no plans or recommendations. The issue of nationalities and regional autonomy was eventually fleshed out in the Constitution of the People's Republic ratified in 1987. I shall discuss this matter in more detail below.

Given the continued civil unrest among nationality groups into 1985, it was evident that these groups had not been appeased in significant numbers by the Derg's social policies, the establishment of the WPE, or the Nationalities Institute. Significant segments of that population continued to question the regime's commitment to democracy and justice. A glaring obstacle to this was the fact that the Politbureau consisted exclusively of Amharas and Tigres: two-thirds of the central committee comes from these groups. Although the Oromo are the most numerous ethnic group in the country, not one of their number is included in the Politbureau, and few are on the WPE central committee. And the lack of religious diversity at all levels of the party is also glaring. David Korn notes; "The current Ethiopian leadership is Christian almost to a man, even down to its secondary level; there is only one Muslim in the Cabinet . . . and only three altogether in the . . . Central Committee of the WPE."[72]

In addition to being dominated by military men and civilian bureaucrats obligated to them, the WPE is under the control of elements of those ethnic groups that historically had been the politically and culturally dominant, the Amhara and individuals from other ethnic groups who have been Amharized. The ethnic factor may or may not be significant in determining the revolutionary commitment of individuals, but some observers consider it extremely significant. The most obvious implication is that these self-styled socialists may be more nationalist than anything else. While they may well be revolutionaries or socialists, they put some vision of "Greater Ethiopia," or the "motherland" above all else, above the correct line, above proletarian internationalism, above the vanguard party. Marxism-Leninism is valued most, then, because it legitimizes the oligarchic rule of a segment of the military and their civilian supporters. As long as Marxism-Leninism does not seem to threaten the rule of this group, it will be used to support the regime's statist development strategy. The ideology, the vanguard party, and other centrally controlled institutions are viewed almost as ingredients in some magical potion that will enable the regime to build a command economy, if not a command society. This strategy is invoked as if in search of administrative efficiency and regime legitimacy. But what remains apparent is the state's "softness."

The Constitution of 1987 and Regime Legitimation

The primary task facing the WPE following its formation in 1984 was to devise a new national constitution that would inaugurate "The People's Democratic Republic of Ethiopia." In the process, the new regime hoped to enhance the twin goals of control and legitimacy. A 191-person constitutional drafting committee was appointed by the WPE. It was dominated by members of the Politbureau and central committee of the party, as well as by carefully selected civilians, soldiers, and bureaucrats, and staffed by the Institute for the Study of Ethiopian Nationalites. For more than a year the committee worked at hammering out the details of the document.

In June 1986 a 120-article draft constitution was issued. A million copies were printed and distributed to kebeles and peasant associations throughout the country. For the next two months the draft was discussed at twenty to twenty-five thousand locations.[73] The regime apparently used this approach in an effort to legitimize the process of constitution making and to test the mood of the general population. In some cases, people attended local constitutional discussion sessions only after pressure from local party cadre, but in others they attended voluntarily. Where popular interest was apparent, it mostly centered around articles dealing with such issues as taxes, the role of religion, marriage, the organization of elections, and citizenship rights and obligations.[74] By far the most controversial provision was Article 38, Chapter 7 of the draft, which outlawed polygamy and caused a furor among Muslims who comprise 40 to 60 percent of the total population. Few questions were raised about the glaring failure of the document to address the nationalities problem and the right to self-determination. According to government officials, however, more than a half million suggested revisions were submitted by the citizenry. In August the drafting committee reconvened for the purpose of considering proposed amendments. In all, the committee accepted ninety-five amendments to the original draft. Most of the changes made, however, were only cosmetic.

The referendum on the Constitution of the People's Democratic Republic of Ethiopia (PDRE) was held on February 1, 1987, and the results of the vote were announced by WPE General Secretary Mengistu three weeks later. He reported that 96 percent of the fourteen million people eligible to participate (all adults eighteen years of age and above) actually voted. Eighty-one percent of the electorate was said to have endorsed the constitution, while 18 percent opposed it.[75] This was the first election in Ethiopia's history based on the principles of universal manhood suffrage. It is important to note, however, that the regime was unable to hold referenda in rural areas of Tigre and Eritrea controlled by the TPLF and EPLF respectively. On the other hand, referenda were possible in urban centers in both provinces and in rural south and central Eritrea, which is government controlled. In other places, such as parts of Wollo and Gondar, the vote took place amid heightened security measures. One cynical observer said it was rumored in the days leading up to the referendum that the government had already prepared a computer printout of favorable results. This contention was never validated, but in January, a month before the referendum, one commission official intimated to me that it was certain that this was the *final* version of the constitution.

The PDRE was officially proclaimed on February 22, 1987, at the time making Ethiopia the latest of six Black African regimes subscribing to the designation people's republic.[76] The constitution resembled a hybrid of the Soviet and Romanian constitutions. The original draft was closely patterned on the Soviet model, but the final version departs from that model in two critical respects. First, the office of the presidency is strengthened and elevated above the authority of the Council of State. This change creates a presidency with powers similar to those of the Romanian chief executive. Second, the Soviet model of self-determination is consciously not endorsed. It was reported that the problem of nationalities was hotly debated in the drafting committee as well as in the WPE central committee, but nothing changed in this regard.[77]

Part One of the constitution defines the social order. The PDRE is declared to be "a state of working peasants in which the intelligentsia, the revolutionary army, artisans and other democratic sections of society participate."[78] The commitment to socialist construction is reaffirmed, and so is the notion of equalitarianism within the context of a unitary state. As in the past, the official language remains Amharic. This section also spells out the procedures for the exercise of "people's power" through the National *Shengo* (assembly of the people) and local *shengos*.

The operating powers of the 835-member National Shengo are spelled out in Part Three. It is declared to be "the supreme organ of state power." Shengo representatives are nominated by cells of the WPE, mass organizations, military units, and "other bodies so entitled by law" from electoral districts each averaging seventy-five thousand people in rural areas and fifteen thousand in urban centers. They serve terms of up to five years. The National Shengo is responsible for electing the president, vice-president, and the vice-presidents of the Council of State. On recommendation from the president, the Shengo elects the prime minister, deputy prime ministers, other members of the Council of Ministers, and other officers in the national executive and judicial branches of government. The National Shengo convenes as a whole once a year; but it functions year-round through standing commissions. The Council of State is said to be the permanent organ of the National Shengo, and the president of the PDRE is the president of the Council. From this position, the president can exercise a great deal of power and influence. The twenty-four-member Council of State oversees the day-to-day operations of government and is complemented by twenty ministries, seven permanent commissions, and the party.

The president of the PRDE is granted sweeping powers in the new constitution. Like the emperor of the deposed imperial regime, he has extensive appointive and dismissal powers. In addition to nominating ministers to the Shengo for ratification, he also nominates the chief judicial officers in the country and the head of the workers' control commission and the chief auditor—important investigative positions in the WPE. Furthermore, he appoints members of and chairs the defense council and has broad powers in the area of foreign affairs. The president can appoint or dismiss, at will, any ministers, high-level judicial officers, and even the attorney general, and after the fact simply submit his decisions to the National Shengo for ratification.

Part Two of the constitution deals with "Citizenship, Freedoms, Rights and Duties." Among the rights guaranteed are work and leisure; free education; health care; "inviolability of the person" and "the home"; due process; trial by court; free legal counsel when needed; franchise; free assembly and expression; peaceful demonstration; property ownership; and religious freedom (as long as it is not exercised in a manner contrary to the interest of the state and the revolution).

The implementation of most of the provisions of the new constitution required new legislation. Some of the needed laws were quickly formulated in September 1987 once the National Shengo was elected and held its first sessions. As soon as the new constitution was approved, however, the WPE appointed a number of committees to study various aspects of existing laws and procedures and to recommend changes. These committees had completed a good deal of the drafting of guidelines and laws that were enacted at the inaugural session of the Shengo.

The final congress of the Provisional Military Administrative Council was held in the PMAC's Congress Hall on September 3, 1987, and theoretically the Derg was dissolved. However, its presence is still heavily felt in all areas of government and the party. There was a seemingly conscious effort to achieve an ethnic balance in the upper levels of the new government, but the continuing influence of Amhara cultural orientation was unmistakable.[79] Those who held the most important positions, as in the past, were steeped in the dominant Amhara tradition.

The new government was inaugurated with Comrade Mengistu Haile Mariam as president of the People's Democratic Republic on September 10, 1987. Within one week the Shengo issued a proclamation concerning the administrative reorganization of the country and the creation of twenty-four administrative regions and five so-called autonomous regions.[80] This was an effort to defuse nationalist discontent, particularly in Eritrea, Tigre, and the Ogaden. The five autonomous regions created were Eritrea, Tigre, Assab, Dire Dawa, and Ogaden. By granting autonomous status to Assab and Dire Dawa, the regime effectively retained the economic cores of Eritrea and the Ogaden respectively.

Despite this gesture of regional reorganization, the response of most nationalist movements fighting the Derg was negative and swift.[81] The EPLF perceived the move to be nothing but "old wine in new bottles" and a continued effort on the part of "Ethiopian colonialists" to deprive the Eritrean people of their right to self-determination. The EPLF continues to call for a referendum and UN intervention into the situation. The TPLF and OLF were not as outspoken as the EPLF, but both groups also saw what the new regime considered to be a momentous move as insignificant. The Somalis saw the creation of the autonomous region of Ogaden as nothing more than tokenism, since it does not incorporate a large number of Ogaden Somalis. The Afar Liberation Front at first lauded the regional reorganization plan, but then roundly condemned it as nothing new.

According to this plan, each region will have its own assembly and the populace will be able to elect its own executive body. In general, regional governments have some control over culture, health, education, taxation, and local economic development. Additional powers are given to the so-called autonomous regions, but even among these Eritrea is clearly considered a special case.

The newly created province of Eritrea, apart from being stripped of Assab and its environs, is divided into three subregions in the north, west, and central parts of historic Eritrea. The new subprovince in the west consists of what were the provinces of Barka, Keren, and Sahel, in which the main language is Tigre and the predominant ethnic group is the Beni

Amir. Perhaps it is not insignificant that this is the region where the EPLF is strongest. The official government in the area is limited to the cities of Keren and Agordat. It has no presence at all in Sahel. The rest of the area is firmly in the control of the EPLF. Some observers suggest that this arrangement may make it easy for the regime to give up this area to the EPLF in future negotiations for an independent Eritrea while retaining access to the Red Sea afforded by control of Assab and the rest of Eritrea.[82] It is important to note that the new Assab autonomous region includes portions of what were once districts in eastern Tigre and Wollo provinces.

The westernmost subregion of Eritrea is populated by the Naranga and Kunama peoples, who have been extremely supportive of the revolutionary government. The central subregion is comprised mainly of Tigrinya-speaking people who have historically identified with the Ethiopian heartland.

The regime, in an effort clearly to highlight the uniqueness of the region of Eritrea, gave the regional government expanded authority in the areas of industrial development and education. The regional government is allowed to draw up its own budgetary and taxation plans and to implement them on approval from the central administration. This contrasts sharply with the practice in other regions, which do not have any extensive powers in this area. In the area of education, the Eritrean regional government has authority up to the junior college level. In other regions the local government controls education only up to the secondary level.

By late 1987, administrative reorganization was a reality only on paper. Despite these reforms, the nationalist opposition seems determined to continue the struggle. This is particularly the case with the EPLF, the TPLF, and to a lesser extent the OLF. Moreover, the EPLF and TPLF seem to have the capacity to render these new reforms moot in the areas they currently control. Both groups have large, well-trained fighting forces that continue to keep major portions of the north out of effective government control. Rather than endorse the new reforms and recognize the new regime as legitimate, people in these areas are likely to continue to struggle for self-determination and social justice for the foreseeable future.

Conclusion

The new government of Ethiopia has engaged in social and political policies intended to consolidate state power while at the same time enhancing the state's legitimacy. In approaching both these objectives the regime is severely constrained by its limited resource capacity. With the steady growth of the state bureaucracy and the inauguration of a vanguard party, the problem of a lack of trained and ideologically disciplined agents of the Afro-Marxist state has at least been partially addressed. However, the regime continues to lack access to the ample, autonomous reservoir of monetary resources necessary to implement its development strategy free from donor pressure and without external dependence.

Ironically, the regime was able to turn the drought and famine of 1984–1986 to its advantage. The substantial foreign relief assistance that poured into the country relieved pressure on the government's own resources. Rather than having been weakened by the crisis, then, the regime emerged from it stronger than ever before. In spite of the catastrophe, it was able to keep opposition groups relatively in check, to begin consolidating the vanguard party, and to enhance central control over the general population through the villagization and resettlement programs.

The regime's efforts to implement socialism from above have been costly in both financial and human terms. The enactment of new projects like resettlement and villagization will do little to change the situation. Critics argue that, if anything, these policies will make matters worse. Moreover, the inauguration of the WPE and the constitution of 1987—new institutions intended at least in part to enhance the regime's legitimacy—promise to have immediate meaning for few, if any, members of the general population. Especially in the eyes of opposition movements like the OLF, TPLF, and EPLF and their supporters, the regime is as illegitimate as it ever was.

IX

TOWARD ECONOMIC
SOCIALIZATION

Even though the Derg did not have a clearly formed ideology when it seized power, it was committed to dismantling the structure of power and privilege that had characterized the ancien régime. At first this translated into stripping the traditional privileged classes of their control over rural property and surplus production and ousting the few but significant multinational firms that had penetrated Ethiopia after World War II. There was no indication as to where the nationalization of foreign firms would lead at the time these actions were taken. After the announcement of the Program for the National Democratic Revolution, there was a firm commitment to a statist development strategy that rejected the idea of an open capitalist economy and endorsed the notion of intensive state leadership and direct involvement in economic activities. Such an approach has come to be associated with socialist countries guided by some variant of the Soviet model. Like the scientific socialist ideology the regime has adopted, and that allows for rule by clique, this approach was seen as an integral aspect of a state-socialist development strategy.

The Derg, it can be argued, calculated the short-term if not long-term advantages of closely identifying with the Soviet bloc as well as attempting to adapt the Soviet economic model to suit Ethiopia's circumstances. This model requires the elimination of the private ownership of the key means of production and the transference of this ownership to "the people." The state, until it withers away, "owns" this property and is responsible for managing it for the masses. Closely related to the state ownership of the means of production is the requirement that it control the productive, distributional, and exchange processes for the common good. This could only be achieved through an all-embracing, planned economy. An essential component of the state's orchestration of socialist economic development is, in theory, the collectivization of agriculture.

The language and the form of Soviet-style scientific socialism was eagerly adopted by the Derg, more because of what they enabled the regime to do or to justify than because of a blind faith in Marxist-Leninist doctrine. This could be clearly seen in the fact that the type of socialism in Ethiopia

245

between 1976 and 1987 was fraught with contradictions. The regime seemed more attracted to the enhanced nature of control it was afforded by this approach than by its truths. Even then, the inherent "softness" of the state prevented it from assuming the dominant, instrumentalist role that it sought.

The purpose of this chapter is to assess critically the Derg's attempt to socialize the economy. Particular attention is paid to the agricultural sector. As in other parts of Africa, agriculture is the "engine" that drives the country's economic development. Therefore, it would seem logical that the Derg's first order of priority in the road to economic socialization would be the harnessing of productive forces in the agricultural sector. The Derg tried this but failed in the first ten years of its rule. The state's limited resource capacity, coupled with multiple environmental constraints, served to short-circuit its ambitious plans.

The State, Production, Distribution, and Exchange

Even before the Derg endorsed the doctrine of scientific socialism, it began the process of seizing control of the "commanding heights" of the Ethiopian economy. The nationalization of privately owned industrial and commercial enterprises in the mid-1970s was the first step in that direction. By 1982 the state was at least nominally in control of the industrial sector. It controlled, in whole or in part, all large-scale manufacturing firms, and of the 1,586 registered small-scale firms only 216 were private manufacturing concerns.[1] The state enterprises were reorganized into thirteen corporations and five share companies; for the most part, these came under the control of the Ministry of Industry.

Merely achieving tenuous hegemony in the industrial sector was not enough to enable the Derg to utilize rapid industrialization as a stimulant to economic development. The existing industrial base was simply too small. In total, the industrial sector accounted for only about 22 percent of the gross domestic product (GDP) in 1978; and by 1982 its share of the GDP had fallen five points to 17 percent. Only between 7 percent and 9 percent of industry is represented by manufacturing, usually the most dynamic part of the industrial sector.

Significantly, the regime could not seize absolute control of the industrial sector even if it had wanted to. It simply did not have the capacity to do so. When foreign companies were nationalized, most of their expatriate employees vacated their posts and were replaced by indigenous managers and technicians. The pool of qualified local manpower was quickly exhausted, and the government had to retract some of its original decisions. For example, only a few days after having nationalized all the major food-processing firms, the Derg announced that food processing would be left in private hands. It also had to denationalize the fuel distribution industry when it proved too difficult for the state to manage. By 1982, however, the state owned 80 percent of the industrial sector.[2]

Initially, no attempt was made to seize control of the import-export sectors, but by 1981 the state was involved in 65 percent of the export trade and 77 percent of the import trade. Private enterprise was allowed to continue in certain strategically important sectors such as coffee export, pharmaceuticals, and construction, although the state seized control of portions of these activities as well. Retail and wholesale remained largely in private hands.[3]

Over the past decade of the revolution, the Derg came to realize that it could not do without foreign private investments. In 1983, after having settled most of the compensation claims resulting from the nationalization of foreign firms, it began to invite in entirely new foreign capital in an effort to stimulate the economy.[4]

As if to convince prospective investors and donors that the commitment to scientific socialism and all that it implies had not changed Ethiopia's economic policy instincts, after the appeal went out for more Western capital, the governor of the National Bank of Ethiopia remarked,

> The government is not intending to nationalize . . . we should be given credit for being wise enough to appreciate that capital is a very shy animal and that if you play the game wrongly you will lose. We have decided we need [foreign companies] to invest and can be expected to act accordingly.[5]

Further assurances to the owners of private property in Ethiopia—particularly local property owners—are provided in the newly enacted Constitution of the People's Democratic Republic of Ethiopia. The constitution guarantees that government will not nationalize private property without compensation.

The continued importance of private capital in the Ethiopian economy would seem to contradict the principles of scientific socialism. However, this is officially justified by the fact that Ethiopia is at the developmental stage of the national democratic revolution. This stage is said to be very complex and often characterized by apparent contradictions. But with vigilance and careful state guidance, it is argued, these paradoxes will be worked out in the long run. For the moment, the government is forced by circumstance to tolerate some private investments, but it regulates them closely and sets ceilings on the level of private investment. Where possible, joint ventures are encouraged between the state and private investors, particularly foreign concerns.[6]

In January 1983 the government issued a new joint investment code intended to encourage private foreign capital to return. At the same time, the code gave the state a measure of control over foreign investors that went far beyond what existed under Haile Selassie. Joint ventures are now possible in areas that introduce technology and know-how or make positive contributions to foreign exchange generation and employment, economic, and social development. Foreigners are forbidden from investing in public utilities, banking, insurance, precious metals, transport, and domestic trade. All joint ventures are required to be with the public sector, and the government must possess at least 51 percent of the shares of a given venture. From the Ethiopian state's point of view, the decision to encourage joint ventures between itself and foreign capital would serve two main purposes. First and foremost, such ventures would stimulate the industrial and agro-industrial sectors of the economy. Second, they would provide a vehicle for training Ethiopian technicians and managers and contribute to a diffusion of technology and managerial expertise. With careful state guidance, it is believed, Ethiopia will become more and more self-reliant and independent of foreign economic interests in the long run. Critics charge that this dependency could become an addiction.[7] While the joint venture strategy does involve some dependence on foreign capital, the government claims that by maintaining controlling shares, it can exercise a good deal of leverage over foreign investors.

Foreign capital was gradually returning to Ethiopia by 1987, but by any standard the level of foreign investments at the time was still "miniscule."[8] There was apprehension among some prospective investors over the sincerity of the regime's claim that it would not utilize its nationalization option capriciously. On its part, the government provided potential investors with the incentives of attractive tax holidays of up to five years as had been the case under the previous regime; no indirect taxes at all on investment goods; spare parts, raw material, and other inputs; and the opportunity to repatriate 10 percent of their dividends to their countries of origin. Some critics contend that such a liberal investment policy represents nothing more than a reincarnation of the imperial regime's preference for foreign investment capital over local entrepreneurship.[9] Such a charge, however, is hard to substantiate.

In 1970 only two of the top fifty-one manufacturing firms were wholly owned by private Ethiopian investors. Of that number, thirty-three firms were characterized by 50 percent or more foreign ownership. Thirty-eight of these firms were foreign-owned or foreign-operated or both, and accounted for 57 percent of the value added in the whole of manufacturing in Ethiopia. At that time the state owned eight of the top firms and participated in an open economic environment.[10] By 1984 the economy was largely closed and the state was the dominant economic actor. Almost all medium- and large-scale manufacturing, all large-scale trade and service enterprises, and all financial institutions were under state control. Private capital was confined to small-scale manufacturing, cottage enterprises, and petty trade. Significantly, the state controlled the distributional system in which all traders had to function. State enterprises employed 94 percent of the 362,054 employed by such concerns, and they accounted for 2 percent of the total value of exports, whereas the contribution of private firms was negligible.[11]

The state's dominance in the economy, however, was not entirely decisive. It was still not in a position to implement its plans with any degree of absolute certainty. This could clearly be seen in agricultural policy, which will be discussed below. But the profound effect of the state's limited resource capacity could also be seen in the implementation of industrial policy. A 1983 International Labor Organization report, for instance, noted that in 1980–1981 actual public sector expenditure was only 57 percent of the amount budgeted and only 65 percent for the following year. This is a clear indication that the public sector is unable to absorb these investments and thus adequately assume its assigned leadership role in industrial development.[12]

The public sector, as well as the private sector, was faced with numerous problems, such as a lack of spare parts, foreign exchange, and poor transport equipment and infrastructure. In addition, planning, management, and coordination were generally poor. It was common for some projects to be started and remain unexecuted, resulting in a wastage of the allocated funds. On the whole, industry was unable to satisfy not only the demands of agriculture, but also its own.[13]

Beyond the fact that the Derg was not able to gain complete control of the forces of production in the industrial sector, other problems emerged. The nationalization of industry, for example, was accompanied by more disruption than the nationalization of land in terms of output, investment, and employment. The economic downturn was attributed in part to the necessary dislocation that accompanies nationalization and in part to the civil unrest that gripped the country beginning in 1976. Initially, the main problems related to management and management-worker relations. In the first place, the Derg soon found itself in the position of having to employ the former owners of certain firms—the very class the revolution was supposed to get rid of—at relatively high salaries, simply because of the dearth of qualified managers among the supporters of the revolution. Second, the responsibility for managing nationalized firms should in theory have been shared between workers and managers. One of the main industrial problems the regime had to face initially was the corporate grievances of Ethiopia's small wage-labor force. Labor protests forced the Derg to ban the Confederation of Ethiopian Labor Unions (CELU) and to institute a new labor code. The code alluded to the encouragement of workers' councils that would provide a voice for labor in the management of nationalized firms. In practice, however, these councils came to be nothing more than grievance committees.[14]

Agriculture is the motor force of the Ethiopian economy, and it is in that sector that the Derg's policies had the most immediate and long-term effect. Initially, the new regime was more concerned with the redistribution of wealth and property in the countryside than with managing economic development. In addition to nationalizing major urban-based industries, the Derg nationalized an estimated five thousand commercial farms covering about seventy-six thousand hectares. Although this represented only 2 percent of all land under cultivation, commercial farms monopolized the production of such significant import-substitution crops as sugar and cotton. About ninety-five hundred hectares of this property were redistributed to landless peasants, and the remainder was converted into large-scale mechanized state farms. By early 1981 about 330,000 hectares had been reserved for state farms.

The State Farm Development Authority, based in the Ministry of Agriculture and Settlement, was created to staff and oversee the activities of these farms. At the time, the hope was (and continued to be) that state farms would make a vital contribution to agricultural production for export, but to date they have not approached this expectation.

Peasant agriculture has historically been Ethiopia's most vital economic resource, but it had been stifled by the oppressive conditions of feudalism and crude, highly exploitative, nascent capitalism. The Derg claimed that through its land reform edict it sought to unleash this pent-up potential of rural producers and to empower the peasantry. The expectation seems to have been that peasant farmers would naturally make their contribution to development without state intervention by selling the surplus produce that used to go to landlords in the market economy or by voluntarily producing because the "motherland" required it. All that had to be done was to explain the goals of the revolution to them. The *Zemacha* was expected to be a substitute for a vanguard party of committed socialists, but this expectation, for the reasons discussed in chapter 7, quickly proved unrealistic.

The Derg, following the restoration of relative political quiesence in the wake of the Red Terror, attempted more resolutely to create institutions and implement policies that allowed it to plan rationally for economic development. Rational planning, however, was not enough to guarantee desired results in the industrial or agricultural sectors.

The Imperative of Central Planning

In theory, scientific socialism requires a centrally planned economy. However, the Derg initially rushed to consolidate the revolution without giving much thought to this priority. In fact, it seemed almost an afterthought. Perhaps this was because the problems encountered by the imperial regime in its efforts to plan development were well known and had not been resolved. Faced with poor administrative coordination and desperate economic problems, the Derg made its first halting steps toward the establishment of a centrally planned economy in 1978. In October of that year the regime issued a "Proclamation to Provide for the Establishment of the

National Revolutionary Development Campaign and Central Planning," which was viewed as signalling a "second *Zemacha*" or the "Green *Zemacha*."[15]

The objective of this reform was to begin the process of long-term economic planning, with peasant agriculture serving as the basis of economic development and with industrialization relegated to a secondary priority. To the extent that the expansion of the manufacturing sector would be stressed, it was expected that concentration would be placed on light and cottage industries. It was not that the heavy industrial sector was deemed unimportant, but that for the moment Ethiopia should concentrate on increasing production in its strongest sector, agriculture.

The proclamation established a Central Planning Supreme Council (CPSC) under the direction of Provisional Military Administrative Council chairman Mengistu. The organization consisted of a committee, a secretariat, a Provincial Development Campaign and Planning Office, plus similar offices at the regional and district levels. Delegates to the Council Congress and employees in the other institutions represented all major interests in the society. The permanent staff of the National Revolutionary Development Campaign (NRDC) was around one thousand by the end of 1981 and included seven or eight Soviet advisers.[16] However, it is important to note that this new organization, as in other new institutions created around this time, was top-heavy with military personnel and bureaucrats, far outnumbering workers and representatives from other mass organizations.

In contrast to the first *Zemacha*, this second campaign was a serious effort to plan policies and programs systematically and thoroughly and to implement them efficiently. The state planning body was to set goals and coordinate the activities of the multiplicity of agencies involved in attempting to stimulate development in the field.

In its first year of operation, the CPSC planned to expand the area of land under peasant cultivation dramatically, at the same time boosting production of grain by 170,000 tons. By 1980 it projected that new state farms would be operating on 250,000 acres of land set aside for that purpose. In the industrial sector, a 40 percent increase in production in the 132 most important state-owned enterprises was targeted. As for coffee, the most important export commodity, it projected that production levels would reach 100,000 tons.

By the end of 1979 the Derg was claiming success. It had planned annually for two years and claimed that its industrial targets fell short by only 7 percent and agricultural targets by only 1 percent. Coffee exports did not reach the projected 100,000 tons, falling 15,000 short, but the growth in that sector and others was satisfactory to the regime. The overall economic growth rate jumped from below 1 percent at the beginning of 1978 to over 5 percent at the end of 1979.

Despite this remarkable growth in Ethiopia's economy, it continued to be in crisis. In fact, the crisis seemed to deepen even as impressive production targets were almost being met. There were many reasons for this, but chief among them were worldwide inflation, declining coffee prices, and dwindling foreign exchange reserves. In 1980 Ethiopia exported almost 87,000 tons of coffee that netted about $342 million. Coupled with this was a worldwide decrease in demand for Ethiopia's second most important export commodity, hides and skins. As a result, earnings from exports in that year were sufficient only to cover about 70 percent of the cost of imports. By the end of the year it was estimated that the country had only $122 million in foreign currency reserves.[17] By March 1981 reserves had plummeted to about $60 million.[18]

Exacerbating these foreign exchange problems was an external debt that had grown by 80 percent to $691 million. Most of this was debt owed by the central government, which had invested heavily in arms as well as social services since 1976. The balance of payments deficit for 1979–1980 climbed to more than $200 million. This was mostly due to an overall increase in import prices and the growing demand for imported items. By far the most costly of imported items was fuel, which accounted for one-fourth of total imports and cost almost 60 percent of export earnings. All of this must be considered against an annual inflation rate of 25 percent.

Using this crisis as a backdrop, Mengistu convened a congress of the NRDC in July 1981. The Derg apparently was heartened by the success of the campaign thus far in implementing central planning and decided to take this process one step further. In his opening remarks, Mengistu emphasized such internal problems as poor management, low productivity, a lack of organizational capacity, and the shortage of necessary equipment and spare parts, rather than problems relating to the international market. He went on to make an appeal to international donor agencies and friendly governments to assist Ethiopia in the inauguration of a ten-year development plan.

The cost of executing this plan was projected at more than $8 million annually. Over the plan period, investments would have to increase by 21 percent, most of which would have to come from foreign aid. This would be complemented, it was posited, by a dramatic increase in domestic saving until it accounted for 16 percent of the GDP. Domestic saving was expected to be realized by holding government expenditures constant while increasing revenues, thus creating a surplus that could then be saved. Public enterprises were counted on heavily in the plan to raise government revenues to 30 percent of the GDP, a rise of 12 percent from the 1980 level. It was further expected that public enterprises would contribute about half of the total public sector domestic saving.

The main objectives of the ten-year plan were as follows: (1) to raise the GDP at the 1979–1980 market prices from $2.5 billion to $6.8 billion; (2) to provide employment for five million people; (3) to increase agricultural production by 60 percent; (4) to increase industrial production; (5) to augment export earnings in real terms by 260 percent; (6) to provide basic health services to cover 85 percent of the rural population; (7) to eradicate illiteracy and provide polytechnic education from grades one through eight for about nine million children; (8) to construct 45,000 housing units each year or about 450,000 in ten years; and (9) to increase the annual growth rate from 5.6 percent to 7.5 percent. Sectoral growth targets were identified as 4.5 percent for agriculture, 13.6 percent for industry, and 7.5 percent for services.[19]

What was most striking about the plan was its heavy reliance on foreign aid. In its initial formulation, the plan required 55 percent of all investment to come from foreign sources. There were numerous potential pitfalls in the pursuit of such a strategy, only one of which had to do with ideological orthodoxy. Some critics argue that if the massive amounts of foreign capital envisaged were to flow into Ethiopia, the result would be to promote *antisocialist* rather than socialist tendencies. Additional possible problems might ensue. First, poor coordination: Foreign aid funds are usually tied to projects, to products, or to uses according to the desires of donors. Loans generally have similar lender expectations: Both grants and loans secured from foreign sources are often on terms that do not mesh with those of the recipient country. Therefore, Ethiopia could conceivably have its plans delayed if not derailed by its blind pursuit of foreign capital. Second, as mentioned above, assuming Ethiopia could attract the massive amounts of foreign aid needed to make the plan work, it is unlikely that it could absorb these funds smoothly. This point was vividly demonstrated at the height of the catastrophic drought and famine of 1984–1986. Third, most of the funds would be used to pay for foreign inputs and spare parts, or, as in the past, they might be used to pay for increased expenditures in social services, administration, and defense. Fourth, the industrial sector that would grow out of this plan would be large and capital intensive. Thus it would not address the problem of urban unemployment and most likely would exacerbate it. A small, relatively highly paid work force would emerge largely comprised of workers in the public sector, worsening the very inequities that socialism is supposed to eliminate.[20]

The regime delayed inaugurating the Ten-Year Guiding Plan (TYGP) until the tenth anniversary of the revolution. Five annual plans, centered around the concept of the "development campaign," preceded this announcement. At the time, the NRDC and CPSC were phased out and replaced by the Office of the National Committee for Central Planning.[21] The most authoritative unit in this new body is the twenty-member national committee, headed by Mengistu and dominated by Politbureau members. Significantly, no peasants or workers are represented on this committee, but technocrats are well represented. This committee assigns duties and provides guidelines to the executive committee responsible for providing actual leadership in the organization.

The national committee is responsible for standardizing plan procedures and targets and for generally defining the parameters of economic development. Also, it reviews and evaluates plans from various central government agencies, mass organizations, and regional offices. The day-to-day work of the office is conducted by the executive committee and the Politbureau.

There are seven regional planning offices that represent the national committee in the regions. These offices are designed mainly to collect data and research, which is processed by the secretariat, and the executive and national committees in the course of formulating short-, medium-, and long-term plans. Regional planning offices are also responsible for ensuring plan implementation, follow-up, and evaluation in their respective areas. At that level, the most important institutions are regional planning councils, headed by Workers' Party of Ethiopia representatives in the regions and comprised of government officials and the leaders of mass organizations, regional planning committees, and regional secretariats. This pattern is repeated down to the *awraja* level and in that respect parallels party and government.

The Derg seems either to have recognized the overambitiousness of the initial formulation of the ten-year plan, to have learned from experience, or to be responding to criticism when it produced the TYGP. Even though it is still an ambitious plan, its goals have been somewhat tempered.[22]

The TYGP is to run from 1984–1985 to 1993–1994. The overall annual growth rate is now expected to be 6.5 percent as compared to the 7.5 percent anticipated in the perspective plan. Although the regime claims that agriculture is the top priority, the TYGP makes clear its determination to improve the capacity of urban-based industry. By the end of the plan period it is anticipated that agriculture's share of total output will drop to 39 percent, and industry's share is expected to rise to 24 percent.[23] Despite the intention to improve the performance of industry, the new plan places its emphasis on increasing agricultural output, promoting capital accumulation, improving the overall standard of living, and achieving food security. Most of the other goals articulated in the perspective plan are retained.

The devastating drought and famine of 1984–1986 contributed substantially to a precipitous decline in food production among the peasantry. This was accompanied by a rising rate of population growth. In this period, population grew at a rate of almost 3 percent annually, while agriculture's average annual rate of growth was only 1.7 percent. If only for political reasons, then, the regime must be sensitive and responsible to the welfare needs of the general population.

An initial three-year public sector investment program is expected to cost almost $3 million. Fifteen percent of this amount will go to agriculture and 10 percent to transport, communications, and water development.[24] Peasant cooperatives are expected to lead this drive, but state farms are also charged to expand production and improve productivity. The historic difficulty of harnessing agriculture, however, has proved a menace to the best intended plans and policies.

The Pitfalls of Planning Agricultural Development

Despite the fact that Ethiopia's economy thrives on the agricultural production of the peasantry, the regime has almost been forced to invest a great deal of resources and attention in state farms. It realized from the start that it could not turn large-scale farms organized as plantations over to the peasantry. This would certainly have resulted in unwise economic disruption in the production of export and import-substitution commodities. Large-scale grain farms were also maintained intact because they provided the regime with the most reliable source of staple products for the urban sector. As far as the peasant sector has been concerned, the state merely attempted to gain a measure of organizational control over peasant producers and to provide them with positive and negative incentives to move toward collective production.

Citing the fact that the rate of economic growth had dropped below the rate of population growth, Mengistu clearly spelled out the Derg's short run economic development rational at the second COPWE congress in early 1983.[25] He expressed disappointment in peasant-based agriculture and emphasized the need to turn more toward large-scale agriculture. In the short run, he said, the commitment would be to emphasize the expansion and strengthening of state farms. Such enterprises were expected to "not merely produce the raw materials and crops required for domestic consumption and foreign trade and to meet the foodstuff needs of urban centers [but also] to speed up agricultural development . . . by introducing better farming technology and organization, by supplying choice seeds and in general setting an example."[26]

The Derg's reaffirmed and stronger commitment to state farm development was emphasized when the Ministry of State Farms was created in 1979, thus phasing out the State Farm Development Authority. The ministry consists of seven semiautonomous, regionally based corporations that could coordinate their activities through the ministry but in practice are quite autonomous in making management decisions. Within two years of the establishment of the new ministry, the amount of state farmland under cultivation had been expanded to 245,000 hectares, and by 1984 state farms occupied 300,000 hectares. This amounted to about 4 percent of the total land under cultivation.

The expansion of state farms has proven to be very costly. The work force needed to maintain such operations is substantial, and the large numbers of laborers involved results in a sizable wage bill. State farms employ both permanent and seasonal workers and provide many employees with housing, medical, and other social services. In addition to unskilled and semiskilled labor, mechanized farming requires highly qualified manpower, and this provides an additional financial burden. Labor costs comprise about two-thirds of the total cost on state farms. The income per individual worker, however, is not very high, and this has been a major contributor to low morale and inefficiency in the labor force.[27]

State farms consume about sixty thousand tons of fertilizer per year or 82 percent of all fertilizer imports. This is important because Ethiopia does not have the capacity to produce most of the fertilizer it needs and must expend foreign exchange to meet its needs. Over 73 percent of the improved seeds distributed annually by the government (sixteen thousand tons) goes to state farms. Perhaps more important, the state farm sector consumes about 80 percent of the credit provided by the Agricultural and Industrial Development Bank (AIDB).[28] It is important to note that state farms and producer cooperatives have preferential access to all inputs, since the Derg has chosen to rely on them to lead economic development. Peasants in areas of Shoa, Arussi, and Hararge that are firmly in government hands fare a little better than those in other areas in terms of their access to credit, improved farm inputs, and extension services.

The government further subsidizes state farms by providing them with preferential prices for their produce. They are required to sell their production to the Agricultural Marketing Corporation (AMC), as are peasant producers, but they are paid about 20 to 50 percent more than peasants for similar goods.

Despite their high cost and inefficiency, state farms have contributed greatly to the elimination of shortfalls in food production and to the safeguarding of the production of such major cash crops as cotton and sugar. By 1983 state farms accounted for 10 to 15 percent of all the grain sold in the wholesale market, but most important are the markets for which this grain was intended. State farms play a strategic role in supplying such crops as wheat, maize, and sorghum to such consumers as civil servants, the armed forces, and certain residents of urban areas. The Derg has a vested interest in keeping these groups politically quiescent, if not loyal.[29]

Ironically, the state grants regional state farm corporations considerable autonomy in managing their respective operations. It has taken the lead, however, in dictating the pace of change. This contrasts sharply with the experiences of the Soviet Union and other Eastern European countries with state farm systems where the state exercises a high degree of control over production as well as marketing. Part of the reason for limited state control is its sheer lack of capacity for rigid control. In official circles the hope is that once state farms have become established and efficient enough they can move naturally into large-scale collectives. The architects of this strategy trust this will come about even as they avoid the bloodshed that accompanied the Soviet Union's consolidation of its control over the agricultural sector. This rationale allows the regime to justify the short-term reliance on state farms, since there is nothing inherently *socialist* about them.

The most important sector of the economy continues to be peasant agriculture. Instead of emphasizing the productive capacity of this sector as a whole, the government has chosen to emphasize the development of the cooperative system as a first step along the road to collectivization. On March 3, 1978, the "Proclamation to Provide for the Establishment of Cooperative Societies" was issued. The objectives of cooperatives were to promote self-reliance among cooperative members, put the means of production under the control of cooperatives and to transform them gradually into collectives, increase production, expand industries, conduct political agitation, eliminate reactionary culture and customs, participate in building a socialist economy, and accumulate capital and mobilize human resources to sustain economic development.[30] The idea was to create conditions for the voluntary acceptance of collective ownership and collective production and to skip completely a phase characterized by individual capitalism.

Although the 1978 proclamation more clearly spelled out the organizational and legal details associated with cooperatives, such institutions had been encouraged since the land reform proclamation three years earlier. Originally, two main varieties of cooperatives were considered: service and producer cooperatives. The response of the peasantry at the time was not overwhelming. By 1978 a handful (twenty-one) of producer cooperatives at an advanced state of development, with at least 75 percent of their land collectively owned, were officially registered. Twenty-two more were at the initial stage of organization and were not registered.

The response to service cooperatives was somewhat better, but also meager. In 1978 there were 343 registered service cooperatives with 1,846 in the process of being formed. After that time, however, the number of service cooperatives grew rapidly, and the number of producer cooperatives increased at an even more dramatic rate, although they were still less popular than service cooperatives. By the summer of 1984 3,651 service cooperatives served almost five million peasant households and over one thousand producer cooperatives at various stages of development.[31] It is envisioned that service cooperatives will eventually transform themselves into elementary producer cooperatives and then, over time, be further transformed into advanced producer cooperatives. Although the government denies that the resettlement and villagization programs are intended to speed up this process, its real intentions are clearly to do just that.

Service cooperatives serve strictly economic functions such as marketing, the provision of credit, the encouragement of savings, and the distribution of consumer goods. Producer cooperatives control the instruments of production more directly. There are three levels of producer cooperatives: the *malba, welba,* and *weland* levels. The malba level is the elementary stage, and at that level members are required to transfer most of their private holdings to the cooperative. They are allowed to keep one-fifth of a hectare for their individual cultivation. Farm implements and draft animals, such as donkeys and oxen, may continue to be privately owned. The cooperatives simply pay rent to the owners of these inputs for their use.

A welba or advanced producer cooperative level is reached when all land becomes communal property and when draft animals and implements become the property of the cooperative, which has a legal "personality." Individuals are allowed to cultivate up to one-tenth of a hectare privately. The cooperative at this stage buys the draft animals and implements from the individuals, and they become communal property. Any peasant association or a minimum of thirty of its members may form a welba. Service cooperative members within a given peasant association may choose to join producer cooperatives. When several of these institutions within a peasant association have been created, they may unite and form an "association of producer cooperatives." When most of the peasants belonging to the peasant association are organized into producer cooperatives at the welba level and are members of an association of producer cooperatives, they may unite to form a new institution called a weland. In a weland the average landholding is four thousand hectares and the membership involves about twenty-five hundred individuals. Each weland then takes on the personality of a *habre* or brigade. The goal is gradually to transform service cooperatives into communes and to convert peasant associations into brigades. It is expected that this will take some time. Originally the regime said that it expected to have achieved more than 50 percent of collectivization by 1985. As of 1984, no welands were in existence.[32] By 1987 the target had been revised downward, and the government was saying that it expected that the number of collectives would only triple by 1989.

Until recently the government was not able to exercise firm control over local peasant associations. Particularly before the vanguard party was formed and began to penetrate the far corners of the country, peasant associations often had considerable autonomy. In fact, they were originally created as vehicles for peasant empowerment. After 1978, however, the government began systematically to try to curb the autonomy peasant associations enjoyed. The idea was to absorb peasant associations gradually into the cooperative network. This was encouraged mainly by providing incentives, especially for the development of producer cooperatives. For example, all public distribution and service agencies and public officials are now required by law to give priority to the needs of cooperatives before they address the needs of individuals.[33] Also, when a producer cooperative is formed within a particular peasant association area, the key leadership within the association must be elected from among the members of the cooperative if those who form the cooperative are not already leaders in the association. All communal property the association possesses, such as grazing land, woodland, equipment, or other fixed property, must be transferred to the cooperative. Any service cooperatives in the area are required to provide loans of 25 percent of their surplus to the producer cooperative, and they must give priority to meeting the needs of the producer cooperative for inputs such as fertilizers and high yield seed.[34]

Service cooperatives, then, are to facilitate the development of producer cooperatives and to move in the direction of forming themselves into collectives. In 1983 the government attempted to encourage this process further by redeploying some of its trained agricultural agents to districts where they could concentrate on assisting service cooperatives in high potential areas.

Significantly, most peasants do not belong to producer cooperatives. This no doubt will change as the villagization program matures. Peasants until now have tended to participate more in service cooperatives. Some observers suggest that these institutions are favored because they allow peasants to maintain a certain amount of autonomy over their land and productive activities, while at the same time allowing them to gain access to valued farm inputs and credit that otherwise they would have difficulty in obtaining. Service cooperatives also facilitate the marketing of peasants' crops. It is estimated that more than five million farm families utilize service cooperatives but less than 100,000 belong to producer cooperatives.

The popularity of all forms of cooperatives among the peasantry is closely related to the level of community support for the regime. The same is true for peasant associations. Peasant associations and producer and service cooperatives are all poorly endorsed in Tigre and Eritrea and most popular in Shoa and parts of the south, areas historically characterized by tenancy and absentee landlords. (See Table 9.1.)

The fact that the government has attempted to channel its inputs to the peasant sector through service and producer cooperatives should not be construed as significantly enhancing or promoting peasant production. What is more striking is the apparent neglect of that sector by the state. For instance, John M. Cohen found that only 8 percent of the government's agricultural budget allocated for agriculture is directed to peasant production. Moreover, that sector receives less than 20 percent of the agricultural credit provided by the AIDB, and only 25 percent of the land farmed by peasants is treated with enriched fertilizer provided through government agencies.[35] This pattern is influenced in part by the fact that the government simply does not have the capacity to do what it must to stimulate peasant agriculture, and in part it is an indication that the state wants to deal more closely with those segments of the economy over which it has at least minimal control.

Even as it committed itself and its resources to large-scale agricultural production, the Derg attempted to involve itself with the peasant sector. This was manifested not so much in the quality of policy making, but in the expanded scope of its activities. Building on the success of the Minimum Package Program (MPP) established by the government in 1971 with Swedish government and World Bank aid, the Derg inaugurated a program

TABLE 9.1

Peasant Associations, Service and Producer Cooperatives by Region, 1984

Region	Population	Peasant Associations	Peasant Association Membership	Service Cooperatives	Producer Cooperatives
Hararge	3,043,000	1,352	383,991	259	96
Sidamo	2,735,000	1,488	719,242	235	84
Shoa	6,195,000ª	5,346	1,327,522	1,055	167
Bale	856,000	519	106,190	128	89
Tigre	2,105,000	157	55,988	56	3
Arussi	1,119,000	1,086	235,501	142	85
Illubabor	795,000	961	148,959	186	77
Eritrea	2,363,000	188	38,537	13	5
Kaffa	1,573,000	1,612	370,042	242	54
Wollega	1,966,000	2,123	216,698	347	90
Wollo	2,544,000	1,132	535,001	258	75
Gemu-Gofa	977,000	795	179,267	81	18
Gondar	2,000,000	1,052	320,859	411	120
Gojjam	1,984,000	1,750	520,082	411	120
Total	30,050,000	19,579	5,164,178	3,651	1,006

SOURCE: Tegegne Teka, "Cooperatives and National Development: The Ethiopian Experience," Institute for Development Research Working Paper, No. 18 (Addis Ababa, 1984).
ª Does not include Addis Ababa.

known as MPP II with help from the World Bank in 1981.[36] The original project was centered in the Chilalo and Wolaita districts and involved the integrated development of peasant agriculture in those areas. The projects provided peasant farmers in a limited area with such inputs as hybrid seeds, fertilizer, credit, and extension services and encouraged them to adopt modern farming techniques using area-specific appropriate technology. This approach was abused by some better-off farmers who tried to enhance their positions at the expense of the poorest peasants, but it did prove to be effective in stimulating peasant production. Consequently, the regime has made an MPP-type program the center of its agricultural strategy. As the state's resource capacity improves and as the villagization and resettlement programs consolidate, the government expects to involve more peasants in such programs.

Agricultural extension services were expanded in the early 1980s to cover 469 districts in the arable highland areas, but this was done without increasing trained manpower assigned to such tasks. About 80 percent of the Ministry of Agriculture's workload came to be absorbed by this project, but even this amounted to no more than one extension agent per two thousand farm families. Agents must direct their attention to peasant associations rather than individual farmers.[37] The World Bank estimated in 1984 that out of fifteen thousand Ministry of Agriculture staff involved in providing agricultural services, less than two thousand had had at least two years of professional training and another two thousand had had only a few weeks to nine months of practical training.[38] The poor quality of extension and support services was exacerbated by the weakness of available technology that could be disseminated to farmers. This problem has been compounded with the push toward villagization and resettlement. Although there are a few model villages, resettlement communities, and integrated development zones, the majority of the peasantry is untouched by government programs to stimulate peasant production.

Peasants are traditionally risk-averse no matter where they are found.[39] However, they might still respond to new technologies if such inputs can be demonstrated to improve the quality of their lives with a minimum of risks. The Ministry of Agriculture has been generally unable to provide adequate amounts or varieties of improved seeds to stimulate farmer demand for these inputs. Less than 20 percent of the improved cereal seeds produced in 1981–1982, for example, went to peasants. Most of the four thousand tons that were supplied to them was nearly a decade old and had lost its potency.[40]

With regard to commercial fertilizer, peasants would use this input if it were readily available and reasonably priced. But, as I mentioned above, relatively small amounts of fertilizer are made available to peasants, and what is available tends to be expensive for the average peasant. This acts as a brake on wider distribution.[41]

Peasants were further discouraged from producing for the market by low producer prices and high consumer prices and by regulations governing the sale of their products. Since 1977 the government has fixed the prices the AMC will pay for peasant crops, and peasants are required to sell their goods to the AMC and only within their districts. They deliver their produce through their neighborhood associations at fixed quotas.[42]

Peasant associations are expected to be the lowest level of governmental administration, and the regime has increasingly attempted to bring them under control by influencing appointments to leadership positions. For the most part, this policy has had only limited success. Increasingly, however, these institutions serve more as agencies of state control than of peasant participation. They adjudicate land and civil disputes, set up and administer local defense squads and development committees, and represent the central planning office at the neighborhood level.

In many areas peasants have lost the enthusiasm they initially had for peasant associations. This tendency has increased as the demands on the peasantry have increased and as peasant associations have proven incapable of providing the kind of leadership needed to stimulate and sustain the rapid expansion of peasant production. Peasants today often participate in association activities more because they fear being penalized than because they feel them efficacious.[43]

Faced with lower producer prices, growing restrictions, and coercion, the majority of peasants—because of the nature of the "soft state" and Ethiopia's transitional society—are free to exercise their "exit option" or to retreat to the "economy of affection" and away from the market economy.[44] By 1983 they tended to produce less and to consume more of what they produced as market conditions worsened for them. In some cases, they joined informal, parallel markets and sold their products clandestinely at more advantageous prices.[45] This was true not only of food crops, but also of cash crops like coffee. In 1987 a vigorous coffee-smuggling trade from Ethiopia to Djibouti was reported. High taxes and low producer prices drove peasants in coffee-producing areas into the informal market. In the process, Djibouti became a net coffee exporter even though it does not possess a single coffee tree![46] Further evidence of the state's inability to control the peasantry is found in the fact that as much as 82 percent of rural produce is either withheld for private consumption or sold in the informal market.[47]

As the villagization and resettlement projects mature, peasant autonomy is likely to diminish and state control should increase. This is already evident in resettlement areas set up after the drought of 1973–1974. Peasants in resettlement areas must farm collectively. Party cadre are a part of the community's administrative framework. They are responsible not only for political agitation, but also for stimulating and monitoring production. Peasants pool their produce and are rationed food on a weekly basis according to the number of "work points" they have accrued in that time. A similar practice exists in producer cooperatives. It seems reasonable to expect that this could become the pattern for villagized communities as well.

Conclusion

In general, the Ethiopian government's mixed success in central planning must be viewed in the context of the state's limited resource capacity, bureaucratic immaturity, and severe political and social pressures emanating from the environment in which it must operate. The major problems facing the Derg were the political instability it had to cope with continuously since 1976 and the "uncaptured" peasantry.

The areas of most intense opposition to the government, Eritrea and Tigre, were also areas most affected by the drought of 1984–1986. Thousands upon thousands of innocent victims of war and drought were dislocated from their farms and forced into refugee camps by ensuing famine, disease, and malnutrition. Opponents of the regime demonstrated that they had the will *and* the capacity to undermine its policies and would do so no matter what the price. The state's limited resources were taxed to their ultimate limits during this period, and it survived only with the help of foreign-based relief efforts. It could not have survived on its own.

In spite of the state's progress in consolidating its power, its inability to crush its opponents militarily or to have them recognize the regime as legitimate have clearly demonstrated that it remains a "soft state." It still possesses limited political, economic, managerial, and technological capacity. Rational planning and bureaucratic management do not guarantee effective policy making.

The "softness" of the state is also demonstrated in its inability to harness peasant producers. Numerous policies have been introduced to address this problem, but peasants as a group have still not been captured by the market to any significant degree. They continue to exercise considerable autonomy and move in and out of the formal market at will. Low producer prices and high consumer prices exacerbate the problem for the state. The villagization and resettlement programs could well change this pattern, but there is no guarantee that this will happen. Without the proper incentives, the peasantry will continue to exercise their "exit option" to avoid exploitation in the market place.

The argument here is not that a centrally planned economy based on collectivized agriculture and the heavy involvement of the state in economic production, distribution, and exchange is inherently flawed. Rather, what is being suggested is that because of the Ethiopian state's limited resource capacity, its inability to cope with uncertainty, and its limited ability to ensure citizen compliance, the regime's development policy has largely failed to achieve the economic goals it set for itself. The very best that can be said of the attempt to socialize the economy is that it is ill-timed. Moreover, a top-down development strategy that only represents the façade of democratic participation and legitimacy is destined to fail in the future.

X

FEUDALISM IS DEAD! LONG LIVE DEPENDENCE!

In many ways the Ethiopian Revolution resembles the classic social revolutions of the modern era—the French Revolution of the late eighteenth century and the Russian and Chinese revolutions of the early twentieth century—more than it resembles other Third World social revolutions. The "great revolutions" resulted from contradictions that emerged and became unmanageable for "well established imperial states with proven capacities to protect their own hegemony and that of the dominant classes against revolts from below."[1] This characterization could well be applied to the Ethiopian empire-state that consolidated itself after 1855 and matured over the next century. Under the weight of pressures resulting from internal social contradictions, the administrative and military coherence of the Ethiopian Empire broke down. Popular unrest set this process in motion. As revolt transformed naturally into revolution the movements spontaneously emerged. In the case of Ethiopia, this leadership was represented in the Derg. Revolutionary leaders were faced with resolving unleashed political and class conflicts and with the challenge of reestablishing society on new structural and ideological foundations. All of these features were common to the Russian, French, and Chinese revolutions.

While the Ethiopian Revolution resembles the "great revolutions," except for the fact that it emerged from the breakdown of an imperial system, it could be argued that the Ethiopian Revolution has more in common with the modern social revolutions that have occurred in the Third World (i.e., Cuba, Vietnam, Mexico), particularly those occurring in Africa (i.e., Algeria, Guinea-Bissau, Angola, Mozambique). The Ethiopian Revolution, like those in other parts of Africa, took place in a state that was in a relatively weak and dependent position in the world economic and political order. Structurally, it was organized much as were the colonial systems found in most of the rest of Africa. Moreover, the imperial state was constrained from asserting its unquestioned autonomy in making domestic policy by its limited resource capacity. This is a fundamental difference between modern Third World revolutions and the "great revolutions."

In her seminal work, *States and Social Revolutions,* Theda Skocpol argues that in the case of the French, Russian, and Chinese revolutions, the new states that were formed were stronger and more autonomous in their domestic positions as well as in their positions in the world economy. They were more centralized, bureaucratic, and powerful both at home and abroad.[2] Yet Skocpol cautions that analysts should not attempt mechanically to formulate a general theory of revolutionary transformation based on the model suggested by the "great revolutions." Instead, they should be sensitive to the peculiar, idiosyncratic features of the societies under observation. Limited generalizations are acceptable. For instance, the highly vulnerable and dependent positions of modern African states in the world capitalist economy and in the international community of states is a common denominator that places all of them, regardless of their ideological propensities, into a common category. African states tend to be "soft," dependent states that experience difficulty in implementing their strategies even when they have planned rationally. Moreover, they tend to be inhibited from autonomous policy making by low resource capacities and/or low levels of legitimacy.

The analysis in this book has been informed by the structuralist perspective offered in Skocpol's work. An effort has been made to focus less on ideological rhetoric than on the objective relationships that exist between the state and social classes and the state and other states. The Ethiopian state's pursuit of autonomous decision making, then, has been analyzed in the context of dependency. Despite the fact that new states of the Third World that are products of revolutions like the one occurring in Ethiopia are dependent and constrained from autonomous decision making, there are opportunities for some state autonomy depending on the circumstance and the relative strength of the state. These regimes are highly dependent on economic and military aid from abroad for their very survival. Yet they do tend to be relatively stronger and more autonomous than the regimes they displaced. Skocpol notes that Cuba, for example, overcame extreme dependence on the United States and eventually was able to pursue more autonomous and egalitarian policies for economic development.[3] This is not to say that Cuba became truly self-reliant after the overthrow of the Batista regime. In fact, it merely shifted patrons from the U.S. to the Soviet Union. But the Soviet alliance seems less constraining than the former one with the U.S., particularly in domestic economic matters.

A similar process has occurred in the Ethiopian situation. Even though the new state continues to be dependent and lacks absolute autonomy, it does possess some leverage and political power depending on the circumstance. Moreover, just as had been the case with the imperial regime, the Afro-Marxist regime has diligently worked to strengthen its autonomy relative to domestic as well as international actors.

The introduction of a scientific socialist ideology to replace the myth of the Solomonic divine right and the monarchical absolutist state was a conscious effort on the part of the Derg to enhance its legitimacy and thus give it the freedom to pursue its statist development strategy. Social policies and economic reform were also a part of this design. Bureaucratic restructuring, expansion, and consolidation were all intended to strengthen the regulative, extractive, redistributive, and coercive capacity of the state. These changes have improved the capacity of the state for autonomous decision making in the formulation, if not the execution, of public policy.

In the formulation of domestic development policy, the state seems to possess its most significant opportunity for autonomous decision making. "Formulation" is emphasized because the state seems less able always to implement the policies it articulates. For instance, there is no doubt that the Derg has been successful in destroying the institutional vestiges of the old order and has been able to replace these with new socialist institutions. Most notably, the landed aristocracy has been eliminated, land has been redistributed, and new relations of production have been introduced. The role of private capital has changed as the state has assumed a dominant role in industrial production. Central planning is now being attempted in all sectors of the economy, a vanguard party has been put in place, and a people's democratic republic has been enshrined in a new constitution. These are only a few of the changes the regime has succeeded in accomplishing, often in the face of opposition from internal and external forces.

However, the implementation of new policies and the consolidation of new institutions have been more difficult. In the area of domestic transformation, for example, the state's lack of capital has forced it to be heavily dependent on foreign capital, most of which comes from the West. Publicly, Ethiopia's leaders claim a disdain for Western capitalism, but in reality, they must take a pragmatic approach to economic development and this, at least for the moment, has required a reliance on foreign capital. Viewed from another angle, the regime is not able to ensure a centrally planned economy and tight state control of the forces of economic production, distribution, and exchange. There are two main reasons for this. First, the state bureaucracy and the party are not sufficiently extensive or consolidated to allow such tight management. Second, the most important producers in society, the peasantry, are "uncaptured" and continue to make production and exchange decisions largely on their own. The state is unable to force peasants to form collective farms, even though it favors collectivization of peasant producers. For the moment, the government seems content to get peasants simply to move into villagized settlements. There, the agitation of party cadre over time is expected to convince peasants that collectivized farming is best for them. The state's autonomy in domestic policy making is further compromised because it has failed to recognize the importance of a resolution of the "national question" in building legitimacy for the new order. Ethnic and ideological opponents of the Afro-Marxist regime have the capacity, and indeed the will, to engage in protracted struggle on behalf of their respective causes.

Rather than emphasizing a negotiated political solution to the claims of nationality groups that call for self-determination or of opponents who demand popular democracy, the regime has responded with force and bureaucratic centralism. Between 1976 and 1987, the state consistently worked for the elimination or neutralization of such groups. Force and co-optation, however, did not result in the regime's achieving widespread legitimacy among civilian intellectuals of either rightist or leftist persuasion; nor was it able to convince large segments of the non-Amhara ethnic population that their interests were being addressed forthrightly.

The formation of the Workers' Party of Ethiopia, the creation of the Nationalities Institute, and the inauguration of the People's Democratic Republic were all measures intended to present the illusion of official concern for democratic rights. The regime claims to be dedicated to the creation of a society based on the principles of scientific socialism and democratic centralism; instead, what seems to be developing is an authoritarian system characterized by bureaucratic centralism.

The continued opposition being faced by the government over its vision of the New Ethiopia has resulted in a strengthening rather than a lessening of its military and economic dependence. To what extent has this trend interfered with the state's efforts to enhance its autonomy? Related to this is the question of self-reliance. Have the declarations of self-reliance and non-alignment and the rejection of dependence on Western capital resulted in more or less autonomy for policy makers in economic matters?

External dependence is the one area that has been unaffected by the new regime's transformation strategy. In fact, in both military and economic matters, Ethiopia's dependence grew over the first decade of the revolution. The United States had provided Ethiopia with just over $200 million in military aid over a twenty-two year period. In less than half that time, the Soviet Union provided US$4 billion in military assistance.[4] This was complemented by military sales or aid in the form of advisers, troops, weapons, and equipment from such countries as Libya, Italy, Israel, South Yemen, Cuba, Czechoslovakia, East Germany, and other Eastern bloc countries. Between 1975 and 1983, the Ethiopian government purchased $3.5 billion worth of arms, representing 72 percent of the cost of all imports during this period.[5]

The availability of this military aid is as essential—if not more essential—to the Derg than it was to Haile Selassie. The new regime has found it necessary to expand dramatically the armed forces in order to contain opposition forces and to provide itself some limited freedom to institute its development strategy. The standing army grew from 55,000 in 1974 to over 300,000 by 1987, with the institutionalization of the people's militia and national conscription. Military expenditure grew from $38 million to almost $400 million annually.[6]

Clearly, then, the regime's ability to develop its military policy free of internal or external pressures is nonexistent. Opposition groups have forced the regime to borrow extensively, particularly from the Soviet

Union, to maintain a level of military preparedness sufficient to keep itself in power and to keep intact the geographic boundaries of what it considers "Greater Ethiopia." Critics have charged that Ethiopia under the Derg consistently sides with the Soviets in the international diplomatic arena. For example, Ethiopia was one of the few non-Soviet bloc countries to support the Soviet occupation of Afghanistan in 1979, and in 1984 it was the only African country to boycott the Los Angeles Olympics along with the Soviet Union and other Eastern bloc countries. Other observers, however, suggest that these actions were a small price to pay to ensure continued Soviet military aid.[7]

Military dependence on the Soviet Union has not been so important as to make Ethiopia a mere pawn. Despite public displays of allegiance to their Soviet "friends" and despite the fact that the Afro-Marxist regime has been attempting to copy the Soviet model as no other African country has, there have been occasions when it was evident that it would not tolerate Soviet interference in domestic matters. As early as 1977, for instance, the Soviet Union and Cuba were attempting to bring about negotiated settlements to the Eritrean and Ogaden conflicts, but in each case the Derg balked at such efforts at diplomacy.[8] In another situation in 1978, the Soviet Union and Cuba tried to pressure the Derg to make amends with its civilian leftist opposition in preparation for the creation of a civilian-based vanguard party, but the initiative backfired when the Cuban ambassador was asked to leave the country and accused of interfering in Ethiopian domestic affairs.[9] In 1979, however, the Derg did set up a commission to begin making plans for the creation of a vanguard party. Four years later the party was created, but it was hardly "civilian-based." Instead, it was top-heavy with military personnel and had relatively few workers and peasants in the general membership.

The Afro-Marxist regime is apparently willing to side with, or give in to, the Soviet Union in matters that do not threaten its own ruling position or its concept of the Ethiopian "nation-state." Conceivably, the Soviets could gain more influence over domestic policy making in Ethiopia if they could afford to make the regime more dependent on Soviet economic aid.

The volume of trade between socialist countries and Ethiopia grew significantly in the 1980s. Before 1974, the total volume of trade with Eastern bloc countries never exceeded 4.5 percent. By 1982, 17 percent of Ethiopia's exports went to its socialist friends, and 28 percent of its imports flowed from them.[10] In addition, other socialist countries such as Bulgaria, Yugoslavia, Poland, Romania, Hungary, North Korea, Cuba, and South Yemen provided technical and/or economic support to Ethiopia. This aid is facilitated through economic, scientific, and technical commissions that established bilateral relations between Ethiopia and individual socialist states and through treaties of "friendship and cooperation." It is important to note that further economic interaction between Ethiopia and Eastern bloc countries is inhibited by the fact that Ethiopia has only observer status in COMECON, the main agency for economic cooperation and development in the Eastern bloc.

The types of development aid covered under bilateral agreements with socialist countries range from factories and assembly plants to geological surveys; from doctors and teachers to construction engineers. By 1983 it was estimated that about $300 million of credits had been allocated by Eastern bloc countries in Ethiopia, with half of this total being pledged by the Soviet Union. Most of this aid was in the form of loans with terms very close to commercial rates. However, no more than about $30 million per year is actually given to Ethiopia in the form of project financing.[11] The meagerness and high cost of Eastern bloc economic aid has been a source of displeasure among Ethiopian officials and has acted as a drag on the possibility of even closer ties. Yet the regime is kept somewhat in tow because of its heavy military dependence on its Eastern bloc supporters. Because of this, the Soviets are virtually assured that Ethiopia's nonalignment in international diplomatic matters will be nothing more than rhetoric with little if any basis in fact.

Even if the Soviet Union and its allies were interested in providing Ethiopia with more economic aid, it is unlikely that they could, since they do not possess the foreign exchange to be too generous, nor the regular food supplies that could be used to address the problems caused by drought and famine in Ethiopia. Some of these countries are in fact net importers of grain themselves. They are better able to provide equipment and technical help. As a result, rather than being able to get assistance in the form of capital that could then be used to buy equipment on the open market, Ethiopia is forced to take the equipment the donor country offers. In many cases this technology has been found to be either of low quality or inappropriate to local conditions.[12]

Because Eastern bloc countries in general and the Soviet Union in particular cannot provide the level of foreign aid that would be necessary to stimulate the Ethiopian economy adequately, the door has remained open for Western capital and, to a certain extent, Western influence. To the displeasure of pro-Soviet elements in the regime, this has inhibited a complete break with the West. Pro-Western elements feel that it has conveniently allowed them to resist being driven firmly into the Soviet camp. The massive amount of Western relief aid between 1984 and 1986, followed by the establishment of new permanent offices in the country by those foreign organizations who had been involved in the relief effort for the purpose of engaging in development projects, further opened the doors of Afro-Marxist Ethiopia to the West.

Soviet bloc economic limitations and Ethiopia's severe economic crisis have forced the government to act pragmatically in its international economic policy in spite of its public condemnation of dependency on Western capitalism. The Ten-Year Guiding Plan reinforces the regime's heavy reliance on foreign aid and private foreign capital. Most of this aid is expected to come from Western bilateral and multilateral aid donors, such as the European Economic Community (EEC), the International Monetary Fund (IMF), and the World Bank.

Some Western aid has been forthcoming, but it is not as much or as extensive as the regime had hoped. However, as Ethiopia began to settle claims with those countries that suffered through the nationalization measures, external bilateral, multilateral, and private aid began to return to the country. Although the amount of new private capital that entered Ethiopia after 1984 has been small, capital from public sources has been quite significant.

The EEC continues to be Ethiopia's most significant source of Western aid. In 1980–1981 Western sources accounted for more than 90 percent of Ethiopia's foreign aid; most of this came from the EEC. Since then Eastern bloc countries have come to account for a larger share of Ethiopia's aid (about 20 percent), and other multilateral and bilateral donors have also begun to provide more aid. The World Bank, for instance, after having refrained from giving aid to Ethiopia between 1975 and 1981, pledged over $250 million in project aid. The European Development Fund promised about $300 million, and the IMF agreed to a loan of almost $100 million. The Derg took this IMF loan even though it claimed to disagree with IMF policies. These are but a few examples of the aid agreements that were concluded with Western donors and lenders.[13] The joint venture law and a new foreign investment policy stimulated a gradual return of external private investors.

Ethiopia, then, is heavily dependent on Western economic aid, from project aid to loans, grants, and even humanitarian aid. At the same time, no Western donor is able to influence day-to-day economic policy on a regular basis. For instance, the World Bank, the Swedish International Development Agency, and other donor agencies favor the development of agricultural cooperatives, but organized on the principles of a free market. The Ethiopian regime is attempting to develop cooperatives that transform into socialist collectives and that are an integral part of a centrally planned and directed economy. As a matter of policy, the World Bank and other foreign aid agencies eschew a heavy-handed approach to influencing a country in determining economic strategy. In Ethiopia the practice has been for such donors to stay out of domestic affairs. Bilateral donors from the West and East may have influence when they operate in policy-making bodies at the request of the Ethiopian government, but this does not necessarily indicate a controlling influence. Like the imperial regime before it, the new government has attempted to play a multiplicity of donors against one another and thereby to maximize certain benefits without a complete surrender of sovereignty. Even though Ethiopia is dependent, then, there are opportunities for autonomous choice making on the part of policymakers under certain conditions. For instance, if the regime is willing to contradict its strict adherence to scientific socialism and its proclaimed disdain for Western capitalism, it is able to secure at least some of the development capital it needs from the West without totally abandoning its ideological course. Although ideology is important in determining some aspects of Ethiopia's domestic economic policy, pragmatism clearly guides its behavior in the international economic arena. Western donors and lenders see Ethiopia as a relatively low-risk debtor. It has a long-standing reputation as a country with a well-managed (if poor) economy. It has an excellent debt-servicing record, and its leaders have been known to pay their debts and to exercise financial prudence.

The Ethiopian Revolution has set in motion a process of social transformation that ensures there will be no return to the modernizing autocracy created by Haile Selassie. A new society is being created based on a variant of state socialism and the principles of Marxism-Leninism. The development strategy the new regime has chosen, as well as its new social myth, is valued most because of the amount of control the state is afforded. The Afro-Marxist regime appears to be more autonomous than its predecessor, but its autonomy is not absolute. Ethiopia today is characterized by *dependent autonomy;* the state's ability for autonomous behavior is often circumscribed by its external dependence. Even if it were to solve the "national question," it would still be extremely dependent on external assistance because of its endemic resource scarcity.

NOTES

Introduction

1. See Christopher Clapham, *Haile-Selassie's Government* (New York: Praeger, 1969), 47–51. I borrow the term *historical bureaucratic empire* from S. N. Eisenstadt, although I do not choose to bind myself to his functionalist framework. Here a historical bureaucratic empire is seen as a state system that stands somewhere between "premodern" and "modern" political systems. Authority, as in premodern societies, is predominantly based on religio-traditional values and symbols, but there are the beginnings of secularization of authority and an ever-expanding bureaucratic, compartmentalized mode of administration. See S. N. Eisenstadt, *The Political System of Empires* (London: Free Press of Glencoe, 1963) for a fuller discussion of this type of political system. I will return to this concept later.

2. See G. K. N. Trevaskis, *Eritrea: A Colony in Transition, 1941–1952* (London: Oxford University Press, 1960).

3. This is especially true of the southern segments of the Oromo group. See Patrick Gilkes, *The Dying Lion: Feudalism and Modernization in Ethiopia* (London: Julian Friedmann, 1975); and P. T. W. Baxter, "Ethiopia's Unacknowledged Problem: The Oromo," *African Affairs*, 77 (July 1978), 283–96.

4. J. Drysdale, *The Somali Dispute* (New York: Praeger, 1964).

5. Crane Brinton, *The Anatomy of Revolution* (New York: Random House, 1938), 180–206.

6. Peter Amman, "Revolution: A Redefinition," *Political Science Quarterly*, 77 (March 1962), 47.

7. The question of the relevance of the feudal paradigm to Ethiopia has been the subject of much debate, and the issue remains unresolved. Some scholars suggest that what appeared at first glance to be feudalistic relationships such as characterized medieval Europe were merely "feudal-like" relationships that could not stand the rigorous application of the feudal paradigm. See G. Ellis, "The Feudal Paradigm as a Hindrance to Understanding Ethiopia," *Journal of Modern African Studies*, 14 (1976), 275–95. Others staunchly maintain that prerevolutionary Ethiopia was feudal in character or at least "semi-feudal." See Legesse Lemma, "Review," *Ethiopianist Notes*, 2 (1978). I will consider this issue in greater detail in chapter 3.

8. See Margery Perham, *The Government of Ethiopia* (London: Faber and Faber, 1948); and Samuel P. Huntington, *Political Order in Changing Societies* (New Haven: Yale University Press, 1968), 140–91.

9. See Jack Shepard, *The Politics of Starvation* (New York: Carnegie Endowment for International Peace, 1975); Colin Legum, *Ethiopia: The Fall of Haile Selassie's Empire* (New York: Africana Publishing Company, 1975); and David Ottaway and Marina Ottaway, *Ethiopia: Empire in Revolution* (New York: Holmes and Meier, 1978).

10. Christopher Clapham, "Centralization and Local Response in Southern Ethiopia," *African Affairs*, 74 (Jan. 1975), 72–81; J. Harbeson, "Toward a Political Theory of the Ethiopian Revolution," (typescript, 1978); P. Koehn, "Ethiopian Politics: Military Intervention and Prospects for Further Change," *Africa Today*, 22 (April 1975), 7–21.

11. Gilkes, *Dying Lion;* Z. Gyenge, *Ethiopia on the Road of Non-Capitalist Development* (Budapest: Institute for World Economics, 1976); M. Stahl, *Ethiopia: Political Contradictions in Agricultural Development* (Stockholm: Raben and Sjogren, 1974);

273

Addis Hiwet, *Ethiopia: From Autocracy to Revolution* (London: Merlin Press, 1975); John Markakis and Nega Ayele, *Class and Revolution in Ethiopia* (London: Spokesman, 1978).

12. Notable exceptions are the class analysis approaches of Markakis and Ayele and of Fred Halliday and Maxine Molyneux, *The Ethiopian Revolution* (London: Verso, 1981).

13. This is not to suggest that traditions *must* succumb to the forces of modernization. But their coexistence is dependent on a minimization of potentially divisive contradictions. See C. S. Whitaker, "A Dysrythmic Process of Political Change," *World Politics*, 19 (Jan. 1967), 190–217. For Ethiopia, the point is nicely made by Donald Levine, *Wax and Gold: Tradition and Innovation in Ethiopian Culture* (Chicago: University of Chicago Press, 1965).

14. Eisenstadt, *Political System of Empires*, 10. Here the terminology "historical" or "centralized bureaucratic empire" is Eisensadt's, but this analysis goes beyond his original formulation.

15. Ibid., 19.

16. Ibid., 360.

17. Huntington, *Political Order of Changing Societies*, esp. 140–91.

18. See, for example, Charles Tilly, *From Mobilization to Revolution* (Reading, Mass.: Addison-Wesley, 1978).

19. See George Pettee, "The Process of Revolution," in C. Paynton and R. Blackey, *Why Revolution?* (Cambridge, Mass.: Schenkman, 1971), 31–56; and H. Lubasz, "What is Revolution?" ibid., 253–59.

20. Tilly, *From Mobilization to Revolution*, 210.

21. Pettee, "Process of Revolution," 44–45.

22. Amman, "Revolution," 39.

I. Ethiopia as a Bureaucratic Empire

1. S. N. Eisenstadt, *The Political System of Empires* (London: Free Press of Glencoe, 1963), 21.

2. Taxation policy in Ethiopia, as in other bureaucratic empires, was often used as a means for undermining economically and politically powerful groups such as the aristocracy, the gentry, or the merchant classes. Relatively high taxes might enhance the ability of the emperor to engage in social and economic policies that strengthened his position at the expense of other power blocs. Monetary and financial devices such as the manipulation of currency might also serve this purpose. See ibid., 126.

3. See Donald Levine, *Greater Ethiopia: The Evolution of a Multiethnic Society* (Chicago: University of Chicago Press, 1974), 70–71.

4. See Yuri M. Kobishanov, *Axum* (University Park: Pennsylvania State University Press, 1979), 35–122.

5. Richard Greenfield, *Ethiopia: A New Political History* (London: Pall Mall Press, 1965), 20. It is about this time that the people who inhabited the area around Aksum began to be referred to as "Abyssinians" and their kindom as "Abyssinia." The Amharas and Tigreans together constitute the "Abyssinians" proper. See D. Buxton, *The Abyssinians* (Southampton: Thames and Hudson, 1970).

6. Tadesse Tamrat, *Church and State in Ethiopia, 1270–1527* (London: Oxford University Press, 1972), 21–68; Sergew Habte Sellassie, *Ancient and Medieval Ethiopian History to 1270* (Addis Ababa: United Printers, 1972).

7. Greenfield, *Ethiopia*, 27.

8. Sellassie, *Ancient and Medieval Ethiopian History*, 175–78.

9. Implications are discussed in Levine, *Greater Ethiopia*, 70–71.

10. Ethiopian mythology traces the founding of Ethiopian society to the off-

spring (Menelik I) of an illicit union between King Solomon and the Queen of Sheba (Makeda). This is detailed in the *Kebra Nagast*, the Ethiopian national epic. Emperors who could prove their pedigree in this line were the most revered. We shall return to this point later. See E. A. Wallis Budge, *The Queen of Sheba and Her Only Son Menelek* (Oosterhout, Netherlands: Anthropological Publications, 1966).

11. Selassie, *Ancient and Medieval Ethiopian History*, 289–92.

12. Levine, *Greater Ethiopia*, 73.

13. Ibid.

14. *Amharization* is a term that is well known and much used among Ethiopianists. It refers to the acceptance of Amhara culture and custom by non-Amharas. This process is facilitated through education, language, the Coptic religion, and the taking of Amhara Christian names. There is a great deal of ethnic chauvinism involved, as those other ethnics who readily accept Amharization are more fully integrated into the mainstream of society and have better life chances as a result. See D. Levine, "Ethiopia: Identity, Authority and Realism," in L. Pye and S. Verba, eds., *Political Culture and Political Development* (Princeton: Princeton University Press, 1965), 245–82.

15. See J. S. Trimingham, *Islam in Ethiopia* (London: Oxford University Press, 1952), 76–97.

16. See Edward Ullendorf, *The Ethiopians* (London: Oxford University Press, 1965), 71–75.

17. Buxton, *Abyssinians*, 49–53.

18. Levine, *Greater Ethiopia*, 78.

19. See, for example, Herbert Lewis, *A Galla Monarchy* (Madison: University of Wisconsin Press, 1965), 23; and Levine, *Greater Ethiopia*, 79–80. Lewis suggests that it is not known why the Oromo migration began when it did. Levine, on the other hand, argues that the expansion was not politically or culturally motivated but was triggered by a need to carry out ritually prescribed military expeditions against enemies and population pressures.

20. Levine, *Greater Ethiopia*, 80.

21. Levine notes that, "In Shoa the Tulema Galla adopted plow cultivation of grains and Monophysite Christianity from the Amhara, but they maintained Gallinya (Oromo) as their mother tongue . . . the Wello and Yejju Galla tribes adopted many Amhara practices and the Amharic language as well, but kept their separateness by becoming Muslims during the eighteenth century." Ibid., 82.

22. See A. H. M. Jones and Elizabeth Monroe, *A History of Abyssinia* (New York: Negro Universities Press, 1969), 118–19.

23. See James Bruce, *Travels to Discover the Source of the Nile* (Edinburgh: J. Ruthven, 1790), 595–706. Ioas even went so far as to make Oromo the official language of the court.

24. See M. Abir, *Ethiopia: The Era of the Princes* (London: Longmans, 1968).

25. Sven Rubenson, *King of Kings: Tewodros of Ethiopia* (Addis Ababa: Oxford University Press, 1966), 19.

26. David Mathew, *Ethiopia: The Study of a Polity, 1540–1935* (London: Eyre and Spottiswoode, 1947), vi–vii; Bruce, *Travels*.

27. Sven Rubenson, *The Survival of Ethiopian Independence* (London: Heinemann, 1976), 35.

28. Ibid., 271.

29. Fredrick Myatt, *The March to Magala: The Abyssinian War of 1868* (London: Leo Cooper, 1970), 30.

30. See E. J. Hobsbawm, *Bandits* (New York: Delacorte Press, 1969).

31. Rubenson, *King of Kings*, 36.

32. Ibid.

33. Around this time, conflicts among northern princes and kings were intense

and Ali was in the thick of things. He was also occupied with the advancing Turks. See Rubenson, *Survival of Ethiopian Independence*, 55–171.

34. Rubenson, *King of Kings*, 41–42.

35. Ibid., 43–44.

36. Ibid., 48.

37. See Greenfield, *Ethiopia*, 76–77, for a discussion of Tewodros's sensitivity on this issue and the hesitancy of the reigning Archbishop of the Ethiopian Orthodox Church to recognize his claim.

38. Levine, *Greater Ethiopia*, 157.

39. Harold G. Marcus, *The Life and Times of Menelik II: Ethiopia, 1844–1913* (Oxford: Clarendon Press, 1975), 14–16.

40. W. Plowden, *Travels in Abyssinia* (London: Longmans, Green, 1868), 58.

41. Richard K. Pankhurst, *Economic History of Ethiopia* (Addis Ababa: Haile Sellassie I University Press, 1968), 11.

42. Myatt, *March to Magdala*, 35.

43. Ibid.

44. Rubenson, *King of Kings*, 54.

45. Ibid., 68.

46. Ibid., 69.

47. See Rubenson, *Survival of Ethiopian Independence*, 208–87; and Myatt, *March to Magdala*.

48. Zewde Gabre-Sellassie, *Yohannes IV of Ethiopia* (London: Oxford University Press, 1975), 17–53.

49. Ibid.

50. Rubenson, *Survival of Ethiopian Independence*, 259.

51. Ibid., 260.

52. Gabre-Sellassie, *Yohannes IV of Ethiopia*, 29.

53. An exception to this rule was the appointment of some outsiders to critical posts along the borders of the periphery. See Gabre-Sellassie, *Yohannes IV of Ethiopia*, 250–57.

54. See James Scott, *The Moral Economy of the Peasant: Rebellion and Resistance in Southeast Asia* (New Haven: Yale University Press, 1976).

55. Gabre-Sellassie, *Yohannes IV of Ethiopia*, 84–121.

56. Ibid., 44–45.

57. Ibid., 54–83.

58. Ibid., 122–51.

59. Ibid., 94–95.

60. Levine, *Greater Ethiopia*, 160.

61. Ernest Work, *Ethiopia: A Pawn in European Diplomacy* (New York: Macmillan, 1935), 51–97.

62. Gabre-Sellassie, *Yohannes IV of Ethiopia*, 248–49.

63. Sven Rubenson, *Wichale XVII* (Addis Ababa: Haile Sellassie I University Press, 1964), 46–47.

64. Harold Marcus, "Menelik II," in Norman Bennett, ed., *Leadership in Eastern Africa* (Boston: Boston University Press, 1968), 31; Haggai Erlich, *Ethiopia and the Challenge of Independence* (Boulder: Lynne Rienner, 1986), 27–42.

65. Work, *Ethiopia*, 102–103.

66. Marcus, *Life and Times of Menelik II*, 169.

67. Rubenson, *Wichale XVII*, 12.

68. Rubenson, *Survival of Ethiopian Independence*, 395–97; Rubenson, *Wichale XVII, passim.*

69. Rubenson, *Wichale XVII*, 21.

70. Marcus, *Life and Times of Menelik II*, 120–21.

71. Richard Pankhurst, "Fire-Arms in Ethiopian History (1800–1935)," *Ethiopia Observer*, 6 (1962), 165.

72. These are Rubenson's figures. As with other statistics of this era, there is wide variation from one source to the next. Contrast, for example, Rubenson, *Survival of Ethiopian Independence*, 402; and Marcus, *Life and Times of Menelik II*, 164.

73. Again, statistics concerning this battle vary, but here I refer to those given in Rubenson, *Survival of Ethiopian Independence*, 403.

74. Marcus, *Life and Times of Menelik II*, 176–77.

75. Work, *Ethiopia*, 249.

76. Marcus, *Life and Times of Menelik II*, 179–81.

77. Ibid.

78. Ibid., 181–82.

79. Marcus, *Life and Times of Menelik II*, 174–213.

80. See Mesfin Wolde Mariam, *The Background of the Ethio-Somalia Boundary Dispute* (Addis Ababa: Berhanenna Selam Press, 1964), 32–35; and John Drysdale, *Somali Frontier Dispute* (New York: Praeger, 1964).

81. Marcus, *Life and Times of Menelik II*, 28–173.

82. Ibid., 218.

83. Donald Levine, *Wax and Gold: Tradition and Innovation in Ethiopian Culture* (Chicago: University of Chicago Press, 1965), 262–63; "The Military in Ethiopian Politics," in H. Bienen, ed., *The Military Intervenes* (New York: Sage, 1968), 5–34.

84. Pankhurst, *Economic History of Ethiopia*, 556. Similar figures are given by Robert Skinner, *Abyssinia of Today* (London: Longmans, 1906), 174.

85. R. H. Kofi Darkwah, *Shewa, Menelik and the Ethiopian Empire, 1813–1889* (London: Heinemann, 1975), 116.

86. Pankhurst, *Economic History of Ethiopia*, 562.

87. Margery Perham, *The Government of Ethiopia* (London: Faber and Faber, 1948), 160–75.

88. Pankhurst, *Economic History of Ethiopia*, 571–72; Skinner, *Abyssinia of Today*, 174.

89. Ibid., 551–52.

90. See R. A. Caulk, "Armies as Predators: Soldiers and Peasants in Ethiopia, c. 1850–1935," *International Journal of African Historical Studies*, 11 (1978), 457–93.

91. Darkwah, *Shewa, Menelik and the Ethiopian Empire*, 123–30; Skinner, *Abyssinia of Today*, 146–48.

92. Levine, *Wax and Gold*, 187–88.

93. Perham, *Government of Ethiopia*, 270–71.

94. See Charles W. McClellen, "The Ethiopian Occupation of Northern Sidamo: Recruitment and Motivation," typescript, 1978.

95. Ibid.

96. Marcus, *Life and Times of Menelik II*, 229.

97. See Richard K. Pankhurst, "Tribute, Taxation and Government Revenues in Ninteenth and Early Twentieth Century Ethiopia (Part I)," *Journal of Ethiopian Studies*, 5 (1967), 43.

98. Marcus, *Life and Times of Menelik II*, 192–94.

99. Ibid., 227–28.

100. Pankhurst, *Economic History of Ethiopia*, 478–86.

101. Ibid., 194–98.

102. See Eisenstadt, *Political System of Empires*. Eisenstadt notes that the manipulation of currency, banking policies, and taxation policy has often been used as a means for undermining economically and politically powerful groups such as the aristocracy. For example, relatively high taxes might enhance the ability of the monarchy to engage in social and economic policies that strengthen its position at the expense of other power blocs. Another example might be policies relating to

what currency is given the highest value within a given society. There is clear evidence that Menelik followed both strategies.

103. Achaber Gabre Hiwot, *La verite sur l'Ethiopie* (Lausanne, 1931), 32. Richard Greenfield, in personal communication to me, questions the authenticity of this quote.

104. Pankhurst, *Economic History of Ethiopia*, 674.

105. Richard K. Pankhurst, *Ethiopia: A Cultural History* (Woodford Green, Essex: Lalibela House, 1955), 534–652.

106. See Marcus, *Life and Times of Menelik II*, 249–81.

107. Leonard Mosley, *Haile Selassie* (London: Weidenfeld and Nicholson, 1964), 96.

108. John Markakis, *Ethiopia: Anatomy of a Traditional Polity* (Oxford: Clarendon Press, 1974), 229–30.

109. Mosley, *Haile Selassie*, 127–42.

110. Ibid., 140–41.

111. Ibid., 151–63.

II. The Structure of Politics

1. See Taddesse Tamrat, *Church and State in Ethiopia, 1270–1527* (London: Oxford University Press, 1972); and Sergew Habte Sellassie, "Church and State in the Aksumite Period," *Proceedings of the Third International Conference on Ethiopian Studies* (Addis Ababa: Institute of Ethiopian Studies, 1969), 5–9.

2. Sellassie, "Church and State in the Aksumite Period," 6. The link between kingship and divine ordination predates this, but the point here is that the Christian Church was from this point on given a legitimate role in this process.

3. Margery Perham, *The Government of Ethiopia* (London: Faber and Faber, 1948), 104.

4. Donald Levine, *Greater Ethiopia* (Chicago: University of Chicago Press, 1974), 109–110; A. Davis, "The Orthodoxy of the Ethiopian Church," *Tarieh*, 2 (1967), 62–69.

5. See Tamrat, *Church and State in Ethiopia*, 66–68.

6. A. H. M. Jones and Elizabeth Monroe, *A History of Ethiopia* (Oxford: Clarendon Press, 1955); E. A. Wallis Budge, *A History of Ethiopia, Nubia and Abyssinia* (Oosterhout, Netherlands: Anthropological Publications, 1966).

7. Wallis Budge, *History of Ethiopia*, 220–27.

8. See Richard Greenfield, *Ethiopia: A New Political History* (New York: Praeger, 1965), 340.

9. See Robert Skinner, *Abyssinia of Today* (London: Longmans, 1906), 151–52.

10. See Perham, *Government of Ethiopia*, 105–106.

11. Ibid., 108.

12. Donald Levine, *Wax and Gold: Tradition and Innovation in Ethiopian Culture* (Chicago: University of Chicago Press, 1965), 154.

13. For an example of the variance in estimates of Church landholdings, see *Ethiopia in Revolution* (Addis Ababa: Ethiopian Revolution Information Center, 1977), 6; and John M. Cohen and Dov Weintraub, *Land and Peasants in Imperial Ethiopia* (The Hague: Van Gorcum, 1975), 64, 68.

14. Allan Hoben, *Land Tenure among the Amhara of Ethiopia: The Dynamics of Cognatic Descent* (Chicago: University of Chicago Press, 1973), 18.

15. Cohen and Weintraub, *Land and Peasants*, 31.

16. Ibid.

17. Fred V. Goricke, *Social and Political Factors Influencing the Application of Land Reform Measures in Ethiopia* (Saarbrucken, West Germany: Verlag Breitenbach, 1979), 12–13.

18. See, for example, Hoben, *Land Tenure among the Amhara;* Cohen and Weintraub, *Land and Peasants;* F. C. Gamst, "Peasantries and Elites without Urbanism: The Civilization of Ethiopia," *Comparative Studies in Society and History,* 12 (1970), 373–92; and Lionel Cliffe, "Capitalism or Feudalism? The Famine in Ethiopia," *Review of African Political Economy,* 1 (1974), 34–40.

19. Goricke, for example, notes that the families of Ras Makonnen of Hararge and Ras Darge of Selale held quasi-hereditary *gult* titles under Menelik and Haile Selassie. See *Social and Political Factors,* 22.

20. See Harold G. Marcus, *The Life and Times of Menelik II: Ethiopia, 1844–1913* (Oxford: Clarendon Press, 1975), 190.

21. See Cohen and Weintraub, *Land and Peasants,* 33–34.

22. Ibid., 31, 64–65.

23. Richard K. Pankhurst, *State and Land in Ethiopian History* (Addis Ababa: Oxford University Press, 1966), 55.

24. See John Markakis, *Ethiopia: Anatomy of a Traditional Polity* (Oxford: Clarendon Press, 1974), 110–13.

25. Cohen and Weintraub, *Land and Peasants,* 40–43.

26. Perham, *Government of Ethiopia,* 284.

27. Pankhurst, *State and Land,* 38.

28. John Cohen, "Ethiopia after Haile Selassie: The Government Land Factor," *African Affairs,* 72 (Oct. 1973), 369.

29. Pankhurst, *State and Land,* 31.

30. Cohen and Weintraub, *Land and Peasants,* 45.

31. Gene Ellis, "The Feudal Paradigm as a Hindrance to Understanding Ethiopia," *Journal of Modern African Studies,* 14 (1976), 275–95.

32. See, for example, Marc Bloch, *Feudal Society,* Vol. II (Chicago: University of Chicago Press, 1964), 447; and Rushton Coulborn, ed., *Feudalism in History* (Princeton: Princeton University Press, 1956).

33. Bloch, *Feudal Society,* Vol. II, p. 443.

34. Ibid.

35. See Gamst, "Peasantries and Elites without Urbanism," 384; and Bloch, *Feudal Societies,* Vol. II, pp. 441–47.

36. Coulborn, ed., *Feudalism in History,* 4–5.

37. The idea of considering feudalism as having intimately linked political *and* economic features is also endorsed in Perry Anderson, *Passages from Antiquity for Feudalism* (London: New Left Books, 1974), 447.

38. Coulborn, ed., *Feudalism in History,* 5–6.

39. Gamst, "Peasantries and Elites without Urbanism," 384–86.

40. Coulborn, ed., *Feudalism in History,* 6.

41. Bloch, *Feudal Society,* Vol. II, p. 445.

42. Anderson, *Passages from Antiquity to Feudalism,* 447.

43. Markakis, *Ethiopia,* 101.

44. Michael Stahl notes the Sidamo had been deprived of a great deal of its original population between 1882 and 1886 through a combination of wanton massacre by Menelik's troops and the migration of fleeing Oromos to the Bale highlands to escape this oppression. Michael Stahl, *Ethiopia: Political Contradictions in Agricultural Development* (Stockholm: Raben and Sjogren, 1974), 40. Pankhurst, *State and Land,* 143, described the style of Ethiopian rule in Sidamo as "a real system of military colonialism."

45. Richard K. Pankhurst, *Economic History of Ethiopia* (Addis Ababa: Haile Sellassie I University Press, 1968), 147.

46. Christopher Clapham, "Centralization and Local Response in Southern Ethiopia," *African Studies,* 74 (Jan. 1975), 76.

47. See Markakis, *Ethiopia,* 251.

48. Christopher Clapham, "Ethiopia and Somalia," in *Conflicts in Africa: Adelphi Papers, No. 93* (London: International Institute for Strategic Studies, 1972), 6.

49. Perham, *Government of Ethiopia*, 296.

50. Goricke, *Social and Political Factors*, 55–56.

51. Pankhurst, *State and Land*, 136.

52. Goricke, *Social and Political Factors*, 64.

53. For the first few decades of the twentieth century, *siso arash* was the most common form of tenancy relationship in the south. By the 1960s, however, *ekul arash* became the most prevalent. Goricke, *Social and Political Factors*, 65.

54. Ibid., 61–62.

55. For a discussion of the mannerisms of "colonial ethnic elite groups," see Horace Orlando Patterson, *Ethnic Chauvinism: The Reactionary Impulse* (New York: Stein and Day, 1977), 35–112.

56. Richard K. Pankhurst, "Tribute, Taxation and Government Revenues in Nineteenth and Early Twentieth Century Ethiopia (Part I)," *Journal of Ethiopian Studies*, 5 (1967), 43.

57. See Edmond J. Keller, "Ethiopia: Revolution, Class, and the National Question," *African Affairs*, 80 (Oct. 1981), 519–50.

III. Policy and the Politics of Survival in the Absolutist State

1. See Robert Hess, *Ethiopia: The Modernization of Autocracy* (Ithaca: Cornell University Press, 1970), 68.

2. Margery Perham, *The Government of Ethiopia* (London: Faber and Faber, 1948).

3. Theda Skocpol has advanced a similar argument about the origins of certain social revolutions. See *States and Social Revolution: A Comparative Analysis of France, Russia, and China* (London: Cambridge University Press, 1979).

4. See S. N. Eisenstadt, *The Decline of Empires* (Englewood Cliffs, N.J.: Prentice-Hall, 1967), 2–3.

5. See Barrington Moore, Jr., *Social Origins of Dictatorship and Democracy: Lord and Peasant in the Making of the Modern World* (Boston: Beacon Press, 1966).

6. S. N. Eisenstadt, *The Political System of Empires* (London: Free Press of Glencoe, 1963), 116–17.

7. Ibid., 18.

8. Perham notes that initially 133 million lire was set aside for the development of infrastructure in Ethiopia, and an annual subvention of 10 million lire was allocated for the recurrent cost of administration. Perham, *Government of Ethiopia*, 180.

9. Ibid., 182.

10. Hess, *Ethiopia*, 68.

11. See Legesse Lemma, "Political Economy of Ethiopia, 1875–1974: Agricultural, Educational, and International Antecedents of the Revolution" (Ph.D. diss., University of Notre Dame, 1980), 105.

12. See Harold G. Marcus, "The Infrastructure of the Italo-Ethiopian Crisis: Haile Selassie, the Solomonic Empire and the World Economy, 1916–1936," typescript, 1978.

13. The constitution was drafted for the most part by the then minister of finance, Bajerond Takla-Hawariyat. It was felt that Japan, as a modernizing empire, was the closest to Ethiopia's own political position. See Christopher Clapham, *Haile-Selassie's Government* (New York: Praeger, 1969), 34–35.

14. John Markakis, *Ethiopia: Anatomy of a Traditional Polity* (Oxford: Clarendon Press, 1974), 271–72.

15. Ibid., 280–81.

16. Ibid., 273.

17. This is a typical tactic of the leaders of historical bureaucratic empires. See Eisenstadt, *Political System of Empires*, 132.

18. See Marina Ottaway, "Social Class and Corporate Interests in the Ethiopian Revolution," *Journal of Modern African Studies*, 14 (Sept. 1976), 471. See also *The Autobiography of Emperor Haile Sellassie I: My Life and Ethiopia's Progress, 1892–1937* (London: Oxford University Press, 1976), 179–81.

19. See Peter Schwab, *Decision-Making in Ethiopia: A Study of the Political Process* (Rutherford, N.J.: Fairleigh Dickinson University Press, 1972).

20. See the text of the 1931 Constitution in Peter Schwab, *Ethiopia and Haile Selassie* (New York: Facts on File, 1972), 12–16.

21. Ibid., 12.

22. Ibid.

23. Ibid., 13–14.

24. *Autobiography of Haile Sellassie I*, 178.

25. Marcus, "Infrastructure of the Italo-Ethiopian Crisis," 6.

26. See Richard Greenfield, *Ethiopia: A New Political History* (New York: Praeger, 1965), 173.

27. Perham, *Government of Ethiopia*, 248.

28. There is some disagreement as to the fate of young people in this category during the occupation period. Perham and others contend that most were massacred by the Italians in 1937. Clapham, on the other hand, claims that instead of only 125 graduates in 1937, there were more than 250, and most of these survived the war. I would suggest (and I assume) that the discrepancy between the figures of these two scholars has to do with the fact that Perham was referring to those actually in the country and Clapham to all those with a college education. See Perham, *Government of Ethiopia*, 249; and Clapham, *Haile-Selassie's Government*, 19–20.

29. John H. Spencer, *Ethiopia at Bay: A Personal Account of the Haile Selassie Years* (Algonac, Mich.: Reference Publications, 1984), 112.

30. Perham, *Government of Ethiopia*, 343–46.

31. Ibid., 190–216.

32. John H. Spencer, *Ethiopia, the Horn of Africa, and U.S. Policy* (Cambridge, Mass.: Institute of Foreign Policy Analysis, 1977).

33. John M. Cohen and Peter H. Koehn, *Ethiopian Provincial and Municipal Government: Imperial Patterns and Post Revolutionary Changes* (East Lansing, Mich.: African Studies Center, 1980), 8–9.

34. Ibid., 25.

35. Ibid., 12, 28.

36. Perham, *Government of Ethiopia*, 346–52.

37. Ibid., 126–36.

38. Ibid., 130–33; Clapham, *Haile-Selassie's Government*, 82–83.

39. See John Cohen and Dov Weintraub, *Land and Peasants in Imperial Ethiopia: Social Background to a Revolution* (The Hague: Van Gorcum, 1975), 61; and Lemma, "Political Economy of Ethiopia," 185.

40. James Scott, *The Moral Economy of the Peasant: Rebellion and Resistance in Southeast Asia* (New Haven: Yale University Press, 1976). Scott suggests that peasants tend to be "risk averse" under normal circumstances. They would rather not tamper with a social institution that has served them well—at least to the point of ensuring the family's survival—even when a new institution promises more benefit in the long run. See also Allan Hoben, *Land Tenure among the Amhara of Ethiopia: The Dynamics of Cognatic Descent* (Chicago: University of Chicago Press, 1973).

41. See Richard K. Pankhurst, *Economic History of Ethiopia* (Addis Ababa: Haile Selassie I University Press, 1968), 176–79; and Richard K. Pankhurst, *State and Land in Ethiopian History* (Addis Ababa: Oxford University Press, 1966), 197–202.

42. Peter Schwab, *Haile Selassie I* (Chicago: Nelson-Hall, 1979), 77; Markakis, *Ethiopia*, 119.

43. Schwab, *Haile Selassie I*, 78.

44. Markakis, *Ethiopia*, 252–59.

45. Spencer, *Ethiopia at Bay*, 97–98.

46. Perham, *Government of Ethiopia*, 171.

47. Spencer, *Ethiopia, the Horn of Africa, and U.S. Policy*, 22; Harold G. Marcus, *Ethiopia, Great Britain, and the United States* (Berkeley: University of California Press, 1983), 42–116.

48. "Statement of Ambassador Edward Korry, Former Ambassador to Ethiopia," in *Hearings before the Subcommittee on African Affairs of the Committee on Foreign Relations, U.S. Senate* (August 4, 5, and 6, 1976) (Washington, D.C.: U.S. Government Printing Office, 1976), 36. At the height of U.S. aid to Ethiopia, six to seven thousand personnel were represented in a large Military Assistance and Advisory Group mission, a large U.S. mapping mission, Kagnew Station, the largest Peace Corps contingent in the world at the time (1962), and other small programs.

49. Senator Dick Clark, "Opening Statement: Ethiopia and the Horn of Africa," in *Hearings before the Subcommittee on African Affairs of the Committee on Foreign Relations*, 2.

50. Lemma, "Political Economy of Ethiopia," 213.

51. Marcus, *Ethiopia, Great Britain, and the United States*, 89.

52. See Ibid, 79–115; and "Statement of Ambassador Edward Korry," 37. Korry testified, "The policy was to do only enough to keep Kagnew and we deliberately dragged our feet on military and economic assistance."

53. Spencer, *Ethiopia, the Horn of Africa, and U.S. Policy*, 22–23. The value of Kagnew to the Americans diminished with the advance in satellite communications technology.

54. See "Statement of Ambassador Edward Korry," 36.

55. See George W. Bader, "Testimony," in *Hearings before the U.S. Senate Subcommittee on U.S. Security Arrangements and Commitments Abroad: Ethiopia* (Washington, D.C.: U.S. Government Printing Office, 1970), 1935.

56. John H. Spencer, "Haile Selassie: Leadership and Statesmanship," *Ethiopianist Notes*, 2 (1978), 36.

57. Clapham, *Haile-Selassie's Government*, 68.

58. Ibid.

59. Markakis, *Ethiopia*, 143–59. Although the emperor's name is now commonly spelled with one "l" in Selassie, he spelled it with two "l"s. The university follows his preference for the spelling of his name.

60. John Markakis and Nega Ayele, *Class and Revolution in Ethiopia* (London: Spokesman, 1978), 50.

61. Clapham, *Haile-Selassie's Government*, 64–65.

62. Markakis, *Ethiopia*, 187.

63. Greenfield, *Ethiopia*, 306–307.

64. Spencer, *Ethiopia at Bay*, 256–60.

65. Schwab, *Haile Selassie I*, 85–86.

66. Spencer, *Ethiopia at Bay*, 257.

67. Clapham, *Haile-Selassie's Government*, 123–24.

68. Ibid., 120.

69. Ibid., 121.

70. Ibid.

71. Ibid., 36–46.

72. The only exception to this was the legislature's right to veto decrees that had been promulgated by the emperor during recess. Even though it had this power, it had never been exercised by parliament by 1955. Ibid., 140.

73. Ibid., 142.

74. Ibid., 143.

75. Markakis, *Ethiopia*, 278n28.

76. Not until the election of 1973 did the landed classes seem to make a come back in the Chamber, and this was during a period of intense concern over land reform. See Colin Legum, *Ethiopia: The Fall of Haile Selassie's Empire* (London: Rex Collings, 1975), 10; and Clapham, *Haile-Selassie's Government*, 143.

77. Central Statistical Office, *Ethiopia: 1972 Statistical Pocket Book* (Addis Ababa: Central Statistical Office, 1972), 11.

78. Samuel P. Huntington suggests that for most traditional monarchies of the twentieth century, security is of primary importance. See Samuel P. Huntington, *Political Order in Changing Societies* (New Haven: Yale University Press, 1968), 155, 162–66; and Christopher Clapham, "Ethiopia and Somalia," *Conflicts in Africa: Adelphi Papers, No. 93* (London: International Institute for Strategic Studies, 1972), 3.

79. Menelik had negotiated the borders of Ethiopia with the British, French, and Italians in a series of separate treaties between 1897 and 1908. As a result of these agreements, the scope of Italian sovereignty in Eritrea and Italian Somaliland was agreed on; France and Ethiopia came to terms with reference to French Somaliland and its hinterland; and Britain and Ethiopia agreed on the boundaries separating Menelik's sphere of influence in the south and east in relation to British Somaliland and Kenya's northern frontier district. See I. M. Lewis, *A Modern History of Somalia: Nation and State in the Horn of Africa* (London: Longman, 1980), 40–41; and Bereket Habte Selassie, *Conflict and Intervention in the Horn of Africa* (New York: Monthly Review Press, 1980), 97–125.

80. *Autobiography of Emperor Haile Sellassie I*, 298–312.

81. Spencer, *Ethiopia, the Horn of Africa, and U.S. Policy*, 17–22; Spencer, *Ethiopia at Bay*, 139–58.

82. Lewis, *Modern History of Somalia*.

83. Selassie, *Conflict and Intervention in the Horn of Africa*, 102–103.

84. See Abdulqawi A. Yusuf, "The Anglo-Abyssinian Treaty of 1897 and the Somali-Ethiopian Dispute," *Horn of Africa*, 3 (Jan.-March 1980), 39.

85. Spencer, *Ethiopia, the Horn of Africa, and U.S. Policy*, 20.

86. Spencer, *Ethiopia at Bay*, 249–50.

87. There is some disagreement over whether a "vote" was actually taken in the Eritrean Assembly on this occasion, but at least one author claims that an eyewitness confirmed this. See Tesfatsion Medhanie, *Eritrea: Dynamics of a National Question* (Amsterdam: B. R. Grüner, 1986), 306n68. See also R. Lobban, "The Eritrean War: Issues and Implications," *Canadian Journal of African Studies*, 10 (1976), 339.

88. Spencer, "Haile Selassie," 36.

89. Schwab, *Haile Selassie I*, 101–14.

90. Spencer, *Ethiopia at Bay*, 305–309.

91. Ibid.

92. Hess, *Ethiopia*, 238–39.

93. See "Ethiopia Severs Its Diplomatic Relations with the [*sic*] Portugal," *Ethiopia Information Bulletin*, 2 (July 1963), 5–6.

IV. The Political Economy of a Modernizing Bureaucratic Empire

1. S. N. Eisenstadt, *The Political System of Empires* (London: Free Press of Glencoe, 1963), 33–49.

2. World Bank, *Ethiopia and the World Bank* (Washington, D.C.: World Bank, 1976), 10. The World Bank surmised that with its dominant subsistence agricultural

sector, geographic isolation, and unexploited mineral potential, Ethiopia was in a much less advantageous position than many other less developed countries.

3. Richard K. Pankhurst, *Economic History of Ethiopia* (Addis Ababa: Haile Sellassie I University Press, 1968), 304.

4. Margery Perham, *The Government of Ethiopia* (London: Faber and Faber, 1948), 178–79.

5. Ibid., 178.

6. David C. Korten, *Planned Change in a Traditional Society: Psychological Problems of Modernization in Ethiopia* (New York: Praeger, 1972), 29–32.

7. John H. Spencer, *Ethiopia, the Horn of Africa, and U.S. Policy* (Cambridge, Mass.: Institute for Foreign Policy Analysis, 1977), 32.

8. Patrick Gilkes, *The Dying Lion: Feudalism and Modernization in Ethiopia* (London: Julian Friedmann, 1975), 76.

9. Assefe Bequele and Eshetu Chole, *A Profile of the Ethiopian Economy* (London: Oxford University Press, 1969), 84–90.

10. Irving Kaplan et al., *Area Handbook of Ethiopia* (Washington, D.C.: U.S. Government Printing Office, 1970), 403.

11. Legesse Lemma, "Political Economy of Ethiopia, 1875–1974: Agricultural, Educational, and International Antecedents of the Revolution" (Ph.D. diss., University of Notre Dame, 1980), 105.

12. *Ethiopia and the World Bank*, 20.

13. Kaplan et al., *Area Handbook*, 413.

14. *Ethiopia and the World Bank*, 19–20.

15. *Second Five-Year Development Plan, 1963–1967* (Addis Ababa: Berhanenna Selam Printing Press, 1962), 51.

16. *United Nations Statistical Yearbook* (New York: United Nations, 1978), 470–71.

17. Kaplan et al., *Area Handbook*, 352–53.

18. Ibid.

19. Ibid., 350.

20. Ibid., 354.

21. Ibid., 353–54.

22. *Second Five-Year Development Plan*, 45.

23. Bequele and Chole, *Profile of the Ethiopian Economy*, 19.

24. *Third Five-Year Development Plan* (Addis Ababa: Berhanenna Selam Printing Press, 1968), 47; *Second Five-Year Development Plan*, 102.

25. *Third Five-Year Development Plan*, 47.

26. Ibid., 189.

27. Ibid., 192–93. Significantly, however, the amount allocated to such projects was only 1 percent of the total projected expenditures during the plan period.

28. Ibid., 392–97.

29. *Ethiopia: Statistical Abstract, 1975* (Addis Ababa: Central Statistical Office, 1975), 140.

30. Perham, *Government of Ethiopia*, 204.

31. Robert S. Love, "Economic Change in Pre-Revolutionary Ethiopia," *African Affairs*, 78 (July 1979), 348.

32. William Abraham and Seilu Abraha, "Ethiopia's Public Sector: Structure, Policies, and Impact," *Ethiopia's Journal of Development Research*, 2 (April 1975), 2.

33. Ibid., 2–3.

34. Ibid., 3–4.

35. Gilkes, *Dying Lion*, 139.

36. Robert L. Hess, *Ethiopia: The Modernization of Autocracy* (Ithaca: Cornell University Press, 1970), 100. Hess calculated that between 1950 and 1970, Ethiopia had received almost $600 million in foreign loans and credits, more than half of which came from the United States (US$211.9 million) and the Soviet Union

(US$100 million). If the contribution of the World Bank (US$121 million) were added to this figure, nearly 70 percent of all loans and credits Ethiopia received over the twenty-one-year period would be accounted for.

37. Rumman Faruqi and Peter O'Brien, "Foreign Technology in the Growth of the Modern Manufacturing Sector in Ethiopia, 1950–1970," *Africa Development*, 1 (Sept. 1976), 24.

38. Gilkes, *Dying Lion*, 160.

39. Mohammed Duri, "Private Foreign Investment in Ethiopia, 1950–1968," *Journal of Ethiopian Studies*, 7 (July 1969), 74–75.

40. Korten, *Planned Change*, 33.

41. Abraham and Abraha, "Ethiopia's Public Sector," 1.

42. Ibid.

43. Ibid., 5.

44. Ibid., 4–7.

45. Richard K. Pankhurst, *An Introduction to the Economic History of Ethiopia* (Woodford Green, Essex: Lalibela House, 1961), 307–21.

46. *Ethiopian Herald*, December 2, 1946, quoted in Perham, *Government of Ethiopia*, 188–89.

47. Taffara Deguefe, "Strategy for Trade and Investment in Ethiopia," *Addis Ababa Chamber of Commerce* (June 1970), 18–20.

48. Ibid., 30.

49. See Glen Bailey, *An Analysis of the Ethiopian Revolution* (Athens, Ohio: African Program, 1980), 43.

50. Faruqi and O'Brien, "Foreign Technology," 32. See also Hess, *Ethiopia*, 88; and Kaplan et al., *Area Handbook*, 346.

51. Duri, "Private Foreign Investment," 55.

52. Faruqi and O'Brien, "Foreign Technology," 27.

53. *Second Five-Year Development Plan*, 183.

54. Faruqi and O'Brien, "Foreign Technology," 27–28.

55. Ibid., 28.

56. See Duri, "Private Foreign Investment," 55; and Bequele and Chole, *Profile of the Ethiopian Economy*, 54.

57. Bequele and Chole, *Profile of the Ethiopian Economy*.

58. Gilkes, *Dying Lion*, 138–39. The most up-to-date official statistics available to me at the time of writing place the percentage of the GDP represented by manufacturing at 4.5 percent in 1972–1973. *Ethiopia: Statistical Abstract, 1975*, 137.

59. Duri, "Private Foreign Investment," 71.

60. Ibid., 73.

61. Ibid., 73–74.

62. Ibid., 59.

63. Ibid.

64. Ibid., 60. See also Gilkes, *Dying Lion*, 150.

65. Gilkes, *Dying Lion*, 151.

66. Duri, "Private Foreign Investment," 65–66; *Ethiopia: Statistical Abstract, 1965/66* (Addis Ababa: Central Statistical Office, 1966), 137.

67. Gilkes, *Dying Lion*, 152.

68. *Ethiopia: Statistical Abstract, 1975*, 111. The most dramatic positive effect of the development of the sugar industry was that it led to an improvement in social services in sugar-growing areas, as the companies came to provide for the health and welfare of their permanent employees. It also aided in the development of feeder roads in remote areas. Duri, "Private Foreign Investment," 68.

69. Lars Bondestam, "Notes on Foreign Investment in Ethiopia," in Carl Widstrand, ed., *Multinational Firms in Africa* (Uppsala: Scandinavian Institute of African Studies, 1975), 34–35.

70. Kaplan et al., *Area Handbook*, 424.

71. See Thomas Biersteker, *Distortion or Development? Contending Perspectives on the Multinational Corporation* (Cambridge, Mass.: MIT Press, 1978).

72. There is disagreement in the literature about the level of U.S. private capital involvement in Ethiopia at this time. John Markakis and Nega Ayele, *Class and Revolution in Ethiopia* (London: Spokesman, 1978), 34, estimate that in the late 1970s there were more than two hundred American firms active in Ethiopia. Kaplan et al., *Area Handbook*, 424, on the other hand, suggest that there were no more than ten.

73. Daniel Teferra, "The Phenomenon of Underdevelopment in Ethiopia" (Ph.D. diss., University of Wisconsin, 1979), 57.

74. Evidence of this is provided in the fact that in 1969, the government raised the excise tax on sugar more than 200 percent, even though this was certain to drive down the domestic demand for that product. See George A. Lipsky et al., *Area Handbook for Ethiopia* (Washington, D.C.: U.S. Government Printing Office, 1960), 526.

75. See Bequele and Chole, *Profile of the Ethiopian Economy*, 78; and *Ethiopia: Statistical Abstract, 1975*, 141.

76. Lipsky et al., *Area Handbook* (1960), 527.

77. Ibid. One of the main exceptions here was the tax on domestic and imported salt. The tax on the former was much higher than the latter so as to stimulate local salt production.

78. Bequele and Chole, *Profile of the Ethiopian Economy*, 79.

79. Kaplan et al., *Area Handbook*, 444.

80. Bequele and Chole, *Profile of the Ethiopian Economy*, 75.

81. See Peter Schwab, *Decision-Making in Ethiopia: A Study of the Political Process*, (Rutherford, N.J.: Fairleigh Dickinson University Press, 1972), 89–140.

82. Ibid., 91–92.

83. Gilkes, *Dying Lion*, 66–68.

84. John M. Cohen and Dov Weintraub, *Land and Peasants in Imperial Ethiopia* (The Hague: Van Gorcum, 1975), 39–40.

85. Ibid., 40.

86. Ibid., 55–57.

87. See Allan Hoben, *Land Tenure among the Amhara of Ethiopia: The Dynamics of Cognatic Descent* (Chicago: University of Chicago Press, 1973), 208–209; and Fred V. Goricke, *Social and Political Factors Influencing the Application of Land Reform Measures in Ethiopia* (Saarbrucken, West Germany: Verlag Brietenbach, 1979), 79–80.

88. Schwab, *Decision-Making*, 129–40.

89. Ibid., 125–26.

90. Ibid., 158–69.

91. *Ethiopia: Statistical Abstract, 1975*, 141.

92. Kaplan et al., *Area Handbook*, 425. Kaplan found that between 1963 and 1966, exports accounted for only 11 percent of the GNP, while imports averaged between 12 and 14 percent of the GNP. This did not include taxes on foreign trade. The World Bank estimated that exports averaged 10 percent of the GDP between 1965 and 1975. See *Ethiopia and the World Bank*, 10.

93. Lemma, "Political Economy of Ethiopia," 217.

94. *United Nations Statistical Yearbook*, 470–71.

95. *Ethiopia and the World Bank*, 10.

96. See Bequele and Chole, *Profile of the Ethiopian Economy*, 60; *Ethiopia: Statistical Pocketbook, 1968* (Addis Ababa: Central Statistical Office, 1969), 59; and *Ethiopia: Statistical Abstract, 1975*, 119.

97. *Ethiopia: Statistical Abstract, 1975*, 119.

98. Ibid.

99. *Ethiopia: Statistical Pocketbook, 1967* (Addis Ababa: Central Statistical Office, 1968), 59.

100. *Ethiopia: Statistical Abstract, 1975,* 119.

101. Ibid., 122–23.

102. *Ethiopia: Statistical Abstract, 1964* (Addis Ababa: Central Statistical Office, 1964), xix; *Ethiopia: Statistical Abstract, 1975,* 111.

103. Gilkes, *Dying Lion,* 141.

104. Peter Schwab, *Ethiopia and Haile Selassie* (New York: Facts on File, 1972), 82.

105. See Gilkes, *Dying Lion,* 141–42; and Bondestam, "Notes on Foreign Investment," 126.

106. Taye Gulilat, "Coffee in the Ethiopian Economy, II," *Journal of Ethiopian Studies,* 1 (Jan. 1963), 49.

107. Bailey, *Analysis of the Ethiopian Revolution,* 45.

108. Gilkes, *Dying Lion,* 132–33.

109. Ibid., 131–32.

110. World Bank, *World Bank Development* (Washington, D.C.: World Bank, 1970), 9.

111. *Second Five-Year Development Plan,* 70–71.

112. See Michael Stahl, *Ethiopia: Political Contradictions in Agricultural Development* (Stockholm: Raben and Sjogren, 1974), 94–113.

113. Gilkes, *Dying Lion,* 128–30.

114. Stahl, *Ethiopia,* 98; Cohen and Weintraub, *Land and Peasants,* 16.

115. Stahl, *Ethiopia,* 103–105.

116. See Abdul Mejid Hussein, "Political Economy of Famine," in A. M. Hussein, ed., *Drought and Famine in Ethiopia* (London: International African Institute, 1976), 13.

117. Gilkes, *Dying Lion,* 160–61.

118. See Teferra-Worq Beshah and John W. Harbeson, "Afar Pastoralists in Transition and the Ethiopian Revolution," *Journal of African Studies,* 5 (Fall 1978), 249–67.

119. Bondestam, "Notes on Foreign Investment," 137–38.

120. See Aiden Foster-Carter, "The Modes of Production Controversy," *New Left Review* (Jan.-Feb. 1978), 63; and "Marxism and the Fact of Conquest," *African Review,* 6 (1976). Foster-Carter notes that, as a rule, the transition to capitalism in Africa differed significantly from the European pattern. Instead of capitalism being born of feudalism in Africa as in Europe, it was imposed from outside by force. Moreover, rather than destroying traditional modes of production and social relationships, in many cases colonial capitalism utilized these structures to advance its own objectives. This is reflective of what happened in Ethiopia.

V. Development and Social Contradictions: The Seeds of Revolution

1. Jeanne Contini, "The Winds of Change and the Lion of Judah," *Reporter,* May 25, 1961, p. 31.

2. See, for example, Robert L. Hess, *Ethiopia: The Modernization of Autocracy* (Ithaca: Cornell University Press, 1970), 144; Peter Schwab, *Decision-Making in Ethiopia: A Study of the Political Process* (Rutherford, N.J.: Fairleigh Dickinson University Press, 1972), 90–91; and Donald N. Levine, "Prepared Statement of Donald N. Levine," in *Ethiopia and the Horn of Africa: Hearing before the Subcommittee on African Affairs of the Committee on Foreign Relations, U.S. Senate* (August 4, 5, and 6, 1976), 7.

3. For detailed discussions of the coup, see Richard Greenfield, *Ethiopia: A New Political History* (London: Pall Mall Press, 1965), 269–458; and Harold G. Marcus, *Ethiopia, Great Britain, and the United States, 1941–1974: The Politics of Empire* (Berkeley: University of California Press, 1983), 116–69.

4. Greenfield, *Ethiopia;* Marcus, *Ethiopia, Great Britain, and the United States,* 120.

5. Greenfield, *Ethiopia,* 343.

6. Marcus, *Ethiopia, Great Britain, and the United States,* 118.

7. Greenfield, *Ethiopia,* 372.

8. Ibid., 372–73.

9. Ibid., 398–99.

10. Ibid., 412–14; Marcus, *Ethiopia, Great Britain, and the United States,* 116–49.

11. Marcus, *Ethiopia, Great Britain, and the United States,* 156–57.

12. See John Markakis, *Ethiopia: Anatomy of a Traditional Polity,* (Oxford: Clarendon Press, 1974), 359; and Peter Koehn and Louis D. Hayes, "Student Politics in Traditional Monarchies," *Journal of Asian and African Studies,* 12 (Jan.-April 1978), 36.

13. Christopher Clapham, "Centralization and Local Response in Southern Ethiopia," *African Affairs,* 74 (Jan. 1975), 75–78.

14. Markakis, *Ethiopia,* 51n3, 337.

15. Donald Levine, *Greater Ethiopia: The Evolution of a Multiethnic Society* (Chicago: University of Chicago Press, 1974), 181.

16. Clapham, "Centralization and Local Response," 73–76.

17. Ibid.

18. See Patrick Gilkes, *The Dying Lion: Feudalism and Modernization in Ethiopia* (London: Julian Friedmann, 1975), 83–84.

19. Quoted Schwab, *Decision-Making in Ethiopia,* 53.

20. Ibid., 141–80.

21. See *Second Five Year Development Plan, 1963–1967* (Addis Ababa: Berhanenna Selam Press, 1962), 315–18; and Markakis, *Ethiopia,* 327.

22. Gilkes, *Dying Lion,* 147.

23. William I. Abraham and Seilu Abraha, "Ethiopia's Public Sector: Structure, Policies and Impact," *Ethiopian Journal of Development Research,* 2 (April 1975), 8–9.

24. Central Statistical Office, *Statistical Abstract of Ethiopia,* (Addis Ababa: Central Statistical Office, 1975), 209.

25. P. T. W. Baxter, "Ethiopia's Unacknowledged Problem: The Oromo," *African Affairs,* 77 (July 1978), 292–93; Markakis, *Ethiopia,* 379.

26. Markakis, *Ethiopia,* 379.

27. Mordechai Abir, "Education and National Unity in Ethiopia," *African Affairs,* 75 (1970), 55.

28. Eileen Stommes and Seleshi Sisaye, "The Development and Distribution of Health Care Services in Ethiopia: A Preliminary Review," *Canadian Journal of African Studies,* 13 (1980), 493.

29. Ibid., 488.

30. See John Markakis and Nega Ayele, *Class and Revolution in Ethiopia* (London: Spokesman, 1978), 28; Horace Orlando Patterson, *Ethnic Chauvinism: The Reactionary Impulse* (New York: Stein and Day, 1977); Addis Hiwet, *Ethiopia: From Autocracy to Revolution* (London: Merlin Press, 1975); and Bereket Habte Selassie, *Conflict and Intervention in the Horn of Africa* (New York: Monthly Review Press, 1980).

31. On "the fact of conquest," see Aiden Foster-Carter, "Marxism and the Fact of Conquest," *African Review,* 6 (1976), 49–75.

32. See James Scott, *The Moral Economy of the Peasant: Rebellion and Resistance in Southeast Asia* (New Haven: Yale University Press, 1976), for a discussion of such economies.

33. Paul Brietzke, "Law, Revolution and the Ethiopian Peasant," *Rural Africana,* 28 (Fall 1975), 14.

34. Allan Hoben, "Social Anthropology and Development Planning: A Case

Study in Ethiopian Land Reform Policy," *Journal of Modern African Studies*, 10 (1972), 580–81.

35. John M. Cohen and Dov Weintraub, *Land and Peasants in Imperial Ethiopia* (The Hague: Van Gorcum, 1975), 61.

36. Ibid., 55–56.

37. Allan Hoben, "Perspectives on Land Reform in Ethiopia: The Political Role of the Peasantry," *Rural Africana*, 28 (Fall 1975), 59.

38. Cohen and Weintraub, *Land and Peasants*, 51–52.

39. Irving Kaplan et al., *Area Handbook of Ethiopia* (Washington, D.C.: U.S. Government Printing Office, 1970), 396–97.

40. See George A. Lipsky, *U.S. Army Area Handbook for Ethiopia* (Washington, D.C.: U.S. Government Printing Office, 1964), 510; and *Ethiopia: Statistical Abstract, 1977* (Addis Ababa: Central Statistical Office, 1979), 79.

41. Markakis, *Ethiopia*, 173–74.

42. Gilkes, *Dying Lion*, 166; Markakis, *Ethiopia*, 174. From this point on, this syndicate functioned as a quasi union.

43. Markakis, *Ethiopia*, 175.

44. Ibid., 176.

45. Gilkes, *Dying Lion*, 166.

46. Seleshi Sisaye, "Urban Migration and the Labor Movement in Ethiopia," unpublished paper, 1978, p. 20.

47. Marina Ottoway and David Ottoway, *Ethiopia: Empire in Revolution* (New York: Africana, 1978), 23.

48. Sisaye, "Urban Migration," 20.

49. Markakis and Ayele, *Class and Revolution*, 46–47. The authors suggest that while manufacturing expanded at an average annual rate of 11.1 percent during the 1960s, the rate of absorption in the sector reached a point of insignificance by 1970.

50. Markakis, *Ethiopia*, 7; Richard L. Sklar, "Political Science and National Integration: A Radical Approach," *Journal of Modern African Studies*, 5 (May 1967), 1–12.

51. Selassie, *Conflict and Intervention*, 49. For a brief period between the fifteenth and sixteenth centuries, the Abyssinians (Ethiopians) established limited control over the Eritrean highlands, but the period was characterized by sporadic resistance to alien rule.

52. Gerard Chaliand, "The Horn of Africa's Dilemma," *Foreign Policy*, 30 (Spring 1978), 124. For a very brief time, the Egyptians succeeded the Ottomans (1872–1890), but they met heavy resistance from Eritrean "patriots" with the aid of some Tigrean allies. See also G. K. N. Trevaskis, *Eritrea: A Colony in Transition, 1941–1952* (London: Oxford University Press, 1960).

53. Marcus, *Ethiopia, Great Britain, and the United States*, 8; John H. Spencer, *Ethiopia at Bay: A Personal Account of the Haile Selassie Years* (Algonac, Mich.: Reference Publications, 1984), 86–99.

54. Selassie, *Conflict and Intervention*, 55; E. Sylvia Parkhurst, *Eritrea on the Eve* (Woodford Green, Essex: "New Times and Ethiopia News" Books, 1952).

55. See Tesfatsion Medhanie, *Eritrea: Dynamics of a National Question* (Amsterdam: B. R. Gruner, 1986), 17–18.

56. Richard Sherman, *Eritrea: The Unfinished Revolution* (New York: Praeger, 1980), 25; Spencer, *Ethiopia at Bay*, 188–242.

57. Lloyd Ellingson, "The Emergence of Political Parties in Eritrea, 1940–1950," *Journal of African History*, 18 (1977), 261–81.

58. Sherman, *Eritrea*, 26.

59. Selassie, *Conflict and Intervention*, 60.

60. See Sherman, *Eritrea*, 26–28; and Richard Lobban, "The Eritrea War: Issues and Implications," *Canadian Journal of African Studies*, 10 (1976), 339.

61. See Yohannis Abate, "Africa's Troubled Horn: Background to Conflict," *Focus*, 28 (Jan.-Feb. 1978), 1–10; and Selassie, *Conflict and Intervention*, 62–63. Selassie suggests that the Ethiopian military, with U.S. and Israeli aid, was used to intimidate the assembly and to maintain law and order during the vote on annexation.

62. Medhanie, *Eritrea*, 25–26.

63. Ibid.

64. Selassie, *Conflict and Intervention*, 61–62.

65. Gilkes, *Dying Lion*, 197–98.

66. See Sherman, *Eritrea*, 72–77; Michael and Trish Johnson, "Eritrea: The National Question and the Logic of Protracted Struggle," *African Affairs*, 80 (April 1981), 181–95; James Firebrace and Stuart Holland, *Never Kneel Down* (Trenton, N.J.: Red Sea Press, 1985); and Haggai Erlich, *The Struggle Over Eritrea, 1962–1978* (Stanford: Hoover Institution Press, 1983).

67. Selassie, *Conflict and Intervention*, 66.

68. David D. Laitin and Said S. Samatar, *Somalia: Nation in Search of a State* (London: Gower, 1987); I. M. Lewis, *A Modern History of Somalia: Nation and State in the Horn of Africa* (London: Longman, 1980), 18–39. The Somali belong to a number of clan families (Darod, Dir, Isaq, Hawiye, Sab), but they enjoy a cultural, linguistic, and religious identity and consider themselves a "nation." This, however, has been disputed. See, for example, Mesfin Wolde Mariam, "The Ethio-Somalia Boundary Dispute," *Journal of Modern African Studies*, 2 (July 1964), 189–219.

69. Selassie, *Conflict and Intervention*, 99.

70. David D. Laitin and Olusola Ojo, "The OAU and the Ogaden Question: Towards a Solution," unpublished paper, July 1980, p. 2.

71. John H. Spencer, *Ethiopia, the Horn of Africa, and U.S. Policy* (Cambridge, Mass.: Institute for Foreign Policy Analysis, 1977), 17–19. The historical record now shows that Bevin himself was not in favor of this plan but was duty-bound as Foreign Secretary to represent the British government's position.

72. E. Sylvia Parkhurst, *Ex-Italian Somaliland* (London: Watts, 1951).

73. Markakis, *Ethiopia*, 368; Abate, "Africa's Troubled Horn," 14.

74. "Emperor Haile Selassie's Speech in the Ogaden, 25 August 1956: Extracts," *Ethiopian Observer* (December 1956).

75. Ibid.

76. "The Ethiopian Government Aide Memoire," *Ethiopian Ministry of Foreign Affairs, Press Release*, November 14, 1963.

77. Gilkes, *Dying Lion*, 215–16.

78. Ottaway and Ottaway, *Ethiopia*, 92–93.

79. See Crane Brinton, *The Anatomy of Revolution* (New York: Vintage Books, 1965). Brinton suggests that the most critical phase of revolutions is the transition from the "reign of terror" to the phase of "thermidorian reaction" as the polity begins to stabilize once again.

80. "A Brief History of Oromo Resistance against Abyssinian Colonialism, 1855–1900," *Waldaansso: Journal of the Union of Oromo Students in North America*, 3 (Aug. 1979), 3–5.

81. There is considerable academic disagreement as to the development—even existence—of a single Oromo national consciousness prior to recent years, let alone the significance of a confederated union of Oromo peoples. Donald Levine, for example, suggests that there was no sense of "Oromo-ness" among the Oromo until very recently. The clan was more important as a terminal community. On the other hand, Bereket Selassie argues that Oromo nationalism has historic roots. See Levine, *Greater Ethiopia*, 128–32; and Selassie, *Conflict and Intervention*, 77–78.

82. See Asmarom Legesse, *Gada: Three Approaches to the Study of African Society* (New York: Free Press, 1973); Karl E. Knutsson, *Authority and Change: A Study of the Kallu Institution among the Macha Galla of Ethiopia* (Gotenborg, Sweden: Etnografiska Museet, 1967); Richard Greenfield and Mohammed Hassan, "Interpretation of Oromo Nationality," *Horn of Africa*, 3 (1980), 3–14; and "Toward Understanding the Gada System," *Waldaansso*, 4 (1980), 3–24.

83. "Oromia: Displacement and Resettlement," *Horn of Africa*, (1981), 35–41.

84. Margery Perham, *The Government of Ethiopia* (London: Faber and Faber, 1948), 220.

85. Baxter, "Ethiopia's Unacknowledged Problem," 288.

86. Clapham, "Centralization and Local Response," 76; Gilkes, *Dying Lion*, 223; Markakis, *Ethiopia*, 136–37.

87. See, for example, Schwab, *Decision-Making in Ethiopia*, 171–72.

88. On the significance of the "fact of conquest," see Foster-Carter, "Marxism and the 'Fact of Conquest.'"

89. Gilkes, *Dying Lion*, 206.

90. See "Brief History of Oromo Resistance," 7; and Greenfield and Hassan, "Interpretation of Oromo Nationality," 11.

91. Gilkes, *Dying Lion*, 225–26.

92. See Ottaway and Ottaway, *Ethiopia*, 91; Clapham, "Centralization and Local Response," 80; and Selassie, *Conflict and Intervention*, 80–81.

93. See Ottaway and Ottaway, *Ethiopia*, 92–93.

94. Selassie, *Conflict and Intervention*, 107–10.

95. See Gilkes, *Dying Lion*, 218; and Selassie, *Conflict and Intervention*, 108.

96. "Oromia Speaks: An Interview with a Member of the Central Committee of the Oromo Liberation Front," *Horn of Africa*, 3 (1980), 24.

97. Ibid.

VI. Politics, Economics, and Class Conflicts:
The Precipitating Causes of Revolution

1. See Joel S. Migdal, *Peasants, Politics, and Revolution: Pressures toward Political and Social Change in the Third World* (Princeton: Princeton University Press, 1974); and Ted R. Gurr, *Why Men Rebel* (Princeton: Princeton University Press, 1970).

2. See Thomas H. Greene, *Comparative Revolutionary Movements* (Englewood Cliffs, N.J.: Prentice-Hall, 1984); Mark N. Hagopian, *The Phenomenon of Revolution* (New York: Dodd, Mead, 1975); Eric R. Wolf, *Peasant Wars of the Twentieth Century* (New York: Harper and Row, 1969); Barrington Moore, Jr., *Social Origins of Dictatorship and Democracy: Lord and Peasant in the Making of the Modern World* (Boston: Beacon Press, 1966); Jeffery M. Paige, *Agrarian Revolution: Social Movements and Export Agriculture in the Underdeveloped World* (New York: Free Press, 1975); Theda Skocpol, *States and Social Revolutions: A Comparative Analysis of France, Russia, and China* (London: Cambridge University Press, 1979); S. N. Eisenstadt, *The Political System of Empires* (London: Free Press of Glencoe, 1963); and Karl Marx and Friedrich Engels, *Selected Works* (New York: International Publishers, 1968).

3. See Greene, *Comparative Revolutionary Movements*, for an illuminating survey of such factors.

4. See, for example, Gurr, *Why Men Rebel;* Clifford T. Paynton and Robert Blackey, eds., *Why Revolution?* (Cambridge, Mass.: Schenkmann, 1971); James C. Davies, "Toward a Theory of Revolution," *American Sociological Review*, 27 (Feb. 1962), 5–19; and James Scott, *The Moral Economy of the Peasant: Rebellion and Resistance in Southeast Asia* (New Haven: Yale University Press, 1976).

5. Marina Ottaway and David Ottaway, *Ethiopia: Empire in Revolution* (New York: Africana, 1978), 3.

6. See Julius Holt and John Seaman, "The Scope of the Drought," in Abdul Mejid Hussein, ed., *Drought and Famine in Ethiopia* (London: International African Institute, 1976), 2.

7. Jack Shepard, *The Politics of Starvation* (New York: Carnegie Endowment for International Peace, 1975), 37; John Markakis and Nega Ayele, *Class and Revolution in Ethiopia* (London: Spokesman, 1978), 80.

8. Holt and Seaman, "Scope of the Drought," 5.

9. Abdul Mejid Hussein, "The Political Economy of Famine in Ethiopia," in Hussein, ed., *Drought and Famine in Ethiopia,* 33.

10. Shepard, *Politics of Starvation,* 60. Shepard notes that Crown Prince Asfa Wossen was found to have "bulging warehouses of grain" in Wollo, and other private entrepreneurs also had large surpluses.

11. Relief and Rehabilitation Commission, *Drought Rehabilitation in Wollo and Tigre* (Addis Ababa: Relief and Rehabilitation Commission, 1974), 26.

12. Shepard, *Politics of Starvation,* 63. Shepard notes that grain exports doubled in 1973 over the previous year to nine thousand metric tons.

13. Lionel Cliffe, "Capitalism or Feudalism? The Famine in Ethiopia," *Review of African Political Economy,* 1 (1974), 36–37; Shepard, *Politics of Starvation,* 3.

14. Colin Legum, *Ethiopia: The Fall of Haile Selassie's Empire* (London: Rex Collings, 1975), 12.

15. Hussein, "Political Economy of Famine in Ethiopia," 16–17.

16. Shepard, *Politics of Starvation,* 14.

17. Ibid., 26–27. It is also suggested that the United States was more concerned with not contributing to a destabilization of the Ethiopian government. See Willeme Johnson, "Food and Politics: A Case Study of Ethiopia," *Horn of Africa,* 2 (Jan.-March 1979), 33.

18. Shepard, *Politics of Starvation,* 17.

19. Legum, *Ethiopia,* 11–13.

20. Shepard, *Politics of Starvation,* 33.

21. Ibid., 34.

22. Markakis and Ayele, *Class and Revolution,* 78–79.

23. Shepard, *Politics of Starvation,* 22.

24. Ibid., 33.

25. Alan Rake suggests that the inflow of foreign export earnings in late 1973 was enormous, but the government tried to get more and more in order to keep up with inflation. Alan Rake, "Winds of Change," *African Development,* 8 (1974), p. E5.

26. "Selassie's Riches Go to Drought Aid," *Denver Post,* (Dec. 10, 1974). This money was allegedly voluntarily signed over to the drought relief campaign in late 1974.

27. See Blair Thomson, *Ethiopia: The Country That Cut Off Its Head* (London: Robson Books, 1975), 22–27.

28. Ottaway and Ottaway, *Ethiopia,* 33. See also Philip H. Combs with Manzoor Ahmed, *Attacking Rural Poverty: How Non-Formal Education Can Help* (Washington, D.C.: IBRD, 1974).

29. Ottaway and Ottaway, *Ethiopia,* 33.

30. See Teshome G. Wagaw, *Education in Ethiopia: Prospects and Retrospect,* (Ann Arbor: University of Michigan Press, 1979), 183–97; and Christopher Davis, "Focal Point of Ferment," *African Development,* 8 (1974), p. E36.

31. Charles Tilly suggests that the most crucial coalition among the whole range of possible coalitions that arise in revolutionary situations is the one that allies the challengers directly with a significant portion of the military. Charles Tilly, *From Mobilization to Revolution* (Reading, Mass.: Addison-Wesley, 1978), 210.

32. Irving Kaplan et al., *Area Handbook for Ethiopia* (Washington, D.C.: U.S. Government Printing Office, 1971), 498–99.

33. Detailed vivid accounts of the military crisis can be found in Legum, *Ethiopia;* and Thomson, *Ethiopia.*

34. Legum, *Ethiopia,* 33.

35. Ibid., 34.

36. Rake, "Winds of Change," p. E5.

37. Thomson, *Ethiopia,* 29–30.

38. Legum, *Ethiopia,* 35.

39. Peter Calvert, *A Study of Revolution* (Oxford: Clarendon Press, 1970), 4.

40. Legum, *Ethiopia,* 39.

41. See Legesse Lemma, "The Ethiopian Student Movement, 1960–1974: A Challenge to the Monarchy and Imperialism in Ethiopia," *Northeast African Studies,* 1 (1979), 8–24; and Ethiopian Student Union of North America, "Historical Development of the Ethiopian Student Movement," prepared for the Twentieth Congress of ESUNA by the Northern California Chapter, August 24, 1972.

42. Peter Koehn and L. Hayes, "Student Politics in Traditional Monarchies," *Journal of Asian and African Studies,* 13 (Jan.-April 1978), 36.

43. Lemma, "Ethiopian Student Movement," 32.

44. Thomson, *Ethiopia;* Markakis and Ayele, *Class and Revolution,* 95.

45. Seleshi Sisaye, "Industrial Conflict and Labor Politics in Ethiopia: A Study of the March 1974 General Strike," *Plural Societies,* 8 (Summer 1977), 53–54.

46. See Legum, *Ethiopia,* 43; and Markakis and Ayele, *Class and Revolution,* 93–98.

47. Markakis and Ayele, *Class and Revolution,* 93.

48. Legum, *Ethiopia,* 42.

49. Markakis and Ayele, *Class and Revolution,* 94.

50. Ibid., 98.

51. Sisaye, "Industrial Conflict."

52. Ibid., 60–64.

53. Gurr, *Why Men Rebel,* 47.

54. Ibid., 51.

55. Calvert, *Study of Revolution,* 4.

56. Chalmers Johnson, *Revolutionary Change* (Boston: Little, Brown, 1966), 151–55.

57. See Gerard Chaliand, *Revolution in the Third World: Myths and Prospects* (New York: Viking Press, 1977).

58. Pliny the Middle-Aged, "The PMAC: Origins and Structure, Part I," *Ethiopianist Notes,* 2 (1978–79), 2.

59. Haggai Erlich, "The Establishment of the Derg: The Turning of a Protest Movement into a Revolution," typescript, 1978, p. 8.

60. Markakis and Ayele, *Class and Revolution,* 89.

61. Pliny the Middle-Aged, "PMAC," 3.

62. Legum, *Ethiopia,* 39–42.

63. Erlich, "Establishment," 13.

64. Markakis and Ayele, *Class and Revolution,* 102–104.

65. Pliny the Middle-Aged, "PMAC," 6.

66. Ibid., 8; Erlich, "Establishment," 16.

67. Erlich, "Establishment," 16. Originally, each of the forty-two units chose three people to represent them, but one representative was allegedly arrested before he assumed his post. Each delegation was supposed to consist of one junior officer, one NCO, and one private from each unit.

68. Erlich, "Establishment," 17.

69. Legum, *Ethiopia,* 45.

70. See Erlich, "Establishment," 21; and Ottaway and Ottaway, *Ethiopia,* 134.

71. Ottaway and Ottaway, *Ethiopia,* 135.

72. Pliny the Middle-Aged, "PMAC," 9.

73. Thomson, *Ethiopia*, 74.

74. Ibid., 76.

75. Markakis and Ayele, *Class and Revolution*, 111.

76. Erlich, "Establishment," 13.

77. Legum, *Ethiopia*, 46.

78. Ibid., 44.

79. Pliny the Middle-Aged, "PMAC," 10.

80. Ottaway and Ottaway, *Ethiopia*, 56.

81. Legum, *Ethiopia*, 47; Thomson, *Ethiopia*, 90–102.

82. Bereket Habte Selassie, *Conflict and Intervention in the Horn of Africa* (New York: Monthly Review Press, 1980), 28.

83. Thomson, *Ethiopia*, 102.

84. Ottaway and Ottaway, *Ethiopia*, 57.

VII. The Quest for a New Social Myth

1. "Ethiopia Tikdem: Declaration of the Provisional Military Government of Ethiopia," Addis Ababa, Dec. 20, 1974.

2. "Development through Cooperation Progress Report: Call of the Motherland," Addis Ababa, Aug. 1975.

3. Dessalegn Rahmato, *Agrarian Reform in Ethiopia* (Trenton, N.J.: Red Sea Press, 1985), 37–73.

4. See Marina Ottaway and David Ottaway, *Ethiopia: Empire in Revolution* (New York: Africana, 1978), 182.

5. See Alula Abate, "Peasant Associations and Collective Agriculture in Ethiopia: Promise and Performance," *Erdrunde*, 37 (1983), 119.

6. "Proclamation to Provide for the Organization and Consolidation of Peasant Associations," Addis Ababa, Dec. 14, 1975.

7. See Alula Abate and Tesfaye Teklu, "Land Reform and Peasant Associations in Ethiopia: Case Studies of Two Widely Differing Regions," *Northeast African Studies*, 2 (Fall 1980), 21–22.

8. Fred Halliday and Maxine Molyneux, *The Ethiopian Revolution* (London: Verso, 1981), 99–100.

9. See V. Solodovnikov and N. Garilov, "Africa: Tendencies of Non-Capitalist Development," *International Affairs* (Moscow, March 1976); V. Solodovnikov, "The Soviet Union and the African Nations," *Political Affairs* (Moscow, July 1978); R. A. Ulynavsky, "Lenin's Concept of Non-Capitalist Development," *Political Affairs* (Moscow, 1970); and A. S. Shin, *National Democratic Revolutions: Some Questions of Theory and Practice* (Moscow: Nauka, 1982).

10. See Berhanu Bayih, "People's Gains in the Ethiopian Revolution," *African Communist*, no. 74 (1978); and W. Jones, "Problems of the Ethiopian Revolution," ibid., no. 69 (1977), 15–28.

11. Although the plans for the commission were revealed in September 1979, the turning point in this choice was what has been termed as the "historic general meeting of the armed forces" in mid-June, marking the first time the rank and file of the military had been gathered en masse, and a subsequent meeting of military cadre and commissars, who are responsible for politicizing the rank and file of the armed forces, which occurred in August. At the first meeting the policies of the Derg and *Abyot Seded* were resoundingly endorsed, and at the second Mengistu was endorsed as the head of whatever party would unfold.

12. *Toward Party Formation* (Addis Ababa: [Committee for the Organization of the Workers' Party of Ethiopia], 1979), 25.

13. See Bereket Habte Selassie, *Conflict and Intervention on the Horn of Africa* (New York: Monthly Review Press, 1980), 24–25.

14. *Program for the National Democratic Revolution* (Addis Ababa: Committee for the Organization of the Workers' Party of Ethiopia, 1976).

15. See "Democracy and the Question of Nationalities in the Ethiopian Revolution," *Maskarem*, 3 (Dec. 1982), 98–99.

16. "Statement of William Schaufale, Jr., Assistant Secretary for African Affairs," in *Hearings before the Subcommittee on African Affairs of the Committee on Foreign Relations, U.S. Senate* (August 4, 5, and 6, 1976) (Washington, D.C.: U.S. Government Printing Office, 1976), 121.

17. Negussay Ayele, "The Horn of Africa: Revolutionary Developments and Western Reactions," *Northeast African Studies*, 2 (1980–81), 3 (1981), 22.

18. Aryeh Yodfat, "The Soviet Union and the Horn of Africa, Part II," *Northeast African Studies*, 2 (1980).

19. Jeffrey A. Lefebvre, "American Foreign Policy and the Horn of Africa: A Cold War Reaction?" *Northeast African Studies*, 2 (1980–81), 3 (1981), 36–39; Ahmed Y. Al-Kasie, "Mubarak's Africa Policy," *Africa Reports*, 27 (March-April 1982), 30.

20. See Colin Legum and Bill Lee, *The Horn of Africa in Continuing Crisis* (New York: Africana, 1979), 78; and *Newsweek*, Sept. 26, 1977, pp. 42–43.

21. Mark Urban, "Soviet Intervention and the Ogaden Counter-Offensive of 1978," *RUSI*, 128 (June 1983), 42–46.

22. Captain Gary D. Payton, "The Soviet-Ethiopian Liason: Airlift and Beyond," *Air University Review*, 31 (Nov.-Dec. 1979), 66–73.

23. Urban, "Soviet Intervention," 44.

24. "Rehabilitation Scheme in Full Swing in Ogaden," *Ethiopian Herald*, Jan. 19, 1982; "Tours Development Project," ibid., Nov. 1, 1983.

25. "Ethiopia: The Revolution Struggles to Consolidate Gains," *Africa Contemporary Record, 1979–80* (New York: Africana, 1981), p. B191.

26. See "Red Star Campaign: Eritrea Region on the Path of Peace and Reconstruction," *Ministry of Foreign Affairs News Bulletin*, Addis Ababa, Feb. 1982, pp. 2–5.

27. See "The Horn: Sand against Wind?" *Africa Confidential* 23, No. 20 (Oct. 1982), 3.

28. "Achievements of Red Star Campaign Noted," *Addis Zemen* [Amharic], May 25, 1982.

29. See "Eritrea Becomes Hub of Socio-Economic Activities," *Ethiopian Herald*, Sept. 3, 1983; and "Eritrean Development Investments Reported," ibid., Sept. 10, 1983. The regime changed the denomination of Ethiopia's currency from "dollars" to "Birr" in 1976.

30. "COPWE Organization Said to be Strengthened," *Ethiopian Herald*, Sept. 10, 1983.

31. "Eritrea Becomes Hub of Socio-Economic Activities."

32. Ibid.; Berhane Gebre-Hiwot, "Mass Organizations and the Revolution," *Ethiopian Herald*, March 1, 1983.

33. See "Ethiopia: Well on the Road to Moscow," *Africa Contemporary Record, 1981–82* (New York: Africana, 1983).

34. See, for example, Tigre People's Liberation Front, "Concluding Declaration of the Second Organizational Congress of the TPLF: May 10–16, 1983" (transcript); and OLF, *Storm: Somali, Tigre and Oromo Resistance Monitor*, 2 (March 1982).

35. "Ethiopia: Well on the Road to Moscow," p. B135.

36. Ibid., p. B131.

37. See, for example, EPLF, "The EPLF and Its Relations with Democratic Movements in Ethiopia" (Feb. 1985), transcript; and "A Marxist-Leninist League of Tigre Declared," *Ethiopia Profile*, 4 (Oct. 1985), 1.

38. The international community responded generously to Ethiopia's cry for relief aid to tackle the drought and famine that began in 1983. Ironically, this took pressure off the Derg, which did not have to worry much about spending its precious foreign exchange on food and could use it instead to pursue other social objectives (i.e., resettlement, villagization) as well as its political and military ones.

39. See "Ethiopia's Foreign Policy," *Yekatit Quarterly,* 8 (Sept. 1984), 3–5; and Michael C. Hudson, "Reagan's Policy in Northeast Africa," *Africa Reports* (March-April 1982), 4–10. Reagan continued the "encirclement strategy" begun by Carter in the Horn which involved the development of military alliances with Ethiopia's neighbors (i.e., Somalia, Kenya, Sudan, Oman, and Egypt) and the conduct of periodic joint military exercises with them. The centerpiece of this policy was the development of the Rapid Deployment Force, units of the U.S. military that could be used to project U.S. military power into the Middle East and the Persian Gulf while using the above-mentioned countries as staging grounds. The U.S. would provide the militaries of these countries with arms, equipment, and training and would assist them in developing local military facilities. The ultimate aim of the policy from the point of view of the countries involved was for the U.S. to reward its "friends" and to serve notice to its "enemies" that the U.S. would seriously challenge any effort by the Soviets to expand their influence in the region. This posture caused Ethiopia, South Yemen, and Libya to come together in a show of solidarity and to dedicate their collective resolve to repulse any efforts by the U.S. or its proxies to intervene in their countries.

40. U.S. Arms Control and Disarmament Agency, *World Military Expenditures and Arms Transfers, 1985* (Washington, D.C.: U.S. Arms Control and Disarmament Agency, 1985).

41. "Proclamation on the National Military Service, the Military Commissariat and Territorial People's Militia," *Negarit Gazeta* (May 1983).

42. "Invulnerable Defense Force," *Yekatit Quarterly,* 8 (Sept. 1984), 34.

VIII. Socialism from Above? Power Consolidation in a "Soft State"

1. See Edmond J. Keller, "The State Policy and the Mediation of Ethnic Conflict in Africa," in Donald Rothchild and Victor A. Olorunsola, eds., *State versus Ethnic Claims: African Policy Dilemmas* (Boulder: Westview Press, 1983), 251–80.

2. See Michael F. Lofchie, "Political Constraints on African Development" in Michael F. Lofchie, ed., *The State of the Nations: Constraints on Development in Independent Africa* (Berkeley: University of California Press, 1971), 9–18.

3. Gunnar Myrdal, *Asian Drama: An Inquiry into the Poverty of Nations* (New York: Twentieth Century Fund/Pantheon Books, 1968).

4. For an excellent description of these tendencies among the African peasantry, see Goran Hyden, *Beyond Ujamaa in Tanzania: Underdevelopment and the Uncaptured Peasantry* (Berkeley: University of California Press, 1980).

5. See Donald Rothchild and Victor A. Olorunsola, "Managing Competing State and Ethnic Claims," in Rothchild and Olorunsola, eds., *State versus Ethnic Claims,* 1–24.

6. Y. Dror, *Public Policymaking Reexamined* (San Francisco: Chandler, 1968), 111.

7. Naomi Caiden and Aaron Wildavsky, *Planning and Budgeting in Poor Countries* (New York: John Wiley, 1974), 57, 62–63.

8. See Jerry Hough, *The Struggle for the Third World* (Washington, D.C.: Brookings Institution, 1986).

9. See David Lane, *The Socialist Industrial State* (London: George Allen and Unwin, 1976), 13. Lane cogently identifies the essence of state socialism. The essential elements include the dominance of the values of Marxism-Leninism;

peculiar institutions that stem from state ownership of the means of production; and a Communist party that theoretically heads the working class and provides authoritative interpretation of the laws of historical development. The *state* in this case consists of the government, including the cen..ral bureaucracy and the party. These are the dominant institutions of society.

10. See Dessalegn Rahmato, *Agrarian Reform in Ethiopia* (Trenton, N.J.: Red Sea Press, 1985); and John M. Cohen and Peter H. Koehn, "Rural and Urban Land Reform in Ethiopia," *African Law Studies*, 14 (1977), 3–61.

11. See Marina Ottaway and David Ottaway, *Ethiopia: Empire in Revolution* (New York: Africana, 1977).

12. See John Cohen, "Agrarian Reform in Ethiopia: The Situation on the Eve of the Revolution's Tenth Anniversary," *Development Discussion Paper No. 164: Harvard Institute of International Development* (April 1984), 9.

13. See Marina Ottaway, "Land Reform in Ethiopia, 1974–1977," *African Studies Review*, 20 (Dec. 1977), 79–90; and Patrick Gilkes, review of Marina Ottaway and David Ottaway, *Ethiopia: Empire in Revolution, Northeast African Studies*, 1 (1979), 88.

14. See Fassil Gebre Kiros, "Agricultural Land Fragmentation: A Problem of Land Distribution Observed in Some Ethiopian Peasant Associations," *Ethiopian Journal of Development Research*, 4 (Oct. 1980), 1–12; and Rahmato, *Agrarian Reform*, 55–56.

15. See "Ethiopia," *Africa Contemporary Record, 1978–79* (New York: Africana, 1980), p. B239.

16. "Thousands On Waiting Lists for Homes," *Africa AFP*, Aug. 27, 1982.

17. See *Ethiopia: A Decade of Revolutionary Transformation* (Addis Ababa: Ministry of Culture and Guidance, 1984).

18. See "Ethiopia," *Africa Contemporary Record, 1978–79.*

19. *Ethiopia: Statistical Abstract, 1980* (Addis Ababa: Central Statistical Office, 1982), 165–70.

20. International Labor Organization, "Socialism from the Grass Roots: Accumulation, Employment and Equity in Ethiopia," internal document, Addis Ababa, 1983, p. 242.

21. Scott Kraft, "Wave of Defections Reveals Marxist Failure in Ethiopia," *Los Angeles Times*, Dec. 24, 1986, p. 10.

22. While the achievements in this area as in others are remarkable, these figures must be placed in perspective. For at least fifteen years Ethiopia's population was estimated at thirty to thirty-two million. The official census of 1984 placed the total population at forty-two million. This has obvious implications for illiteracy estimates. See Office of the Population and Housing Census Commission, *Ethiopia 1984: Population and Housing Census Preliminary Report* (Addis Ababa, Sept. 1984); and Gudeta Mamo, "The National Literacy Campaign in Ethiopia," *Prospects* (1982), 191–97.

23. "Literacy Campaign to Cover 5 More Nationality Languages," *Ethiopian Herald*, March 9, 1982.

24. Personal note from Richard Greenfield to author, December 1986.

25. "Ethiopia's Campaign against Illiteracy," in The World Bank, *Accelerated Development in Sub-Saharan Africa: An Agenda for Action* (Washington, D.C.: World Bank, 1981), 84.

26. *Ethiopia: A Decade of Revolutionary Transformation*, 52.

27. Ibid., 53.

28. See "The Evolution of a Socialist Educational System in Ethiopia," *Meskarem: A Marxist-Leninist Theoretical Journal*, 3 (1982), 1.

29. "Workshop for Political Teachers Organized," *Ethiopian Herald*, Oct. 22, 1983, p. 1.

30. Kraft, "Wave of Defections."

31. *Ethiopia: A Decade of Revolutionary Transformation*, 56.

32. "Ethiopia Revisited," *Africa: Recovery*, 1 (Feb.-April 1987), 7.

33. See James Brooke, "Ethiopia's Post-Famine Goal: Self-Sufficiency," *New York Times*, March 10, 1987, p. 1.

34. See David A. Korn, *Ethiopia, the United States and the Soviet Union* (London: Croom Helm, 1986), 117–54; and Jason W. Clay and Bonnie K. Holcomb, *Politics and the Ethiopian Famine, 1984–85* (Cambridge, Mass., Cultural Survival, 1985).

35. See Marcus Colchester and Virginia Luling, *Ethiopia's Bitter Medicine: Settling for Disaster* (London: Survival International, 1986), 40.

36. See "Ethiopia: More Resettlement," *Africa Confidential*, 28 (March 18, 1987).

37. Open letter from Médecins Sans Frontières to RRC Deputy Commissioner, Berhanu Deressa, Nov. 19, 1985, cited in François Jean, *Ethiopie: Du Bon Usage de la Famine* (Paris: Médecins Sans Frontières, 1986), 86.

38. See Robert D. Kaplan, "Ethiopia: Africa's Killing Fields," *Wall Street Journal*, Oct. 1, 1985.

39. See Jean, *Ethiopie*, 72; *Human Rights and Food Aid in Ethiopia: Hearing before the Subcommittee on Human Rights and International Organizations and the Subcommittee on Africa of the Committee on Foreign Affairs, House of Representatives, October 16, 1985* (Washington, D.C.: U.S. Government Printing Office, 1985), 108; and Jerry Gray, "Ethiopia Resettlement Sparks Controversy," *Santa Barbara News-Press*, Jan. 19, 1986.

40. Dessalegn Rahmato, "Some Notes on Settlement and Resettlement in Mettekel Awraja (Gojjam Province)," typescript, 1986.

41. "Villagization Unfolds New Way of Life in Bale Region," *Ethiopian Herald*, March 25, 1983, p. 1; John M. Cohen and Nils-Ivar Isaksson, "Villagization in the Arsi Region of Ethiopia," *Report to the Swedish University of Agricultural Sciences*, (Uppsala: International Rural Development Centre, 1987).

42. Brooke, "Ethiopia's Post-Famine Goal," p. 4.

43. Cohen and Isaksson, "Villagization," 8–11.

44. Ibid., 18; and various personal interviews conducted in Addis Ababa in September 1986.

45. See "Ethiopia: Villagization Success," *New African*, No. 235 (April 1982), 24.

46. Personal interview with Dag Hareide, UN Office for Emergency Operations in Ethiopia, Sept. 17, 1987.

47. Philip Revzin, "African Migration: With Famine Easing, Ethiopians Are Fleeing Collectivizing of Farms," *Wall Street Journal*, May 27, 1986.

48. "Ethiopia: Villagization Success," 24.

49. Cohen and Isaksson, "Villagization," 7–8.

50. Political agitation by party cadre takes place at the peasant association level to encourage peasants to form producer cooperatives voluntarily. In many cases they have no choice but to engage in collectivized activities and to participate in food rationing programs.

51. Cohen and Isaksson, "Villagization."

52. See Kenneth Jowitt, "Scientific Socialist Regimes in Africa: Political Differentiation, Avoidance, and Unawareness," in Carl G. Rosberg and Thomas Calleghy, eds., *Socialism in Subsaharan Africa* (Berkeley: Institute of International Studies, 1979), 133–73.

53. Ottaway and Ottaway, *Ethiopia*, 174.

54. John M. Cohen and Peter H. Koehn, *Ethiopian Provincial and Municipal Government: Imperial Patterns and Post-Revolutionary Changes* (East Lansing: Michigan State University Press, 1980).

55. "A Proclamation to Provide for the Organization and Consolidation of Peasant Associations," *Negarit Gazeta*, Dec. 14, 1975.

56. *Ethiopia: A Decade of Revolutionary Transformation*, 40.

57. Ibid., 38.

58. Fred Halliday and Maxine Molyneux, *The Ethiopian Revolution* (London: Verso, 1981), 112.

59. Ibid., 122–23.

60. "Ethiopia," *Africa Confidential*, 24 (1983) 5.

61. Roberto Correa Wilson, "On the Eve of the Establishment of the Party," *Verde Olive* [Havana], Oct. 13, 1983, pp. 18–19.

62. "Ethiopian Communist Party is Set Up, with Mengistu at the Helm," *New York Times*, Sept. 11, 1984; Korn, *Ethiopia, the United States and the Soviet Union*, 172; James Brooke, "Ethiopians Officially Joining Ranks of Communist Nations," *New York Times*, Feb. 23, 1987.

63. "Development Strategy Outlined," *Yekatit Quarterly*, 4 (March 1981), 4.

64. "Defending the Revolution," *Yekatit Quarterly*, 5 (Sept. 1981), 6.

65. This information was provided in interviews I collected in 1983 among exiled Ethiopian nationals who had been in a position to know.

66. "Ethiopia: Farewell to Marx?" *Africa Confidential*, 25 (Oct. 1, 1984), 1–2.

67. "Ethiopia: Last Tango in Addis," *Africa Confidential*, 25 (Oct. 15, 1984), 1. Korn, *Ethiopia, the United States and the Soviet Union*, 172.

68. "Mengistu's Gang of Four," *New African* (Nov. 1985), 20.

69. "Ethiopia," *Africa Confidential*, 25 (Oct. 15, 1984), 1.

70. "Government Deals with Nationalities Question," *Africa Now* (May 1983), 22.

71. By claiming that there are as many as eighty nationalities in Ethiopia, the regime essentially rejects the claims of the Eritreans and Oromos to self-determination.

72. Korn, *Ethiopia, the United States and the Soviet Union*, 172.

73. See "Ethiopia: Some Constitution," *Africa Confidential* (June 18, 1986), 6–7.

74. See "Ethiopia: Constitutional Debate," *Africa*, No. 180 (Aug. 1986).

75. Brooke, "Ethiopians Officially Joining Ranks of Communist Nations."

76. See Edmond J. Keller and Donald Rothchild, eds., *Afro-Marxist Regimes: Ideology and Policy* (Boulder: Lynne Reinner, 1987).

77. "Ethiopia: Timetable," *Africa Confidential*, 27 (October 1, 1987).

78. *The Constitution of the People's Democratic Republic of Ethiopia (PDRE)* (Addis Ababa: n.p., 1987).

79. Radio Voice of Ethiopia [in Amharic], Sept. 18, 1987.

80. See "Ensuring the Rights of Nationalities" (Addis Ababa: Committee for the Founding of the People's Democratic Republic of Ethiopia, September 1987).

81. See "Ethiopia: Redrawing the Map," *Africa Confidential*, 28 (November 18, 1987); and Eritrean People's Liberation Front, "Statement on the 'Regional Autonomy' of the Derg's Shengo" (Washington, D.C.: EPLF, September 1987).

82. Ibid.

IX. Toward Economic Socialization

1. International Labor Organization [ILO], "Socialism from the Grassroots: Accumulation, Employment and Equity in Ethiopia," internal document, Addis Ababa, 1983, p. 130; Central Statistical Office, *Results of the Survey of Manufacturing Industries, 1974 E.C.* [1981–1982 G.C.] (Addis Ababa, June 1984). Small-scale industries are those with fixed assets of less than $80,000.

2. Alan Rake, "Ethiopia: Investment Opportunities," *Africa Research Bulletin* (Oct. 15–Nov. 14, 1982), 6617.

3. Ibid.

4. See Don Kabebe, "Western Aid to Boost Ethiopia's Development Bid," *New African*, 174 (1982).

5. "Ethiopia," *Africa Research Bulletin* (April/May 1983), 6836.

6. *Negarit Gazeta*, Jan. 22, 1983.

7. ILO, "Socialism from the Grass Roots," 11.

8. Scott Kraft, "Wave of Defections Reveals Marxist Failure in Ethiopia," *Los Angeles Times*, Dec. 24, 1986, p. 10.

9. Addis Tesfa, "Ethiopia's Joint Venture Law," *Ethiopian Profiles*, 2 (July 1983), 11–12.

10. Rumman Farugi and Peter O'Brien, "Foreign Technology in the Growth of Modern Manufacturing Sector in Ethiopia, 1950–1970," *African Development*, 1 (Sept. 1976), 33.

11. See ILO, "Socialism from the Grass Roots," 127, 259; and Dessalegn Rahmato, "The Political Economy of Development in Ethiopia," in Edmond J. Keller and Donald Rothchild, eds., *Afro-Marxist Regimes: Ideology and Policy* (Boulder: Lynne Reinner, 1987).

12. ILO, "Socialism from the Grassroots," 10.

13. "Some Further Critical Remarks on the Ten Year Investment Plan," *Ethiopian Profiles*, 2 (July 1983), 8.

14. Fred Halliday and Maxine Molyneaux, *The Ethiopian Revolution* (London: Verso, 1981), 109.

15. "Proclamation to Provide for the Establishment of the National Revolutionary Development Campaign and Central Planning," *Negarit Gazeta* (Oct. 1978).

16. Jay Ross, "Ethiopia's Economy on a Treadmill," *Washington Post*, Jan. 5, 1982.

17. *Ethiopia: Statistical Abstract, 1980* (Addis Ababa: Central Statistical Office, 1982), 215.

18. See "Ethiopia," *Africa Research Bulletin: Economic Affairs* (1981), 5899.

19. ILO, "Socialism from the Grassroots," 9.

20. Ibid., 11–13.

21. "Office of the National Committee for Central Planning—Establishment Proclamation," *Negarit Gazeta* (Addis Ababa, 1984).

22. "High Level Group Studies Ten Year Draft Plan," *Ethiopian Herald*, March 16, 1984.

23. Rahmato, "Political Economy of Development in Ethiopia."

24. "Ethiopia: Well on the Road to Moscow," *Africa Contemporary Record* (New York: Africana, 1984), pp. B149–B150.

25. "Closing Statement of the Second COPWE Congress Delivered by Mengistu Haile Mariam," *Documents and Resolutions of the Second COPWE Congress* (Addis Ababa: COPWE, 1983).

26. Ibid., 41; *Ministry of State Farm Development: Its Role, Organization, Present and Future Activities* (Addis Ababa: Ministry of State Farm Development, 1984).

27. The discussion of state farms is based on interviews I conducted in Addis Ababa in July-August 1984 and on a World Bank report: *Ethiopia: The Agricultural Sector: An Interim Report*, Volume I (Washington, D.C.: World Bank, 1983), 19–21.

28. World Bank, *Ethiopia: Recent Economic Developments* (Washington, D.C.: World Bank, 1983), 23.

29. See Henock Kifle, "State Farms and the Socialist Transformation of Agriculture: A Comparative Analysis," unpublished manuscript, July 1983; and John M. Cohen, "Agrarian Reform in Ethiopia: The Situation on the Eve of the Revolution's Tenth Anniversary," Development Discussion Paper, No. 164 (Cambridge, Mass.: Harvard Institute for International Development, 1984).

30. "Proclamation to Provide for the Establishment of Cooperative Socieites," *Negarit Gazeta*, March 3, 1978.

31. *Ethiopian Herald*, July 2, 1984.

32. See Alula Abate, "Peasant Associations and Collective Agriculture in Ethiopia: Promise and Performance," *Erdkunde*, 37 (1983), 120–38, for a good discussion on the collectivization process.

33. *Negarit Gazeta,* March 3, 1978, p. 46.

34. Abate, "Peasant Associations and Collective Agriculture," 125.

35. Cohen, "Agrarian Reform," 37, 50.

36. Ibid., 34–36.

37. Ibid., 138; interview with World Bank official, Nairobi, July 20, 1984.

38. World Bank, *Ethiopia: Recent Economic Developments,* 27–28.

39. See James Scott, *The Moral Economy of the Peasant: Rebellion and Subsistence in Southeast Asia* (New Haven: Yale University Press, 1976).

40. World Bank, *Ethiopia: Recent Economic Developments,* 27.

41. Dessalegn Rahmato, *Agrarian Reform in Ethiopia* (Trenton: Red Sea Press, 1985), 65.

42. World Bank, *Ethiopia: Recent Economic Developments,* 23, 29; Rahmato, *Agrarian Reform,* 66.

43. Interview, August 3, 1984, Addis Ababa; Rahmato, *Agrarian Reform,* 92–96.

44. The "economy of affection" is Goran Hyden's term and refers to the socioeconomic lifestyle of the peasantry. Peasants are subsistence producers who rely heavily on kith and kin to ensure a bountiful harvest and to act as insurance against catastrophe. The guiding principles of this economy are cooperation, reciprocity, and mutual respect. As long as peasants are allowed or otherwise able to maintain a subsistence level of production in the context of a viable peasant socioeconomic network, they can choose to "escape" from the pressures of the outside world (i.e., the market economy). This is especially possible when the state is "soft" and unable to insure compliance, or when the market economy is unable to provide an unlimited range of incentives for peasants to produce for the market. See Goran Hyden, *Beyond Ujamaa in Tanzania: Underdevelopment and an Uncaptured Peasantry* (Berkeley: University of California Press, 1980), 18–19.

45. World Bank, *Ethiopia: Recent Economic Developments,* 30–33.

46. James Brooke, "Ethiopia's Post-Famine Goal: Self-Sufficiency," *New York Times,* March 10, 1987.

47. Rahmato, *Agrarian Reform,* 67.

X. Feudalism Is Dead! Long Live Dependence!

1. Theda Skocpol, *States and Social Revolution: A Comparative Analysis of France, Russia, and China* (London: Cambridge, University Press, 1979), 285.

2. Ibid., 285–88.

3. Ibid., 289–91.

4. Scott Kraft, "Wave of Defections Reveals Marxist Failure in Ethiopia," *Los Angeles Times,* Dec. 24, 1986, p. 10.

5. U.S. Arms Control and Disarmament Agency, *World Military Expenditures and Arms Transfers, 1985* (Washington, D.C.: U.S. Arms Control and Disarmament Agency, 1985), 103.

6. Ibid., 61.

7. See "Ethiopia Becomes USSR's Biggest Toehold in Africa, But How Strong is Link to Kremlin?" *Christian Science Monitor,* Sept. 13, 1984.

8. See Marina Ottaway, *Soviet and American Influences in the Horn of Africa* (New York: Praeger, 1982), 113–14.

9. Ibid., 141–42. On occasion, the Ethiopians have gone so far as to expel Soviet diplomats accused of interference in domestic affairs. See "Mengistu Visits Moscow to Firm Up Shakey Ethiopian-Soviet Alliance," *Africa Reports* (May-June 1984).

10. See "Proletarian Internationalism and the Ethiopian Revolution" [in Amharic] prepared for the Second COPWE Congress, Tah as 1975 (December 1982), 32.

11. See John M. Cohen, "Foreign Involvement in Land Tenure Reform: The Case of Ethiopia," in John D. Montgomery, ed., *International Dimensions of Land Reform* (Boulder: Westview Press, 1984), 196.

12. Ibid., 217.

13. After 1980 Ethiopia signed twenty-five major economic aid agreements with Western governments or Western-based international agencies and only a few with non-Western agencies. "Ethiopia," *Africa Contemporary Record, 1980–81,* (New York: Africana, 1982).

INDEX

Abyssinia: early history, 16–21; use of term, 274n

Africa: Pan-African unity and Haile Selassie, 92–93; power consolidation and state building, 213–14

Agriculture: pre-war tenancy, 62; subsistence production and primitive technology, 98; five-year plans, 100–101; foreign investment, 110; income and taxation, 115; export earnings, 119; commercial farming and peasant production, 124–27; land tenure and class contradictions, 142–46; commercialization and drought, 166; commercial farming and evictions, 168; nationalization of commercial farms, 249–50; state farms, 255–57; peasant production, 257, 259–61. *See also* Land tenure; and Peasants

Aman Andom: supported by Mengistu, 185; minister of defense, 186; chairman of Derg, 187, 192; arrest and death, 192; Eritrea, 202

Amhara: class system and assimilation, 63–64; attitude toward commerce, 112; national integration, 136–37, 150; educational opportunities, 139; Oromo, 158; Nilots and Negroes, 160; literacy campaign, 220; dominance of WPE, 239. *See also* Ethnicity

Atnafu Abate: politicization of military, 182, 183–84

Banking: Menelik II, 40–41; money economy, 96; foreign investment, 110

Bevin, Ernest: on partition of East Africa, 90; Somali nationalism, 156–57

Borders: Menelik II and treaties with European powers, 35–36, 88, 283n. *See also* Nationalism

Bureaucratic empire: concept discussed, 6–7; distinguishing features, 15; history of Ethiopia as, 9; emergence under Menelik II, 36; Chinese, Ottoman, and Carolingian compared to Ethiopian, 66–67; economic expansion, 94; defined, 273n

Capitalism: feudalism and social contradictions, 127–28; class contradictions, 142

Carter, Jimmy: curtailed arms sales, 200; Derg and human rights, 204–205

Centralization: Tewodros II, 25; Menelik II, 38–39; local administration under post-war decree, 74–75

Chamber of Deputies: Constitution of 1931,

70, 71; size and turnover, 87–88; opposition to tax policy, 117–18; landed classes, 283n

Christianity: early schisms, 17; Amharic expansion, 18; Yohannes IV, 28, 29, 30; conversion of Aksum, 46. *See also* Church

Church: Tewodros II, 26, 27; controversy and Yohannes IV, 29–30; education under Menelik II, 41; Abuna Mateos, 43; relationship with state, 46–50; land tenure, 54–55; Haile Selassie after World War II, 75–76; land tax reforms, 77; 1960 coup d'etat, 134; lack of response to famine, 170; protest of clergy against public authority, 178; Derg and land reform, 217

Class: ethnicity, 45, 59–64, 142, 162; land tenure and agricultural policy, 142–46; urban formation and industrialization, 146–49; expectations and revolution, 179–80; Marxism and Derg ideology, 198

Coffee: pre-war commerce, 95; monoculture economy, 98, 109, 121–23; tariffs and state revenues, 114; government response to drought, 167; economic planning, 251, 252; peasant production and smuggling, 262

Colonialism: expansionism and character of state, 45; class and ethnicity in periphery, 59–64; independence movements, 83; foreign policy of Menelik II, 88; Haile Selassie and African independence, 92; diplomatic relations with Portugal, 93; Oromo *Gada* and Ethiopian expansionism, 159–60

Commission to Organize the Party of Working People of Ethiopia (COPWE): announced, 201; Eritrea, 209; hinterland, 211; party formation and political penetration, 234–37

Confederation of Ethiopian Labor Unions (CELU): organization and effectiveness, 148, 149; demands and general strike, 177–78; politicization, 218; banned, 249

Constitution

—1931: Haile Selassie and constitutional monarchy, 69–70

—1955: Orthodox Church as state religion, 76; international image of Haile Selassie, 84–88; tax reform and Chamber of Deputies, 117–18; suspended in Eritrea, 153

—1987: regime legitimation, 239–43; nationalization, 247

Cooperatives: marketing of coffee, 123; peasant production, 196, 257–58, 258–59;

Eritrea, 209–10; peasant participation, 259, 298n

Cuba: relations with Derg, 205, 268; military aid, 206, 207

Debt: government involvement in public sector and foreign capital, 104; growth and economic crisis, 252

Decremental deprivation: defined, 179–80

Derg: legitimacy, 3–4; emperor, 185, 186–87; Endelkatchew government, 185–86; social myth, 191; radicalism, 192–93; civilian criticism, 196–97; ideology and civilian Left, 197–201; Eritrean liberation movement, 202–203; United States, 203–205; Eritrea and Red Star campaign, 208–10; nationalism, 210–11; "soft state," 214–15; labor, 219; education, 221–23; health care of, 223; reorganization of bureaucracy, 230–32; dissolution, 242; formulation and implementation of policy, 266

Dimbleby, Jonathan: documentary on famine, 169–70, 187

Drought: cause of revolution, 166–70; social policies, 211; "soft state," 223–25; resettlement, 225–27; foreign relief and state, 244; decline in peasant food production, 254; opposition to governmental policies, 262. *See also* Relief

Economic development: Italian investment, 97; capital expenditures, 101–102; government involvement in public sector, 103–104; foreign investment, 106–13; tax policy, 113–18; foreign trade, 118–23; integration and definition of development, 138; commercial farming and land reform, 167; villagization policy, 227–30; ideology, 245

Economic planning: five-year plans, 99–100; bureaucracy and military, 251; growth and goals, 251–52; ten-year plan, 252–53; regional planning, 254; mixed success, 262; "soft state," 263; dependence on foreign aid, 269–70

Education: Menelik II, 41; Haile Selassie, 72; military role in bureaucracy, 81, 82–83; third five-year plan, 101; ethnic and regional inequalities, 138–40; language in Eritrea, 153; government reform and popular discontent, 171–73; Derg policy, 221–23

Egypt: aggression and Tewodros II, 22; Yohannes IV, 29; Church, 46–47

Elections: Constitution of 1955, 87–88; Constitution of 1987, 240

Emperor: centralization of authority and bureaucratic empire, 15–16; office under Menelik II, 40; head of Church, 49; *gult*

rights, 53; land distribution, 55; Constitution of 1931, 71; Constitution of 1955, 86

Endelkatchew Makonnen, Lij: formation of government, 175–76; statement on reforms, 179; attempts to curb radicalism, 182–83; loss of control of military, 184; ouster and arrest, 186

Eritrea: nationalist movement, 2, 150–55; Haile Selassie and partition of East Africa, 91; autonomy and Unionist Party, 152–53; nationalist organizations, 154, 155; Aman Andom, 192; liberation movement and Derg, 202–203; Red Star campaign, 208–10; autonomous region under Constitution of 1987, 242–43

Ethiopia Tikdem: proclamation and Derg ideology, 193

Ethiopian People's Revolutionary Party (EPRP): attempt to undermine Derg, 197; ideological conflict, 199

Ethnicity: class, 45, 59–64, 142, 162; Haile Selassie and Empire, 91; nationalist organizations, 135, 150; illegitimacy of state, 191; Derg and nationalism, 202–203; Politbureau and WPE, 238, 239; Amharization, 275n. *See also* Nationalism

Famine. *See* Drought; Relief

Fetha Nagast: Church and codification of law, 48–49; authority of emperor, 50; emperor and land tenure, 52

Feudalism: imperial power, 45; *gult*, 52; Medieval Europe paradigm, 55–59, 273n; colonialism, 64; Haile Selassie and land tenure, 76; money economy, 114; coffee, 123; foreign advisors and commercial farming, 124; agricultural policy, 126, 127; capitalism and social contradictions, 127–28; landed classes, 144; land reform and Derg, 194, 217–18; reorganization of bureaucracy, 231; capitalism in Africa, 287n

Foreign aid: Haile Selassie and United States, 79–81; economic development, 100; public debt, 104; ten-year economic plan, 253; Derg dependence on, 267, 284–85n; current sources, 269–71. *See also* Soviet Union; United States

Foreign policy: Tewodros II and Europe, 26; Yohannes IV, 28–29; European recognition, 34, 35; Haile Selassie and Menelik II, 88–89; British presence, 89–90; partition of East Africa, 90–91; United States, 91–92; Pan-African unity, 92–93

Governors: authority under Menelik II, 38, 39; powers under post-war administrative decree, 74, 75

Grain: production and distribution during drought, 167; export during drought, 167,

292n; 1987 harvest, 225; state farms and urban supply, 255, 256

Great Britain: foreign policy and Tewodros II, 26–27, 27–28; Menelik II and boundaries; reconstruction, 73–74; military aid, 78–79; liberation and continued presence, 89; partition of East Africa, 90–91; Eritrean self-determination, 151; Somali nationalism, 156–57

Gult: defined, 52–53; feudal vassalage, 57; abolishment and land tenure, 116–17, 145, 146

Haile Selassie: international image, xi, 1, 83–84; contradictions, 2–3, 146; tradition and modernity, 4; regency, 43–44; modernization, 66, 131, 143, 165; pre-war reforms, 69; British during reconstruction, 73–74; Church, 75–76; land-tax reforms, 76–77; limited success of early reforms, 78; United States, 79–81; education, 82, 221; Constitution of 1955 and international image, 84–88; foreign policy compared with Menelik II's, 88–89; speech on Italian occupation at League of Nations, 89; British, 89–90; control of periphery after annexation of Eritrea, 91–92; Pan-African unity, 92–93; political economy, 94–95; transportation and money economy, 96–97; economic independence, 105; government involvement in public sector, 105–106; on rapid industrialization, 106; absolutist state and economic development, 107; conservatism of economic policy, 113; overview of economic policies, 127–28; protests, 135; national political integration, 136–38, 149–50, 157, 160; Eritrea, 153; famine, 170; education policy and imperial authority, 172–73; support among military, 173–75; formation of Endelkatchew government, 175–76; demands of Derg, 185; deposed by Derg, 186–87; state and popular demand, 214

Health care: regional inequalities, 140–41; doctor/population ratios, 223, 224

Human rights: violations by Derg, 200; resettlement policy, 226–27; villagization, 229

Industrialization: official policy and foreign investment, 106–107; trade deficit, 119; urban class formation, 146–49

Industry: government involvement, 105; growth and foreign investment, 107–108, 109; import substitution, 109; sugar and GDP, 111–12; regional concentration, 138; nationalization, 194, 246–47; foreign capital, 247–48; state control, 248–49

Islam: Christianization and Yohannes IV, 30; Lij Yasu, 42; public protests, 178; Politbureau representation, 239; polygamy and

Constitution of 1987, 240; Shoan Oromos, 275n

Italy: European expansionism, 30; Menelik II, 31–34; occupation, 65, 68; elimination of educated, 72–73, 281n; invasion and League of Nations, 89; road construction, 97; control of Eritrea, 150–51

Japan: bureaucratic empire compared to Ethiopia, 67; Constitution of 1931, 280n

Kebra Nagast: myth of Church and Crown, 47–48; Constitution of 1931, 69

Labor: union organization and government suppression, 147–49; Derg and unions, 219; grievances after nationalization, 249. *See also* Confederation of Ethiopian Labor Unions

Land tenure: Tewodros II and Church, 26; Church, 50, 54–55; *rist,* 51–52; *gult,* 52–53; private ownership, 54; feudalism, 56–57; colonialism and class, 61–62; reform and Haile Selassie, 76–77; five-year plans, 101; tax policy and *gult,* 116–17; peasants and commercial farming, 126; class contradictions, 142–46; Oromo, 161; drought and government response, 167; nationalization of rural land, 194–95, 217–18. *See also* Agriculture; Peasants

Language: education and ethnic alienation, 140; Eritrea, 153; suppression of Oromo, 160; Amhara and literacy campaign, 220

League of Nations: international image of Haile Selassie, xi; admission of Ethiopia, 43, 68; speech by Haile Selassie on Italian occupation, 89; Western Oromo Confederation, 161

Literacy: Derg priority, 219–20; population estimates, 297n. *See also* Education

Marxism: Derg ideology, 193, 198; Zemacha ideology, 195; nationalist movements, 211

Media: demand for free press, 177; politicization of military, 181; military control, 183

Meison: public debate, 197; ideological conflict, 199

Menelik II: Yohannes IV, 27, 28, 29, 30–31; Italy, 31–34; France, 35; borders and treaties, 35–36, 88, 283n; territorial expansion, 36–37; military, 37–38; centralization, 38–39; taxation, 39–40; office of emperor, 40; monetary policy, 40–41; education, 41; succession, 42; *rist gult,* 53; private ownership of land, 54; expansionism and emergence of class, 59–60; foreign policy compared with Haile Selassie's, 88–89; Italy and Eritrea, 150–51

Mengistu Haile Mariam: leadership of Derg,

184–85; initial conservatism, 192; foreign policy, 200; response to invasion of Ogaden, 207; on national military service, 212; on housing construction, 218; on ideology and COPWE, 236; key positions in COPWE, 237; conference on economic crisis, 252; on state farms, 255

Military: attitude and revolution, 8; Tewodros II, 25; Menelik II, 33, 37–38; colonialism and class, 60, 61; professionalization, 72, 78–79; United States aid, 79–81; 1960 coup d'etat, 132, 133, 134; Eritrean annexation, 153, 155; control of Ogaden, 156; support for Haile Selassie, 173–75; politicization, 181–82; guerillas, 210; build-up, 211–12; national military service, 234; politicization and COPWE, 236; domination of WPE, 238; Derg policies, 267–68

Modernization: selective introduction, 4; bureaucratic empire, 7; Haile Selassie, 44, 58, 66, 83, 131, 143; Constitution of 1955, 84; highway system, 97; demand for imports, 98; public sector, 103–106; tax policy as instrument, 113; tax reform and Chamber of Deputies, 118; commercial farming and drought, 166

Mussolini, Benito: occupation of Ethiopia, 65, 151; Somali nationalism, 156–57

Nationalism: challenge to myth of Haile Selassie, 1–2; integration policies of Haile Selassie, 136–38, 149–50, 157; development of new movements, 210; resettlement policy, 226; WPE study, 238–39; Constitution of 1987, 242, 243; Derg policies, 266–67. *See also* Ethnicity

Nationalization: industrial sector, 193–94, 246–47; urban lands, 196, 218; rural land policy, 217–18; foreign firms, 245, 246; disruption of industry, 249; commercial farms, 249–50

Newaye, Girmame: 1960 coup d'etat, 132–35, 181

Newaye, Mengistu: 1960 coup d'etat, 132, 134, 181

Ogaden: nationalist movement, 155–58; invaded by Somalia, 206–207. *See also* Somali

Oil: exploration by foreign firms, 109; refining capacity and imports, 120; shortages and political economy, 171–80

Oromo: nationalism, 2, 158–63; influence on Abyssinian history, 19–21; expansionism, 60, 275n, 279n; class system and assimilation, 63, 64; integration into upper echelons, 136; nationalist organizations, 163; refugees and villagization, 229; Politbureau representation, 238; national consciousness, 290n

Peasants: military under Menelik II, 40; land tenure and colonialism, 61–62; Land Tax Proclamation, 115; land tenure and *gult,* 117; coffee, 123; five-year plans and productivity, 125; commercial farming, 126–27; land reform and class contradictions, 143–46; protests against public authority, 178; land reform and production associations, 194–96; land reform expectations, 217; associations and bureaucracy, 232; economic potential of agriculture, 250; associations and government control, 258–59; participation in cooperatives, 259, 298n; associations and government administration, 261; autonomy and state control, 261–62; "soft state," 263; socioeconomic network and production, 301n

Politbureau: political groups as members, 199; ethnicity, 238, 239

Population: urban growth and housing, 218; literacy, 297n

Portugal: aid to Abyssinia, 19; Haile Selassie and diplomatic relations, 93

Presidency: Constitution of 1987, 241

Red Terror: Derg and violence, 200; *kebeles* and violence, 234

Relief: corruption and inefficiency, 167, 168, 170; documentary on famine, 169–70; famine aid and Derg, 224, 225, 296n. *See also* Drought

Resettlement: Derg and drought victims, 225–27; peasant agriculture, 262

Revolution: causes, 7, 164–65; facilitating factors, 7–8; class, ethnicity, and colonialism, 64; 1960 coup d'etat, 132–35; decremental deprivation, 179–80; process of interrelated actions, 180–87; classic social revolutions and Ethiopia, 264–65

Rist: defined, 51–52; peasants and land reform, 217

Roads: construction during Italian occupation, 68–69; economic development, 97–98

Senate: Constitution of 1931, 70, 71

Social myth: concept discussed, 8–9; Derg and legitimacy, 191, 265–66

Socialism: Derg ideology, 197–99, 215–16; education policy, 222–23; reeducation of bureaucrats, 231; economic development, 245; private investment as contradiction, 247

"Soft state": defined, 214; drought and famine, 223–25

Solomonic dynasty: early history of Ethiopia, 17–18; Tewodros II, 24; national myth, 275n

Somali: irredentism, 2, 158; common

heritage and nationalism, 156, 290n. *See also* Ogaden

Somalia: territory ceded to Menelik II, 35–36; British and partition of East Africa, 90; independence and conflict with Ethiopia, 157–58; relations with United States, 205–206; invasion of Ogaden, 206–207

Soviet Union: Derg ideology, 197–99, 215–16, 245; relations with Derg, 200–201, 205, 267–68; military aid, 204, 206–207; Constitution of 1987, 240; state farms, 256; economic aid, 269

Students: demonstrations, 135; famine, 169; oil shortages, 171; radicalism and popular discontent, 176–77; links with Derg, 186

Sugar: economic development, 110–12, 285n

Tariffs: foreign investment, 108–109; state revenues, 113–14

Taxation: Tewodros II, 26; Menelik II, 39–40; Haile Selassie and land tax reforms, 76–78; income tax, 78; money economy, 96; concessions to foreign investors, 108; policy and economic development, 113–18; manipulation of policy, 274n, 277–78n

Teachers: foreign nationality and unrest, 140; popular discontent, 172–73; general strike, 178

Tewodros II: early life and rise to power, 21–24; establishment of modern Ethiopian state, 24–27; compared to Yohannes IV, 28

Third World: Haile Selassie and international image, 84; import trade, 120; compared to "great revolutions," 264–65

Trade: foreign domination, 95–96; balance of payments deficit, 98, 119, 252; economic development, 118–23; socialist countries, 268–69

United Nations: Ethiopia as member, 68; Ethiopia and Eritrea, 91, 151–52, 154; commercial farming, 124

United States: strategic alliance, 68; military and economic aid, 79–81, 282n; Constitution of 1955, 84–85; Haile Selassie and control of periphery, 92; import trade, 119–21; famine relief, 170, 225; human rights, 200; relations with Derg, 203–205, 211; relations with Somalia, 205–206; military policy in East Africa, 296n

Villagization: economic development, 227–30

Wolde, Aklilu Habte: resignation of government, 175; arrest of cabinet ministers, 182

Workers' Party of Ethiopia (WPE): proclamation and membership, 235–36; party formation and political penetration, 237–39; Constitution of 1987, 239

World Bank: investment in highway system, 97; feudalism and commercial farming, 124; agricultural development assistance, 125, 126; agricultural extension services, 260–61; foreign aid, 270

Yejju dynasty: influence on Abyssinia, 21; Tewodros II, 23

Yekunno Amlak: restoration of Solomonic dynasty, 18; supported by Church, 47

Yohannes IV: British occupying force, 27–28; as emperor, 28–30

Zauditu: as empress, 42–43; Ras Tafari as regent, 43

Zemacha: public indoctrination, 193; land reform and ideology, 195, 217, 232; villagization, 228; Derg and bureaucracy, 231; peasant agriculture, 250; economic planning, 251